MODERNIZATION AND

BRITISH COLONIAL RULE

IN EGYPT, 1882-1914

PRINCETON STUDIES ON THE NEAR EAST

MODERNIZATION AND BRITISH COLONIAL RULE IN EGYPT, 1882-1914

BY ROBERT L. TIGNOR

PRINCETON, NEW JERSEY

PRINCETON UNIVERSITY PRESS

1966

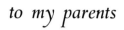

to my parents

PREFACE

THIS BOOK is a study of the impact of the British administration upon Egyptian society. Consequently, the focus is limited to the government as an agency of change. Traditionally the government played a major role in all aspects of Egyptian life, and the British certainly did not alter this pattern radically. This volume, then, does not deal with all the agencies of change in Egypt, most notably the missionaries, the foreign financial community, or the indigenous Egyptian groups outside the government, except for the leaders of the nationalist movement. In one chapter (XI) it deals with the relationship of the foreign financial community to the administration. It should not be assumed, of course, that these groups were not important transforming elements in Egypt. They certainly were, and I would hope that other scholars would study their role in the development of modern Egypt.

This study assumes that in general the British administration had a modernizing impact on Egypt. It does not argue, however, that the British administrators were bent upon the complete modernization of Egyptian society. Indeed, the reverse was the case in many crucial areas of Egyptian development. I have tried to show in what areas the British administrators did serve as modernizers, in what areas they had little or no effect, and in what areas they even impeded the pressures for change. The impact of British rule is compared against the characteristics of modernized societies in order to indicate the specific patterns of change occurring in Egypt. Since what men intend and what in fact takes place in history are often quite different things, I will also point out some of the unintended consequences of British rule for the development of Egypt.

A note on the transliteration from Arabic is in order. I have used the most prevalent English-language spelling for Egyptian place names. This should present no problems because most of the place names like Cairo, Alexandria, and Aswan are well-known. Most of these place names can be found in *Webster's Geographical Dictionary*. In the transliteration of proper names and titles and authors of books in Arabic I have used no diacritical markings. I believe that the scholar who knows Arabic should not have any difficulty in finding the works referred to.

During the research and writing of this manuscript I have incurred many obligations to friends and fellow scholars. It is my great pleasure, now, to acknowledge their help. In the preliminary stages of my work three mentors at Yale University gave willingly of their time and wisdom: Professors Harry Rudin and Franz Rosenthal and the late Ralph E. Turner. I would like to express a special note of gratitude to the late Professor Turner whose consuming interest in the non-Western world was infectious. Five years of teaching and associations at Princeton University have proved immensely stimulating. Professors Jerome Blum, Robert Collins, L. P. Curtis Jr., Raymond Grew, Manfred Halpern, Marion Levy, Arno Mayer, F. C. Shorter, and Walter Struve have all read parts of the manuscript and have offered criticisms. I should like to acknowledge an intellectual debt to Professor Cyril E. Black for many of his ideas on the concept of modernization. I should further like to record my indebtedness to Robert Birrell for reading sections of the manuscript with great care and interest.

This work owes more than I can indicate to the kindness of foreign friends. The late Professor Shafiq Ghurbal and the faculty of the American University of Cairo paved the way for me in Egypt. Albert Hourani of

St. Antony's, Oxford, was a mine of information about sources for the topic. While I was in England I was especially fortunate to be able to interview a number of men who had served in Egypt before the First World War. They provided me with firsthand personal knowledge which I have tried to weave into the manuscript. And they were not to be outdone in their hospitality to me. I record my gratitude to them with great pleasure: Andrew Holden, W. Allard, V. L. O. Sheppard, Harold E. Hurst, H. W. Jarvis, Humphrey Bowman, and P. M. Tottenham.

This manuscript was based heavily on personal papers. Many of these papers were located in public archives. Others were to be found with living relatives, and it is to this latter group that I would like to acknowledge a special measure of thanks for allowing me to see their papers. Mrs. R. K. Thomas made available to me the papers of her father, Sir Eldon Gorst. Lady Dorothea Russell kindly enabled me to see the letters of her husband, Sir Thomas Russell Pasha, and Mrs. Clara Boyle permitted me to look at the papers of her husband, Harry Boyle. At Christ Church College in Oxford I was able to see the Salisbury Papers; at New College, Oxford, the Milner Papers; at the British Museum, the D'Abernon Diaries and Papers; at Durham University, the Wingate Papers; at the Public Records Office in London, the Cromer and Granville Papers and the Foreign Office files; and at the Foreign Office, the Papers of Edward Grey. I would like to express my thanks to the staffs and libraries of these institutions, especially to Richard Hill at Durham and J. F. A. Mason at Christ Church, Oxford.

I also wish to acknowledge permissions to republish in modified form portions of articles which have appeared in the following periodicals: *American Historical Review*, *Agricultural History*, and *Journal of British Studies*.

PREFACE

This project could never have been completed without the financial support of the Ford Foundation, which enabled me to spend a year in England and Egypt, the Princeton University Research Fund, the Princeton University Committee on Regional Studies, and the Princeton University Near East Program.

I would like to thank Mrs. John Harrison, Mrs. Ronald Keene, and Miss Patricia LaRue for the patient typing of the entire manuscript. Mr. Roy Grisham deserves special mention for his care in editing the manuscript and seeing it through to completion.

CONTENTS

xi

MODERNIZATION AND

BRITISH COLONIAL RULE

IN EGYPT, 1882-1914

CHAPTER I

THE BRITISH OCCUPATION OF EGYPT

A GREAT deal of the transformation and modernization of the non-Western world took place in the nineteenth century under the system of European colonial rule. During this century Europe became increasingly expansionistic, and non-Western countries embraced, in varying degrees, the institutions of the West in an attempt to retain their independence. Certain countries, such as Turkey and Japan, succeeded. The majority, however, were unable to adapt rapidly enough to the new ways, and thus came under European control. It was through colonial rule, therefore, that many countries were exposed and transformed by the West's institutions and techniques.

The vast and impressive body of literature on European colonialism has tended to focus on imperialism as a phenomenon of European history. Studies of the problems have dealt mainly with the reasons for European expansionist tendencies, and with the effect European expansion had on the domestic institutions of Europe. Imperialism must be viewed, however, in a world perspective. The historian needs to determine what effect imperialism had on the non-European world, as well as Europe. During the era of colonial rule there was a vast exportation of European civilization, particularly European science, into the colonies. Whether for good or bad, for humanitarian or for selfish motives, the non-Western world was uprooted and made over during this time. The fact that leaders of the non-Western world today have no desire to return to their traditional societies is some proof that this process cannot be reversed.

The crucial issues under consideration in this book are: the elements of European civilization introduced into the non-European world; the interaction of the new with the established, or traditional, ideas and institutions; the new institutions that emerged from this interaction of the traditional and the European; and the response of the indigenous populations to the new and their attempt to restructure their world. This analysis, therefore, deals with both European and non-European society; an attempt is made to view the collision of two cultures, with a subsequent diffusion of techniques, ideas, and institutions into a more backward society.

There has been a regrettable tendency to regard the modern, non-European world purely as an extension of Europe. Africa and the Middle East have been treated as areas in which Europeans did more or less as they pleased. These areas have often been studied entirely from European documents, almost as if indigenous institutions and traditions did not exist. In reality, whenever well-developed and unbroken cultural traditions existed, there was a constant interaction of cultures when Europe came in contact with the non-European world. As Bronislaw Malinowski has indicated, cultural change is a dynamic process, involving the creative adaptation of the non-European societies to Europe. "The paper programs of European intentions, as crystallized in documents, recorded in proceedings of deliberative bodies . . . are never the actuality of contact. . . . At each stage of history there has existed the practical task of implementing such programs: the working out in reality; the surveying; the interference of the old and the new; and the real occasions of contact."[1] Selected elements were exported to the non-European world. Some were accepted with little change; others met with resistance from

[1] Bronislaw Malinowski, *The Dynamics of Culture Change* (New Haven, 1945), p. 114.

[4]

the traditional culture and were partially changed; and many others were resisted almost completely. Nor were the peoples of indigenous societies content to accept or reject only what European colonial administrators offered them. They travelled in the European world. They became aware of the facets of European tradition that colonial administrators had attempted to filter out of the colonial experience, and often demanded for their own societies what Europe had chosen to deny to them.

Modernization is a useful analytical term for discussing the transformation that has occurred in the non-Western world. According to one historian, "modernization is the process of change from an agrarian to an industrial way of life that has resulted from the dramatic increase in man's knowledge of and control over his environment."[2] Sociologists have shown that all societies perform certain basic functions. Modern societies are characterized by a differentiation between the structures or institutions that perform those functions, and also by a rationalization of these structures or institutions. Modernizing societies, therefore, are societies in which specific structures are developed as ends in themselves, with their own autonomous rationality.[3] As an illustration of a non-modern society, pre-1800 Egypt possessed fairly un-differentiated, self-sufficient, and non-rationalized structures. Some of these structures—notably the kin or family group—discharged a variety of societal functions. The kin group, in fact, was of central importance in providing political authority and stability, and in ensuring economic productivity and distribution. As a result of the social changes of the nineteenth century, many of these

[2] Cyril E. Black, ed., *The Transformation of Russian Society* (Cambridge, Massachusetts, 1960), p. 661.

[3] There is an immense literature on this subject. Attention is called to Marion J. Levy, *The Structure of Society* (Princeton, 1952) and S. N. Eisenstadt, *The Political Systems of Empires* (Glencoe, Illinois, 1963).

functions were gradually taken over by other more specialized institutions in the process of being rationalized. Moreover, recruitment into these new structures was made increasingly on the basis of merit rather than on ascriptive criteria, such as family or class.

It is not the contention of this book that the European colonial rulers favored the full modernization of their colonial societies. Many European administrators of the late nineteenth century were quite pessimistic about the ability of colonial societies to adapt fully to the more difficult requirements of modern life. In many cases, these administrators opposed the demands of the indigenous population for more comprehensive programs of social change. In others, the modernization that resulted in the society was a totally unintended consequence of specific programs sponsored by the colonial administrators. The term *modernization* will be used as an analytical tool, not as description of intended aims and goals of the colonial regimes. As a tool of measurement it can show those areas where European colonial regimes most decisively disrupted the traditional societies, where they either had no effect or tended to impede modernization, and where the pressures for it were resisted within the indigenous society.

The process of modernization involves embracing certain of the ideals and the institutions of more powerful societies and blending them with indigenous elements. Social scientists have generalized on various techniques or models for modernization, such as the liberal, European model, the Marxist or Bolshevik model, the Kemalist, Nehru, and Maoist models. But little attention has been directed to the patterns and problems of modernization that developed within the colonial situation. Europe was placed in the ambiguous position of exporting techniques and institutions which eventually were turned against it. The patterns of social change under colonial rule are, therefore, different from those of a relatively free, indigenous society, such as Russia or Japan. The dominant motive for transforming traditional colonial societies, for instance, is not that found in independent states: the desire to overtake the more advanced states. The programs of change, reflecting the needs of the colonial power rather than those of the subject peoples, tend to be more limited, therefore, than those carried out in independent states.

Egypt offers an ideal example of a case study of cultural contact and change under colonial rule. There is an abundance of material, published and archival, from the British side, all of which gives a clear picture of the policies the British pursued in Egypt, the programs of reform they introduced, and the reasons for their policies. Of equal importance is the amount of Egyptian material, which enables one to generalize about Egyptian society before European contact and the anticipated response of Egypt to British rule. In this sense, countries like Egypt and India are presently more profitable areas in which to study cultural contact than those of Africa, where knowledge of the traditional society and its institutions is still scanty. Egypt, indeed, stands in a most favorable position because of its great homogeneity.

In the view set forth here, technology is regarded as one of the primary factors in the transformation of the non-Western world. Western technological superiority, manifesting itself most forcibly to the East through its military strength, was the major reason for the first attempts by indigenous rulers to modernize their societies. From the technological confrontation of East and West, the non-Western world was driven to seek the sources of strength in the West other than its technology—its economic organization, its ideologies, and its political institutions. The new technology undermined the traditional patterns and institutions of life. Agriculture and hydraulics in Egypt, for instance, were to bring about a closer integration of rural and urban spheres, to put the Egyptian economy on a cash and export basis, and to compel more precise attitudes towards cultivation than the peasantry had ever shown. These were, indeed, far-reaching changes, not only in the routines of the peasants, but also in their mentality and world outlook. The emergence of a new class of intellectuals, by which colonial regimes were brought under attack and through which the process of modernization was often carried forward, is regarded by many as the most significant achievement of colonial rule. But this class was rooted in the technology of colonial administrations. Its members came from new schools, established to produce trained men: lawyers, doctors, civil servants. They were trained to operate the new economic and administrative machinery introduced by the West. Furthermore, this group would have had only a small following among the population if there had been no technological change. Railroads, crop export, and the cash economy brought the countryside into contact with the city. Slumps and booms made the peasantry and urban proletariat alike receptive to the leadership provided by the new educated class.

The programs of social change introduced into colonial areas were related, in turn, to the reasons for the acquisition and domination of these colonies; that is, to the aims and goals of the imperial powers. The technological apparatus introduced into colonies depended upon the nature and causes of the imperialism involved. The most commonly accepted interpretations of imperialism have stressed four major reasons for European imperialism in the late nineteenth century: (1) economics, (2) strategy or defense, (3) national prestige, and (4) the migration of populations. It should be clear that the predominant factor in the acquisition and continued domination of a colony governed the manner in which that colony was developed by the colonial power. In a colony acquired for economic reasons, for instance, the resources of the colony were developed rapidly and integrated into that of the mother country, often disrupting radically the traditional patterns of life. In a colony of prestige the administrative program was designed not to meet the needs or even the potential of the colony, but to reflect favorably upon the home state. In white-settlement colonies modernization was rapid, but usually carried out by, and confined to, the settlers. Conscious efforts were made to exclude the subject peoples from the entire process, or where this solution proved impossible, to use them in the least responsible and least rewarding tasks. Finally, in colonies of defense the overriding concern of colonial administrations was to maintain the tranquility of the colonial populations. In these colonies, therefore, the pace of social change was slowed for fear that fundamental changes might disrupt the traditional patterns of life and, by increasing the possibilities of revolution, thereby threaten the position of the colonial power. Colonies acquired for defensive and strategic reasons were governed generally as vast, holding operations.

Colonies did, of course, shift from one type to another as they developed. It was not unusual for a colony acquired for strategic reasons to develop into a colony of economic exploitation if its resources were found to be rich. Moreover, in no colony did one of these factors operate to the exclusion of all others. In the Union of South Africa all four motives existed. Yet it is often possible to isolate that factor which was predominant and which most determined the nature and pace of modernization.

Account must also be taken of the influence on social

change of private or non-governmental groups. They were often responsible for the most active programs of social change in colonial areas, directly or through the pressure they exerted on colonial administrations. Two of the important non-official agents of change were the foreign merchants and the missionaries. It could certainly be argued that these elements were in favor of more rapid social changes than the administrators. Yet they were also subject to the influence of the colonial administrations and often were forced to tailor their interests accordingly. Indeed, in many colonies the private sphere tended to be an arm of the administration, as was the case in Leopold II's Congo Free State.

Since European expansion and social change in colonial areas are so closely related, it is necessary to examine in some detail the motives for the British acquisition of Egypt. Egypt has, in fact, served as a leading illustration of the economic interpretation of imperialism. But this interpretation has been increasingly subject to general criticism. In a recent study a group of British scholars have made a new and bold effort to re-examine British imperialism in Africa. Focusing their interpretations sharply on Egypt, they have argued that the British government, despite great hesitation, occupied Egypt because of its location on the route to India, and not for economic reasons.[4]

In reality, it seems quite clear that economic and political factors intertwined to produce the conditions leading to the British occupation of Egypt. The export of European ideas and European capital into Egypt affected the foundations of traditional Egyptian society. Economic factors were fundamental causative forces in creating the conditions of turmoil and political disequilibrium. The paralysis of Egyptian government in the

---

[4] Ronald Robinson and John Gallagher, with Alice Denny, *Africa and the Victorians* (New York, 1961).

1870's, and the Arabi revolt followed closely on the heels of the disruptive effects of European capital on Egypt's basic institutions. The final decisions to invade Egypt, however, were political and strategic: Egypt was occupied in order to protect the route to the East and to forestall occupation of the country by any other power. Specifically, the British invaded Egypt to crush an indigenous proto-nationalist movement—the Arabi revolt—which threatened the security of Britain's major route to the East, the Suez Canal. Egypt's extravagant ruler, Khedive Ismail (1863-1879), had borrowed heavily from Europe for his reform programs, mortgaging most of his country's resources to European financiers. Driven to the verge of bankruptcy by 1875, Ismail sold his remaining, important asset: Egypt's shares in the Suez Canal Company. But the sale provided only temporary relief. A year later the Khedive found that he could no longer meet his debt payments and, under European pressure, created an international financial body, known as the *Caisse de la Dette*. The *Caisse* represented the financial interests of England, France, Austria, and Italy; its responsibility was to receive Egyptian revenues for the interest payments and the amortization of Egypt's debt. It was an administrative body, destined to grow from these "comparatively small beginnings . . . to be an important and ubiquitous factor in the government of the country."[5] As representatives of the leading creditor countries, the British and French members quickly established a predominant power.

Britain and France had a long-standing interest in Egypt. French interest had reached its peak at the end of the eighteenth century with Napoleon's grandiose invasion of Egypt. Although the French were subsequently driven out, they continued to maintain close political and cultural ties with Egypt. Egypt's early

[5] Lord Milner, *England in Egypt* (London, 1892), p. 23.

[*11*]

attempts at modernization, under Muhammad Ali (1805-1848) and Ismail, drew heavily on French thought and institutions. Egypt's evolving legal system, its education, and the social life of its upper classes reflected France's cultural influence. Moreover, French capitalists were heavy investors in Ismail's modernization programs. France perhaps unjustifiably regarded Egypt as a cultural colony, as a territory in which France's *mission civilatrice* was to be realized. The more aggressive imperialists in French society, and particularly their most vocal representatives in the French parliament, were anxious that nothing should jeopardize France's position in Egypt. They were jealous of Britain's role in Egypt, and even before the occupation were anxious that the British not be permitted to achieve dominant influence.

British interests in Egypt were as firm as those of the French, but of a slightly different order. Like the French, the British had important investments in Egypt. Basically, however, Egypt represented to the British a strategically located territory on the route to the East. With the construction of the Suez Canal and the introduction of steam power in shipping, Egypt's significance increased. By 1880 the bulk of shipping passing through the canal was British. Also, the canal made the trip from England to India shorter. As it developed into an important diplomatic problem, the Egyptian question became a burning issue in British politics. Even before the Arabi revolt in Egypt, British statesmen were aware that firm policies would have to be developed. The attempt to formulate policies for Egypt tended to sharpen the divisions of left- and right-wing forces in Britain. The right wing was inclined to see opportunity in Egypt's difficulties and to call for expansionist policy. Right-wing opinion, represented by journalists like Edward Dicey, argued that Egypt must be made secure under British rule. They contended that the only way Britain could safeguard the route to the East was to force French influence out of Egypt and establish British paramountcy.[6]

The left wing of the Liberal party, on the other hand, feared that British expansion into Egypt would set in motion unrestrained imperialist forces and involve the country in controlling and administering a vast African empire. They predicted that further imperial responsibilities would turn England into a garrison state and would direct attention away from the solution of pressing social problems at home. In 1877 Gladstone wrote an article in *The Nineteenth Century,* "Aggression on Egypt and Freedom in the East," in which he stated: "The root and pith and substance of the material greatness of our nation lies within the compass of these islands and is, except in trifling particulars, independent of all and every sort of political domination beyond them."[7] The opinions of the left reflected the Cobdenite approach to foreign affairs. They were based on the assumptions that the governance of other peoples against their will was immoral, that foreign policy was often manipulated by the privileged classes to the detriment of the people, and that England contained within itself the essential sources of its own well-being. Moreover, the economy-minded Gladstonians feared that colonial ventures would place heavy financial burdens on the home government.[8]

The policy followed by the British before the outbreak of the Arabi revolt in Egypt was that established

[6] There is a collection of Dicey's articles from this period in Edward Dicey, *England and Egypt* (London, 1881).

[7] W. E. Gladstone, "Aggression on Egypt and Freedom in the East," *The Nineteenth Century,* II (August, 1877), 153.

[8] The attitude of the left toward imperialism, among other issues, is discussed by A. J. P. Taylor, *The Trouble-Makers* (London, 1957).

by Lord Salisbury. It was based on the proposition that while Britain had no wish to govern Egypt, it could not allow France to gain an upper hand. Lord Salisbury described his policy in a letter of September 16, 1881: "As to our policy—the defence of it lies in a nutshell. When you have a neighbor and faithful ally who is bent on meddling in a country in which you are deeply interested—you have three courses open to you. You may renounce—or monopolize—or share. Renouncing would have been to place the French across our road to India. Monopolizing would have been very near the risk of war. So we resolved to share."[9] For this reason the British worked with the French when the *Caisse* was established in 1876, then when British and French controllers, or ministers, were appointed to help run the Egyptian government, and finally when Khedive Ismail was deposed in 1879 in favor of his son, Tawfiq (1879-1892), for trying to upset these international arrangements.

Financial difficulties were to prove the stumbling block of Anglo-French cooperation. They forced the British and the French to increase their control over internal affairs in Egypt until they were virtually running the government. England and France controlled the all-important Ministries of Finance and Public Works. Of greater significance was the fact that the near-bankruptcy of the government produced a situation of administrative chaos. Taxes were raised and collected sometimes twice a year. The peasantry suffered acutely from the tax burden, and from the breakdown of the hydraulic system. 1879 was a tortuous year for the people. The Nile flood, upon which the peasantry depended for the irrigation of crops, was unusually low, and much otherwise arable land could not be irrigated; yet taxes remained at previous high levels and were collected only

[9] Lady Gwendolyn Cecil, *Life of Robert, Marquis of Salisbury* (London, 1921-1932), II, 331-32.

by the cruelest methods. Government officials were not paid regularly. Many of them had salaries as much as two years in arrears. The educational system, because of financial cutbacks, was disrupted and most of Ismail's expensive programs of modernization were either curtailed or completely discarded. It was within the context of this frightening financial and administrative breakdown that the Arabi revolt occurred.

The Arabi revolt has been viewed by many observers as one of the earliest nationalistic uprisings in the Middle East. There is some validity in this estimate. The earliest exponents of Egyptian and Islamic nationalism had helped to create an intellectual renaissance influenced by Western ideas and desirous of modernizing Egypt and the Islamic world along Western lines. The most prominent figure in this intellectual movement was Jamal al-Din al-Afghani, an Islamic activist and reformer who had lived in Egypt from 1871 to 1879. He helped to energize Egypt's budding intelligentsia. He called for a political revival of the East, the union of Islamic states, the assimilation of the superior science and military technology of the West and some of its institutions for the purpose of resisting Western encroachment in the Islamic world. His followers had organized small activist societies with the avowed purpose of revitalizing the East and resisting the West.[10] Ahmad Arabi, a colonel in the Egyptian army and the actual leader of the revolt, would hardly have fitted the modern image of an intellectual and a modernizer. Of Egyptian peasant stock, he knew no European languages and had apparently read only a few Western books in Arabic. His exposure to higher educa-

[10] There is no recent study of the Arabi revolt, but a plethora of works on Jamal al-Din al-Afghani and some of the other intellectual leaders in Egypt. For Jamal al-Din, the reader is referred to the two most recent interpretations: Sylvia G. Haim, *Arab Nationalism* (Berkeley, 1962) and Albert Hourani, *Arabic Thought in the Liberal Age, 1798-1939* (London, 1962).

[15]

tion was limited to a few years spent at al-Azhar, the leading Islamic institution of learning in the Middle East. But he had acquired enough understanding of the new currents of thought to be sympathetic to the new intellectual class and their demands for the renewal of Egypt along Western lines. He put himself in touch with the constitutionalists who hoped to introduce Western parliamentary institutions into Egypt. According to Blunt, a pro-Egyptian observer whose evidence must be treated with great caution, Arabi was reputed to have rebuffed Khedive Tawfiq at one stage of the revolt by saying: "We are not slaves and shall never from this day forth be inherited."[11]

The so-called nationalistic agitation in Egypt was, however, only a thin veneer of the total movement of revolt. The intelligentsia was a tiny class compared with that which would develop in the Middle East in the twentieth century. Its exposure to the West and its understanding of Western civilization was not deep. Many of the leaders tended to see the West purely in terms of its superior military technology and its parliamentary institutions. Many, like Arabi himself, knew no European language and had never travelled in Europe. Arabi's last cabinet before his military defeat by the British had only a few members who could converse fluently in a Western language.[12] Not surprisingly, therefore, the ideology of the intelligentsia retained many traditional elements, such as its appeal to the unifying power of Islam, and coupled them with catch phrases derived from a limited knowledge of the West, such as Egypt for the Egyptians and the demand for a constitution. The political agitation in the army began among the native-born

[11] Wilfrid Scawen Blunt, *Secret History of the English Occupation of Egypt* (New York, 1922), p. 150.

[12] Abd al-Rahman al-Rafii, *al-Thawrah al-Arabiyah* [The Arabi Revolt] (Cairo, 1949), p. 204.

Egyptian officers who resented the fact that the highest positions in the army were reserved for Turks and Circassians. At first the movement was anti-Circassian, not anti-Western, and the officers limited their demands to corrections of abuses in the army. It was only after some of these demands had been rejected that the scope of the agitation was expanded and threatened to undermine the entire administration, including the privileged position of the European powers.[13] Among the leaders of thought at this time there was little agreement on what form the new society was to assume. Some wanted a parliamentary regime; others a constitutional monarchy; still others, and especially the army offices, merely wanted to eliminate the most glaring abuses in the army or in the administration. Those influenced by Afghani sought to make Egypt a base for the revival of the East and for a holy war against the Christian West. The most conclusive proof of the weakness of the nationalist movement was the rapidity with which the British suppressed it, as well as the fact that Egyptian nationalism reappeared only after a new generation of intellectuals had come to the fore.

Basically, the Arabi revolt was a movement of discontent against an established authority that affected most segments of society. The peasants (*fellahin*) were drawn into it because of the oppressive taxes. They saw in Arabi a leader who would release them from their tax obligations, and who would also liberate the country from foreign, Christian oppressors. Their action must be seen largely as a traditional peasant uprising against oppressive and weakened political authority; it was part of the usual rural hostility toward urban rule, which traditionally manifested itself in its more acute forms when this authority had been undermined.

[13] Donald Mackenzie Wallace, *Egypt and the Egyptian Question* (London, 1883), pp. 58ff.

[*17*]

The urban masses in Cairo were motivated by the same desires, especially by the call to defend Islam against "infidel" invaders. The intellectuals and the military wanted to rectify personal grievances against the ruling aristocracy and to modernize the country so that it could withstand foreign encroachments. The revolt resulted from the breakdown of administrative order in the country and the inability of the traditional ruling class—mostly of foreign origin—to suppress any longer classes having heavy grievances. The sophisticated form of Egyptian and Islamic nationalism was an ideology of a relative few, a thin veneer that was quelled, or at least driven underground, when the revolt was put down and its leaders exiled.

The Egyptian army, its discontented junior officers led by Arabi, first began to cause trouble in the crisis leading up to the deposition of Ismail in 1879. By 1881, the young officers had begun to play a decisive role in Egyptian politics. They forced the dismissal of the Minister of War, who had discriminated against native Egyptian officers in the army. Then, at the end of the year, they brought down the Ministry and established a new one, dominated by Arabi and a fellow officer, Sami al-Barudi. By the end of 1881 the situation was sufficiently embroiled to require a clarification of British policy.

The Gladstone cabinet, however, was paralyzed in the face of these rapid developments. It was incapable of defining a policy for two reasons: Gladstone's campaign pledges of 1880, and divisions within the cabinet. In the election campaign of 1880, considered by some to have been Gladstone's most triumphant moment, the leader of the Liberal party had launched a stinging attack upon Disraeli's foreign policy. During the campaign Gladstone had set forth the principles on which he believed a nation's foreign policy should be based. He argued for the maintenance of peace, the equality of all nations, and the right of nations to settle their own problems. Since the Arabi revolt was being described by some observers as a genuine nationalistic movement, it was difficult for Gladstonians in the cabinet to agree to repressive measures.

The second problem facing the cabinet was its internal divisions. The Liberal cabinet of 1880 was a ministry of great talents, but bitterly divided on important domestic and foreign policies. On the right were Lord Hartington and Lord Northbrook. They favored the maintenance of traditional *laissez-faire* economic policies and close attention to international affairs for the purpose of safeguarding the empire. The left wing of the party, represented by Chamberlain and Dilke, were opponents of a *laissez-faire* economy and supported vigorous government intervention in the social and economic life of England. While neither was anti-imperialist, both, at this stage of their careers, were suspicious of right-wing elements using imperialism to divert attention from much needed reforms at home. They were also determined that British power should not be used to support overseas financial ventures of the financial classes in England. In the middle, trying to maintain unity within the cabinet, were Gladstone and Granville. Already, before the Egyptian question had become acute, the cabinet had split over Chamberlain's radical "unauthorized program," and over the Irish question. The divisions and tendencies in the cabinet were further intensified by the Arabi revolt. The more conservative Whig politicians, led by Hartington and Northbrook, called for forthright measures to stamp out the revolt. To them Arabi was nothing more than a military adventurer. The new radicals of the party, led by Chamberlain and Dilke, were at first hesitant to support strong measures. They tended to see Arabi as a well-meaning nationalist. More important, because of their own radical social policies and concern for the welfare of the masses, they were violently opposed to any action that might be interpreted as aiding Egypt's foreign bondholders. They feared that the demands for an expeditionary force were actually being put forward by the bondholders and that an invasion of Egypt would prove beneficial only to the wealthy classes in England and France. Gladstone and his Foreign Secretary, Granville, held a middle position. As in previous questions, they were primarily interested in maintaining unity in the cabinet.[14]

Ultimately, the event that irrevocably committed Europe to stamping out the revolt was the famous Joint Note of January 6, 1882. The French Prime Minister, Gambetta, persuaded the British to dispatch a note identical with the French note to the Egyptian government to warn agitators against undermining the authority of Khedive Tawfiq. The Note met with a violent response in Egypt, where it was regarded as an undue interference in Egypt's internal affairs. Gambetta had foreseen such a reaction, and was in fact prepared to collaborate with the British to crush the revolt. At this moment, however, the French Chamber of Deputies overthrew Gambetta and installed a weaker government. It was well-known that the Chamber, worried about France's position in Europe, was not anxious to become embroiled in Egyptian affairs along with the British. Thus, the field was left open to the British. But even as the agitation in Egypt increased in tempo, the British remained reluctant to take any aggressive steps. The cabinet, which had been quite unprepared for the hostile reception given the Joint Note in Egypt, was still violently divided. Its first plan was to encourage the Ottoman Turks to suppress the revolt, but so many restrictions were placed on

[14] The clearest discussion of the divisions within the cabinet over the Egyptian question is Robinson and Gallagher, *Africa and the Victorians*, pp. 76-121.

the proposed Turkish military expedition that the Turks were reluctant to agree. An international conference at Constantinople, called to examine the Egyptian question, failed to reach an agreement. Faced with a worsening situation in Egypt, riots, and jeopardy to the Suez Canal, the British bombarded Egyptian forts at Alexandria in July, landed troops from the Suez Canal, and defeated the Egyptian army at Tell el-Kebir on September 13, 1882. The following day, British troops occupied Cairo and returned Khedive Tawfiq to his throne.

❉

Certain basic attitudes toward Egypt were established during the Egyptian crisis and the early years of the occupation, attitudes which influenced the nature of British rule in Egypt and the programs of reform carried out during this period. Even after the occupation, Egypt remained a burning issue in British domestic politics. The left felt that the Gladstonian ministry had betrayed its own principles in invading Egypt. The critics of imperialism argued that Egypt had been occupied in order to save the European bondholders and in violation of the principle of self-government. In the light of later developments, they generally regarded the occupation of Egypt as the first and decisive step toward British expansion into the rest of Africa. Passions were aroused every time the Egyptian question was raised in the English Parliament or the English press.[15] It was, therefore, necessary for the British administrators in Egypt to keep Egypt calm, in order to permit few opportunities for keeping the issue alive in England. The British in Egypt were reluctant to sponsor programs which might create strong opposition in Egypt, thus setting off new

[15] One of the most outspoken critics was Henry Labouchere. Excerpts from his parliamentary speeches are printed in Algar Thorold, *The Life of Henry Labouchere* (London, 1913).

criticism at home. The British representative in Egypt considered one of his major responsibilities to be that of maintaining quiet in Egypt and not raising questions embarrassing to the cabinet.[16]

The reason given by the British for occupying Egypt was the danger to the Suez Canal and the desire to restore order in Egypt. The Liberal government promised that as soon as order had been restored, the troops would be withdrawn. The first decade of British rule, when the programs of reform were being developed, was influenced by the possibility of evacuation.[17] For this reason, the British confined themselves primarily to programs requiring immediate attention and to those which they felt might be carried on by the Egyptians after British withdrawal. Moreover, the administration in Egypt was hesitant to bring forward programs which might be interpreted by critics at home as postponing the date of evacuation. Such a policy created great difficulties. Even reforms that could have hastened evacuation were not introduced because they would have been misrepresented in England as part of a trend to keep Britain in Egypt. Suggestions that British influence in the Egyptian Ministry of the Interior be increased, for instance, met with opposition both at home and in Egypt. English critics argued that such a step was intended to turn Egypt into a British colony. The dilemma con-

[16] In 1890 Baring wrote the following to Foreign Secretary Salisbury: "Since I have been in Egypt my earnest endeavor has always been to ensure the local treatment of local questions, that is to say, to prevent any Egyptian question, in itself of comparatively slight importance, from creating a diplomatic disturbance which might extend outside Egypt." Baring to Salisbury, No. 56, February 22, 1890, Public Records Office (hereafter cited as PRO), Foreign Office (hereafter cited as FO), 78/4308.

[17] As late as 1890 a British official, Alfred Milner, spoke of the unsettling effect of the temporary nature of the occupation on the British administrators in Egypt. Milner to Goschen, June 22, 1890, Milner Papers, Box 6.

fronting the British was that the attitudes toward Egypt at home, especially among leftist critics, precluded an active reform program. Yet without vigorous reforms, Egypt could not be reorganized, and the British could not withdraw with the confidence that an independent Egyptian government would not again be undermined by revolt.

In his study of imperialism, Hobson uses the British occupation of Egypt as a key example of the economic causes of imperialism. He argues that capitalists with heavy investments in Egypt compelled the British government to assume political control of the country in order to safeguard these interests.[18] A more careful scrutiny of the economic and non-economic factors is required, however. The Egyptian state debt of nearly £E100 million was extremely large by any standards.[19] British and French capitalists controlled most of this debt. These financial groups were well-organized; the Council of Foreign Bondholders, a private British group, had been established in the 1860's for the express purpose of protecting the overseas investments of English creditors. There is undeniable proof that the first encroachments in Egypt were brought about largely by pressure from these financial groups. As noted earlier in this chapter, the bankrupt Egyptian government was forced to create an international financial body, the *Caisse de la Dette*, to control Egyptian finances pledged to the debt, and then allowed the establishment of Anglo-French control over the Egyptian administration. The Arabi revolt had its roots in the financial dislocations in Egypt which resulted in oppressive taxes and an administrative breakdown. Even in some of the last stages, the influence of the financial elements was apparent. Gambetta's government was driven into an aggressive policy by various

[18] J. A. Hobson, *Imperialism, A Study* (New York, 1902).
[19] An Egyptian pound was worth £1 0s 6d in English currency.

[23]

interested groups, including the French bondholders. But these groups were not strong enough to carry the day in France. Similarly in England, although the bondholders applied pressure, the final decision to invade the country was made because the administrative chaos in Egypt threatened the Suez Canal. Egypt was occupied primarily for strategic and defensive reasons. The radicals in the cabinet agreed to the dispatch of the expeditionary force only when they were convinced that Arabi was, in fact, a military adventurer and that the rest of the Empire was threatened by events in Egypt. Egypt was occupied because of India, not because of the bondholders. The subsequent policies of reform and control in Egypt reflected the defensive nature of the occupation. The primary concern of the administrators in Egypt was to maintain the tranquility of a country considered important because of its strategic location.

CHAPTER II

EGYPT IN 1882

Two GENERALIZATIONS about Egypt in 1882 are pertinent to the general framework of this study. The first is that Egypt had already begun a conscious policy and drive toward redressing its material strength vis-à-vis the West; that is, Egypt had already begun to modernize. The encounter with France in 1798 had been shattering to the traditional society. Egypt's subsequent rulers, particularly Muhammad Ali (1805-1848) and Ismail (1863-1879), had launched programs of limited modernization, designed to bring Egypt into better military and technological balance with the West. Second, agents of social change—carriers of modernization—had been created during this push toward modernization. These agents, both foreign and indigenous, favored the continuation of development programs within Egypt.

There were two crucial groups involved in the modernization of Egypt before 1880. The first was the foreign commercial and financial class, attracted to Egypt by its investment and developmental opportunities. Because of their number, their ability to dispose of foreign capital, and their peculiarly privileged legal status in Egypt, foreign financiers had a considerable influence over the determination of Egyptian policy. The second class was the Western-educated Egyptian intellectuals, those trained in the Westernized schools of Egypt and in European schools. Although this class was still small and relatively new, its goals were clearly interlocked with those of a more modernized Egypt. Therefore, the British, when they occupied the country, were brought into contact with a society already undergoing change and with relatively activist segments of that society favoring programs of change.

There is a growing consensus among theoretical sociologists about the major characteristics of a relatively modernized society. According to the literature on the subject, such a society can be characterized by the differentiation of its structures or institutions. These structures are more specialized and perform more specific functions in a modernized society than in a relatively nonmodernized society. The modern bureaucracy has often been cited to illustrate this kind of a development; in a sense it is a mirror of the larger society. It tends to be divided into numerous, specialized agencies, each with a rather specific task to perform. This analysis does not imply that there is not a problem of integration of the specialized institutions in modernized societies. The modernized society must, in fact, attain high levels of integration and solidarity if the society is to function effectively. For this reason, certain institutions must secure the proper relationships between specialized units. Their functions, then, must be highly general and integrative. This analysis merely suggests that in a modernized society there are more specialized and interdependent units than in a non-modernized society. Moreover, accompanying this growth of specialization, there is a breakdown of self-sufficiency among the structures of the modernized society along with a growth of interdependence. Another important characteristic of the modernized society relates to recruitment of personnel into these differentiated structures. Personnel are recruited on the basis of their ability to perform the rather specialized tasks of the institution. Recruitment and advancement depend on demonstrated capacities of merit, rather than ascriptive criteria such as birth.[1]

In contrast, the relatively non-modernized society is characterized by a lack of differentiation, lack of special-

[1] In this chapter I must indicate my indebtedness to Marion J. Levy, *Modernization and the Structure of Society* (Princeton, 1965).

ization of structures, high degrees of self-sufficiency, and low levels of interdependence among the institutions. Here, individual institutions tend to perform diffuse and non-specialized functions. Recruitment is on the basis of ascription rather than merit. The individual is judged by who he is rather than by how well he performs specific tasks. In these societies the family, or kinship, system is the prototype structure. It performs a wide range of basic functions: socialization, political and economic allocation. In one sense, the modernization process can be seen as the disengaging of many of the functions once performed in the family, and the incorporation of them into more specialized and differentiated institutions.

Egypt before the Napoleonic invasion was an example of what S. N. Eisenstadt refers to as an historic bureaucratic empire, in his work, *The Political Systems of Empires*. It was not a completely traditional society; that is, one dominated by undifferentiated structures, by great self-sufficiency of the units, and by recruitment to the various structures by ascription. Mixed with the traditional, it already had elements of modernity. As Eisenstadt has pointed out, in these more developed societies a certain amount of differentiation had taken place in many of the most important institutions. Egypt's political institutions—particularly the bureaucracy—had been disembedded from the traditional political structures and from the kinship system. In the economic sphere there had developed relatively autonomous and rationalized market exchange systems. Furthermore, recruitment into all of these structures emphasized qualities of merit as well as ascription.

Nevertheless, the vast majority of the population belonged to the traditional and undifferentiated structures of the Egyptian society. As the French scholars who accompanied Napoleon showed, most of the population lived on the land, producing only subsistence crops. The irrigation system of the Nile basin was rudimentary compared with the developments of the nineteenth and twentieth centuries. The land was irrigated only once a year—during the flood season. Consequently, it supported a single crop, usually a grain, most of which was consumed locally. Very little capital was generated. In many areas market exchange systems were hardly known. Almost no cash crops were grown. Artisans did, of course, exist, but were mostly confined to the larger cities and towns. With their crude techniques and rudimentary machines, they produced goods distributed mostly to small, privileged groups in the cities.[2]

The kinship system was the basic institution of traditional Egyptian society. It discharged many of the society's fundamental functions, those performed by more specialized structures in a modernized society. It played the dominant role in socializing its younger members. The kinship system also played a large role in the allocation of political authority and economic resources. A person's financial responsibilities and his share of political power were determined largely by his place within the family by age, relationship to other members of the family, and by his or her sex. Economic and political power usually went to the more aged, the patriarchs of the kin group, while the more onerous duties fell to the younger members. The political and economic organization of the village tended to be an extension of the kinship system. The most responsible political or administrative positions went to certain of the more venerated families. The *Umdah* (headman) of the village, and

[2] The best picture of Egypt at the end of the eighteenth century is that of the French savants contained in *Description de l'Égypte, État Moderne* (Paris, 1809-1812). A more general analysis of the Ottoman Empire in the eighteenth century is H. A. R. Gibb and Harold Bowen, *Islamic Society and the West* (London, 1950-1957).

[28]

the various *shaykhs* were chosen with great attention to birth, and with considerably less attention to merit. There were, of course, more technically demanding tasks performed in the village, such as that of the barber (a medical practitioner) and the teacher at the village school. Certain minimal requirements of efficiency were expected, but training for these jobs and recruitment into them were governed largely by the prescriptive rights of certain families. The allocation of economic resources was also thoroughly intertwined with the kinship system. The communal nature of land ownership and its redivision at various times secured the rights of all members of the village community, but tended to place a low priority on rewards for the most efficient cultivation of the land.[3]

Coexisting with the largely undifferentiated and unspecialized structures of rural Egypt were the more developed institutions of the central government, the central economy, and the religious organization. The religious institution seems, in some respects, to have been the most disembedded from the traditional structures. It was centralized more by its commitment to basic religious beliefs than by its administrative hierarchy. The religious organization in Egypt was clearly not as centralized in its bureaucracy as, for example, the Catholic Church of the Western world. The religious organization was probably the most open in its recruitment of talent, emphasizing merit far more than qualities of birth. Among the members of the religious institution there tended to develop what might be called autonomous goals and rationality; that is, goals pursued for maximizing the power, efficiency, and status of the religious organization alone. The centralized religious

[3] Agricultural practices in this period have been studied by Helen Rivlin, *The Agricultural Policy of Muhammad Ali in Egypt* (Cambridge, Massachusetts, 1961).

structures penetrated into the rural areas, where they were one of the most important means of cutting across the fundamental orientations of the traditional, rural society. It was almost the only institution through which members of this society could move into the centralized and differentiated structures.[4]

Egypt had been ruled almost continually by alien conquerors—in the period before the Napoleonic invasion, by delegates of the Ottoman Empire based at Constantinople, and by the Mamluk military oligarchy, also brought in from foreign territories. These conquerors dominated the central government, particularly the bureaucracy and the military, monopolizing the upper ranks of the bureaucracy and the military. But within the ranks of the privileged there were rewards for performance and merit to be had. The bureaucracy and the military, then, reflected the admixture of the traditional and the more modern so common to eighteenth-century Egypt.[5]

Pressures by the members of the government and religious institution to maximize their political and economic power were instrumental in forcing the rural communities to make available some of the villages' human and economic resources. The centralized and differentiated structures were thus able to free resources from the control of rural structures. Taxation was the most effective technique. Since the desired wealth inevitably depended upon agricultural productivity, the government also requisitioned manpower in the form of the *corvée* to keep the canals in working order. Security was also a desideratum, necessary if the government was to obtain revenue from the rural areas. Members of the

[4] Gibb and Bowen, *Islamic Society and the West*, especially ii, 70-80.

[5] Stanford Shaw, *The Financial and Administrative Organization of Ottoman Egypt, 1517-1798* (Princeton, 1962) and A. N. Poliak, *Feudalism in Egypt, Syria, Palestine, and Lebanon* (London, 1939).

lower bureaucracy were given some responsibility for securing at least minimal levels of public security. In addition, some efforts were made to regulate the behavior of village officials for the purpose of controlling villages. To a limited extent, the government was able to introduce criteria of merit and performance in the recruitment and rewarding of these village officials. For the purpose of securing the three basic goals of taxation, manpower, and security, the more differentiated structures interpenetrated with the less differentiated, leading to a reduction in village self-sufficiency. The religious organization, because of its more universal criteria of recruitment, was also a direct link between the traditional and the more developed structures of the society. Nevertheless, except in these relatively restricted ways, these two quite different set of structures were isolated from each other.

Egypt's encounter with the French in 1798 was to prove the beginning of the end of the old order. The French themselves were not in Egypt long enough to make much of an impact. Although Napoleon had taken with him a host of scholars to study Egypt and effect changes, he was never in a strong enough position to carry out reforms. Nevertheless, the invasion proved sufficiently disruptive for the Mamluk and Ottoman rulers of Egypt that they could not reassert their authority. After a short interim, during which there was a struggle for power, Muhammad Ali came to the fore. He was to lead a program of Egyptian modernization during his long period of rule (1805-1848).

Muhammad Ali, who had been sent to Egypt with the Ottoman troops to defeat the French, stayed on with his troops after the French evacuation and engaged in a three-cornered struggle with the Mamluk soldiers and the representative of the Ottoman Empire for control of Egypt. By 1805 he had consolidated his position in Lower

Egypt, and by 1811 had removed from competition the chief contenders for authority—the Mamluks. He then proceeded to gather full authority in himself and rule the country. Although relatively uneducated, Muhammad Ali recognized the superior power of the West and determined to embrace Western institutions to increase the power of Egypt. He was not a nationalist or a pan-Islamist; rather, he treated Egypt as a tax farm or exploitable personal property much as the Mamluks had done before him. His goal was personal aggrandizement. In spite of this limited outlook, Muhammad Ali's influence on Egypt's development was impressive. The areas most touched by his reform plans were the military, education, agriculture, and industry.[6]

The touchstone of Muhammad Ali's forced modernization was his military reform. All other considerations were subordinated to his desire to make Egypt a strong military base from which to exercise influence throughout the Middle East, even over Constantinople. In an effort to modernize the military Muhammad Ali brought in European, particularly French, military advisers. He created military schools from which a new group of officers were graduated. The modernization of the military also included the development of an Egyptian navy. An arsenal was built at Alexandria. After part of the Egyptian navy was destroyed at the Battle of Navarino, in the Greek War of Independence, Muhammad Ali undertook to rebuild the navy with the aid of French advisers. The military reorganization was an immediate success. The army was used to put down the Wahabbis in the Arabian peninsula, served creditably on the Ottoman

[6] James Heyworth-Dunne, *An Introduction to the History of Education in Modern Egypt* (London, 1938), gives a reliable estimate of Muhammad Ali's aims and intentions in Egypt. Gabriel Guermard, *Les Réformes en Égypte* (Cairo, 1936), presents a general description of the many-faceted reform programs of Muhammad Ali.

side in the Greek War of Independence, extended Egyptian control over the Sudan, and was successful in later campaigns against Ottoman troops. These last campaigns were to prove the undoing of Muhammad Ali, however. In the Egyptian-Turkish War of 1839-1840, advancing Egyptian armies were halted by the major European powers, and Muhammad Ali was forced to sign a treaty, which, while recognizing his position and that of his family in Egypt, forced him thereafter to drastically reduce the size of his army. Muhammad Ali's grandiose expansionistic aims were thus brought to an end by the limitation on the size of his army. With the opportunity for further expansion blocked, the campaign for modernization was slowed. In the last years of his reign there was a dwindling of reform programs at all levels.

Educational reform was intertwined with the military requirements of the country. The first Westernized schools were military schools where young Turkish officers were trained. In time, educational reform was broadened. A School of Medicine and Veterinary was created in the 1820's, mostly for the benefit of the army. A School of Engineering followed shortly. As the administration had to be run efficiently and men had to be trained in the knowledge of Western languages and other Western skills, the School of Languages was started in the 1830's. Its goal was to turn out future administrators and officials who could translate foreign languages and would be familiar with Western administrative techniques. One of the most important tasks of the graduates was to translate books from European languages into either Arabic or Turkish. To give talented students the opportunity to develop their skills further, educational missions were sent to Europe. A generation of students was educated in medicine, engineering, military science, and administration in France, Austria, and England. Problems of conveying European subjects to Egyptian students who did not know European languages were, of course, tremendous. Since Egypt had almost no native-born trained personnel, teachers were brought to Egypt from Europe. Their lectures, which were, of course, written in European languages, were translated either into Turkish or Arabic, depending upon the medium of instruction of the particular school. The effectiveness of the courses depended, in large part, on the skill of the translators, the majority of whom were poorly equipped to render European words into Arabic or Turkish. According to a government committee on schools, "the lessons which were taught by foreign teachers ignorant of Arabic or Turkish were given to the students by translators who knew nothing of their meaning. Thus, clarification was impossible because of their lack of familiarity with the subject. This was the one reason for the backwardness of the students."[7]

In spite of the difficulties in educational reform, there were a number of positive achievements. A tradition of providing Westernized education was established in Egypt during this period. Primary, secondary, and higher education was organized to give a restricted but Western type of education. Certain schools established under Muhammad Ali have had a long life in Egypt. The famous School of Medicine, founded by Clot Bey, has existed except for brief periods since that time. The School of Engineering dates to this time. But even more important than these changes was the fact that the graduates of these schools came to form a nucleus of a new educated class. These men, educated in Westernized schools in Egypt and in some cases in Europe itself, had a new understanding of the West and were advo-

[7] Jamal al-Din al-Shayyal, *Tarikh al-Tarjamah wa Harakah al-Thaqafah fi Asr Muhammad Ali* [A History of Translations and Cultural Development in the Reign of Muhammad Ali] (Cairo, 1949), p. 19.

cates of the introduction of Western institutions. They constituted a corps of trained personnel, whose talents the government could utilize in later periods. The most famous representative of this new intelligentsia was Rifaa Badawi Rafi al-Tahtawi.[8] An Azhari *shaykh*, he accompanied an educational mission to Paris in 1826, serving as the religious leader (*Imam*) of the group. He studied on his own in Paris, met noted Western scholars, including France's leading orientalist, Silvestre de Sacy, and was impressed with the attainments of the West. He was convinced that Egypt must make a creative adaptation to the life of the West. When he returned to Egypt, he became a leader of the Westernization movement. Tahtawi served for a time as a translator at the School of Medicine; in 1836 he helped to found the School of Languages, which became the most influential in Egypt. It was in this school and through the influence of Tahtawi that a great many of the new intelligentsia received their first authentic exposure to the West. Tahtawi continued to serve Egypt in his role of a modernizer after the death of Muhammad Ali. Later he incurred the disfavor of Abbas, and was exiled to the Sudan; but he returned to Egypt under Said.

Rapid modernization under Muhammad Ali depended upon the development of Egypt's agricultural economy. It was not surprising, therefore, that Muhammad Ali's regime made some of its most notable contributions through development of the agricultural resources of the country.[9] Two far-reaching changes were the introduction of new, long-staple, high-quality cotton, known as *Jumel*; and the development of perennial irrigation. The new cotton had been developed by Jumel, a Frenchman. The Jumel strain was raised almost nowhere else in the world and was ideally suited for the Egyptian soil

[8] Hourani, *Arabic Thought in the Liberal Age*, pp. 67-84.
[9] See Rivlin, *The Agricultural Policy of Muhammad Ali in Egypt*.

[35]

and climate. Also Muhammad Ali found cotton to be an ideal export product by which to finance his modernization programs. The first exports were made in the 1820's. The cultivation of cotton was extended rapidly throughout Lower Egypt and soon became Egypt's primary export item. In certain good years cotton exports accounted for well over half of Egypt's total exports. In such a fashion Muhammad Ali began the transformation of Egypt from a subsistence to a cash-crop export economy.

Since cotton was grown only in the summer during the low stage of the Nile and required extensive and frequent waterings, major changes in the irrigation system were necessary. In Lower Egypt, where cotton was the primary crop, perennial irrigation was substituted for the old basin system which existed when land was irrigated only by the floodwaters. Under the basin system, the lands along the banks of the Nile, having been suitably prepared, received the Nile floodwaters. After the water had been in the basins for a certain number of days, it was allowed to run back into the Nile, or if necessary on to other basins. The basin system which allowed only one irrigation of the soil and one crop a year, was altered under Muhammad Ali. Deep, summer canals were constructed for the purpose of carrying low-level water from the Nile to the fields. Pumps were also installed to raise water from the low-lying canals. These changes permitted the watering of the soil in the summer, and thus the raising of cotton then.

But the alterations in the basic pattern of the Egyptian economy took their toll among the peasants. The summer canals required more attention than the basin system, since they had to be carefully maintained and cleaned of silt every year—duties that became the lot of peasant, forced (*corvée*) labor. Moreover, the peasantry were not the beneficiaries of the increased productivity of the soil, for most of the increased wealth of Egypt was absorbed by its ruler's expensive programs of military modernization. The duties of the peasants were simply increased; they were compelled to work the soil more frequently and more carefully; they were called out for the onerous *corvée* operations more regularly.

Muhammad Ali's most bizarre experiment in modernization was his effort to industrialize the country.[10] In keeping with the military requirements of the state, the Egyptian ruler sought to make his country independent of Europe for some of its basic industrial needs. He brought in European engineers, created a shipbuilding plant at Alexandria, and set up textile and armaments factories throughout Egypt. Since the country was lacking in fuel, animals were used to supply the motive power. Because most of the factories were run at a substantial loss, the experiment proved costly. The climate, and particularly the dust, caused breakdowns in the machinery, usually with no one to repair it.[11] The defeat of Muhammad Ali's troops in 1840, and the application of the treaty limiting the size of the army, brought a rather dismal conclusion to this most enterprising effort at forced industrialization. The industries disappeared almost immediately after government supports were withdrawn. By the time of the British occupation almost nothing remained of them. The country was still essentially agricultural; industrial development was again restricted to a few extractive and processing industries.

The modernizing efforts of Muhammad Ali, although made by an alien ruler in an effort to make his country of conquest a more powerful instrument with which to pursue his personal aims, had a far-reaching influence

[10] An exaggerated and flattering estimate of these efforts can be found in Mustafa Fahmy, *La Révolution de l'Industrie en Égypt et ses Conséquences Sociales au 19ᵉ Siècle* (Leiden, 1954).

[11] Michaud and Poujoulat, *Correspondance d'Orient* (Paris, 1834), VII, 33.

on Egypt. The industrial reforms collapsed with the defeat of the Egyptian troops, but the educational and agricultural-hydraulic reforms continued to determine the path followed by Egyptian modernization. Increased cotton production and perennial irrigation were established as the techniques for developing the potential wealth of the country. Education produced an elite, an intelligentsia, aware of the West and Egypt's need to adapt to it. The elite were later to serve as an administrative element through which Egyptian modernization was to be implemented. Its members were also to become leaders of the new press and the developing educational establishment; eventually some were to place themselves in alliance with the revolutionary aspirations of Arabi and his young Egyptian military officers.

The rate of modernization slowed during the reigns of Abbas and Said, but a flourishing of activity began anew under Egypt's most flamboyant ruler, Ismail (1863-1879). The funds for Muhammad Ali's reforms had been generated within the Egyptian economy itself by means of rigid control over the agricultural life of the country. Under Ismail, on the other hand, the Egyptian government borrowed heavily from European capitalists.[12] The extravagances of Ismail's reign have caught the attention of many historians—the lavish expenditure on the ceremonies for the opening of the Suez Canal in 1869, the new palaces, the misuse of state lands—but extravagance should not obscure the immense changes wrought in Egypt's life.[13] In agriculture the changeover from basin system to perennial irrigation continued

[12] The mechanisms of international finance in Egypt are discussed by David Landes, *Bankers and Pashas, International Finance and Economic Imperialism in Egypt* (Cambridge, Massachusetts, 1958).
[13] Studies of the reforms carried out under Ismail may be found in M. G. Mulhall, "Egyptian Finance," *Contemporary Review* (1882), pp. 525-36; Angelo Sammarco, *Le Règne du Khedive*

apace. Parts of Middle Egypt and most of Lower Egypt were perennially irrigated, supporting cultivation the year round by the time of the British occupation. Cotton production was steadily extended throughout these areas. The American Civil War, coming at the beginning of Ismail's reign, established cotton as Egypt's great export commodity. England's textile mills, unable to obtain cotton from the blockaded Southern states, paid top prices to countries like Egypt.[14] The value of cotton exports in 1870 was five times what it had been in 1860. Even before the British occupation Egyptian cotton exports in certain good years had accounted for as much as 80 percent of all Egyptian exports.

Ismail also extended educational reforms. Schools which had been closed at the end of Muhammad Ali's reign were reopened; educational missions were resumed on a large scale. Egypt's growing intelligentsia were revitalized by the educational activity, and the country experienced a great intellectual flourishing under Ismail.[15] Al-Azhar, the leading Muslim institution, was stirred by the teaching and ideas of the pan-Islamic reformer and agitator, Jamal al-Din al-Afghani. Students who studied with Afghani or who were influenced by his ideas were to play an important role in the modernization of Egypt and the development of Egyptian nationalism. They included Muhammad Abduh, Sad

Ismael (Cairo, 1937); Abd al-Rahman al-Rafii, *Asr Ismail* [The Reign of Ismail] (Cairo, 1948) and A. E. Crouchley, *The Economic Development of Modern Egypt* (New York, 1938). These are rather uncritical works and accept the statistics of the period without questioning their accuracy.

[14] Statistics from this period, and later periods as well, are treacherous, but they can be used as indications of general trends. The cotton statistics here are taken from Landes, *Bankers and Pashas*, p. 332.

[15] Heyworth-Dunne, *Introduction to History of Education in Modern Egypt.*

[39]

Zaghlul, al-Muwaylihi, al-Nadim, and others. During these years the first private Egyptian newspapers were founded, the most influential being *al-Ahram,* founded in 1875, *Abu-Naddara,* the various newspapers of the famous journalist, al-Nadim, and *al-Mahrusah* of Salim al-Naqqash. This intellectual revival was to culminate in the Arabi revolt.

Under Muhammad Ali's successors, particularly Ismail, foreign capital and foreign financiers were welcomed to Egypt. As David Landes has shown in his book, *Bankers and Pashas,* these groups were not slow to take advantage of the opportunity. There was a remarkable growth of foreign banking, commercial and trading houses, and real estate companies during Ismail's reign. The men who came were a new breed of aggressive investors, on the fringe of the more sedate European financial world. These men, as represented by Edouard Dervieu, were primarily interested in making money as fast as they could by exploiting the current conditions in Egypt. Many of them had important entrees into the financial world of Europe. Dervieu, for instance, was well-connected with Alfred André, the head of Marcuard, André et Cie, one of the oldest private banks in Europe. Although the André firm was known for its essentially conservative financial policies, and although men like André would themselves probably not have engaged in the high-handed financial dealing of Dervieu in Egypt, the firm could not resist the opportunity to provide capital at such marvellously high rates of interest. Moreover, the conditions in Egypt seemed ideal for the foreign investor. The European financier himself enjoyed a privileged legal status in Egypt. As a foreigner he had extra-territorial rights. All cases involving him had to be tried in his own consular courts, and these courts were well known for their bias toward their nationals, especially in cases affecting a foreign national and an Egyptian. The story is told that on one occasion Khedive Said interrupted a conversation with a European business- man to order a servant to close the window. "If this gen- tleman catches cold," he said, "it will cost me £10,000."[16] For the most part the Khedives were quite willing to avail themselves of the capital provided by these foreign groups, no one more so than Ismail whose sometimes forced borrowing, sometimes utter extravagance, ulti- mately brought Egyptian indebtedness to the staggering figure of £E100 million. By that time, Egypt's credit was exhausted, and the country was on the verge of bankrupt- cy. The British invasion was in the offing.

When the debt had reached these astronomical figures, another fact of great importance to Egypt was clear: the presence of a foreign commercial and financial class. Muhammad Ali had tried to control all aspects of modern- ization, even its financing. His successors had adopted the easier expedient of relying on the foreign merchant and his access to European capital. Even had these rulers wanted to dispense with the use of foreign capital, it seems doubtful that they could have done so. The weaknesses inherent in Egyptian society, such as extra- territorial rights and the pressure that was exerted from Europe, would have forced them to rely upon this for- eign commercial class. Foreigners played a dominant role in the banking system, in the whole system of Egyptian finance, in the development of transportation —particularly the movement of goods for export—and in the buying and selling of land. Egyptians had not en- tered these fields in any great numbers and were not to do so until the end of the First World War.[17]

❊

[16] Landes, *Bankers and Pashas*, p. 92.
[17] See A. E. Crouchley, *The Investment of Foreign Capital in Egyptian Companies and the Public Debt* (Cairo, 1936) and M. A. Rifaat, *The Monetary System of Egypt* (London, 1935).

The modernizing efforts of Egypt's rulers should be seen in the light of the categories of analysis presented by the theorists of modernization. Such an examination will clearly demonstrate that while Egypt could not be regarded in any way as a modernized society, it had made impressive gains in that direction. The most apparent change was the amount of differentiation and specialization within the economic sphere. With the introduction of large-scale cotton cultivation and the development of a greatly improved irrigation system, part of the agrarian economy produced for export. Cotton was exchanged for money or goods at local markets, from which it was eventually exported to Europe. The resulting specialization in production tended to break down the self-sufficiency of rural Egypt. The rural economy was brought into a much closer and interdependent relationship with the urban economy. There was, of course, an accompanying increase in the systems of exchange. Money transactions were gradually replacing the old barter exchange. It should be added, however, that the economic differentiation tended to take place on the larger estates in Egypt, among the wealthy, landholding aristocracy who were more responsive to the economic incentives of the modernizing market system. The vast majority of the Egyptian peasantry lived at the same levels as before, producing only subsistence crops. But there was a growing agricultural work force, the result of population increase and the growth in size of the estates. In this important respect, specialization and interdependency affected some of the smaller peasantry.

In the agricultural sphere there was also a very substantial increase in the use of inanimate sources of power. A series of dams and barrages, so essential to perennial irrigation, was being constructed along the Nile. There was an increase in the number of steam pumps for raising water from the canals and a more elaborate use of machinery for cultivation, harvesting, and digging new canals. Nevertheless, because of the relatively large population and the effective techniques of recruiting this potential work force, manpower was still the basic source of power within the agrarian sector.

Within the central government there was a remarkable development of the army and bureaucracy. The pressures of modernization called for an increased specialization of these institutions and rationalization of their development. The military colleges prepared engineers to serve with the army, trained a medical corps, and gave a much more specialized technical training in the weapons and strategy of warfare than Egypt had had before. Higher levels of expertise were also required for the running of the bureaucracy; mastery of a European language became a basic requirement for the upper levels. It was, of course, in the interest of the ruling elite, mostly of foreign origin, to keep these institutions under control and to monopolize the positions of power in both establishments. The pressures of modernization, however, drove in an opposite direction. Talent, rather than birth, was required for the efficient running of these organizations. Concessions were made to the demands of merit, especially because many members of the old Turkish aristocracy were reluctant to obtain a Westernized education. For this reason, many Egyptian-born men who were fortunate enough to gain access to the education system, pushed their way into upper levels of both the bureaucracy and the army. Within both, there was a development of cohesiveness among certain groups and a pursuit of autonomous goals. In many respects, the Arabi revolt was produced by the drives for autonomy and open recruitment in these two organizations. The Arabists in the army were anxious to open the upper ranks of the army to all members of the society. These activists were joined in time by certain segments of the

Egyptian bureaucracy seeking the same goals for their institution.

The educational institution also reflected the movement toward a relatively more modernized society. Of course, the old Islamic educational system remained, and in fact was somewhat altered in response to the pressures of the West. It continued to provide access to the religious structures of the society and to recruit its membership on the basis of fairly open and universal criteria. Coexisting with it was the modernized and Westernized education system. This system ranged from the primary schools to the technical colleges, which gave a functionally more specific type of education than was provided elsewhere. They equipped the graduates with the knowledge necessary to function in a more specialized society. Since the government financed the educational system, entry into the schools was perhaps as open as it was to be for a long time. Under the British, tuitional charges were re-imposed, thus blocking entry into the schools from the less wealthy segments of the society. Since advancement in school was dependent on achievement, the school system tended to accelerate the development of the notion of judgment by merit rather than by birth.

As might be expected, the family unit was subject to tension during this process of change. The more differentiated economic, political, and educational institutions performed some of the former functions of the family. The gradual breakdown in the isolation of rural Egypt from the urban environment resulted in more centralized political control over the rural populace. This control, such as the establishment of some judicial controls over rural areas, meant that the family played a functionally lesser role in the allocation of political power in Egypt. The economic exchange system, the development of an agricultural wage-labor force, the cultivation of cash crops, and the sale of these crops reduced the influence of the family over the allocation of economic resources. The spread of education into rural Egypt also implied a less significant family control over the whole socialization process of the children.

Nevertheless, the extent of the change must not be exaggerated. Even in the most modernized sectors of the economy the family played a major and diffuse role in socialization, role differentiation, political and economic allocation. On the peasantry, furthermore, there had been little impact from the modernizing reforms of the ruling elite. This vast majority of the population lived much as it had before, little affected by economic modernization or changes in the political institutions, probably having little access to the more extensive education system of the state.

The British, therefore, entered a country already considerably influenced by the Western world. They were in a favorable position to build on programs and to follow the direction already established by Egypt's first efforts at modernization. The development of agricultural resources through perennial irrigation and the extension of cotton cultivation were already well under way. The British only accelerated this process when they transformed other areas into perennial irrigation and when they encouraged the cultivation of cotton throughout the entire country. Most important was the fact that in the previous half-century educational reforms had been introduced and an educated elite had been trained. Although Egypt had only a fraction of the technical skills Europe possessed, Egyptians could run a complicated, modernizing economy and administration if certain technical deficiencies were filled in from Europe. For instance, in contrast to some of the new independent countries, Egypt had well-trained doctors, engineers, and lawyers who could discharge their responsibilities for public health, public works, and legal reform.

On the other hand, the difficulties encountered by the British in Egypt cannot be exaggerated. Ismail's extravagance had brought Egypt to the brink of disaster and threatened to undermine the achievements attained up to that point. His impressive reform programs, designed to increase the wealth of the country and to extend the educational system, required large capital outlays. As long as money was forthcoming from Europe, the program was a success.[18] By 1875, however, it was apparent to Ismail's European creditors that Egypt was not in a position to meet its debt obligations. No new credits were extended and the inability to obtain much needed capital jeopardized the reforms. Under the Anglo-French dual control of Egypt from 1876 to 1882, there were cutbacks in every branch of the administration. The programs of reform suffered seriously. Schools were closed; the hydraulic system was not tended properly; the system of public health began to break down. Administrative modernization was being replaced by administrative chaos.

When the British assumed control, they were faced with the problem of a country in the process of regressing into an earlier condition, on the verge of administrative collapse. Until the financial system was brought under control, the budget balanced, confidence in the economy restored so that Egypt could utilize the financial resources of Europe, Egyptian modernization could not go forward. The first years of the British occupation, therefore, dealt with these problems. By strict

[18] Egypt's public debt is discussed by Landes, *Bankers and Pashas* and Abdel Maksud Hamza, *The Public Debt of Egypt, 1854-1867* (Cairo, 1944).

financial controls such as better allocation of existing revenues, the British saved the important achievements of Ismail's reign. Although a steady development of Egypt's resources can be seen in the period 1882 to 1914, it would be a mistake to assume that such a progression was inevitable or even easily attainable. Without financial and administrative acumen, economic and political chaos might, in fact, have gained the upper hand and undermined the earlier modernizing efforts.

CHAPTER III

THE SEARCH FOR A POLICY, 1882-1888

THE MAJOR aim of British policy in Egypt was evacuation of the country as soon as its administrative and economic life permitted. The Liberal government, because of its campaign promises and traditional friendship with France, had no desire to make the occupation permanent. Its chief goal was to secure the stability and tranquility of Egypt so that it would not be torn by internal disturbances and thus threaten England's strategic route to the East. Within this context the British government was well aware that Egyptian stability could be attained only by reviving and strengthening its traditional institutions where they were still viable, and where they were not, by replacing them with institutions more suitable to the needs of Egypt. There was considerable hope that this task might be carried out in a relatively short span of time—perhaps a year, but no more than five. The administrative activity carried out in the early years of the occupation, then, was mainly an effort to achieve stability in Egypt, and not an attempt to develop Egypt's resources for European exploitation. The drives for modernization and administrative reform were relatively restricted in this period of British rule. Many of them were initiated by British officials in Egypt far less concerned with overall British foreign and imperial policy, and they often met with strong opposition from London.

European economic groups, particularly the European bondholders, maintained a constant interest in the affairs of Egypt and favored policies congenial to their interests. The bondholders were able to make their influence felt in the determination of British policy on a number of important occasions, but it is quite clear that they did not control the British administration and that in many instances their interests were subordinated to the strategic aims of the British government.

Evacuation was the policy agreed upon by the Liberal cabinet.[1] Even the most imperialist-minded segment of the party counted Egypt as a greater burden than an asset. Yet, the cabinet was decisively split on the best methods for attaining the goal of Egyptian autonomy. Disputes within the cabinet focused largely on the amount of administrative reform and modernization to be sponsored by the British. The Whig members favored a fairly strong reforming policy. They demanded that the British assume full responsibility for Egyptian affairs and introduce modern Western institutions, arguing, with a great deal of justification, that since the Arabi revolt had discredited and undermined the traditional pattern of life, evacuation could only be effected after a fundamental reorganization of Egyptian society. The radicals and the moderate Liberals, however, feared that such policies would have the opposite effect; they would, in fact, have the British entrench in Egypt, making evacuation impossible. Consequently, they favored more moderate reform, a refurbishing of the traditional institutions, and light control by the British administrators in Egypt.[2]

[1] John Morley, *Life of William Ewart Gladstone* (London, 1903), III, 120.

[2] The position taken by the various groups in the cabinet can be studied in the following works: Joseph Chamberlain, *A Political Memoir, 1880-92*, ed. by C. H. D. Howard (London, 1953); A. G. Gardiner, *The Life of Sir William Harcourt* (London, 1923); Stephen Gwynn and Gertrude M. Tuckwell, *The Life of Sir Charles Dilke* (New York, 1917); and Agatha Ramm, *The Political Correspondence of Mr. Gladstone and Lord Granville, 1876-1886* (Oxford, 1962). Much of this material and additional evidence has been summarized by Robinson and Gallagher, *Africa and the Victorians*, pp. 122-59.

The confusion of British policy was compounded further by the fact that the British did not have a free hand in Egypt. Since the occupation was deemed temporary, no major changes in the international status of Egypt could be made. Egypt remained, as it had since the reign of Muhammad Ali, an autonomous state within the Ottoman Empire. The Khedive continued as the formal ruler of the country. The Ottoman delegate at Cairo was the representative of the Porte and theoretically the most powerful foreign personage. The British were represented by a Consul-General whose powers, ostensibly, were no greater than those of the consuls of other powers. The Consul-General, in accordance with the international status of Egypt, was an agent of the Foreign Office, not the Colonial Office. In fact, until the outbreak of the First World War, Egyptian policy was determined by the Foreign Office. Of course, in practice, the British Consul-General had considerably greater powers than the other foreign delegates. But Egypt, until 1914, was characterized by its anomalous international status. The Egyptian governmental apparatus was retained. Egyptian officials held the administrative positions, at least in name, although they were subject to varying degrees of control by the British. This book will show the considerable degrees of Egyptian independence from British control, although it will make clear the growing British control over all branches of the administration in the years prior to World War I. Nevertheless, British control was always far from complete, and the British never ruled Egypt directly from 1882 to 1914.

A second factor inhibiting the power of the British was the considerable right of interference other European states possessed over Egypt's internal affairs. Ismail had granted the leading European nations considerable control over the financial life of his country. The British were able to restrict some, but not all, of the foreign power exercised over Egypt's finances.[3] In particular, the *Caisse de la Dette*, created by Ismail in 1876 to represent the interests of the foreign bondholders to the Egyptian government, remained. It received revenues pledged to the payment of the debt. Changes in the allocation of these pledged revenues required the assent of the European states. The French, bitter opponents of British rule in Egypt, were not willing to relinquish any powers to the British; nor were they inclined to accept changes in financial regulations beneficial to British interests.

The capitulations were another stumbling block to administrative progress. The Ottoman Empire had granted capitulatory rights to European citizens and their protégés early in its history. These rights had been developed more extensively in Egypt than anywhere else in the Empire, particularly under the encouragement of Muhammad Ali. By the time of the British occupation, European criminal offenses were tried in European consular courts, no new tax could be applied to Europeans without the consent of the individual powers, no house or building owned by a European could be entered without the consul of the subject being present, and no administrative ruling could be applied to Europeans without the consent of the powers. These restrictions meant, in effect, that almost all new legislation had to have the assent of the foreign powers if it was to be applicable to European subjects. Since European subjects and their protégés did play an important role in the Egyptian economy, it was necessary for the Egyptian

[3] The decision to allow the dual control to lapse and to be replaced by the Financial Adviser was not easily arrived at by the British. Gwynn and Tuckwell, *Dilke*, I, 547. French reaction to this change can be seen in Duclerc to Tissot, No. 92, October 28, 1882, France, Ministère des Affaires Étrangères, *Documents Diplomatiques, Affaires d'Égypte, 1882-1883*, Vol. CXIII.

government to consult and negotiate with the European governments before any new piece of legislation could be applied effectively in Egypt. For this reason, an easy method of obstruction was presented to powers such as the French, that were opposed to British rule.[4]

The first efforts to establish a policy for Egypt and to determine the amount of British interference required were made in the Dufferin mission of 1882-1883. Lord Dufferin, British ambassador at Constantinople, was sent as a special agent to Egypt to examine the existing conditions and suggest the best method for restoring order and stability to the country. With the cabinet still torn by dissension over policy, Foreign Secretary Granville gave Dufferin some general instructions to guide his investigations. These instructions clearly indicated the British emphasis on securing the tranquility of the country. Granville told Dufferin that "the reorganization of the Egyptian administration should be undertaken on a basis which will afford satisfactory guarantees for the maintenance of peace, order, and prosperity in Egypt, for the stability of the Khedive's authority, for the judicious development of self-government, and for the fulfillment of the obligations towards foreign powers." Dufferin was further instructed that the principal questions to be examined were: army and police, substitution of a new system for the dual control, reduction of the foreign element in all branches of the administration, improved system of justice for Egyptians, equal taxation for Europeans and Egyptians, development of political institutions, prevention of the slave trade, and the Suez Canal.[5] It was anticipated that, if these problems were

[4] There are numerous discussions of the capitulations. The reader is referred to the short summary in Jaspar Yeates Brinton, *The Mixed Courts of Egypt* (New Haven, 1930), pp. 1-19.

[5] Granville to Dufferin, No. 18, November 31, 1882, *House of Commons Sessional Papers* (hereafter cited as *HCSP*), Egypt No. 2 (1883), Vol. LXXXIII, c. 3462.

solved, British troops could be withdrawn without concern for future disturbances.

Dufferin's famous report served as a blueprint for British activity in the early years of the occupation.[6] It also gave the impression, as Gladstone had hoped it would, that British rule need not be an extended one. Dufferin said little of the financial problems which were basically international issues. But he felt that Egypt's prosperity depended upon control of the Nile and full utilization of its waters for irrigation purposes. For this reason he advised the Egyptian government to procure the services of a group of Anglo-Indian hydraulic engineers to initiate necessary reforms in this branch of the administration. By means of their expertise, Dufferin expected the irrigation system to be remodelled and the agricultural productivity of the country thereby increased. In response to his advice the Egyptian government contacted Colin Scott-Moncrieff, a former hydraulic engineer in India and Burma, and brought him to Egypt, where he was immediately placed in charge of Egyptian irrigation. Dufferin further indicated the need for police and military reform under British auspices, so that these organizations might preserve order in the country without themselves becoming organs of revolutionary discontent. In addition, he advised reforms in education and taxation, particularly in the tax laws applying to Europeans. Like so many other British officials, the British ambassador to Turkey spoke of the need for judicial reforms. He felt that one of the chief causes of discontent in the country was the lack of well-defined laws and a system of courts for settling disputes cheaply and efficiently. Before Egypt could become an orderly country, it would have to have a modern set of

[6] Dufferin's report is to be found in Dufferin to Granville, No. 38, February 6, 1883, *HCSP*, Egypt No. 6 (1883), Vol. LXXXIII, c. 3529.

laws and courts serving the mass of the population. Dufferin also recognized that one of the basic reasons for the Arabi revolt was the growing peasant indebtedness, which, he felt, had resulted from unwise borrowing and heavy financial obligations. A discontented peasantry was a threat to political stability. Dufferin offered no solution to this difficult problem, aside from a general raising of the standard of living, but he did recognize that its solution was a pressing need.

Perhaps the most influential of Dufferin's recommendations were those relating to political institutions. In 1866 Ismail had created Egypt's first representative institution on a national level—the Council of Notables.[7] This body, which represented the ruling and wealthy land-owning elements of Egyptian society, had met sporadically from then until 1882. It had been at the center of the Arabi revolt, when its members demanded the right to debate the Egyptian budget. For this reason, the British were hesitant to allow it to remain in existence. In its place Dufferin recommended three levels of political institutions—a Legislative Council, a General Assembly, and provincial councils. The provincial councils, their model based partly on previous Egyptian provincial bodies and also on Indian local representative bodies, were to represent the upper classes in the provinces. They were to have consultative powers over a wide range of local problems, mainly relating to the use and distribution of irrigation water. The Legislative Council was also based partly on Indian models. It was half-elective, half-appointive—a consultative body which met six times a year to advise the government on problems submitted to it by the administration. High property qualifications for voting and for eligibility to serve in the Council ensured that the Legislative Council,

[7] Parliamentary institutions in Egypt are discussed by Jacob Landau, *Parliaments and Parties* (Tel Aviv, 1953).

like the provincial councils, represented the established classes rather than the masses. The General Assembly was a large elective body which was to meet once every two years. Dufferin agreed to the creation of this institution only in response to Egyptian demands that the country be endowed with a body more truly representative of the country than the Legislative Council. Its sole, non-consultative power, however, was the right to veto new taxes or increases in pre-existing taxes.[8]

The British were not sanguine about their experiment in maintaining even these attenuated representative bodies.[9] They feared that the autocratic tradition in Egypt would militate against them. Nor did they want an Egyptian element to be able to undermine Britain's position in Egypt. Because of this, the representative institutions were given severely limited powers. Membership in them was confined to the established, wealthy classes, who, while not necessarily supporters of the occupation, were not likely to espouse radical economic or political doctrines.[10]

Dufferin's report proved to be a shrewd compromise of the different tendencies within the cabinet. Its proposals for the restoration of order in Egypt struck a balance between basic administrative modernization under British auspices, favored by the right wing of the cabinet, and the refurbishment of the traditional Egyptian institutions, a program sponsored by the more moderate Liberals. The report anticipated considerable British interference in and reform of agriculture, hydraulics, the police, the military, and the judicial system. The

[8] The decrees creating the new political institutions and defining their powers are to be found in HCSP, Egypt No. 19 (1883), Vol. LXXXIII, c. 3733.

[9] Alfred Lyall, The Life of the Marquis of Dufferin (London, 1905), II, 47.

[10] See the interpretation advanced by Abd al-Rahman al-Rafii, Misr wa-l-Sudan [Egypt and the Sudan] (Cairo, 1948), pp. 41-51.

moderate Liberals were appeased by the fact that Dufferin did not favor complete administrative control by the British; nor did the report suggest that the British alter the financial system of Egypt or assume full financial control of the country. Implicit in the report was the idea that the British should attempt to utilize the traditional ruling classes and institutions for their reform programs wherever possible. It was expected that after the country had been set on its feet, authority would gradually be returned to these classes. Although some astute observers doubted whether such a comprehensive program could be carried out in a short period of time, Dufferin argued that these reforms could be inaugurated rapidly and that the day of evacuation would not be distant.

Dufferin called for a limited and controlled modernization of Egypt. Although the heavy emphasis on hydraulics and agriculture, for instance, might be interpreted as an effort to exploit Egypt's resources for European purposes, it seems clear that by these reforms the British intended to secure the material contentment of the country and thereby its general stability. The great interest in the institutions for the maintenance of public order and the suppression of disturbances, namely the courts, the police and the military, also reveal the emphasis upon obtaining order, stability, and tranquility. Considerably less attention was devoted to items that would have come in for a detailed analysis if the British goals in Egypt had been purely economic—railroads, currency, banks, markets, actual and potential exports, industrial resources, and so forth. Dufferin's report clearly did not view Egypt as a supplier of raw materials to Great Britain or as a market for manufactured products or European capital. Egypt was valued as an area of imperial defense because of its strategic location.

The concern for institutions designed to ensure the

contentment of the masses and the suppression of possible internal disturbances revealed Britain's fundamental interest in Egypt as an area of imperial defense. Considerably less attention was paid to education, and virtually nothing was said about public health. Dufferin foresaw that the reforms he proposed would require a staff of British officials and technicians; in certain cases he suggested that British officials trained in India would have the requisite experience.[11]

There were rumors that Dufferin would assume full responsibility for Egyptian affairs and become Great Britain's Consul-General at Cairo. This suggestion was rejected, however, because it was felt that Dufferin's services were required at Constantinople. Other names were considered, including Lord Lansdowne and Lord Derby, before the government finally decided to appoint Sir Evelyn Baring.[12] Sir Evelyn was to serve as Consul-General of Egypt from 1883 to 1907 and was to be regarded as one of the makers of modern Egypt. Baring was of the famous Baring banking family. It must, however, be stressed that Baring himself was not a member of the banking firm, nor did the Baring Brothers banking house have any financial interests in Egypt in 1883.[13]

[11] There is Dufferin's statement from the report: "Had I been commissioned to place the affairs in Egypt on the footing of a subject state, the outlook would have been different. The masterful hand of a resident would have quickly bent everything to his will and in the space of five years we should have greatly added to the material wealth and well-being of the country by the extension of cultivated land and the consequent expansion of its revenue, by the partial, if not the total abolition of the corvée and slavery, by the establishment of justice and other beneficent reforms."

[12] Ramm, *Political Correspondence of Gladstone and Granville*, I and II.

[13] The Baring Brothers Banking House is described in Ralph W. Hidy, *The House of Baring in American Trade and Finance: English Merchant Bankers at Work, 1763-1861* (Cambridge, Massachusetts, 1949).

In fact, Baring Brothers never invested in Egypt; the one time that the question was raised later in his career, Evelyn Baring opposed the suggestion that Baring Brothers invest in Egypt.

Evelyn was the twelfth child in a family of thirteen. His father had worked in Baring Brothers for part of his life, but had later left the company, apparently because of gambling extravagances.[14] While the family had connections with the upper class of English society, it was certainly not wealthy. Evelyn was given a military education at the Royal Military College at Woolwich. He claimed that he learned almost nothing in school, and that his scholarly attainments, which were an impressive sidelight to his political career, were the result of self-education. Baring served as an artillery subaltern at Corfu and then in the War Office. His still uneventful career was altered when his cousin, Lord Northbrook, was appointed Viceroy of India in 1872 and took Baring along as his private secretary. Early in his Indian experience he demonstrated both his administrative skills and his autocratic nature. As private secretary he assumed so many of the administrative responsibilities of the Viceroy that he soon was known as the "vice-Viceroy."[15] Later, in Egypt, he was to be known as "over-Baring" because of his authoritarian nature.

Baring's work in India opened doors of opportunity to him. In 1877, when the Egyptian government was looking for an individual to represent England's financial interest on the *Caisse de la Dette*, one of his sponsors at the India Office, Louis Mallet, suggested Baring's name. In Egypt he became a great power in a position of limited authority. He was directly responsible for limiting the arbitrary power of Khedive Ismail, for

[14] For details of Baring's life see the biography by the Marquis of Zetland, *Lord Cromer* (London, 1932).

[15] *Ibid.*, p. 53.

negotiating changes in the financial arrangements, and for forcing the Khedive to turn over his personal estates to the state. If later, when he was at the helm in Egypt, he used to complain that he was forced to work a system of government which had been set up to shackle a corrupt and inept government, he could not forget that he himself was responsible for introducing many of these restrictions.

In 1880 when the Liberal government appointed Lord Ripon as Viceroy of India. Baring was sent as his financial adviser. From 1880 to 1883 Baring and Ripon were intimately associated in a plan for reorganizing and liberalizing the Indian administration.[16] Baring's name was most closely tied to the reduction of Indian tariffs, budgetary reforms, and the development of Indian railways. The reputation of Ripon's administration was also derived from the extension of the powers of local self-governing bodies, educational reforms, and the controversial and unpopular Ilbert Bill. This last was a bill which would have empowered Indian judges to try cases involving Europeans. It was bitterly opposed by the European population and eventually withdrawn by the administration in the face of such an adverse reception. Baring wrote an important article in defense of the government's position, although in later life he admitted that he had not been consulted fully on the matter before it became controversial.[17]

[16] Ripon and Baring favored many of the same policies—abolition of customs, substitution of direct for indirect taxes, and the encouragement of private enterprise. Nevertheless, there was a certain amount of tension between them. Ripon wrote to Northbrook, November 14, 1881: "On most parts we [Baring and I] agree in principle. It may perhaps be said that the great distinction between us is that he is Doctrinaire and I am not." Lucian Wolf, *The Life of the First Marquess of Ripon* (London, 1921), II, 75. Baring, on the other hand, found Ripon's ideas and reforms "rather extreme." Zetland, *Lord Cromer*, p. 76.

[17] The article he wrote in defense of the bill was published as

Baring carried a wealth of experience with him to Egypt. His autocratic tendencies were already well known and feared, but the government felt that these could be controlled. In addition to his proven financial capabilities, his earlier experience in Egypt made him familiar with its financial and administrative problems. His experience in India suited him ideally for working with the host of Indian officials being brought to Egypt and for guiding administrative programs based largely on Indian experience. Not the least of his assets were his own avowed liberal sentiments. At one point in his career he had thought of standing for Parliament as a Liberal, only to be dissuaded by Gladstone.[18] He was, in fact, highly regarded as a representative of the Liberal party's imperial policy. Louis Mallet, one of his early patrons at the India Office and a bitter critic of an expansionist foreign policy, felt that Baring was "the best and strongest anti-jingo agent" of the party, the only man who could be trusted to effect Britain's evacuation of Egypt with proper haste.[19] In a letter of congratulation on his appointment, Mallet wrote: "All the advantages which we have hitherto . . . derived from our insular position will be at an end [if we remain in Egypt]. We deliberately adopt a land frontier, constantly liable to attack which will inevitably carry us further and further into the heart of Africa. We are doomed forever to be a great fighting empire, dependent on the support of subject races who may turn against us any day when they have learned their strength."[20] Baring, in fact, was

---

"Recent Events in India," *The Nineteenth Century* (1883), pp. 569-89.

[18] Cromer, "The Politician Wordsworth," *Political and Literary Essays*, Third Series (London, 1916), p. 262.

[19] Louis Mallet to Baring, No. 220, January 21, 1884, The Cromer Papers, PRO, FO 633/7.

[20] Mallet to Baring, No. 222, April 9, 1884, *ibid.*

known to be in sympathy with the general aims of the government at this stage. He saw Egypt as a great impediment to England's foreign and imperial policy and felt that the British forces should be withdrawn as rapidly as possible.[21]

Practical exigencies in the form of a revolt in the Sudan shattered Baring's optimistic plans for effecting a rapid evacuation of British troops from Egypt. The Sudan, which was under the control of Egypt at this time, was thrown into turmoil by the Mahdist uprising. Muhammad Ahmad ibn Abdullah, the so-called Mahdi, led a religious movement, calling for a return to a purified Islam and for a religious war against Christians and corrupted Egyptian Muslims. Baring was on the verge of reducing the size of the British garrison and ordering the withdrawal of troops from Cairo to Alexandria when news reached him of the slaughter of the Egyptian army in the Sudan. This defeat altered the situation in Egypt radically. The Mahdi now constituted a military threat to Egypt. Moreover, Baring feared that the discontented peasant populations of Upper and Middle Egypt might rise in revolt in an effort to join forces with the Mahdi. For these reasons, he cancelled the order to evacuate the troops from Cairo to Alexandria.[22]

Up to this point, the British government had not interfered with the Sudanese policy of the Egyptian government, a stance dictated by a desire to leave the Egyptian government to settle most of its own affairs. But following the defeat of the Egyptian army, the Sudan question became of considerable consequence to the British. There were two possible approaches to the problem created by the revolt: either dispatch troops

[21] Dilke mentions a memorandum from Baring submitted to the cabinet arguing against a protectorate or annexation. Gwynn and Tuckwell, *Dilke*, I, 546.
[22] Mekki Shibeika, *British Policy in the Sudan, 1882-1902* (New York, 1952), pp. 79-145.

to crush the Mahdists, or withdraw from the Sudan, leaving it to the Mahdi, and defend Egypt at its natural frontiers. The cabinet felt that the Egyptian army, in the process of reorganization, was not in a position to reconquer the Sudan by itself. The effort to regain the Sudan would therefore require substantial assistance from the British. Most members of the cabinet in London were opposed to extending Britain's obligations further into Africa. They saw a Sudanese campaign as committing Great Britain more firmly to precisely what they feared —an African empire. The liberal and radical members of the government, especially, regarded British support of Egypt in the Sudan as part of a right-wing effort to extend the Empire. Granville, echoing this feeling, wrote about "an immense and powerful combination [attempting] to force us into a more exclusive administration of Egypt: the bondholders, Bismarck, the English and foreign press, the Tories, and the Jingoes."[23] Therefore, this group favored withdrawal from the Sudan and the establishment of a frontier force to protect Egypt from Mahdist attacks.

Baring and a few members of the cabinet saw the issue differently. In the first place, they believed that the presence of the Mahdi and his religious army would constitute a continuing threat to Egypt, necessitating large Egyptian military expenditures and, quite possibly, considerable British assistance in guarding the frontier. Some of the Egyptian ministers, as Baring indicated to Granville, believed that the policy of abandonment was "merely a snare and was recommended in order to render [British] presence permanently necessary in Egypt."[24] Of more importance to Baring was the fact that the Egyptian ministry regarded the maintenance of Egyptian

[23] Granville to Baring, No. 41, April 18, 1884, The Cromer Papers, PRO, FO 633/7.
[24] Baring to Granville, No. 19, December 16, 1883, *ibid.*

[62]

prestige and authority in the Sudan as a matter of great significance. He rightly feared that there would be intense opposition and a possible ministerial crisis if the British forced Egypt to withdraw.[25] Such a crisis could well disrupt political equilibrium and increase the chances of a prolonged occupation. The majority opinion in the cabinet, however, favored withdrawal, and Baring was ordered to instruct the Egyptian government to this effect.

The Egyptian ministry at this time was headed by Sharif Pasha, a man of Turkish origin. He had studied in France; upon his return to Egypt he was one of the leading advocates of a constitutional government.[26] For this reason he was one of the most popular ministers in Egypt. Indeed, he was one of the few popular ministers, for Egyptian ministers were mainly drawn from alien, non-Egyptian classes who had migrated to Egypt under Muhammad Ali and his successors to serve this alien regime. As Baring had predicted, Sharif, angered when the British government ordered Egypt to withdraw from the Sudan, resigned in protest. The ministerial crisis posed an extremely serious problem for the British, especially since they were committed to the policy of propping up the existing government, not ruling Egypt by themselves. The British were afraid that so much odium would be attached to the withdrawal that no Egyptian would agree to assume the reins of the government and that the British would be confronted with the collapse of the existing political structure. Actually, Baring, in the first manifestation of his autocratic nature, suggested that the British should take over the Egyptian ministry and run some of the important departments if cooper-

[25] Baring to Granville, No. 25, January 5, 1884, *ibid*.
[26] Jurji Zaydan, *Tarajim Mashahir al-Sharq* [Biographies of the Great Men of the East] (Cairo, 1922), i, 198-201.

ative Egyptians were not to be found.[27] The cabinet in London was, of course, quite unwilling to go to these extremes. Pressure was exerted on Baring from London, with the desired effect. The famous Armenian minister, Nubar Pasha, who was henceforth to be closely associated with British rule, agreed to form a new ministry and to accept the policy of Egyptian withdrawal from the Sudan.

The revolt in the Sudan forced the British to revise some of their plans for withdrawing troops. The Egyptian army, as reconstituted in 1883 by the British, was not strong enough to protect the country against invasion from the south and also to guarantee its internal security. And the British were unwilling to increase the size of the army so that it could handle both tasks, for fear a large Egyptian army would be a potential revolutionary threat. Therefore, the Egyptian army, with its British officers, was assigned to defend the frontier against the Mahdi, and the British army of occupation was mainly made responsible for guaranteeing the security of the population in Lower Egypt.

Critics of the occupation have argued that Egypt was compelled to withdraw from the Sudan in order to make British military assistance mandatory, and thereby, to delay evacuation. There seems no justification in this charge. The reason the British demanded withdrawal from the Sudan was their fear that British troops would have to go to the rescue of Egyptian forces and would eventually acquire military and administrative responsibility for a growing African empire. But the decision did necessitate postponement of evacuation. And as the British became more involved in Egypt and less willing to evacuate, the Mahdist threat was utilized as a convenient pretext for the maintenance of the army of occupation.

[27] Baring to Granville, January 4, 1884, The Granville Papers, PRO, 30/29/162.

Long after the Mahdists ceased to be a serious threat, Baring was still citing them as a major factor in the continuance of British rule. Mahdist power actually began to wane shortly after the death of the Mahdi in 1885; by 1889, which was the occasion of the last serious attack on the frontier, the Mahdist forces no longer worried the British.[28]

The first ministerial crisis helped to give a preliminary definition to the respective spheres of Egyptian and British authority in Egypt. During the crisis the British government impressed upon the Khedive and his ministers that in matters of importance the British representative in Egypt was to be consulted and his advice was to be followed. As Baring wrote to Granville, "they (the Egyptian ministers) did not thoroughly understand that they must, on important matters, do what they were told. This very essential point will now become clearer."[29] On the other hand, the Egyptian administrative apparatus remained intact. Egyptians continued to hold formal ministerial authority, while the British worked behind the scenes and through the Egyptian ministers. Nubar, in taking office when it was feared that no Egyptian would come forward, was able to take advantage of British discomfiture and drive a hard bargain with the British. He compelled Baring to accept a large measure of independent Egyptian authority in the government, at least for a time. Even as the occupation began to take on more permanent features he fought a retreating battle to limit British influence in the Egyptian administration. He and his successors were mildly successful, since they knew that the British needed them, if only to maintain the facade of Egyptian rule.

[28] P. M. Holt, *The Mahdist State in the Sudan, 1881-1898* (Oxford, 1958), pp. 156-64.
[29] Baring to Granville, No. 20, January 7, 1884, The Cromer Papers, PRO, FO 633/7.

But it would be a mistake to see Nubar or his successor, Riyad, as puppets of British rule. With limited power they struggled to maintain pockets of independent Egyptian authority in the administration. It was not until Mustafa Fahmi became Prime Minister in the 1890's that the British had a puppet minister through whom they were able to govern almost as they wished. In this early stage of the occupation, of course, the establishment of a dependency arrangement was not uppermost in the minds of the British.

＊

Although the plans for the immediate evacuation of Egypt were postponed by the Sudanese disturbances, the long-range goal remained the same. Egypt, as the Dufferin report had indicated, was to be prepared for autonomy by a combination of reorganization of existing institutions and by outright reform. Yet difficulties were encountered in attempting to implement such a policy. Efforts to revive traditional institutions—particularly the position and power of the Egyptian ruling class, and to allow this class to use its traditional, arbitrary techniques of rule—were not popular with British officials in Egypt or with the British public at home.

One of Baring's major tasks in refurbishing the long-standing ruling institutions was the restoration of Khedivial power. The Khedive was, of course, the locus of power—indeed, traditionally the only source of power in Egypt. The various consultative and representative institutions that had been established in the past had not supplanted him as the seat of authority. But Khedivial authority had been weakened in Egypt's disputes with Europe. Ismail had been deposed by the European powers in 1879. His successor, Tawfiq, had been in opposition to the Arabi revolt. Tawfiq had, in fact, been rescued from possible deposition by British troops in 1882 and then placed back on the throne. His position was far from secure, as he was at once the object of hostility from the articulate Egyptian classes and the seeming puppet of British authority. Baring perceived that so long as this situation existed there could be no real restoration of traditional authority in Egypt. His solution to the problem was to allow the Khedive to reassert his authority in the traditional, autocratic fashion if there should be disturbances in the country.[30] The Liberal cabinet at home was, however, reluctant to adhere to this advice. Parliament followed Egyptian events closely, and the cabinet felt that its members would be offended if highhanded and arbitrary techniques of rule were employed.

This clash over policy came to a head during the trial of Arabi and other leading revolutionaries. Khedive Tawfiq wished to mete out death penalties to these men as traitors to the regime.[31] Many British in Egypt favored this policy, since it would give the Khedive a much needed opportunity to reassert his powers. The cabinet in London was, at first, undecided. Gladstone had favored the death penalty for Arabi at one stage, considering him to be only a military agitator responsible for the riots that swept through Egypt in 1882. But Arabi had his defenders in England, who saw him as a sincere nationalist and a reformer. The leading exponent of this view was Wilfrid Scawen Blunt, the champion of many unpopular causes. Blunt, who had an estate just

[30] Baring was aware that "the whole tendency of reforms we now have in hand is to weaken [the authority of the Khedive] still further." But he added, "I do not see why the policy of withdrawal should not be carried out, but it can only be carried out with safety, if, on the first symptoms of disturbance, the Khedive and his government act with vigor and put it down with a strong hand." Baring to Granville, No. 5, October 9, 1883, The Cromer Papers, PRO, FO 633/6.

[31] Granville to Queen Victoria, September 28, 1882, ed. G. E. Buckle, *The Letters of Queen Victoria, 1879-1885* (New York, 1928), p. 342.

outside Cairo, had throughout the revolt supported the aims of Arabi and the nationalists. Blunt obtained the services of two qualified Europeans to defend Arabi at the trial.[32] Pressure exerted by Blunt and others caused a shift in the opinion of the Liberal government. The British now demanded that the Egyptian government prove that Arabi specifically had been responsible for the riots in Lower Egypt, if he was to be executed.[33]

As it became clear that Arabi had not been implicated in the crimes, the Arabi trial proved extremely embarrassing to the Egyptian government. Tawfiq was still anxious to carry out the death sentence, but Dufferin, who was in charge of affairs at the time, compelled Tawfiq to compromise with the wishes of the British government. Arabi was persuaded to plead guilty to leading a military rebellion, for which he was judged a traitor. He was then sentenced to death by the tribunal, but the sentence was commuted to a lifetime exile to Ceylon. Tawfiq was chagrined by this check on his power. Instead of reasserting his authority, he had emerged from this event even more a tool of the British occupation in the minds of the Egyptian populace.

The most serious problems in the first years of the occupation were not connected with attempting to revive unpopular aspects of traditional institutions. They arose from trying to restrain the reforming zeal of British officials in Egypt, who were often only interested in carrying out their own administrative reform programs. It was difficult to make them understand that their plans had to be tailored to the overall needs and goals of the occupation. Only those schemes which contributed to the general stability of the country could be support-

[32] Blunt, *Secret History*, p. 443 and Alexander M. Broadley, *How We Defended Arabi and his Friends* (London, 1884).

[33] Dufferin to Queen Victoria, November 21, 1882, *Letters of Queen Victoria*, p. 362.

ed, while those of a more radical nature would have to be set aside because of their disruptive effects on Egypt. Even Baring, in the opinion of the Foreign Office, was guilty of excessive zeal. Although he recognized the importance of strengthening the established institutions, he was far more excited by the opportunities, however limited, of introducing more radical programs of reform. Baring regarded himself as a colonial administrator of reforming temperament. The fetters on his freedom only made him more impatient for a chance to exert his influence. He wrote numerous and insistent letters to the Foreign Office, full of radical suggestions for manipulating the international and financial bonds in Egypt. Moreover, for all his blustering and lack of tact, he saw clearly that Egypt could not be prepared for evacuation without reform and reorganization of existing institutions, disrupted and discredited by the Arabi revolt. A reform program, he believed, could be carried out successfully in a short period of time only if the restrictions on the Egyptian government's freedom of action were removed. It was quite impossible, he argued, to implement the Dufferin blueprint as long as the French were free to obstruct the British at every step. Perhaps more in exasperation than in seriousness he suggested that a circular be sent to the powers, "explaining our difficulties and saying that we did not propose to consult them any more on each detail.... Give me 2,000 men and power to settle matters between the English and Egyptian governments, and I will guarantee that in twelve months there shall not be a soldier in Egypt and that the country is put in such a position as to render it very improbable that any Egyptian question will be raised again for many years to come at all events."[34] There was, as Baring saw, an incompatibility between

[34] Baring to Granville, No. 8, October 28, 1883, The Cromer Papers, PRO, FO 633/6.

reform leading to rapid evacuation, and all the international limitations which made reform virtually impossible.

The most spectacular conflict over the scope and extent of reforms the British could afford to sponsor came when Clifford Lloyd was sent to Egypt. Lloyd had been a resident magistrate in Ireland, where he had incurred considerable unpopularity. His appointment to Egypt was a gentle push upstairs by the Liberal government, to get him out of Ireland. He was sent to Egypt as Director-General of Reforms and later became adviser to the Ministry of the Interior,[35] where he immediately set to work drafting schemes for the reform of Egypt's internal structure. He drew up projects of such far-reaching implications as to alarm leading Egyptian officials. His program favored bringing the Egyptian police under British inspectors and giving the police administrative responsibilities traditionally wielded by Egypt's provincial officials, the *mudirs* (provincial governors) and the *mamurs* (district administrators).[36] He also developed schemes for public health reform, the improvement of prisons, and the creation of a municipal government at Alexandria. Lloyd was, in the modern parlance, a radical modernizer, in charge of one of Egypt's most sensitive ministries—the Ministry of the Interior, which was the chief administrative branch dealing with the internal life of the country. Under its control were the police and the local and provincial officials, the *mamurs* and the *mudirs*. It also had responsibility for public health and for many features of the urban life of the country. Should Lloyd and the British fully control this ministry,

[35] There is a biographical notice in the *Dictionary of National Biography* and a critical description in Edward Dicey, *The Story of the Khedivate* (New York, 1902), p. 366.

[36] Baring to Granville, No. 32, January 7, 1884, *HCSP*, Egypt No. 5 (1884), Vol. LXXXVIII, c. 3852.

they would be in a position to carry out radical schemes of administrative reorganization.

Clifford Lloyd's reforming zeal had the support of the British administration—including Baring—at first.[37] But, as might have been anticipated, he incurred the enmity of the Egyptian ministers. These men, representing the old order, naturally feared his reforming and modernizing schemes. They rightly saw these programs as a threat to their own power, for the reforms would swing power from the provincial and local administrations into the hands of the British. They viewed Lloyd as representing the activist element among British officials—an element, they felt, that sought to make Egypt into a British colony, in practice if not in name. The lines of battle were drawn, as so often has happened in colonial situations, between the modernizers, represented by certain colonial officials, and the forces of conservatism, represented by the traditional ruling class. In this case the modernizing element was defeated, and for some instructive reasons.

Nubar Pasha, the Prime Minister of Egypt, who had made himself so indispensable to the British during the Sudanese crisis, led the attack against Lloyd. Successive Ministers of the Interior resigned in protest against Lloyd's interference in their domain.[38] Nubar himself lodged numerous complaints with Baring, the main emphasis of his argument being that "the Ministry of the Interior . . . is the private life of a country; a European, no matter what tact he may possess, would introduce confusion."[39] Baring was eventually left little alternative

[37] Baring to Granville, No. 6, October 14, 1883, The Cromer Papers, PRO, FO 633/7.

[38] Abd al-Rahman al-Rafii, *Misr wa-l-Sudan* [Egypt and the Sudan], p. 158.

[39] Egerton to Granville, No. 106, May 19, 1884, enclosing letter from Nubar Pasha, *HCSP*, Egypt No. 25 (1884), Vol. lxxxix, c. 4100.

if he wanted to retain Nubar as Prime Minister. Lloyd, therefore, was asked to leave, and many of his schemes for reform and reorganization had to be put aside. British influence receded from the Ministry of the Interior, Nubar and the other representatives of the ruling class thereby retaining control of the internal life of the country.

There were two reasons for British acquiescence in the resignation of Lloyd. First, because of the temporary nature of the occupation, the British were committed (outwardly at least) to the maintenance of the Egyptian ruling class in positions of power. The resignation of Nubar would have brought a second explosive ministerial crisis in the span of a year. The British this time might not have found anyone willing to assume the reins of government as Nubar had in 1883. Second, the dropping of Lloyd was indicative of the British concern for security and for the maintenance of Egypt as an area of imperial defense, rather than as an area to be modernized rapidly and exploited for its economic potential. The British did not support Lloyd in the face of Egyptian criticism because they did not want to alienate the ruling classes; they sacrificed reform programs of large scope to the desire to preserve tranquility in the country.

British officials in Egypt were reluctant to admit the significance of Lloyd's dismissal and its relationship to their modernizing efforts. They explained his resignation entirely in terms of his admitted tactlessness in dealing with Egyptians, not because of his reform programs. But the real issues were not obscured either for the *London Times* or for Lloyd himself. While the whole question was still unresolved the *Times* observed:

> The strength of Nubar Pasha's position lies in the weakness of our own. Nubar Pasha's rule is a compro-

mise between protection and annexation. Through him we can work protection, without him nothing is visible but a completely European administration.... The only solution which offers even a prospect of success is the undertaking of the entire administration by England.... To dismiss Mr. Clifford Lloyd is—utterly irrespective of whether he has committed faults—a simple reversal of our whole system and a return to the times of Khedive Ismail.[40]

Lloyd saw the problem more clearly. In a letter to Baring he wrote:

I foresaw exactly the opposition and intrigue I have met with and only undertook work with the assurance of the support of Her Majesty's Government so long as you were satisfied with the propriety of my proceedings. To my mind the one point is whether Her Majesty's Government desires to proceed with the reform of their corrupt administration, or, by supporting Nubar Pasha, to let the whole work of the last nine months fall away at one drop. Believe me, it is no question of me or my tact; the real question is whether Her Majesty's Government will now face the inevitable and appoint an English President of the Council, or by withdrawing deal a death-blow to reformation in the country, thereby not only throwing to the winds all our labors and anxieties, but putting the representatives of arbitrary power in a stronger position than perhaps ever held.[41]

*

The overriding issue of the British occupation in its early years—indeed, almost throughout—was the question of finance. It was for this reason that Baring, with

[40] The *London Times*, April 8, 1884.
[41] Lloyd to Baring, No. 32, April 7, 1884, The Granville Papers, PRO 30/29/288/12.

his proven financial skills, was appointed Consul-General. Also for this reason, the British official in the Egyptian government with the most power was the financial adviser. The adviser attended meetings of the Egyptian council of ministers and had a virtual veto power on any project put forward. The first financial adviser was Auckland Colvin, who had served in Egypt before the British occupation and knew the financial situation well. He was succeeded in 1883 by Edgar Vincent, a brilliant young (in his twenties at the time of his appointment) financial expert. Vincent guided the destinies of Egypt through its most difficult years; when he resigned in 1889, the country was safely secured against bankruptcy.

The Egyptian debt, incurred by Ismail and his predecessor Said, totalled nearly £E100 million in 1882. In 1876 Ismail had created the *Caisse de la Dette*. Eventually, Britain, France, Russia, Austria, Germany, and Italy had representatives on it. Egyptian finances were regulated by the Law of Liquidation of 1880. This law, which dealt with the distribution of Egyptian state revenues, divided all Egyptian revenue into two categories: one for payment of the debt and the other for the administrative expenditures of the Egyptian government. The following sources of revenue were designated for debt payment: state railway and telegraph receipts, port dues of Alexandria, receipts of the customs department, proceeds of taxation from four provinces, and proceeds from former Khedivial estates. In addition to the *Caisse*, there were mixed European administrations in charge of the railroads and the former Khedivial estates, further evidence of the international control of Egypt.[42] The remainder of Egyptian revenue

[42] Short, admirable summaries of this complicated problem can be found in Milner, *England in Egypt* and Auckland Colvin, *The Making of Modern Egypt* (New York, 1906). Both men served in

went to the administration and could be expended on its administrative programs. If more money was collected from sources allocated to the debt than was required to cover the interest on the debt, it was applied to the amortization of the debt.

The estimates of revenue, made when the Law of Liquidation was framed, proved, however, to be unrealistic; the government collected less revenue than was anticipated. Funds for the interest and amortization of the debt were adequate, but the money allotted for the administrative needs of the country was insufficient. The budget was barely balanced by the time of the Arabi revolt, and the additional demands on the revenue of the country, produced by the revolt and the campaigns in the Sudan, destroyed this balance. By 1883 the government was in the awkward position of paying interest and amortizing the debt while building up a new floating debt because of the insufficiency of the administrative revenue.[43] Salaries were in arrears. Basic and minimum administrative programs could not be paid for. The major problem confronting the British was how to return the country to financial stability. The only solution was to alter the Law of Liquidation by reducing the interest rate on the debt and the amortization programs so that some of the funds being set aside for the debt could be used for regular administrative purposes. This problem, however, involved the European powers that had negotiated the Law of Liquidation, and represented the interests of their bondholders.

Once again, the British cabinet split over trying to determine its financial policies in Egypt. Baring was in

the financial departments of the Egyptian government and, therefore, knew these problems intimately.

[43] Malet to Granville, No. 81, August 18, 1883, HCSP, Egypt No. 22 (1883), Vol. LXXXIII, c. 3802.

favor of independent action. He advised making alterations in the Law of Liquidation without consulting the
other powers, giving a guarantee that as soon as the
Egyptian situation had returned to normal the British
would withdraw. This plan received no support in London. Baring then suggested that the British government,
on its own authority, float a loan to the Egyptian government. The loan would enable the Egyptian government
to liquidate deficits already accumulated and also to develop Egypt's resources so that no new floating debt
would be incurred. This arrangement would, in effect,
make the British responsible for financial security in
Egypt. It would substitute English control for international authority in the decisive area of Egyptian finance.[44] This plan had the support of the Whig members
of the cabinet, especially Hartington and Northbrook.
But it was opposed by others, particularly the radicals,
on the grounds that France would be forever alienated and English money would be used to support the
foreign bondholders of Egypt's debt.[45] An impasse was
reached in the cabinet. The Whigs favored increasing
British power in Egypt and assuming Egypt's heavy
financial obligations. Liberals and radicals were in general agreement about the need to withdraw as soon as
possible.

In 1884 the British called an international conference
in London to attempt to make changes in the Law of
Liquidation. The French had indicated in advance their
willingness to reduce the rate of interest on the debt
and to abolish the sinking funds. The British, on their

[44] This proposal was put forward on various occasions, but
never so forcibly as when it was sponsored by Lord Northbrook,
who had been sent to Egypt to make recommendations on the
financial question. Northbrook to Granville, No. 183, November
20, 1884, The Granville Papers, PRO 30/29/289/15.

[45] James L. Garvin, *Life of Joseph Chamberlain* (London, 1932-
1951), I, 522.

part, had promised that if these concessions were made, they would withdraw from Egypt at the end of three and a half years.[46] Critics in the French parliament, however, made their influence felt at this point, and the French government withdrew the concessions they had seemed willing to make. From the breakup of the London Conference in the summer of 1884, until another conference was assembled in March, 1885, the financial situation in Egypt worsened. The Egyptian government was eventually forced to divert funds earmarked for external payments in order to take care of pressing administrative expenditures. By 1884 the floating debt was £E2,300,000, in addition to which the Egyptian government had to meet awards of the indemnity commission of £E3,950,000 for losses suffered by the population during the Arabi revolt, and an estimated £E1 million for the abandonment of the Sudan.[47] By this time it was clear to all the foreign powers, including the French, that certain changes would have to be made in the financial laws. To force the European states to make concessions, the British used the threat of bankruptcy and inability to make payments to European subjects in compensation for losses incurred at the time of the Arabi revolt. Alterations were finally made at the 1885 Conference of London.

The changes made at the Conference, coupled with the Law of Liquidation, were to serve as the fundamental regulations of Egyptian finances: The Conference agreed to do away with the sinking funds for the amortization of the Egyptian debts. It also agreed to reduce the rate of interest on the debt one-half percent for a

[46] Protocols of the conference held in London, respecting the finances of Egypt, are to be found in *HCSP*, Egypt No. 30 (1884), Vol. LXXXIX, c. 4130.

[47] Granville to Her Majesty's Representatives at Berlin, Vienna, Paris, Rome, and St. Petersburg, No. 1, April 19, 1884, *HCSP*, Egypt No. 17 (1884), Vol. LXXXIX, c. 4000.

two-year period. If at the end of this period Egypt was not able to meet its regular debt payments, an international commission was to be set up to re-investigate Egyptian finances. The old distinction between debt and administrative revenues was retained. Certain special revenues would still be collected for the payment of the interest on the debt, and other revenues would go to the government. The authorized administrative expenditure was, however, raised slightly and fixed at £E5,237,000. The allocation of surpluses was a crucial issue. If the *Caisse* had a surplus from its revenues and the government had insufficient funds to meet its authorized expenditures, the *Caisse* had to help make up the deficit. Otherwise the total annual surplus from these two revenue sources was divided evenly between the *Caisse* and the government. The surplus turned over to the *Caisse* went for the amortization of the debt, and the government's surplus could be used for additional and non-authorized expenditures.[48]

The regulations laid down by the Conference of London had far-reaching effects on the administration of Egypt and its programs for modernization. The ceiling placed on authorized administrative expenditures meant that the government was severely restricted in the amount of money it could use to develop the country's resources. An administrative expenditure of £E5,237,000 was a bare minimum. Only £E70,000 was allotted for education in the budgetary estimates drawn up at the Conference. For the entire Ministry of the Interior the figure was £E102,000. £E450,000 was set aside for pension payments to superannuated civil servants. The total authorized expenditure could be raised only by consult-

[48] Granville to Her Majesty's Representatives transmitting copies of declarations signed by the plenipotentiaries of the Great Powers and Egypt on the Egyptian financial question, No. 1, March 17, 1885, *HCSP*, Egypt No. 6 (1885), Vol. LXXXIII, c. 4339.

ing the *Caisse* and receiving its agreement. This was difficult, and in 1904, when the financial arrangements were finally altered, the authorized administrative expenditure was only about £E1 million greater than it had been in 1885. Financial adviser Vincent, estimated that out of a revenue of about £E9 million, over £E5 million was composed of fixed charges for tribute and debt. Added to this figure was £E500,000 for pensions and £E300,000 for the civil list; a margin of less than £E3,500,000 was left for the administrative programs.[49] It was, however, possible to finance expensive reform programs through surpluses turned over to the government after debt payments and authorized administrative expenditures had been met. But the division of surpluses between the *Caisse* and the government meant that for every pound that went into non-authorized or special administrative expenditures, two pounds had to be collected; the additional pound was, of course, turned over to the *Caisse*.[50] This awkward situation was adjusted somewhat in 1888 when a reserve fund was created by the *Caisse*. This fund, maintained from surpluses in the hands of the *Caisse*, was not used to amortize the debt, as intended, but was set aside for the development of Egypt's resources.[51] The *Caisse*, nevertheless, had to agree to the way money was spent, and it tended to sanction only those projects which would prove immediately remunerative.

No student of the British occupation can overlook the importance of these financial factors in influencing British policies in Egypt. Financial pressures forced the reform programs in certain directions; basically, of course, that of increasing the wealth of the country. The British

[49] Add MSS 48960-61, D'Abernon Papers—manuscript of a proposed book on Egypt at the British Museum.

[50] There is a clear discussion of this issue in Milner, *England in Egypt*, pp. 191-92.

[51] Lord Cromer, *Modern Egypt* (London, 1908), II, 580.

were unable to pursue the kind of a land policy they otherwise might have favored. The new land being brought under cultivation could not be distributed cheaply to the *fellahin*, as many desired, but had to be sold to the top bidders, the wealthy classes, in order to increase government revenue. Because of financial considerations, the British found compelling reasons to develop the so-called "remunerative resources" in Egypt. Money was allocated for hydraulics and agriculture, where immediate financial returns could be expected. Other branches of the administration, education and public health, were not attended with such care for there money would obviously have helped to develop the financial capabilities of Egypt, but not so rapidly as in the field of hydraulics.

This is not to say that finances predetermined the development of Egypt under the occupation. They merely made certain approaches more obvious and necessary. Overall, the pressure to develop material resources was exceedingly great. It was applied strongly from London, where Egypt was regarded as only one of many imperial problems and where the solution of the financial question was regarded as the leading problem. If finances could be set in order, France would no longer be able to harass the British through its power on the *Caisse*. Egypt would become much more secure as a possession of the greatest strategic importance to the British.

The years 1885 to 1888 were, as Lord Milner has said, the years of the race against bankruptcy.[52] According to the terms of the Conference of London, if Egypt was not able to assume full financial obligations by 1887, an international commission would be convoked. Such a commission, the British had every reason to believe, would fetter Egypt and the British with more inter-

[52] Milner, *England in Egypt*, pp. 172-220.

national obligations. The Conference of 1885 had also raised an international loan of £E9 million, all but one million of which was to be used to liquidate Egypt's floating debt. The remaining million was to be turned over to the Ministry of Public Works to be expended on hydraulic projects for developing the resources of the country. A tense battle against bankruptcy was fought in these years. The budget was not in balance in 1885 or 1886. Vincent, as financial adviser, reorganized the accounting system, pared down administrative expenses to the bare essentials, and worked to increase the potential revenue of the country.[53]

By 1887 Egypt was in a position to assume full financial payments, and the international commission was avoided. The successful resolution of this financial problem must be considered one of the triumphs of British rule. Yet it was not attained without resorting to financial expediency. In order to balance the budget in 1887 the last month's salaries of Egyptian government employees were not paid in December, in the fiscal year of 1887, but put off to January, 1888. The British government made no charge in 1887 for the British army of occupation and also remitted Egypt's payment on the Suez Canal shares, owed to the British government.[54] Only by doing all this was the Egyptian government able to stave off bankruptcy and the international commission of investigation. The situation began to improve, however, as better hydraulic technology began to take effect. By the end of 1888 there was no longer a need for special devices to balance the budget. Vincent, in his last report before resigning his po-

[53] A financial commission of three European financial advisers, headed by Vincent, was created to cut the administrative budget to its barest essentials. This body had autocratic control over budgetary estimates. Add MSS 48948, notations for December 21, 1883 and January 1, 1884, D'Abernon Papers.

[54] Salisbury to Baring, No. 9, April 1, 1887, The Salisbury Papers, A/55.

sition in Egypt, was able to write that it would take a suc-
cession of bad years to place the present financial position in any serious state.[55] By 1889 solvency had been attained, and the Egyptian government was in a position
to undertake more extensive reform programs.

＊

Egypt had been occupied while the Liberal government was in power. The Conservative party was no
more imperialistic than the Liberals at this juncture and
on this issue. Lord Salisbury, the leader of the Conservatives, was extremely critical of the Liberal policy in
1882 and 1883 and was as disinclined as the Liberals
to take responsibility for governing Egypt. While in
opposition, he tended to see Egypt as a millstone of
British foreign policy and as an issue which kept the
British and French from establishing a closer rapport.[56]
Salisbury came to power in 1885, reaffirming the principles set forth by the Liberals, namely that the ultimate goal in Egypt was the restoration of Khedivial
authority and the withdrawal of British troops. Salisbury was no jingo imperialist. He believed in empire,
but not in jeopardizing Britain's position in Europe by
adding unnecessarily to the empire. Conservative policy
under Salisbury's predecessor, Disraeli, had been directed toward using the Ottoman Empire as a bulwark of
British policy in the Middle East. The British occupation of Egypt, of course, weakened the prestige of the
Ottomans, and Salisbury was loath to upset traditional
Middle Eastern policy by continuing this occupation.
Salisbury had been in power for approximately a year
(1885) during which he set in motion the Drummond

[55] Baring to Salisbury, No. 12, December 4, 1888, enclosing
report of Edgar Vincent, financial adviser, *HCSP*, Egypt No. 4
(1889), Vol. LXXXVIII, c. 5718.
[56] Cecil, *Salisbury*, IV, 38.

Wolff mission. Drummond Wolff was dispatched as a special adviser to the Turks in order to negotiate the Egyptian question. When Salisbury was returned to power in 1886, Drummond Wolff was ordered to attempt to reach an agreement with the Turks for the withdrawal of British troops from Egypt.

By the time Salisbury returned to power he had begun to alter his feeling about the British position in Egypt. On one hand he continued to regard the British occupation as an intolerable burden, the most vulnerable part of Britain's foreign policy. He realized that the presence of British troops in Egypt antagonized the French and that as long as France had a seat on the *Caisse de la Dette* and also capitulatory rights in Egypt, it could make the British task of governing Egypt difficult. The opposition of France and Russia on the *Caisse* put the British at the mercy of Germany. With German and Austrian support on the *Caisse* the British could maneuver most of their policies through this body. But the Germans drove a hard bargain, as far as Salisbury was concerned. In order to retain German friendship the British were forced to make numerous concessions in Asia and Africa. For these reasons, Salisbury felt that evacuation from Egypt would remove Britain from an exposed position. He admitted to Drummond Wolff that Bismarck's "policy in a humble walk of life would be called *chantage*. He is perpetually telling us of the offer France is making of reconciliation on the basis of an attack upon England in Egypt and of the sacrifices which Germany makes by refusing these proposals, sacrifices for which, he adds, England must make some return, and then he demands this and that. I heartily wish we had never gone into Egypt. Had we not done so we could snap our fingers at all the world."[57]

[57] *Ibid.*, pp. 41-42. The Liberal Foreign Secretary shared many of the same sentiments. Rosebery wrote to the then Lord Cromer:

On the other hand, Salisbury came increasingly to understand and value the strategic importance of Egypt as the lifeline to the East. By this time he was beginning to lose faith in the recuperative powers of the Ottoman Empire. He feared that under the pressure of an expanding Europe and of local nationalistic movements, the Empire might disintegrate, resulting in a scramble for territory among the European powers. For this reason, he saw the importance of remaining in Egypt and making Egypt, instead of Constantinople, a new strategic center of British power in the Eastern Mediterranean. At Cairo, Baring tended to re-enforce Salisbury's ideas. By this time Baring was arguing that the reconstruction of Egypt could not be effected in a short span of time and that it would be folly to withdraw from Egypt for many years to come. If the British withdrew, he argued, there would be no one to carry on the complicated system of government, and the country would soon be plunged into chaos. "Getting out of Egypt," Baring argued, "is a very different problem from getting out of Afghanistan." There were no great European interests in Afghanistan, but in Egypt there was an "exotic superstructure superimposed on oriental institutions. I do not suppose that Europe will stand by and let this superstructure crumble to pieces."[58] Baring was especially conscious of the tensions within Egyptian society which had manifested themselves most acutely during the Arabi revolt. Also, he felt that there were no Muslim administrators capable of ruling a divided society.[59] The forces that produced the Arabi revolt—

"In Egypt the British nose is in a twitch, the handle of which is at the disposal of every great power." Rosebery to Cromer, No. 138, February 7, 1896, The Cromer Papers, PRO, FO 633/7.

[58] Baring to Granville, No. 8, October 28, 1883, The Cromer Papers, PRO, FO 633/6.

[59] These opinions are most fully developed in two dispatches to Salisbury: No. 157, June 28, 1890, and No. 172, December 11, 1891, The Cromer Papers, PRO, FO 633/6.

proto-nationalism and especially anti-Turkish feeling—
were still alive in Egypt. A French occupation could easily follow British withdrawal, thereby jeopardizing the
British road to the East.

Salisbury's attempt to solve the dilemma—withdraw
from Egypt, yet retain paramountcy—was the Drummond Wolff mission. Drummond Wolff, who had been
sent to Constantinople in 1885, finally did reach a preliminary agreement with the Turks over Egypt. The
convention, negotiated by him with the Turks, stipulated that the British would withdraw from Egypt at the
end of a three-year period, but that they would possess
the right of re-entry if conditions in Egypt became unsettled. What the convention meant was that the British
would control Egypt and the Eastern Mediterranean
through their bases in Malta and Cyprus. If the Ottoman
Empire collapsed, or the Egyptian administration could
not sustain its authority, Britain would have a clear right
to reoccupy the country and govern without the old international fetters. Salisbury blew optimistic then pessimistic over whether the French would accept the agreement. If not, Britain would, of course, have to stay on in
Egypt, for if the French refused to recognize the agreement it would have no value for the British. In a pessimistic mood he wrote to Queen Victoria that "it is very
probable that France will not consent to these proposals
and that negotiations may be protracted, but they will be
acceptable to Turkey which chiefly desires to see the flag
of the infidel disappear, and they will exonerate Your
Majesty's Government from any charge of attempting to
ignore their pledges."[60] The pessimistic outlook proved
correct. The French government, pressured once again
by the imperialistic element in the Parliament, could not
accept an agreement which might eventually result in

[60] *Letters of Queen Victoria, 1886-1890,* pp. 272-73.

the formal, British annexation of Egypt. The French government, with Russian support, put pressure on the Turks, who responded by refusing to ratify the convention.

The failure of the convention did, at least, clear the air in Egypt. The Conservative government, which was to remain in power until the election of 1892, was committed by this failure to the maintenance of British rule in Egypt. Increasingly, Salisbury came to recognize the importance of the British position in Egypt. He saw the growth of German influence at Constantinople and the possibility of the disintegration of the Ottoman Empire. Thus he felt that Cairo, rather than Constantinople, should be the hub of British power in the Middle East.[61] Salisbury's attitude toward Egypt was always conditioned by these larger imperial and foreign policy considerations. He was never greatly troubled by, or committed to, the modernization of Egypt. He favored reforms in Egypt only insofar as they would secure British rule in the country. Like so many other advocates of the British occupation of Egypt, Salisbury considered Egypt important not for itself but for its strategic position. As he indicated, "interference with the internal government [of Egypt] is no part of our political aim and should only be practiced so far as the higher dictates of humanity require. . . . I do not believe in the plan of moulding the Egyptians to our civilization."[62] Salisbury never felt that the British had a moral responsibility to bring Western institutions to Egypt, although he did hold that so long as the British occupied Egypt they should be responsible for its good government.

Baring and the British officials in Egypt had contrib-

[61] The change of attitude is discussed fully by Robinson and Gallagher, *Africa and the Victorians*, pp. 254-73.

[62] Cecil, *Salisbury*, III, 126.

uted substantially to strengthening British intention to remain in Egypt. Although Baring had been sent to Egypt to liquidate the occupation, he quickly came to the realization that the occupation would have to be prolonged if Egypt was to be reorganized and made safe against revolution. He was firmly convinced that the ruling classes in Egypt would not be able to control the rest of the population if British troops were withdrawn. Therefore, he prodded the British foreign ministers to remain in Egypt, by painting a gloomy picture of conditions in an Egypt without British overlordship.

By 1888 the majority of public opinion in England had also solidified around a continued occupation of Egypt. As Salisbury realized full well, "English opinion is not prepared for an evacuation of Egypt, still less for abandonment of it. . . . The national or acquisition feeling has been roused."[63] Up to this point, although there had been a strong element in the country opposed to the evacuation policy, it had not been dominant. Those favoring continuance of the occupation were concentrated in the Conservative party. In the early years of the occupation, the right-wing press, the bondholders, and the new active imperialist groups played an important role in counterbalancing leftist sentiment in favor of evacuation. They neutralized the left, so that the government continued to drift in its Egyptian policy. It would, however, be a mistake to see the occupation primarily as the work of these groups, for they were not able to exercise decisive influence in imperial affairs until later in the decade. The British officials in the technical branches of the administration threw all of their still rather limited influence on the side of prolonged occupation. As was noted earlier, their concern was with administrative progress and efficiency, not with

[63] *Ibid.*, IV, 41-42.

the general aims of Britain's foreign policy; thus, they wanted an extended period in which to carry their administrative and technical programs of reform to a successful conclusion.

It should be quite clear that the reasons for prolonging the occupation were primarily political, rather than economic, in this period. The British desired strategic bases in the Eastern Mediterranean, secure against any foreign encroachment. Indeed, economic groups had begun to turn away from Egypt during the last years of Ismail's reign and the early stage of the occupation. The country was disrupted internally, on the verge of bankruptcy; there was little guarantee for economic activity, especially since the British had indicated their desire to evacuate shortly. Of course, the economic groups that had involved themselves previously were interested in Egyptian affairs. But their influence was limited. The bondholders, by obstructing the administration of Egypt through the control of Egyptian finance, did, in fact, make British rule more difficult. The British government was prepared to sacrifice these interests for its political aims, whenever it could do so. The French government assumed the role of protecting the interests of bondholders, but only because its political interests coincided with the economic interests of the bondholders. They, too, were willing to sacrifice these interests when the occasion demanded, and they did so later, on several occasions, by negotiating changes in the financial regulations of Egypt.

✻

1888 was a turning point in the British occupation. By this date, the occupation, though still formally regarded as temporary, had acquired certain fixed features. While the Liberal government had not intended to remain in Egypt, it had not determined how to evacuate its troops. By 1885 it was supplanted by the Conservatives, who were less squeamish about honoring pledges of withdrawal. The failure of the Drummond Wolff mission had made it clear that British rule had a permanency it had not had before. For the first time it was possible for British administrators to plan long-range programs with some certainty of seeing them through to completion. Baring was the recognized supreme authority in Egypt. He wielded more power than any other British or Egyptian official. British influence was paramount in the Ministries of Public Works and Finance. Accordingly, British efforts were expended mainly on bringing the budget into balance and developing the agricultural resources of the country. Besides Baring, the two most powerful officials in the country were the British advisers to the Ministries of Public Works and Finance. The latter plotted the budget and made decisions on how the resources of the country were to be allotted; while the adviser to the Ministry of Public Works, Scott-Moncrieff was mainly responsible for using whatever funds were available for developing the hydraulic and agricultural potential of the country. These men, with Baring, shaped Egypt's development in this period.

Salisbury and the Conservative government were not committed to transforming Egypt along Western lines. They were basically interested in maintaining British control with as few troops and as little English money as possible—a situation dictated by the exigencies of the colonial situation of the late nineteenth century. The only way rapid modernization could be effected, at least in the early stages of colonial rule, was for colonial powers to be responsible, militarily and administratively, for the impact of radical changes. The colonial power could not expect the established classes of the subject country to carry out programs that would ultimately mean alterations in the class structure and a decline in their own position in society. It was hardly possible during this period when European states were acquiring large empires, to expect them to shoulder the tremendous administrative and financial burdens involved in the rapid modernization of their colonial territories. Rather, it was to be expected that they would attempt to govern through established institutions, to utilize established forms of power to maintain their own position. Thus, the colonial states had to gear their policies to classes that were interested only in certain aspects of modernization.

Full-scale modernization implied education for the masses, the opening up of the class structures so that individuals from the lower classes, if talented, might gain positions of power. It also meant a more equitable distribution of wealth and land, and heavier taxes upon the ruling classes for modernization schemes. The upper classes in colonial areas were not in favor of such programs and would accept such only if forced to by foreign troops. Instead, they favored programs for developing the wealth of the country only as long as the distribution of wealth among the classes was not altered, and the changes did not create discontent against the established classes among the lower classes.

These factors made for a commitment to the status quo in the British occupation. There were other factors, however, favoring governmental development and modernization of the country. First there was the financial plight of Egypt. Egypt was deeply in debt. If it was to be rescued, its resources would have to be developed, in order to produce financial self-sufficiency. As in so many colonies at this time, the need to create a government which could pay its own way forced the British to embark upon a certain amount of modernization. The standard policy at home was that colonies should pay for themselves, a policy rather vigorously enforced in Egypt, because Parliament, watching Egyptian affairs, interpreted financial support of Egypt as an attempt to make Egypt into a British colony.

The second factor was associated with a desire to preserve tranquility in the country. It was difficult for the British to conceal the fact that it was British power, and not Egyptian, that counted. Furthermore, the established classes had been challenged in the Arabi revolt. There was latent discontent against the British overlords among the mass of the population, and against the old, alien ruling aristocracy, now partially discredited. British officials in Egypt saw that the regime must win a certain amount of popularity from the masses. They felt that rising standards of living might be the answer. And rising standards of living could be achieved only by developing the agricultural resources of the country. It must also be remembered that this was the post-Indian Mutiny era. Colonial officials were wary of discontent among subject peoples. They feared the possibility of rural uprisings against alien rule—a feeling especially prevalent in an Egypt that had just experienced an uprising.

Finally, the British officials in Egypt believed in the superiority of European civilization, and felt an obligation to export certain fundamentals of it. They believed that European powers should at least assure good government and a minimum standard of living for their subject peoples. There was a self-generating drive for reform within the bureaucracy. Lower level British administrators, of course, were not concerned with overall British imperial policy. These men demanded an enlarged British staff for their projects. Most were quite oblivious to the possible long-range consequences—to Egypt and to Britain's position in Egypt—of their suggested reforms. Finally, private groups, mostly European, agitated for reform, for the rapid modernization of the country, in the form of railroads, new courts, schools, etc., which would make Egypt a profitable area for investment and trade.

The Egyptian administrative structure in 1888 remained largely as it had been before the occupation. The British ruled behind it, indirectly, much as they did in parts of India and were to do so effectively throughout Africa. They controlled the Ministries of Finance and Public Works, but their efforts to control other departments met with only partial success. Egyptian officials were successful in removing a great deal of British influence from the Ministry of the Interior. The Ministry of Justice, although reformed in 1883, slipped from British control into Egyptian hands. Other departments, such as Education and Public Health, while guided by the British, were largely staffed and run by Egyptians. The Egyptian ruling class attempted to stand by the principle that the internal life of the country was personal and that the British ought to keep their hands off; until 1888 they had been rather effective in realizing this plan.

In 1882 the Liberal government had promised early evacuation from Egypt after the restoration of order. Throughout the next years it searched in vain for a policy through which to bring this about. International fetters in the form of capitulations and the financial powers of other states, divisions within the cabinet, and revolt in the Sudan, complicated the search. The government was not able to decide on a firm policy, except to strengthen the existing authority and to reorganize the administration. It had not been able to fix the date of evacuation, as the French so desperately desired. By 1886 the Conservatives, under Salisbury, had come to power, and the attitude toward Egypt was beginning to alter. Although the Conservative government continued to reaffirm the promises of the temporary nature of the occupation, there was less desire to give those promises concrete form. Egypt was gradually becoming an important imperial link on the British route to the East.

CHAPTER IV

FIRST ADMINISTRATIVE
REFORMS, 1888-1892:
AGRICULTURE AND LAW

BY 1888 Egypt had attained financial stability. A reserve fund had been established by the *Caisse de la Dette* to aid the administrative reform program. By 1895 the reserve fund had at its disposal more than £E1,000,000.[1] Foreign payments, comprising debt and tribute to the Ottoman Empire, had accounted for almost two-thirds of the Egyptian budget in 1880; by 1893 extraneous payments had been reduced to approximately one-half of the budget.[2] Baring's annual reports on the state of Egyptian finance and administration took on a new note of optimism. From 1889 on, he was convinced that Egypt's financial position could no longer be threatened.

With the attainment of financial solvency, the Egyptian government for the first time was able to direct its attention to administrative reform. Nearly every branch of the administration required reform. Education had been hindered by financial cutbacks. The agricultural and hydraulic system of the country had fallen into a dangerous state of disrepair. The sanitary condition of the country demanded immediate attention. Egypt had experienced a frightening epidemic of cholera in 1883, which had carried off many lives.[3] Legal and public security systems had broken down, with alarming increase

[1] Annual Report of Lord Cromer for 1895, *HCSP*, Egypt No. 1 (1896), Vol. xcvii, c. 7978.

[2] Annual Report of Lord Cromer for 1893, *HCSP*, Egypt No. 3 (1893), Vol. cxi, c. 6957.

[3] Salim to Khairy, No. 1875, November 6, 1883, Department of Public Health, Copy Letters, Vol. 4220.

in the crime rate. Indeed, virtually every branch of the administration was starved for funds and was calling for a large part of the administrative surplus. The funds at the government's disposal were obviously not sufficient to embrace all of the country's needs. Major decisions on the allocation of the new surplus revenues were required, decisions that would, of course, influence the patterns of modernization in the country.

The major share of responsibility for allocating resources belonged to Baring. In this sense, then, he played the decisive role in setting the patterns of Egypt's modernization during the occupation. His decisions were not haphazard; they were based on his own well-developed philosophy of colonial administration, adapted to Egyptian conditions. This colonial philosophy was dominated by two elements, his Gladstonian liberalism and his Indian administrative experience.

Baring belonged to the generation of colonial administrators strongly influenced by the Indian Mutiny of 1857. In the early nineteenth century disputes among colonial administrators over colonial rule in India had resulted basically in a decision that India be given European institutions.[4] Administrators like Warren Hastings, who admired the Indian traditions and believed them to be capable of self-renewal, had been defeated by the Westernizers. Macaulay expressed the feeling of the most extreme reformers, in writing on education: "The question now before us is simply whether, when it is in our power to teach this language (English), we shall teach languages in which, by universal confession, there are no books on any subject which deserve to be compared to our own; whether when we can teach European science, we shall teach systems which, by universal confession, whenever they differ from those of Eu-

[4] See George D. Bearce, *British Attitudes Towards India, 1784-1858* (London, 1961).

rope differ for the worse. . . ."[5] The Mutiny of 1857 came as a shock to most British administrators, causing them to recognize the difficulties of forcing Western institutions and techniques on colonial areas. They came to see that the fabric of a traditional society was more resistant to change than they had expected; Indian and other Oriental societies did not adapt easily to the European way of life. Indeed, the introduction of Western reforms only tended to undermine the traditional fabric, creating discontent, instability, and in extreme cases, revolutionary agitation. Men trained in the post-Mutiny period were, therefore, conscious of the strength of the traditional ways of life. While they did not return to Hastings' formula of preserving and rejuvenating the old, they were inclined to move more slowly in establishing Western institutions. They felt that Western patterns should be grafted onto the traditional in a gradual fashion. Many were far more pessimistic, holding that certain of the more elaborate institutions of the West, such as parliamentary government and constitutional freedoms, would never be assimilated by Eastern peoples. These administrators were far more aware of the fact that the introduction of new institutions undermined an old way of life and produced insecurity in the subject peoples, without providing a new orientation, thus creating conditions favorable to revolutionary agitation. The specter that haunted them was spontaneous, peasant revolutionary activity, spurred on by nationalist agitators.

Baring was influenced by these attitudes while serving in India. One of his Indian colleagues, and a friend, was Alfred Lyall. Lyall held a variety of important positions in the Indian civil service and was in the midst of the Mutiny, but had won his reputation as an

[5] *Ibid.*, p. 171.

interpreter and writer on Indian society. In cogent fashion he set forth some of the emerging premises of British officialdom toward Oriental societies. He argued that East and West were profoundly different, that their basic institutions and the roots of their civilizations had come from entirely different sources. The process of Westernizing the Orient could not be stopped, he argued, if only because it had gone too far and educated Indians themselves were demanding the introduction of Western institutions. But at the same time, he feared that such changes would undermine the internal cohesiveness of society and leave Eastern peoples in a disturbed state, at least until a new unity and a new integrated social fabric had been achieved. He cautioned colonial governments, therefore, to expect a great deal of discontent and to carry out programs of reform only as the people were prepared to accept them.[6]

Baring's colonial philosophy rested on these new and evolving attitudes. Its fundamental tenet was a belief in the wide difference between East and West, and—equally important—his assumption of the basic similarity of all Oriental societies. Like so many colonial administrators of his time, he was convinced that techniques developed in one Oriental Society—India—had universal applicability throughout the East. In his major work, *Modern Egypt*, he wrote that "the broad lines which . . . reforms must take are traced out by common place requirements of European civilization and must of necessity present some identity of character, whether the scene of action be India, Algiers, Egypt, Tunisia, or Bosnia."[7]

[6] Lyall set forth many of his ideas in his correspondence with Cromer, included in the Cromer Papers. Among his published works, the most representative of these ideas are *Asiatic Studies, Religious and Social* (London, 1884) and *The Rise and Expansion of the British Dominion in India* (London, 1907).

[7] Cromer, *Modern Egypt*, 1, 5.

One of the dangers to be avoided in governing the East, Baring felt, was to rely on experiences taken from colonies of white settlements, such as Canada and South Africa. The techniques for ruling these countries had been put forth most clearly in the famous Durham Report for Canada. These colonies were to be governed by giving large amounts of responsible self-government; Western institutions were to be introduced as the people demanded them.[8] But Oriental societies could not be entrusted with this same degree of self-government. Nor could they be permitted to determine for themselves when they were ready for more advanced Western institutions. Such decisions had to be made by colonial administrators who would take into account the stage of preparation of the majority of the population. Colonial administrators must not be swayed, Baring argued, by the demands for reform put forth by the most advanced, Westernized segment of the population.[9] If reforms were introduced before the rest of the population was prepared to accept them, the society's cohesiveness would be undermined, plunging the country into revolution. New institutions were to be introduced gradually and grafted onto those already in existence. Colonial administration must be concerned with developing a new unity in society without forcing the country to the verge of revolution.

Administrative reform, according to Baring, had to proceed by stages if the internal stability of the country was to be maintained. In an article written after he left Egypt, Baring (then Lord Cromer) assessed the French experience in Algeria. He argued that the French

[8] Cromer, *Ancient and Modern Imperialism* (New York, 1910), p. 15.

[9] The result of introducing free institutions would be to "enable a small minority of natives to misgovern their countrymen." Cromer, "The Government of Subject Races," *Political and Literary Essays, 1908-13*, p. 28.

had done what any civilized society must do, namely, introduce their superior civilization into a backward country. But he cautioned that the order in which changes were made was decisive.[10] Baring had no doubt that the first stage of administrative reform was to be devoted to the development of material prosperity in the governed country. In another essay, he wrote that "in the absence of ties such as community of race, language, religion, and social customs, the only link between the governors and the governed was to be found in material interests."[11] As a Gladstonian he held that the most effective way to ensure the material well-being of the subject peoples was to lighten the burden of taxation. He wanted money to fructify in the hands of the peasants, to promote feelings of independence and individualism, and to give the peasantry new incentives to develop the country for themselves. Baring was fond of quoting the maxim of Lord Lawrence, one of the Viceroys of India; "Light taxation was the panacea of foreign rule."[12] This formula was practiced in India, and Baring carried it over into Egypt. After the tax burden had been lightened, Baring felt, the government could then direct its attention to administrative reforms. In a country like Egypt this goal would be accomplished most effectively by undertaking agricultural and hydraulic reforms.

Baring was not an advocate of strong, centralized government for European societies. He believed that the distinguishing feature of British society was its individualism and philosophy of self-help. This position is evident in Baring's later career, when as a member of the House of Lords he was known as a bitter opponent of the social legislation sponsored by the Liberal govern-

[10] Cromer, "The French in Algeria," *ibid.*, pp. 250-63.
[11] Lord Cromer, *Abbas II* (London, 1915), p. xxii.
[12] Cromer, *Political and Literary Essays*, Second Series (London, 1915), p. 199.

ment from 1906 to 1914. He felt that such legislation would destroy the foundations of English society and undermine the self-reliance of the English people. By the same token, he felt that one of the weaknesses of Eastern peoples came from their undeveloped sense of individuality and their total reliance upon the government for the well-being of their countries.[13] He believed that the East would not revitalize itself until private individuals took more responsibility for the welfare and actions of their country. This, then, was the Gladstonian influence on Baring's administrative philosophy. It manifested itself in his desire to allow individualism to express itself in education and other spheres of Egyptian life.

But Baring, recognizing the basic economic, political, and geographical differences between East and West, realized that the government must play a larger role in these societies.[14] He was well aware that in Egypt the government was regarded as the only instrument of control and change. At times he was pessimistic about a society with such deep-seated autocratic traditions ever fully embracing individualism and self-reliance. Also, he recognized that India and Egypt had vast hydraulic systems which private groups could not administer effectively. For this reason he did not hesitate to undertake, by means of government activity, vast public works in the fields of hydraulics and transportation. Indeed, the hydraulic system was so important to the prosperity of Egypt that he would not think of giving private interest a controlling hand. In 1883, when

[13] Cromer, *Modern Egypt*, I, 145.
[14] See Cromer's essay, "East and West," *Quarterly Review* (1916), ccxxvi, 21-39, in which he presents a table of the most striking differences between the Orient and the West. First in his list was the despotism of the East in contrast to European free government.

[*100*]

schemes for the reform of Egypt's hydraulic system were being put forward, British officials vetoed a proposal by a private European firm to take charge of the irrigation system of Lower Egypt. Such control, these officials felt, would give a private company a virtual stranglehold on the Egyptian economy.[15] Since Oriental societies were deficient in private capital, compared with Europe, Baring was also willing to permit the government to utilize its resources where private capital was hesitant to venture. It was, therefore, by means of governmental expenditures on important public works and the encouragement of private capital in other spheres of the economy, that Baring hoped to increase the material prosperity of the country.

Only after a minimum level of material prosperity had been ensured, Baring felt, could the "moral and intellectual superstructure" of Western institutions be added. If the government could do a great deal to secure material prosperity, it should play only a limited role in sponsoring these latter developments. Basically these changes had to spring from the desires of the people. In this realm Baring was quite Gladstonian, for he felt that the superstructure of a civilization could not be imposed on the population through governmental decree, and especially by an alien government. By the time material prosperity had been reached, it was hoped that the mass of the population would be contented with foreign rule and that the disrupting effects of exposing society to the intellectual and political life of the West would not be severe. At this stage Baring favored endowing the country with increased powers of self-government, extending education, and giving the educated class

[15] Égypte, Ministère des Travaux Publiques, *Exposé* (Cairo, 1883).

more of an opportunity to participate in government.[16] The great mistake made in India, he felt, was that the process of Westernization had not been undertaken strictly in this sequence. Before material prosperity had been ensured and a new social fabric had emerged, the intellectual content of the West—in the form of higher education and responsible self-government—had been introduced.[17] The result was that a class of nationalists had been created, who had been able to excite the discontented, rudderless mass of the population against British rule. Baring feared the nationalistic demagogue, which he characterized as a half-Westernized, half-Muslim (or Hindu) breed of a person whose only aim was to increase his own following in the country by making irrational appeals to the ignorant masses. By ensuring the well-being of the masses, this type of agitator would not be able to acquire a following among the people.[18]

Baring was not sanguine about whether his type of rule would in fact realize its goals, although he knew no better system. In an essay written after he left Egypt, he argued that the system of introducing Western elements by stages had worked so successfully in Egypt that "the whole nationalist movement has been a mere splutter on the surface. It never extended deep down into the social ranks."[19] In his less optimistic moments, when observing growing nationalistic agitation in all colonial areas, he wondered whether subject peoples would ever be grateful for the benefits he thought were being conferred. Under these circumstances the nationalist agitator would always be able to gain a hearing among the people, no matter how contented. A great

[16] See Baring's essay, "The French in Algeria," *Political and Literary Essays, 1908-13*, pp. 250-63.

[17] Cromer, *Political and Literary Essays*, Second Series, p. 200.

[18] Cromer, *Modern Egypt*, II, 228.

[19] Cromer, "The French in Algeria," *Political and Literary Essays, 1908-13*, p. 260.

problem facing colonial administrators was that new generations of subject peoples would fail to recognize how onerous conditions had been before European rule, and disregarding the advantages of such rule, would judge the colonial administrations by standards applicable only in Europe. If Baring was not confident of securing the colonial countries against nationalist demagogues, he was even less so about the chances of Oriental societies assimilating the moral and intellectual superstructure of the West.[20] Under Western tutelage, countries might develop representative institutions and move in the direction of a free society. But Baring feared that the autocratic traditions were too ingrained, the religious influence too regressive, and the mentality of the people too susceptible to authoritarianism for this system to stand on its own without the support of the colonial administration. He did hope, however, that the material foundations in Egypt and elsewhere were being laid properly so that the country, although without parliamentary institutions, could maintain political and economic stability when independent.

Although for Baring and others, Indian experiences were deeply ingrained and constantly served as models for administrative reform in Egypt, they recognized some fundamental distinctions between Egypt and India.[21] In essence, they felt that India and Egypt had the same natural, political, economic, and social conditions; both being "Oriental societies"; but that the aims of British rule differed in each country. India was ruled directly, and the British assumed more complete responsibility for its administration. Egypt, as an area of defense, was ruled indirectly through its existing insti-

[20] Cromer, "The Government of Subject Races," *ibid.*, p. 25.
[21] See my article, "The 'Indianization' of the Egyptian Administration under British Rule," *American Historical Review*, LXVIII (April, 1963), 636-61.

tutions and leaders. For this reason, Indian experience had to be modified and even discarded in Egypt. Baring's predecessor, Edward Malet, even "deprecated new officials being imported from India." He added: "It is not the right school whence to draw for this service. Were Egypt administered by us, it would be the best; but incapacity to work under native authority is too marked a feature of those who come from it for them to be useful at present."[22] Baring said somewhat the same thing 20 years later, in stating that "the existing circumstances in either country are so great as to render any conclusion drawn from a presumed analogy but of little value."[23]

❋

Although these ideological considerations were important, Baring's philosophy of colonial administration was also rooted in the material conditions and problems of colonial rule facing the British in Egypt. In one sense, Egypt was a vast, holding operation for the British, because of its strategic location. In Egypt Britain was less willing to embark upon radical reform schemes that might endanger the stability of the country, than in a colony like India. Baring's colonial philosophy, therefore, reflected the deep concern among the British for maintaining the tranquility of the population and for not jeopardizing Britain's strategic interests in Egypt by hasty and ill-conceived reforms.

The British army of occupation in Egypt was quite small. At times it totalled less than 5,000 men. Although the Egyptian army was officered by the British, Cromer

[22] Malet to Granville, No. 286, May 29, 1883, The Granville Papers, PRO 30/29/287/10.

[23] Lord Cromer, Annual Report for 1902, HCSP, Egypt No. 1 (1903), Vol. LXXVII, cd. 1529. Cromer was speaking specifically here of the fact that the British did not exercise direct judicial and executive powers in Egypt.

had no great confidence in it should the country be torn by revolution. Therefore, great emphasis was placed on winning the support of the subject peoples. And even greater emphasis was placed on a controlled and limited modernization of the colonial country.

Additionally, Baring's colonial attitudes were determined largely by colonial problems facing the entire British Empire of the late nineteenth century. England's chief concern was its ability to govern a constantly expanding empire with limited technical, military, and financial resources. The only workable technique in this context was that of associating the governed classes with their conqueror by providing for their economic welfare without threatening the traditional structure of life. The British were not in a position to run the risk, when introducing reforms, of plunging the country into an uncontrollable revolution. They did not have the military or technical capacities to buttress rapid modernization, with its attendant shocks to traditional societies in the vast areas under British control. The tension between modernization and the traditional existed in all colonies. Nearly all colonial administrators, including Baring, thought of themselves as reformers, as champions of Western institutions; but none were willing to push the process of modernization to the point where societies would lose their internal cohesiveness. Therefore, they adopted the expedient of attempting to raise standards of living without changing class structures. They attempted to make their authority felt without undermining the position of the traditional ruling classes. They governed behind these ruling classes.

Such a system was bound to cause difficulties. There was friction between the British and the traditional ruling classes. The latter became increasingly captive of the British. Further, as new educated elements came into existence, their demands for Western reform outdistanced the desires of the colonial administrations. Toward the end of almost all British colonial regimes, the administration was under heavy attack because of its conservative position on reform.

There were other more specific considerations that affected the formulation of British policy in Egypt. The most important of these was that British authority in Egypt had not been clarified. International obligations still existed. Moreover, the British had made their promises of evacuation. Because of these limitations they could not govern Egypt directly even if they had so desired.

*

With financial solvency attained, the British turned their attention to administrative changes. Baring's philosophy of colonial rule and the needs of the country dictated that the first step be the lightening of tax burdens. Egypt's revenue was derived from a variety of taxes. There were land taxes, customs, a salt tax, a tax on trees, *octroi* duties, and a variety of minor taxes. The most important source of revenue was the land tax. Since the reign of Muhammad Ali this tax had constantly been increased. There had been increases in 1820, '34, '39, '44, '52, '55, '58, '61, '64, '68, '70, and '71.[24] There were basically two types of land tax, *kharaj* and *ushr*—a distinction that had come into existence in the nineteenth century. As a rough definition, *kharaj* was the tax imposed on land farmed communally and believed to belong to the government, while *ushr* tax was assessed on land believed to be private property.[25] These distinctions

[24] Add MSS 48960-61, D'Abernon Papers, British Museum.
[25] Gabriel Baer, *A History of Landownership in Modern Egypt, 1800-1950* (New York, 1962), pp. 19-20. *Ushr* land was established in 1854. As Baer states: "This is not to be confused with the traditional Muslim distinction between *Ushr* and *Kharaj* land, the most important difference being that traditionally *Ushr* land

began to break down as the peasant tillers of *kharaj* land acquired landholding rights in the nineteenth century. But certain basic distinctions remained, the most important being that *kharaj* land was more heavily taxed than *ushr* land; also that *kharaj* land was mainly worked by small peasantry, *ushr* by the large landowners. A study by an Indian land expert in 1884 showed that the average incidence of taxation on *kharaj* land was £1 6s 4d per *feddan* (roughly an acre); that on *ushr* was 10s 7d.[26] This study further indicated that the average *kharaj* land in Egypt bore much heavier charges than the best agricultural land in India.

A large group of British land officials, impressed by the high incidence of taxation and frightened by the possibilities of revolt, agitated for immediate reform of the land taxation system. They wanted the abolition of the tax differential between *ushr* and *kharaj* and the equalization of tax burdens. They felt that this reduction of taxation could be carried out without disrupting the administrative and revenue needs of the country.[27] Baring and top British financial officials opposed such far-reaching changes. The avowed reason for their opposition was that the abolition of the distinctions and the equalization of burdens could not be undertaken until a new land survey had been made. Until the exact worth of the land was determined, they argued, it would be impossible to fix the rates that individual pieces of land should bear.[28]

---

was held by Muslims only while now many *dhimmis* (adherents to non-Muslim monotheistic religions) and even foreigners paid the *Ushr*."

[26] Baring to Granville, No. 6, July 25, 1884, *HCSP*, Egypt No. 31 (1884), Vol. LXXXIX, c. 4131. A study conducted in 1886 gave approximately the same results. Add MSS 48960-61, D'Abernon Papers.

[27] Egerton to Granville, No. 3, June 2, 1884, *HCSP*, Egypt No. 31 (1884), Vol. LXXXIX, c. 4131.

[28] Cromer to Kimberley, No. 48, April 21, 1895, PRO, FO 78/4668.

Egypt had not had an effective survey of lands since the reign of Muhammad Ali. Funds for such an undertaking were not available in the early years of the occupation, so, if this reasoning were accepted, radical reform of the land tax system would have to be postponed until these funds finally became available.

A more decisive reason—not made public—for not undertaking land tax reform was that changes in the taxation scheme were opposed by the large landholders. Baring's financial adviser, Vincent, realized that the British must trim their program to the desires of the ruling classes, at least in the early years of the occupation. Baring supported Vincent, arguing that "an alien government ... has to be much more circumspect in its action than any native government." He feared that extensive reform would turn "the most important and influential class in the country" against the British.[29] Therefore, the administration decided to delay the revision of the land taxation schedule until the completion of a land and revenue survey. This survey was not completed, in fact, until the first decade of the twentieth century; so it was not until then that new, equal rates went into effect and the remaining distinctions between *kharaj* and *ushr* land were abolished.

Instead of a tax schedule revision, the British undertook minor changes in the land tax. When the budget of 1885 was drawn up, approximately £E200,000 was appropriated for the purpose of land tax reduction.[30] From then until the new tax schedules came into effect, various reductions were made in the land tax, averaging £E100,000 to £E200,000 a year. The reductions were guided by two principles. The first was that nowhere

[29] Baring to Childers, No. 33, January 30, 1885, The Cromer Papers, PRO, FO 633/5.

[30] Egerton to Salisbury, No. 81, October 3, 1885, *HCSP*, Egypt No. 4 (1886), Vol. LXXIV, c. 4768.

should the tax exceed one-third of the rental value of the land. Those landholders who paid a higher rate were released from this obligation, and their tax was reduced at least to the maximum allowed by the British.[31] The second principle was that in areas chronically in arrears, the tax burdens were to be reduced.

Upper Egypt suffered the heaviest tax obligations. Although the system of basin irrigation was still in operation there, tax assessments were almost as high as the perennially irrigated lands in Lower Egypt.[32] The British irrigation inspector for Upper Egypt warned that high taxes could not be collected and that the peasant population was extremely discontented. For these reasons tax reductions were granted first and most generally to the oppressed peasantry of this area. In this sense, then, many of the so-called tax reductions were only paper transactions, a formal recognition that the taxes could not be collected.

Tax reforms in this early period had the effect primarily of bringing the tax schedule into line with the tax-paying potential of the peasantry. The reforms did away with the arrears in taxes but did not effectively give the peasants more money for their personal needs. They did, however, free the peasantry from continual governmental interference for previously unpaid taxes, and they liberated the *fellahin* from the obligation to borrow money from village money-lenders to meet part of this debt. The tax reductions enabled some of the peasants to pull themselves out of debt, but they did not increase the cash in pocket, as some British officials claimed.

[31] A. T. McKillop, *Note on the Readjustment of the Land Tax in Egypt, 1895 to 1907* (Cairo, 1907), published by the Ministry of Finance.

[32] Egerton to Granville, No. 129, May 27, 1884, *HCSP*, Egypt No. 25 (1884), Vol. LXXXIX, c. 4100.

Land tax reform was the most important fiscal reduction, but there were other significant changes in the taxation scheme during these years. From 1890 to 1895 the land tax was reduced by £E430,000, the professional tax by 180,000, the sheep and goat tax by 40,000, the weighing tax 28,000, and small taxes 31,000. In addition, postal and telegraph rates were reduced by 50 percent and there were large reductions in railway rates.[33] One exception was customs, which could not be touched, since they were fixed at 8 percent ad valorem for all parts of the Ottoman Empire, and their receipts were pledged for debt payments. Despite the reductions, the revenue of the country continued to increase as Egypt's resources were developed.

✿

In his report suggesting essential reforms for Egypt, Dufferin laid great stress on hydraulics.[34] His advice was heeded, and in 1884 Colin Scott-Moncrieff was made adviser to the Ministry of Public Works.[35] Scott-Moncrieff's appointment marked the beginning of Anglo-Indian control over Egyptian hydraulics. As Dufferin had pointed out in his report, conditions in Northern India were so similar to those of Egypt that technical skills acquired there could be transferred to Egypt. Scott-Moncrieff was followed by eight other hydraulic engineers, all trained in India. Many, like Garstin, Scott-Moncrieff's successor, and William Willcocks, had been educated at Thomason Civil Engineering College in India and had spent most of their lives in that country. As Scott-Moncrieff said:

[33] Lord Cromer, Annual Report for 1894, *HCSP*, Egypt No. 1 (1895), Vol. cix, c. 7644.

[34] Dufferin to Granville, No. 38, February 6, 1883, *HCSP*, Egypt No. 6 (1883), Vol. lxxxiii, c. 3529.

[35] Details of Scott-Moncrieff's life may be found in Mary A. Hollings, *The Life of Sir Colin C. Scott-Moncrieff* (London, 1917).

Irrigation is an art which there is no occasion to practice in England. But there are few forms of agriculture which are not practiced in one or another of Her Majesty's many possessions, and so it happened that from Northern India Lord Dufferin was able to obtain officers possessing the experience required in Egypt. In Northern India a system of canals exist far greater than in Egypt, and here, too, irrigation is practiced when the heat is the greatest and the canals at their lowest. . . . It was to India, then, that Lord Dufferin looked for engineers to improve the irrigation of Egypt.[36]

Although irrigation engineers were to come from England in the later years of the British occupation, the influence of Indian experience and techniques was never to be erased from the Ministry of Public Works during the occupation.

The pressures for modernizing the hydraulic system came, in these early years, mostly from British officialdom in Egypt. Hydraulic improvement was sponsored because it would increase the wealth of the country, enable the government to balance its budget, and keep the populace reasonably contented. It was also re-enforced by the foreign commercial class in Egypt. This class, temporarily forced into the background by Egyptian bankruptcy, was anxious to regain its predominant position. Its members supported most of the development programs of the administration, although they would have preferred to exercise larger control. It was not until later in the occupation, however, that the interested, foreign groups—land companies, banking establishments, and textile manufacturers—began to play a major role in determining Egyptian irrigation policies. In this early

[36] Colin Scott-Moncrieff, "Irrigation in Egypt," *The Nineteenth Century*, xvii (1885), 344.

period the only outside group capable of exerting constant pressure were the foreign bondholders. Like the British administration, they were anxious to see the wealth of the country increased, so that Egypt would be able to make payments on its foreign debt. Also, the reforms sponsored by the British enjoyed the support of the Egyptian landed class and were tailored to its interests.

At the outset, Scott-Moncrieff encountered opposition from leading Egyptian officials who were concerned about the way in which the British would use their powers in the Ministry of Public Works. They were afraid that British control might mean radical reform of the economic life of the country, which would threaten their positions. In a letter home Scott-Moncrieff wrote that he did not "suppose that the authorities here want reform. I believe they would be delighted to increase my pay and send it to me regularly if I would only go home and never bother them anymore."[37] These obstructions diminished when the Egyptians saw that the British intended no fundamental alterations in landholding or in the distribution of wealth. Egypt's leading minister, Nubar Pasha, became one of the most devoted followers and supporters of Scott-Moncrieff's programs.[38] His reasoning undoubtedly was that reforms would increase the wealth of the established ruling classes and the masses as well, and might even win for him and his class popular support. The British, on the other hand, had no intention of allowing control to pass from their hands back to the Egyptians, as had occurred in the Ministry of the Interior. They believed that the wealth of the country depended on its hydraulic system. If Egypt was to balance its budget, its agricultural resources

[37] Hollings, *Life of Scott-Moncrieff*, p. 158. Also Egerton to Barrington, No. 64, August 18, 1885, Salisbury Papers, A/39.
[38] Najib Makhluf, *Nubar Pasha* (Cairo, 1899), p. 126ff.

would have to be expanded through hydraulic improvements. Even while the duration of the occupation was in doubt, the British were firmly committed to making their influence felt in the Ministry of Public Works. As Baring wrote, "Here [in irrigation and agriculture] we have interfered actively and with great success. It is the most important subject in respect to which the good results of European administration can be readily brought home to the natives. Hence, there is some chance that, in the event of withdrawal, our work would not be wholly undone."[39]

The support the British gave to the Ministry of Public Works in hydraulic projects can be seen in the financial outlays on hydraulics. The Conference of London (1885) subscribed £9 million as an international loan to help Egypt out of its pressing financial difficulties. £8 million was used to pay off past debts, but the remaining million was turned over to the government for irrigation. When this sum was exhausted, a further loan of £800,000 was made available to the Ministry. According to statistics compiled by the British in 1903, covering the 20-year period from 1882 to 1902, approximately 8 percent of Egyptian revenue went for hydraulic and agricultural improvements.[40] The size of this expenditure is only evident when it is realized that nearly half of the Egyptian revenue was set aside for debt and other foreign payments, and another large percentage of the budget went for military expenses incurred in protecting the country against the Mahdi, and then in the reconquest of the Sudan. More important, the Ministry of Public Works was the only department which had regular long-range development programs. It received a large percentage of the surplus accumulated by the *Caisse* in its

[39] Quoted in Zetland, *Lord Cromer*, p. 171.
[40] Lord Cromer, Annual Report for 1902, *HCSP*, Egypt No. 1 (1903), Vol. LXXXVII, cd. 1529.

reserve funds and was the only department with a special budget for these development programs.

Scott-Moncrieff spent the first half-year after his arrival investigating the Egyptian irrigation system. He was appalled by the disrepair he saw, and convinced that Ismail's engineers had not mastered the basic techniques for constructing efficient irrigation canals.[41] Most of the canals were badly aligned and choked with silt. One of the British hydraulics experts assigned to Upper Egypt, Justin Ross, reported that "every year ... drains were abandoned or became useless, and canals became less of artificial and more of natural channels wholly influenced by the natural rise of the Nile."[42] The drainage of excess water from the land was virtually nonexistent in certain places. The British estimated that the level of Lake Fayum had risen because of faulty drainage, thereby submerging large amounts of otherwise arable land.[43] The Ibrahimiyah Canal, which had been constructed in Ismail's reign to bring much-needed summer water to Fayum province in Middle Egypt was improperly looked after. Because of its faulty alignment and silting in the canal bed, it carried only a fraction of the water it should have. No doubt, a great deal of what the British officials reported was exaggerated for the purpose of calling the attention of Baring and Vincent to their reform programs, but even when one discounts the exaggeration, the picture of the existing hydraulic system was alarming. There was ample evidence that Egypt's irrigation system was on the verge of collapse.

Scott-Moncrieff was encouraged by many interested observers to inaugurate the British occupation with a gran-

[41] Malet to Granville, No. 8, June 24, 1883, enclosing report of Scott-Moncrieff, Granville Papers, PRO, FO 30/29/287/11.

[42] Quoted in William Willcocks, *Egyptian Irrigation* (London, 1889), p. vi.

[43] Colin Scott-Moncrieff, "On the Nile," *Proceedings of the Royal Institution of Great Britain*, 1895, xiv, 413.

diose water-storage scheme. Plans for the construction of a huge dam in Upper Egypt were presented to him at this time. But after preliminary investigations he was convinced that the most pressing duty was to put the existing irrigation system into proper working order. The eight hydraulic engineers brought from India were each put in charge of a district, or an "irrigation circle." The duties of the irrigation inspector, as the British engineer was called, were the distribution of water from the headworks of the main canal to the outlets, the maintenance of canals and drains, and the protection of the country from flood.[44]

British irrigation inspectors were to become the arbiters of Egypt's agricultural life. Their responsibilities brought them in contact with local Egyptian officials —the *mudir*, the *mamur,* and the village *shaykh.* The inspectors settled disputes over the division of waters, determined, with the aid of the central office, how often the land was to be watered and how frequently. They arbitrated disputes over where private canals could be constructed and whether pumping apparatus could be installed. When it is kept in mind that irrigation water was the lifeblood of Egypt and that those unable to procure water could not raise their crops, it is possible to understand the vast powers exercised by these officials. On the whole, inspectors were well received by the peasant population. Scott-Moncrieff insisted that his engineers live among the people, and encouraged them to learn the language of the country.[45] Their obvious skills were recognized by the peasantry. Since they were always a

[44] Egypt, Ministry of Public Works, *Irrigation Service* (Cairo, 1921), pp. 30-31.

[45] It was Scott-Moncrieff's ruling that they should live in towns and villages and "not come often to Cairo." Hollings, *The Life of Scott-Moncrieff,* p. 178. There is a detailed account of the life of the British irrigation officer in William Willcocks, *Sixty Years in the East* (London, 1935).

[*115*]

small group, they were therefore unable to stamp out the bribery and corruption so long associated with the distribution of irrigation waters. They themselves were, however, incorruptible and scrupulously honest in their dealings with the people, in spite of numerous temptations. They did all in their power to ensure that the waters were distributed equitably to small and large landowners alike.

The focal point of attention at this time was the repair of the Nile barrage, located below Cairo, where the Nile divides into the Damietta and the Rosetta branches. The idea of constructing a regulating dam or barrage at that point was originally put forward by Linant de Bellefonds, a French engineer, during the reign of Muhammad Ali. The barrage was intended to raise the level of water in the Nile during the summer season, thereby providing summer irrigation for the Nile delta, where Muhammad Ali was hopeful of increasing cotton cultivation. Three large canals with their mouths upstream from the barrage were to carry the irrigation water into the delta provinces. The scheme captured the imagination of Muhammad Ali, and work was begun on it in the 1830's. Unfortunately, construction progress was fitful. An epidemic of plague interrupted work in 1835; the interest of the Khedives flagged from time to time, and, even when high, did not always prove beneficial. The structure was not completed until 1861, at an estimated cost of £E1,880,000, not to mention the unreckoned human cost. As a result of the interruptions and lack of planning, the foundations had been laid hastily. In 1863, when the barrage was first tested, cracks appeared in the masonry, and one section of the barrage moved noticeably downstream. It was, of course, unable to hold the desired level of water in the Nile. After several subsequent attempts to raise the water level had proved unsuccessful, the barrage was pronounced unfit, and, to all intents and purposes, was written off as a costly failure. The Damietta branch of the barrage was left unequipped with regulating gates, and two of the three feeder canals remained unfinished. In the opinion of one of the designers, "the barrage resembled a gangrened body. It was covered with a fine coat, but disease gnawed at its vitals. A major operation was needed."[46]

Considering the barrage to be of little use, the Egyptian government opened negotiations with a private pumping company to supply the delta with irrigation water. The company demanded an initial outlay of £E700,000, and estimated that annual operating expenses would be £E250,000—approximately half the budget of the Ministry of Public Works at that time.[47] It was while the government was in the midst of these negotiations that Scott-Moncrieff arrived in Egypt. Alarmed at the vast expenditures involved, his first reaction was to suggest using these funds to build another barrage; but he soon decided to determine whether the old barrage might still be salvaged.[48] Knowledge that the Egyptian Minister of Public Works had not visited the barrage in 27 years may have helped him to make this decision in the face of much opposition.[49]

As a preliminary step Scott-Moncrieff delegated one of his most capable engineers, William Willcocks, to

[46] This was the opinion of Linant de Bellefonds, quoted in Edward W. C. Sandes, *The Royal Engineers in Egypt and the Sudan* (Chatham, England, 1937), p. 368. There are other discussions of the history of the barrage in Robert Hanbury Brown, *The Delta Barrage of Lower Egypt* (Cairo, 1902) and Helen Rivlin, *The Agricultural Policies of Muhammad Ali in Egypt*, pp. 233-37. One should also consult Linant de Bellefonds, *Mémoires sur les Principaux Travaux d'Utilité Publique Exécuté en Égypte Depuis la plus haute Antiquité jusqu'à nos jours* (Paris, 1872).
[47] Baring to Salisbury, No. 101, June 27, 1890, enclosing report of Scott-Moncrieff, HCSP, Egypt No. 2 (1890), Vol. LXXXIII, c. 6135.
[48] Hollings, *Life of Scott-Moncrieff*, p. 201.
[49] Cromer, *Modern Egypt*, II, 459.

[117]

inspect the work and make temporary repairs. Willcock's investigations confirmed the worst fears of the British engineers. They showed the timber to be rotten, the iron rusted, and the foundations insecure. Nevertheless, it was decided to patch the cracks in the masonry, to equip the Damietta branch with its missing regulating gates, and to attempt to hold up a head of water. Although new cracks appeared and there was a slight shifting in the foundation when the regulating gates were closed, the experiment proved a success. The level of the low Nile was raised higher than it had ever been raised, and water was supplied to the cotton-growing lands of the delta. The cotton crop of 1884 was estimated to be 30,000 tons greater than that of the previous year.[50] The successful trial of the barrage in 1884 proved its fundamental soundness, and it was therefore resolved to undertake a comprehensive restoration.

The basic problem facing the British in the repair of the barrage was how to strengthen the foundations, which had been built upon mud and sand. The greatest fear was that water percolating under the flooring would scour out the mud under the barrage and eventually cause it to collapse. The British experience on the rivers of Southern India now proved of great value. Engineers had encountered similar problems there, and had devised techniques for dealing with them. The scheme suggested by Indian experience was to prolong the foundations, not by deepening the foundations, but by extending them horizontally, upstream and downstream. The purpose was "to stop the water passing under [the barrage] or to compel what little did pass to travel so far either vertically or horizontally that its velocity would be checked. Not only would this prevent its washing out sand and mud, but it would cause it to part with sand or mud brought in with it, so that every year the sub-

[50] Hollings, *Life of Scott-Moncrieff*, p. 203.

stratum would become more and more impermeable, like an old filter."[51]

Work was begun along these lines in 1887. Since all the repairs could not be completed in a single year, it was decided to work on one-fourth of the barrage each year. The portions not being repaired were continued in use, to regulate the level of the Nile. "It was like mending a watch, and never stopping the works," wrote Scott-Moncrieff.[52] In December of each year, when the flood had subsided, the part to be worked on was enclosed by earthen dams and the water pumped out. The actual work on the barrage usually commenced in March and continued without interruption night and day until the end of June, when the flood had to be prepared for. The night work was made possible by electric lights, and nine steam-pumps were employed constantly to keep the bed of the river dry. In this fashion, the old foundations were strengthened, and new foundations were laid upstream and downstream from the old. While the work was going on, two feeder canals were dug as originally planned, and a third was put in sound working order. By 1890 most of this massive undertaking had been completed, thus realizing the earlier, well-conceived plans of Muhammad Ali's engineers. The barrage, regulating the summer irrigation of the delta as intended, made possible in the 1890's the highest cotton yields on record, only to be superseded when the Aswan Dam was completed in 1902.

The barrage, however, required close surveillance even after the general restoration had been executed. "Though off the sick list," wrote one of the English engineers, "the barrage was still of delicate constitution."[53] The old foundations had only been encased,

[51] Baring to Salisbury, No. 101, June 27, 1890, *HCSP*, Egypt No. 2 (1890), Vol. LXXXIII, c. 6135.

[52] *Ibid.*

[53] R. H. Brown, *The Delta Barrage of Lower Egypt*, p. 45. The

with the defects inside remaining; it was widely feared that the pressure of the water on the masonry might eventually cause it to collapse from within. Some of the worst fears were, in fact, confirmed when springs were once again sighted downstream. In 1896, a British engineer was brought out to Egypt to repair two locks on the Ismailiyah Canal by introducing a special kind of clay at high pressure into the works. The engineers working on the barrage decided to use the same technique in an effort to secure its foundations. Holes were bored from the top of the superstructure to the underside of the flooring and clay at high pressure was forced into them. It was hoped that the clay would spread out into the cracks in the masonry and bind them together. The experiment did not work, but the idea of repairing the defects in the foundations by boring and introducing a material under pressure through the bores was not abandoned. An alternative method of employing cement instead of clay produced the desired results, that of binding all that was loose in the old work into a solid, cohesive mass. To be doubly safe, subsidiary weirs were constructed downstream of the barrage to take some of the pressure off the main work.

❊

The *corvée* had been used traditionally to dig and clean Egypt's network of irrigation and drainage canals —a system filled with abuses. Labor was generally recruited unfairly, and was often required to travel long distances from the fields. Laborers were unpaid, poorly equipped, and were forced to sleep out in the open air. On the other hand, *corvées* were called out primarily during the summer season when, before the introduction

---

remainder of the discussion of the barrage is based primarily on Brown's book. Brown was, in fact, the British engineer in charge of the barrage in this latter period.

of perennial irrigation, the land was lying fallow. It could almost have been argued, if the labor requirements had been distributed equitably, that the *corvée* was a tax in kind, paid in return for the irrigation water provided by the government.

With the substitution of perennial irrigation for basin irrigation, the situation was changed completely. The land now demanded constant attention, and it was unfair to the peasants and harmful to the economy to have a proportion of the population absent from the fields for long periods of time. The introduction of perennial irrigation meant that there were many more canals to dig and clean than ever before. Moreover, the *corvée* was both inefficient and expensive. Canals now had to conform to exact measurements in slope, width, and depth; *corvée* labor was found to be incapable of cleaning the canals to meet these rigid measurements.[54] It was also more expensive in many places than dredging machines. The British engineer, Willcocks, estimated that it cost twenty times more to remove slush in one of the major canals by using the *corvée* than with dredgers.[55]

Prior to the British occupation the Egyptian government had considered problems arising from the use of the *corvée*. Its inefficiency was generally conceded; its expense was admitted; but because the government in its financial plight could not find the money with which to pay for dredging operations, it was decided that the *corvée* would have to be continued.[56] This dilemma confronted the British after 1882, especially in view of Egypt's debt payments. At the same time, pressures for

[54] Julien Barois, *Irrigation in Egypt*, tr. from the French by A. M. Miller (Washington, D.C., 1889), p. 45.

[55] William Willcocks, "Egypt during the Forty Years of the British Occupation," *Bulletin de l'Institut d'Égypte*, 1926, p. 21.

[56] Early attempts at abolishing the use of the *corvée* are discussed in Baring to Salisbury, No. 49, December 18, 1889, HCSP, Egypt No. 2 (1890), Vol. LXXXIII, c. 6135.

abolishing the *corvée* began to mount on both practical and humanitarian grounds, for the British engineers were offended as much by the aspect of forced labor as by its inefficiency and expensiveness. The labor levies were traditionally enforced with the use of the *kurbaj*(whip made of hippopotamus hide)—a practice the British suppressed.[57]

In 1885, an opportunity arose to suppress the use of the *corvée* itself. The budget for that year allowed a £E450,000 reduction in taxes. Instead of reducing the tax by this much, it was decided that £E250,000 be retained and applied to the partial abolition of the *corvée* practice. This decision, however, was opposed by France, which, as a member of the *Caisse de la Dette*, still had certain powers over Egyptian finances.

The French objected partly on legitimate financial grounds and partly on purely political grounds. For a moment it appeared that French opposition would block the reform. But through the timely intervention of the Salisbury government in London, the French were persuaded to withdraw their opposition. The use of the *corvée*, gradually reduced in the late 1880's, came to an end in 1889. After that, canal construction and clearance were done either by dredging machines or by paid labor.[58]

The British had made only a beginning in the hydraulic and agricultural transformation of Egypt. Much more had to be done if the entire country was to enjoy the benefits of perennial irrigation. Already there were indications that a vast water-storage scheme would be the next, large hydraulic undertaking. The social consequences of

[57] Baring to Rosebery, No. 175, February 16, 1886, *HCSP*, Egypt No. 4 (1886), Vol. LXXXIV, c. 4768.

[58] This statement refers only to the use of forced labor to clear and dig canals. Actually the *corvée* continued to be used during the Nile flood to watch the banks of the Nile, to prevent their being breached.

these changes for the mass of the peasant population were still little understood and would require attention and skillful handling. Peasant life was being altered radically by the introduction of perennial irrigation and the extension of cotton cultivation. The concomitant social unrest and economic problems would have to be treated. Cotton and other crop yields were high, but because of imbalances in the irrigation reforms these yields were to decline at the turn of the century, creating serious problems for the British hydraulic and agricultural experts.

❋

The modern judicial system of Egypt traces its origin to the establishment of the Mixed Tribunals in 1875. Prior to their creation Egypt had had a variety of judicial systems, administering a set of widely divergent laws. In the first place, there were the Islamic courts. Although their jurisdiction had been steadily restricted throughout the nineteenth century, under the impact of Egypt's modernizing activities, they were still responsible for personal status cases among Muslims in Egypt, such as marriage, divorce, and wills. Foreigners in Egypt, enjoying the benefits conferred by capitulations, were tried in their own consular courts for criminal and civil cases. Criminal, civil, and commercial cases involving only Egyptians as litigants came before the newly-emerging Egyptian secular courts. These courts administered a most ill-defined law. Some of the law was taken over from the reformed Ottoman Empire courts. Other laws were derived from the French *Code Napoléon*. The commercial code, for instance, was taken from the Ottoman code, but when items arose that could not be settled by referring to this code, it was customary to refer to French civil law.[59] Judges were given almost no specialized

[59] *Al-Kitab al-Dhahabi* [The Golden Book] (Cairo, 1937-1938), I, 110.

training, and there were virtually no special qualifications for practicing law before the courts. The real
locus of power still rested with the executive, in spite
of the existence of these courts. The judiciary had no independent existence; courts were created, abolished,
and modified at the whim of the Khedive. At the time of
the British occupation the courts were divided into five
levels: village councils, district councils, first instance
courts, appeal courts, and a kind of court of cassation,
known as *Majlis al-Ahkam*.[60] Educated Egyptians were
well aware that one of the requirements for the continued modernization of the country was a reformed and
independent, secular judiciary.

The nineteenth-century modernizing tendencies in
Egypt had made clear its need for modern, Westernized
law. Islamic law was not suitable to the changing requirements of Egyptian society; its civil and commercial codes
were not nearly so specialized and developed as the
Western codes. Nor did the Islamic law apply to minority
and foreign communities in Egypt. Gradually, Islamic
law was replaced by Western-type law. Foreign communities were able to bring their own codes to Egypt
as a result of the capitulations; these codes, of course,
influenced the evolving Egyptian legal system.

Nubar Pasha, Egypt's Armenian minister, was one of
the leading figures in the modernization of the Egyptian
legal system before 1882.[61] He and other Egyptians
balked at the powers exercised by the consular courts
and the freedom enjoyed by the foreign communities in
Egypt. The consular courts administered their own system of law, and all the powers with capitulatory rights

[60] *Ibid.*

[61] The history of the Mixed Courts can be traced in Jaspar
Yeates Brinton, *The Mixed Courts of Egypt* (New Haven, 1930)
and *Livre d'Or* (Cairo, 1925). The role of Nubar has been discussed by Alexander Holynski, *Nubar Pacha devant l'Histoire*
(Paris, 1886).

in Egypt possessed such courts. Moreover, cases were settled by consular agents whose dispassionate interest in the facts and the merits of the disputes did not always manifest itself. Indeed, foreigners used their own courts to bring suits against the government, a practice that proved extremely costly to the Egyptian government during the reign of Ismail. Nubar took his inspiration for reform from the Mixed Tribunals created in Turkey to replace the capitulatory consular courts. His goal was to persuade the European powers to give up their jurisdiction to an internationally controlled tribunal of mixed European and Egyptian judges. The courts were to administer French law, and European judges were to constitute a majority on the bench. After long negotiations and a great deal of opposition, the foreign powers eventually agreed to the reform scheme, and the new courts, known as the Mixed Tribunals, were established in 1875.

The Mixed Tribunals were divided into two levels: courts of first instance, located at Alexandria, Cairo, and Mansura; and a court of appeal at Alexandria.[62] All courts had several judges, a majority being European. The Egyptian government had the power to select the judges, but always selected individuals on the advice of the European powers involved. The courts, as Nubar had hoped, administered French law which was, in fact, almost an exact replica of the *Code Napoléon*. The task of suiting the law to Egyptian circumstances was assigned to an Alexandrian lawyer, M. Manoury, but since he was not trained for this work, he made almost no basic changes in the French code.[63] The languages of the new courts were French, Italian, and Arabic, with English introduced later. The courts had jurisdiction over commercial and civil cases involving foreigners, and a foreigner and an Egyptian. Nubar had hoped to endow

[62] Brinton, *Mixed Courts of Egypt*, p. 71.
[63] *Ibid.*, p. 83.

the courts with jurisdiction over criminal matters, but the foreign powers were not willing to relinquish this authority. The consular courts, therefore, retained their jurisdiction over criminal and personal status cases.

In a relatively short time the new courts became the most important judicial bodies in the country. As European interests in Egypt increased, the courts became increasingly responsible for the settlement of the most important cases in the country. Indeed, by the turn of the century it was a commonly established practice for the Mixed Tribunals to assert the right to try every single important case. The rationale behind the demand was that the courts had the right to try not only cases involving any foreign subject, but also cases involving any foreign "interest." As the Egyptian judicial adviser indicated in 1899, "the Mixed Tribunals have gradually established a principle (which is nowhere to be found in the law itself) under which they affirm their jurisdiction in all suits where a "mixed interest" is discoverable, although the actual parties to the suit may be natives. It is easy to understand with so vague and arbitrary a criterion of jurisprudence that the powers of these tribunals have been extended in an ever widening circle."[64] Egyptian government officials were powerless to oppose this extension of influence. The Mixed Courts remained foreign controlled, an international judiciary. Various attempts by the Egyptian government to resist the demands of European governments to appoint their own judges did not succeed. The Egyptians had another serious complaint against these tribunals, namely the caliber of men put forward by the European governments to serve as judges. These men were usually rather poorly qualified for judicial work, looking for sinecures to which to retire as rewards for their services to the

[64] Quoted in Brinton, *Mixed Courts of Egypt*, p. 105.

state.[65] Nevertheless, in spite of these drawbacks, the courts operated in a relatively efficient fashion. More important, they set an example for the evolving Egyptian tribunals.

Agitation to reform Egypt's Native Courts culminated just before the occupation. In 1880 leading Egyptian ministers established a committee under the presidency of Husayn Fakhri to draw up a scheme for the reform of these courts.[66] The committee considered a variety of projects. It rejected a proposal that the Native Courts administer the *sharia* (religious law), on the grounds that this law was not suited to modern requirements and should be confined to personal status matters. The members finally decided to reform the existing courts by taking over the *Code Napoléon* and the French judicial system. The *Code* had a rather natural appeal to the Egyptians because of the seeming ease with which a fully codified set of laws could be introduced into Egypt. Indeed, after the Mixed Tribunals had been created, Egyptian scholars had translated a great deal of the French law into Arabic.[67] Moreover, it was hoped that the Mixed and Native Courts might eventually be assimilated into one court system, and Egypt could be spared the problems of a double judicial system. The only way that such a change could be effected, it was argued, was to introduce the same legal system into the Native Courts. Although the work of the committee was interrupted by the Arabi revolt, it reconvened afterward and put forward the same set of recommendations.

The British were reluctant to agree with the recommendations of the Egyptian committee, primarily because their own technical experts were unfamiliar with

[65] Kitchener to Grey, No. 133, December 15, 1911, PRO, FO 371/112, file 6974, No. 51358.

[66] *Al-Kitab al-Dhuhabi* [The Golden Book], I, 151.

[67] Abd al-Rahman al-Rafii, *Asr Ismail* [The Reign of Ismail], II, 239.

French law and were worried about whether French law would be suited to conditions in Egypt. The British judicial expert, Benson Maxwell, who had acquired his own judicial experience in India, would have preferred to see the Egyptian Native Courts employ Anglo-Indian law.[68] But the objections of the British were overcome, and the new Native Courts, based on French law and French procedure, came into existence in 1883. The reason the British accepted the change was twofold: first, they were impressed by the argument that because of the Egyptians' experience with the Mixed Tribunals the only kind of Western law they were familiar with was French law; and at this point they were reluctant to interfere with the domestic life of the country.[69] Most British officials felt that the Egyptians should be allowed to select for themselves the type of law they found most suitable.

The original proposals for the new court system envisaged four levels of tribunals.[70] There were to be summary courts, administering law in the provinces, close to the peasant populations; courts of first instance, located in the major urban centers; two appeal courts, at Asyut and Cairo; and a court of cassation. Actually, when the new courts came into existence, the summary courts and the courts of cassation did not function effectively and were set aside temporarily. There were, therefore, just two types of courts operating in the early years—the court of first instance and the appeal tribunal. The new courts were not introduced into Upper

[68] Baring to Granville, No. 31, January 26, 1884, enclosing report of Benson Maxwell, *HCSP*, Egypt No. 12 (1884), Vol. LXXXVIII, c. 3969.

[69] Dufferin to Granville, January 2, 1883, Granville Papers, PRO 30/29/166.

[70] The decree for the reorganization of the native courts, promulgated June 21, 1883, is contained in Malet to Granville, No. 49, June 22, 1883, *HCSP*, Egypt No. 22 (1883), Vol. LXXXIII, c. 3802.

Egypt until 1889, the legal problems of this area being dealt with by the old courts and by temporary administrative courts. It had been the intention of the reformers even before the British occupation to rely upon foreign personnel to help staff the bench of the new courts.[71] Accordingly, approximately 40 Belgian and Dutch experts were brought to Egypt as judges. French law was translated into Arabic by a group of talented Egyptians, led by Muhammad Abduh and Muhammad Qadri. There was an attempt, of course, to adapt it to Egyptian requirements, especially in the matter of penalties assigned for specific crimes; but, like the codes administered by the Mixed Tribunals, this law was almost an exact replica of French law and was not well suited to the differing conditions in Egypt.[72] The British sought to make their influence felt at the apex of the system by the appointment of a British official as the Procurer-General, the head of the prosecuting office in the Egyptian legal system.

The new courts encountered difficulties from the outset. There was first the problem of finding well qualified personnel. The Belgian and Dutch judges were unfamiliar with Arabic and the peculiar problems and circumstances in Egypt. They found their duties increasingly onerous and unrewarding; by 1890 almost all had resigned to return to more lucrative positions in Europe.[73] The Egyptian judges were, for the most part, poorly trained, since there had been no regular law school in Egypt until the British occupation.[74] In addition, the

[71] See the memorandum of Husayn Fakhri, Minister of Justice, December, 1882, quoted in *al-Kitab al-Dhahabi* [The Golden Book], I, 107-15.

[72] Baring to Granville, No. 31, January 26, 1884, enclosing report of Benson Maxwell, *HCSP*, Egypt No. 12 (1884), Vol. LXXXVIII, c. 3969.

[73] Brinton, *Mixed Courts of Egypt*, p. 272.

[74] Northbrook to Granville, No. 105, October 24, 1884, en-

lawyers and agents who practiced before the bar were not well qualified. Almost the only requisite for practicing in the Native Courts in these early years was indication of some competence in law.[75] Finally, legal proceedings were long, expensive, and inaccessible to the mass of the population.

The British judicial experts were convinced that the basic defect of the new courts was the use of the French legal system. They felt that French law was too rigid for a backward country like Egypt, and that the practice of trying cases before multiple judges, as in French law, made the court system slow and expensive for Egyptians. They found a constant friction between police and judicial authorities, for according to French practice the judicial authorities assumed responsibility for collecting evidence and preparing the case for the prosecution once a crime had been committed. The regular police force was supposed to render assistance to the judicial authorities, but in reality there were innumerable disputes over respective spheres of authority between these two branches of the administration.[76]

The first Procurer-General, Benson Maxwell, wrote that French law was "utterly unsuited to this country," adding that "no person who has a general acquaintance either with the reforms made in our country or with Indian legislation of the last quarter of a century, both in procedure and in the law of evidence, can look upon such a system as rationally calculated to administer jus-

---

closing report of Sami Ullah Khan, one of the judges in the North-Western provinces of India, Granville Papers, PRO 30/29/289/15.

[75] *Al-Kitab al-Dhahabi* [The Golden Book], I, 374. The ruling of 1888 fixed the requirements for the practice of law before the Native Courts. Applicants had to be twenty-one and "competent in law." A committee was formed in the appeal tribunal to test a man's competence, but the test was easy.

[76] A good summary of these criticisms can be found in C. E. Coles Pasha, *Recollections and Reflections* (London, 1918), p. 83.

tice either quickly, cheaply, or efficiently."[77] The British experts agitated for the introduction of reforms based on Anglo-Indian law which they felt was far more suitable to Egypt's stage of development. They proposed the decentralization of the judicial system, the utilization of single, rather than multiple, judges, the creation of summary or executive courts dispensing quick and effective justice for the mass of the population. The prime emphasis of the British suggestions was upon making justice cheaper and more accessible to the Egyptian population. In all of their suggestions the British experts were guided by the model of Anglo-Indian law where summary and administrative justice was already highly developed, where the legal system was not so centralized, and where the British had evolved legal codes which they felt were more suitable to oriental societies than the *Code Napoléon*.

The chief critic of the Egyptian legal system in this early period was Raymond West. West had served as Judge of the High Court in Bombay and had come to Egypt as Procurer-General. Unfamiliar with French law, he immediately became critical of the system in Egypt. Prior to his resignation West drew up a long and detailed report, the essence of which was that French code should be replaced by the Anglo-Indian system.[78] But his criticism and proposals were to no avail, as the British were not ready at this point to assume larger administrative responsibilities in the Ministry of Justice. With the resignation of West in 1886, however, British influence in the Ministry of Justice ceased. The Ministry had not a single British adviser in a position of authority; and it was not until the appointment of John Scott as

[77] Baring to Granville, No. 31, January 26, 1884, enclosing a report by Benson Maxwell, *HCSP*, Egypt No. 12 (1884), Vol. LXXXVIII, c. 3969.

[78] Baring to Rosebery, No. 58, March 27, 1886, *HCSP*, Egypt No. 5 (1886), Vol. LXXIV, c. 4769.

British adviser to the Ministry of Justice in 1890 that the British once again asserted their authority over the judicial life of the country.

The appointment of Scott was occasioned by investigations revealing grave deficiencies in the existing system. In 1884 the British had permitted the creation of Commissions of Brigandage to stamp out lawlessness in the provinces. These were executive bodies, composed of official and nonofficial members of the various communities. Their duty was to ensure that the countryside was not ravaged by groups of brigands, a practice on the rise during this period of administrative turmoil. These bodies were not to be bound by the new codes, as to procedures or punishments.[79] Unknown until 1888, LeGrelle, West's successor as Procurer-General of the Ministry of Justice, issued a scathing indictment of the Commissions. His investigations revealed that they operated in the most brutal and high-handed fashion. Confessions were exacted from persons by torture. The notorious *kurbaj*, which had been long used throughout Egypt and the use of which the British had supposedly abolished, was being employed liberally and indiscriminately on witnesses and on the accused to obtain confessions. The Commissions were found to employ their powers in many cases not for the purpose of stamping out crime, but in order to carry out revenge on enemies or to strengthen one's position in the village community. The majority of persons imprisoned by the Commissions, LeGrelle believed, were innocent men.[80]

The furor among the educated in Egypt caused by these revelations and in the European press compelled the British to redirect their attention to the judicial sys-

[79] Baring to Granville, No. 43, October 16, 1884, *HCSP*, Egypt No. 1 (1885), Vol. LXXXVIII, c. 4278.

[80] Clarke to Salisbury, No. 42, December 1, 1889, *HCSP*, Egypt No. 2 (1890), Vol. LXXXIII, c. 6135.

tem. It also gave Baring and his associates a good rationalization for increasing British control over the Ministry of Justice. The appointment of Scott was resisted bitterly by the Egyptians, jealous to maintain their own control over the department. Baring realized the import of the step he was taking and the amount of opposition he would encounter. He had consulted with Salisbury, the Foreign Minister, long in advance and had prepared the London cabinet for the outcry raised by some of the Egyptians.[81] The Minister of Justice, Husayn Fakhri, one of the leaders in establishing the reformed judiciary in 1883, resigned in protest over the Anglicization of this branch of the administration. Actually, the Egyptian opposition was not totally ineffective. Baring and the British were forced to compromise certain essentials of their programs in the face of this criticism. They had hoped to make Scott judicial adviser with the right to attend meetings of the Egyptian Council of Ministers, as the financial adviser did. They also wanted to bring in a number of British judicial inspectors to control the judicial system in the same fashion that the irrigation inspectors controlled the hydraulic system.[82] These far-reaching changes, which would have left little independent judicial authority in the hands of the Egyptians, were understandably opposed by the Egyptian ministers. The British had to settle for an agreement that Scott, as judicial adviser, would have the right to attend meetings of the Council of Ministers only when judicial affairs were on the agenda. Additionally, the British were not able to appoint judicial inspectors as they wanted, but established, instead, a Committee of Judicial Surveillance composed

[81] Most of the important documents of this correspondence were published in HCSP, Appendix to Lord Cromer's memorandum of July 12, 1906, pp. 25-55, Egypt No. 3 (1906), Vol. cxxxvii, cd. 3086.

[82] Baring to Salisbury, No. 297, November 6, 1890, PRO, FO 78/4312.

of Scott and two other top-ranking European judicial experts, with the right to supervise the operation of the judicial system.[83]

It should not be thought that the only reason for the assumption of control over the Ministry of Justice was the irregularities in the Ministry. By 1890 the British occupation had taken on some permanence. Not only were the British beginning to feel responsibility for the entire Egyptian administration, but they were also aware that many reforms were being jeopardized by defects in the internal administration. Joseph Chamberlain, leader of the Liberal-Unionists and later Colonial Secretary of the Conservative party, made a trip to Egypt in 1889. While impressed with the accomplishments of the occupation government, he indicated in a letter to Baring after he left Egypt that there were still parts of the administration requiring further attention, especially the Ministries of the Interior and Justice.[84] Chamberlain's letter reflected increasing British involvement in Egyptian administrative developments. And the British move into the Ministry of Justice must be seen in the light of British encroachment on other ministries in this period.

John Scott's credentials were more impressive and more suited to Egypt than those of his English predecessors. Having graduated from Oxford, he was called to the bar in 1865. For reasons of health he had gone to Egypt where he served on the bench of the Mixed Tribunals. In 1882 he went to India as a judge and remained there until sent back to Egypt as judicial adviser in 1890. His particular qualifications for the post of judicial adviser were that he was thoroughly versed in both French and Indian law, and knew the Indian and Egyp-

[83] Lord Cromer, Annual Report for 1895, with report of Scott on the Native Tribunals, 1894-1895, *HCSP*, Egypt No. 1 (1896), Vol. xcvii, c. 7978.

[84] This letter is quoted in Joseph Chamberlain, *A Political Memoir*, C. H. D. Howard, ed. (London, 1953), pp. 314-20.

tian court systems equally well. He was therefore better able than his predecessors, who had been hindered by not understanding the fundamentals of the French judicial system, to blend into the existing system reforms based largely upon Indian experience.[85]

The first measures of the new judicial adviser were designed to break up the centralized French system of courts, holding sessions with multiple judges only in the larger cities, thereby making justice more accessible to the population. To this effect Scott conferred upon certain local administrators—the *umdahs*—powers to summarily settle minor civil and criminal cases, subject to appeal, in order to prevent abuses of this power.[86] In addition, he created summary courts of justice to hold sessions under a single, qualified judge in hitherto unrepresented provincial cities. The courts of first instance, which had been the first line of courts until this reform, were restricted to the more important civil and criminal cases and to appellate cases from the lower courts.[87] In order to raise the personnel standards in the courts, Scott also enacted more stringent rulings pertaining to the appointment of judges and the practice of law before the Egyptian courts. A number of Europeans were appointed to the bench. Unfortunately, little could be said for their abilities, for few possessed the requisite qualifications in law and Arabic. In an attempt to provide for higher quality in Egypt's legal profession Scott encouraged the reform of the Egyptian Law School and the increase of its European teaching

[85] There is a short biographical sketch of Scott in *The Dictionary of National Biography*, Second Supplement (London, 1912), III, 280.

[86] *Al-Kitab al-Dhahabi* [The Golden Book], I, 163.

[87] A detailed discussion of Scott's programs, including the opposition he encountered, is found in Baring to Salisbury, No. 297, Nov. 6, 1890, PRO, FO 78/4312.

staff.[88] In 1893, practice before the Native Tribunals was permitted only to those with law degrees from recognized schools.

The majority of these reforms had their inspiration deep in Indian experience. In the first place, the delegation of judicial powers to the *umdahs* was supported by the full weight of Indian practice, where the British had successfully given Indian administrative officials substantial judicial power. The great difference in the systems was that the Indian administrative positions were held by the English while the positions in Egypt were retained by Egyptian officials. The parallels for the creation of the summary courts of justice under a single judge were also to be found both in India and in England. Trial by a single judge was, of course, common practice in England and in India, while summary sessions, used in the lower courts in England, were widespread in India. The reforms had the desired effect of making justice faster, cheaper, and more accessible, although the crime rate showed no signs of declining, as had been hoped.

Court procedure and the rules of evidence had also troubled the British in Egypt. Benson Maxwell and Raymond West, Scott's predecessors at the Ministry of Justice, had criticized the Egyptian system as being inflexible and time-consuming. Both had attempted to introduce changes based on the Indian Rules of Evidence of 1872, but neither had significant success.[89] It was, in fact, not until Scott's appointment that some of these French

[88] Cromer to Rosebery, No. 31, Feb. 18, 1894, enclosing report of Scott, PRO, FO 78/4574.

[89] Before West resigned, he left a detailed report with Nubar Pasha setting forth his criticisms of the existing system, along with his recommendations for reform. These proposals for reform were based largely on Indian procedures. Drummond Wolff to Rosebery, No. 48, Mar. 13, 1886, enclosing report of West on the administration of justice, *HCSP*, Egypt No. 5 (1886), Vol. LXXIV, c. 4769.

practices were modified in the light of Anglo-Indian experience. The preliminary investigation was made less decisive in many cases. The accused was permitted to be represented by counsel during the preliminary hearings and to interrogate his accusers and other witnesses. The court trial became, in this instance, far more important for eliciting the facts and developing the case against the accused. Court procedure was altered to allow for more vigorous cross-examination of the witnesses on the part of the lawyers.[90]

The reform of the judicial system during the British occupation is an extraordinarily complex subject. It is difficult to distinguish the different influences at work: French, English, Indian, purely Egyptian. What is clear, however, is that French law was introduced into the reformed Egyptian courts at the outset, primarily because of long-standing French dominance of Egyptian modernization. The British went along with the French system, though disliking it, until the appointment of Scott as judicial adviser in 1890. Through his energetic reform program, carried out primarily between 1890 and 1895, a considerable amount of Anglo-Indian procedure was grafted onto the French system. Further Anglo-Indian reforms were enacted from time to time after this period. The Egyptian judicial system remained primarily French, but the changes were eventually significant enough to require a separate Egyptian legal commentary on the divergences from the French system.[91]

The foundations of the Egyptian legal system were established in the period 1880 to 1894. The reforms introduced by Scott were designed to improve the caliber

[90] Annual Report, enclosing report by Scott on the progress of the Native Tribunals, 1890-1894, HCSP, Egypt No. 1 (1894), Vol. xc, c. 7308. A few of these reforms in procedure had actually been enacted under Scott's predecessors, Maxwell and West.

[91] Al-Kitab al-Dhahabi [The Golden Book], I, 419.

of personnel responsible for the administration of the law and to decentralize the judicial system so that justice would be accessible to the mass of the population. These tendencies continued after Scott's resignation in 1899. Under his successor, McIlwraith, Assize courts were created in 1904, by which judges from courts of the first instance were sent on circuit into provinces to try criminal cases. It was hoped that the Assize courts would enable peasants to obtain justice from highly qualified judges near their own villages, reasonably soon after crimes were committed.[92] The most far-reaching change was the creation in 1912 of cantonal, or district, courts which were to be staffed by village notables as unpaid magistrates and were not to be bound strictly by the established codes. If a case required, they were to judge and mete out penalties according to the customary law of the land. Such law was, of course, not codified and was subject to review by the higher legal authorities. This reform, it was hoped, would bring justice even closer to the people and make it more understandable.[93] In 1914 the Egyptian judicial structure was composed of the following courts: 8 central tribunals, 90 summary tribunals, 28 *markaz* courts, 235 cantonal courts; with the central tribunals divided into first instance and appeal courts.[94]

❋

The Westernized legal system introduced into Egypt was intended to substitute an orderly system of laws, drawn from Western experience and adapted to the needs of a modernizing country, for the previous arbitrary

[92] Egypt, Ministry of Justice, *Report of the Judicial Adviser, 1905* (Cairo, 1906), p. 36.
[93] Lord Kitchener, Annual Report for 1912, *HCSP*, Egypt No. 1 (1913), Vol. LXXXI, cd. 6682.
[94] Lord Kitchener, Annual Report for 1913, *HCSP*, Egypt No. 1 (1914), Vol. CI, cd. 7358.

and inefficient judicial methods. Although the old procedures, best characterized by the use of the *kurbaj*, were gradually done away with, the new legal system failed to operate as effectively as anticipated. The British had expected the new courts to provide ample means for punishing crime, then, as their effectiveness increased to lead to a decline in the amount of crime. Nevertheless, the crime rate rose in the 1880's. After subsequently slackening for a short period, it began to mount again at an alarming pace. Part of the rise was undoubtedly only on paper, the result of more vigorous detection and reporting of crime. But no one was so optimistic as to believe that the actual increase in crime was completely a matter of statistics. A statistical increase in the number of serious felonies left no doubt that there was a general increase in violence, especially the worst forms, throughout the country.[95]

The British were continually perplexed by the growth of crime in Egypt. At least part of the explanation lay in the internal difficulties and structure of the new courts. Despite efforts to the contrary, the courts were too highly centralized and inaccessible to the populace. Even after the cantonal courts had been created in the smaller provincial centers the peasants were forced to travel what they would have regarded as a long distance to take advantage of these courts. Most of the *fellahin* did not have the necessary leisure time or money, for court procedure was expensive and slow. The courts were always in arrears in their cases. Another partial explanation was the caliber of the court personnel. European judges had difficulty adjusting to the requirements of Egyptian law. Most of them were expert in the law, but understood little or nothing of Arabic and were hope-

[95] These statistics may be found in the *Annual Reports of the Judicial Adviser*. There is a summary of much of this information in Lord Cromer's Annual Report for 1903, *HCSP, Egypt No. 1* (1904), Vol. cxi, cd. 1951.

lessly dependent upon interpreters. The requirements of a knowledge of Arabic were paper requirements, not rigidly enforced in the selection of judges.[96] Those few judges who were skilled in Arabic were unfortunately not trained lawyers and were not fully qualified to serve as judges. Most of the men in this category had been appointed just after Scott introduced his reform program. They were appointed with the understanding that they were to be replaced by more highly qualified judges as soon as such men were available. As it turned out, because of a failure to obtain better qualified men, several of these nonspecialist judges were serving on the bench as late as 1906.[97]

Although the quality of native-born Egyptian judges improved, their positions were not entirely secure. Promotions often were dependent upon obedience to the British judges with whom they worked, and on a suppression of their own individuality. Reports of subordinate English judges were held in absolute fear by their supposed Egyptian superiors.[98] This was especially true when the political atmosphere was heavily charged and Egyptian judges were expected to cooperate with the British. Also, as the British feared, French law was not well suited to Egypt. Much of it was completely incomprehensible to the Egyptian populace as Tawfiq al-Hakim has pointed out so humorously in his novel, *The Maze of Justice.*[99]

[96] J. E. Marshall, *The Egyptian Enigma, 1890-1928* (London, 1928). Marshall, a judge in the Egyptian court of appeal, admitted that he was appointed to the bench without having done well on his Arabic examination, p. 45. He also stated that most of the English judges needed interpreters, p. 59.

[97] See correspondence in PRO, FO 371/248, file 20586.

[98] Ahmad Lutfi, *Safahat Matwiyah min Tarikh al-Harakah al-Istiqlaliyah fi Misr* [Forgotten Pages from the History of the Movement for Egyptian Independence] (Cairo, 1946), p. 27.

[99] Tawfiq al-Hakim, *Yawmiyyat naib fi al-Aryaf* [The Maze of Justice] (Cairo, 1953), p. 30ff.

Law enforcement officers were not nearly as well trained as the system required. On the village level the *umdahs* and the *ghaffirs* (village watchmen) exercised executive authority. These persons were untrained, amateur officials who were not sufficiently qualified to administer such a highly sophisticated set of regulations. Even when given training, as they were in the latter years of the occupation, they were still strikingly inadequate. The more expert officials of the Ministries of Justice and the Interior could do little to enforce laws when they were not supported on the local level.[100]

The British often attributed the increase in crime to deficiencies in the legal system. The increase was, in fact, related to traditional attitudes toward authority in Egypt and also to the stresses brought about as old patterns of life began to give way to new ones. The inadequate courts were a contributing factor in the growth of crime, but not the most important. The new courts were not sufficiently established to control the profound and revolutionary transformations taking place in Egypt during these years. Prior to, and into, the nineteenth century, public order had been maintained in Egypt by arbitrary rule. Local administrators were responsible to the central government for the maintenance of standards of public security sufficient for the collecting of taxes and the maintenance of the hydraulic system. If this level of security was not maintained, the local administrator was in danger of losing his position, and in extreme cases, his life. He terrorized his community, maintaining security in the same fashion as the central administration. The *kurbaj* was the symbol of the tyrannical and arbitrary rule of despotic Egyptian government.[101] The peasantry

---

[100] For a more complete description of Egyptian local officials see Chapter VI.

[101] Arbitrary rule in the nineteenth century is discussed in *al-Kitab al-Dhahabi* [The Golden Book], I, 62-97.

built up a great fear and resentment against centralized authority over the years and did their utmost to isolate themselves from the government. When the new system was introduced, they were not well enough prepared to see its advantages. Peasants were loath to come forward and present evidence in criminal cases, for fear of entanglement with the central government. Their unwillingness to avail themselves of the new courts enabled a few criminals to tyrannize the entire community. In the old days the local administrator would simply have used his superior police powers to rid the community of these trouble-makers. Under the new system, where such individuals had to be convicted in a court of law and were free to do as they liked as long as no one would testify against them, there was little the government could do. Fear of the central government and of reprisals either from the lawless themselves or their friends made the peasants hesitant to become witnesses.[102]

Before the modernization of Egypt, village communities had their own set of rules for keeping public order. These rules probably had evolved to solve questions of village insecurity not solved by the government and also partly to prevent the central administration from being forced to interfere with the life of the community. There were well-defined customs for handling serious crimes. The best known was blood revenge for murder committed against a member of a family: other members of the family took a vow to avenge a death by killing the murderer or one of his relatives. In pre-nineteenth century society this system of customary law existed alongside the arbitrary law of the central administration. When operating efficiently, both had maintained the security and tranquility of the country, although in a bru-

[102] Evidence of these attitudes can be found in the report of a British official at the Parquet, Kershaw, contained in Kershaw to Findlay, September 3, 1906, PRO, FO 371/68, file 43863.

tal way. The new codes forbade the resort to violence, blood revenge, and other techniques and customs of village life. Yet these were so ingrained in the community that the central administration was unable to stamp them out effectively. Moreover, the restrictions placed on the government in dealing with the people made it difficult for the government to interfere in the life of the village community to enforce its own codes. An entire community might be torn by a blood revenge dispute, but no one in the community would give evidence to legal or police authorities. In this sense, then, the new codes were not accepted because they clashed with the established and traditional way of maintaining tranquility —a way the Egyptian peasantry was still unwilling to renounce.[103]

If increases in crime stemmed partly from attempting to apply a Western system of law to an underdeveloped country, another reason was that traditional patterns of life were beginning to disintegrate. The solidarity of the village community was breaking down under the impact of Western economic and technological changes. Private landholding was replacing the communal system. A cash nexus was supplanting the self-subsistence economy of the pre-nineteenth century. Many of the disputes, feuds, and blood revenge struggles were a result of controversies over land and money, stemming from the waning of communal life. Many disputes occurred among members of the same family and led to feuds of long duration. The paradox was that an important factor in the resort to traditional forms of violence and the rise in crime was a consequence of the collapse of the traditional communal-agricultural-village life. The peas-

[103] Various types of village crimes and the importance of blood revenge are discussed by a man who spent much of his life among the *fellahin* as a government public health inspector. Muhammad Fakhr al-Din al-Subki, *Mudhakkirat Tabib fi al-Aryaf* [Memoirs of a Rural Doctor] (Cairo, 1946), p. 140ff.

antry was not sufficiently aware of the value of settling cases peacefully through the new courts. It is, of course, not implied that in eighteenth-century village life there were no disputes over land and within families. But the testimony of the contemporary Arab writers, which is all that is available in the absence of statistics for comparison, is overwhelming to the effect that there was an extraordinary nineteenth-century increase in problems of this nature.[104]

The British saw the problem in similar terms. They felt that the Egyptians, passing through a period of transition, showed the strains of the process by their continual resort to violence. They believed that crime was associated with new land rights and new drives for wealth. As the adviser to the Ministry of the Interior wrote: "The extraordinary prosperity of the *fellahin* has whetted their appetite and created in them a lust for gain. This breeds envy, malice, and hatred. The greatest amount of crime in Egypt can be directly traced to these causes."[105] To some of the British officials the only solution was to resurrect some of the past techniques, particularly flogging and summary punishments, in order to bring the population in line.[106] While admitting that the legal system did not "inspire a sufficient degree of fear amongst the criminal classes," Cromer was disinclined to "relapse into practices of

[104] The relationship of crime to the breakdown of traditional ties is mentioned by al-Subki, *Mudhakkirat* [Memoirs]; Tawfiq al-Hakim, *Yawmiyyat* [The Maze of Justice]; and Ibnat al-Shati, *Qadiyyat al-Fallah* [The Case for the *Fellah*] (Cairo, 1931). These are commentaries from a later period. Ali Yusuf, the noted journalist, observed the same phenomenon around 1890, *Muntakhabat al-Muayyad* [Selections from *al-Muayyad*], I, 502.

[105] Report of Machel of the Ministry of the Interior, in Lord Cromer's Annual Report for 1905, *HCSP*, Egypt No. 1 (1906), Vol. cxxxvii, cd. 2817.

[106] This was the point of view of Kershaw in the Ministry of Justice. Kershaw to Findlay, September 3, 1906, PRO, FO 371/68, file 43863.

the past."[107] Nevertheless, he came under increasing pressure from the British community in Egypt to take more vigorous steps to reduce the incidence of crime.

*

The introduction of the new Egyptian codes and the extension of them into rural areas, although carried out gradually, marked a profound transformation in Egyptian life. The isolated village community, accustomed to settling its own disputes through the family group, was passing from the scene. Village communities were being integrated into the cultural, political, and economic life of the entire country. Legal reform, paralleled by economic, social, and political reform, had the effect of bringing rural Egypt closer to the rest of the country.

[107] Lord Cromer, Annual Report for 1903, *HCSP*, Egypt No. 1 (1904), Vol. cxi, cd. 1951.

CHAPTER V

POLITICAL CRISES, 1892-1894

OVER THE first ten years of British occupation a system of British rule had gradually evolved in Egypt. Baring and other British officials attempted to conceal the power they wielded by channeling it through the traditional rulers and by not challenging the existing class structure. Therefore, British officials were appointed as advisers to the Egyptian ministers or as inspectors in the provinces. Although the reality of their power was not obscured from knowledgeable observers, they officially had only consultative functions in the administration. Moveover, British influence was limited to certain important branches of the administration—the Ministries of War, Public Works, and Finance. After a brief conflict between British and Egyptian authorities, the Egyptians were given great freedom to administer the Ministry of the Interior. In the Ministry of Justice Egyptians effected their own type of legal reform in 1883, in spite of strong opposition from the British. Their influence was dominant in the Ministry until scandals in 1890 gave the British compelling reasons to interject a powerful British element.

The system of indirect rule had evolved in this direction because of the anticipated short duration of the occupation, and the assumption that the Egyptian administration had to be maintained for the day when the British would withdraw. Also, the primary goals of the occupation—the maintenance of tranquility and financial stability—could best be obtained, it was felt, by limited interference in decisive branches of the government.

The political crises of 1892 to 1894, occasioned by the accession of a new Khedive, Abbas II (1892-1914) and his disputes with Evelyn Baring (elevated to the peerage as Lord Cromer in 1892), were to shatter this system of rule. The governmental mechanism rested upon a delicate balance of powers—the willingness of the Egyptians to permit the British to exercise predominant influence in important branches of the administration, in return for Egyptian control over other branches. The British, with their superior military power, were, of course, the dominant power, but they obtained the cooperation of leading Egyptians only by limiting their own influence. The alliance was broken in this period. The Egyptians, under a new efflorescence of nationalist agitation, threatened the English position in Egypt even while the English were attempting to extend their control over previously autonomous branches of the administration. The disputes resulted in the overall growth of British influence. Also, British rule became more open and direct. Even though Egyptian ministers were retained in the top administrative positions, they were chosen now less for their ability than for their willingness to submit to British authority.

The political crises of these years established the nationalist movement in Egypt; consequently, the British were compelled to rely on autocratic techniques more frequently to maintain their position. The clash of authority came about through the simultaneous operation of three factors, all working to upset the administrative system as then constituted: (1) the growth of nationalism, energized and directed by the new Khedive, Abbas II; (2) the increase of British control over the administration and the grievances stemming from this; and (3) the suspected paralysis of British power, a result of the election of the Liberal government in England in 1892.

Non-Western nationalism is a particularly difficult phenomenon to describe.[1] In the nineteenth century, and in its earliest stages, it was not a mass movement, but rather one of the educated elements in a society with some knowledge of the West, a defensive reaction against the encroachment of the West. Under the continuing impact of the West, nationalism grew eventually into a mass movement. It also came to embrace the ideological content of Western nationalism in its secular orientation, with its focus on the nation-state as the basic unit of political organization, and its emphasis on the modernization of institutions. In the earliest stages, nationalistic developments did not necessarily contain these ideological elements. Some of the intellectual leaders in this period wanted to return to past glories. Others sought the revival of society on the basis of a religious renewal and the restoration of power to a religious empire like the Islamic empire. Only a minority were convinced that the solution was to focus attention on the secular nation-state and to adapt Western economic and political institutions to the conditions of the East.

The first real movement of Egyptian discontent against the West had occurred during the Arabi revolt. The defeat of the Egyptian army by the British and the exiling of the leaders of the movement, however, had brought disillusionment. Egypt returned to a quiescent state. Wilfrid Scawen Blunt, a close friend of the Egyptian nationalists, observed in 1888 that the "condition [of the nationalist party] was one of patriotic torpor; as a party they had ceased to exist, being without leaders and without organization."[2] The reputation of Arabi was in eclipse. He was regarded as a coward, a

---

[1] For a fuller discussion of the nationalist movement in Egypt, especially the nationalism of the professional classes, see Chapter VII.

[2] Wilfrid Scawen Blunt, *My Diaries* (New York, 1921), I, 13.

self-seeker, an illiterate, unprincipled intriguer. But the defeat of 1882 had brought only temporary relaxation of nationalist feelings. By 1890 they had regained their momentum. The press carried attacks on the British, called for the British to fulfill their pledges to leave, criticized ministers who cooperated and praised those who obstructed English officials. Religious leaders also began to mount an attack against increasing European influence in Egypt and against the decay of religious institutions and faith. These nationalist and anti-foreign sentiments found a ready acceptance among the student population, particularly in the Law School.

As in the Arabi revolt, the nationalist movement made its appeal on two levels. It revived the secular, nationalist slogan of the days of Arabi: *Misr lil-Misriyin* (Egypt for the Egyptians). At the same time, its leaders played on the religious sentiment of the people, calling on the Muslims to resist the encroachments of the Christian invaders. Egyptian nationalism was largely an emotional effusion, confined to a small, educated, or semi-educated, urban class. It drew its support mainly from the professional classes—lawyers and civil servants—and from the student population; that is, the restricted segment of the population with exposure to Western education. Also, there were nationalist flickerings among the traditional intellectual and religious leaders, a small group alive to the challenge of the West and the need for changes in Egyptian institutions. Rural areas were largely untouched. At this stage, the movement was primarily negative, for the appeal that evoked the most vigorous response was that of throwing off the yoke of foreign domination. As in the days of Arabi, the nationalist fervor was also directed against the Egypto-Turkish ruling aristocracy of landholders and high government officials. "Egypt for the Egyptians" tended to mean Egypt for the Egyptian Arabs, since a large portion of the ruling aristocracy were of Turkish and other non-Egyptian origin. The nationalist position implied a program of social reform, for the desire of the nationalists was to limit the economic and political power of the old aristocracy. The nationalists wanted to open the bureaucracy and army more fully to Egyptians. They supported programs for making education available to a larger segment of the population. Some even favored providing firmer guarantees of landholding rights for the peasantry. But the Egyptian nationalists were not socialists. They were drawn almost exclusively from the wealthier segments of the population; many had landed interests, and all had a commitment to the maintenance of essential features of the existing social system. Consequently, they tended to concentrate their fire on political issues. Their social attitudes were more conservative than their political policies—and never as lucid. A closer connection between nationalism and socialism was to develop later, when nationalists were drawn from the lower strata of society.

There was wide disagreement among the nationalist leaders over methods for attaining Egypt's independence. Many looked for assistance from interested foreign powers like France or Turkey; others hoped to win the support of anti-imperialists in England by agitating and criticizing British rule in Egypt, while the more moderate nationalists thought England would grant independence if the Egyptians cooperated with the British and demonstrated their ability to govern themselves. Few leaders had any concrete ideas about what kind of a nation was to be created once foreign domination had been removed. There were those who wished to see Egypt regenerated along Islamic lines. Others hoped for closer ties with the Ottoman Empire and the fulfillment of a Pan-Islamic dream. Those who favored establishing an independent, secular Egyptian nation would have found it difficult to reach agreement on the form of government for Egypt. There were advocates of a parliamentary system, of a constitutional monarchy, and of a republic. As Blunt recorded in his diary, the nationalist movement "consisted of what elements there were in Egypt either of discontent or of such patriotism as was to be found in the country, half political, half religious, which resented the presence of foreign and Christian rule."[3] Nevertheless, there was always the possibility that all of these disparate elements could be solidified, for a time at least, in their opposition to British rule.

Ali Yusuf, Abdullah al-Nadim, and Muhammad Abduh were the most outspoken of those whose programs were couched in Islamic terms. Each had acquired his education in the traditional Islamic institutions. Ali Yusuf and Muhammad Abduh had both been regular students at the famous Islamic university, al-Azhar, though, like so many of their contemporaries, they had grown progressively disillusioned with the rigidity of their training there. This group of men were also characterized by their considerable political awareness. They were all concerned about the political crises confronting Islamic countries and the gradual loss of independence to the West. They were all attracted to political agitation of one kind or another. Islam was always seen in relation to the political and power considerations of East versus West.[4]

There is a good deal of controversy in the literature today about the religious views of men like Muhammad Abduh and Abdullah al-Nadim. It is certainly true that

[3] *Ibid.*, p. 84.
[4] See the articles by Elie Kedourie, "Nouvelle Lumière sur Afghani et Abduh," in *Orient*, No. 2, 1964. The remarks about political agitation apply less well to Abduh than they do to Nadim and Ali Yusuf. Muhammad Abduh played a role in the Arabi revolt, then tended to confine his efforts to social, educational, and religious reform rather than direct political agitation.

these men did not represent the views of the majority of traditional Egyptian scholars, but they were in much closer contact with the West. Many had been influenced by Masonic orders established throughout the Middle East in the nineteenth century. There are suggestions in the literature that if they were not agnostics, as Cromer said of Muhammad Abduh, they tended to hold ideals similar to those of deism. Often they stressed the basic similarities of the three major religions: Islam, Christianity, and Judaism. Jamal al-Din al-Afghani, the inspiration for many Egyptian religious activists, even went so far as to concede that Islam had obscurantist elements in it. But he also contended that Christianity had the very same characteristic.

In 1889 Ali Yusuf founded a newspaper which was to become one of the most influential in Egypt: *al-Muayyad.* It was to be, according to Ali Yusuf, a daily, nationalist, political organ, written in the language of the people and setting forth for governmental consideration the aspirations of the people. It supported the policies of Khedive Tawfiq and his Prime Minister, Riyad, encouraging them to resist incursions of foreign influence in the government. When Abbas came to the throne, Ali Yusuf supported him and remained one of his staunchest defenders and a close confidant throughout his reign. Early issues of the paper were full of articles defining terms which had come to assume increasing importance in the life of the Egyptian intellectual community: *al-hukumah* (government); *al-ummah* (community); *al-mahkum* (the governed); *al-watan* (the nation); and *wajabat al-awtan* (the duties of the citizens). The ideas of Ali Yusuf, like those of so many other intellectuals, harbored many inconsistencies. On the one hand Ali Yusuf called for an Egypt to be governed by the Egyptians; on the other, his appeal for the unity of the East and for

[*152*]

strengthening the bonds of the Ottoman Empire sounded very much like Pan-Islamism.[5]

Abdullah al-Nadim had long been associated with Egyptian nationalism. He was an outspoken pamphleteer of the Arabi cause and a critic of the British occupation. During the early years of the occupation he travelled incognito through Egypt, to elude the authorities who had condemned him *in absentia* to exile for his inflammatory writing. He was finally captured and exiled, but when Abbas came to the throne he enabled al-Nadim to return to Egypt. On his return he quickly organized a paper, *al-Ustadh,* which again became the mouthpiece of anti-foreign, pro-Islamic, and nationalistic sentiments. His most aggressive article was a bitter, satirical discourse on the evils of European imperialism and its devious ways for keeping the East weak; an indictment of British dominance in Egypt, and a call for the East to rally its forces against the West.[6] Al-Nadim's return to Egypt was to prove short-lived, for in 1893 the authorities again used his remarks as grounds for exiling him.

Perhaps the most attractive of the Islamic reformers, certainly the individual with the greatest influence on the thought of his time, was Muhammad Abduh. Like al-Nadim, he had played a role in the Arabi revolt, for which he was exiled. He returned to Egypt in 1888 and became the leading figure in a movement for reform-

[5] The first issues of the paper were collected by Ali Yusuf and issued in book form under the title, *Muntakhbat al-Muayyad* [Selections from *al-Muayyad*] (Cairo, 1906). The most useful biography, primarily because of its copious extracts from the writings of Ali Yusuf, is Abd al-Latif Hamzah, *Adab al-Maqalah al-Sahafiyah fi Misr* [Journalistic Articles in Egypt] (Cairo, 1951), Vol iv.

[6] The article is printed in Abd al-Fatah al-Nadim, ed., *Sulafah al-Nadim* [Selections from al-Nadim] (Cairo, 1914). It has been analyzed and its impact described in a short biographical study by Ahmad Amin, *Fayd al-Khatir* [Reflections] (Cairo, 1953), vi, 170.

ing Islamic institutions such as al-Azhar and the Islamic law courts. In contrast to Ali Yusuf and al-Nadim he was a moderate nationalist. Believing that the day of independence lay further off in the future, he favored reforming and developing Egypt's institutions so that when independence came, Egypt would be well prepared. He was not a political agitator or a pamphleteer. Indeed, he believed that the Egyptians could work with the British in preparing themselves for eventual self-government.[7]

The Islamic reformers formed one prong of the nationalist movement. The second group was made up of Westernized nationalists, mostly young professional men or students, trained in the Westernized schools and in Europe. They were in closer contact with the West; thus their aspirations for Egypt were more closely inspired by Western values.[8]

*

On January 4, 1892, Khedive Tawfiq retired to his bed with a slight cold. Three days later he was dead of pneumonia. He was succeeded by his son, Abbas Hilmi II, a boy of 18 who at that time was studying at Vienna.[9] Almost with one stroke, the Egyptian political system built up in the first ten years of the occupation was jeopardized. The Khedive was still nominally the apex of the political structure in Egypt. Theoretically, he had the power to remove and appoint ministers and to determine policy. Khedive Tawfiq had relinquished most of

[7] The classic studies of Muhammad Abduh are Rashid Rida, *Tarikh al-Ustadh al-Imam al-Shaykh Muhammad Abduh* [The biography of Muhammad Abduh] (Cairo, 1906-1931), and Charles Adams, *Islam and Modernism in Egypt* (London, 1933).

[8] See Chapter VII for a more detailed discussion.

[9] Abbas had been sent to Vienna, instead of England, to study, so as not to offend the French. Edward Dicey, *The Story of the Khedivate* (New York, 1902), p. 459.

his powers without a struggle to the British, but Abbas was still an unknown quantity. Indeed, there were rumors circulating in Cairo before the accession of Abbas that he had not been content with his father's policies, that he called his father "le défunct," and had vowed to resist growing British influence.[10] It was difficult, but not impossible, for the British to remove a recalcitrant Egyptian minister; the removal of the Khedive was an entirely different matter since this would inevitably touch off an international crisis, with the French firmly opposing the British.

It is hardly surprising that the new Khedive was the object of solicitations from all the foreign powers. None were more energetic in protestations of good will than France. The French Consul-General in Egypt, Reverseaux, ingratiated himself with Abbas and let him know that France was displeased with increasing British dominance of the Egyptian administration. Reverseaux also pointed out that France was no longer isolated, having reached an understanding with Russia in 1891, and that it would count for more in the international scene henceforth.[11] He was undoubtedly pleased to learn from the French ambassador at Vienna that Rouiller, who was known for his pro-French feelings and who had been Abbas's teacher in political economy at Vienna, was to head the European section of the Khedivial special cabinet. Rouiller had also reported that Abbas "had only one idea—rid his country of the English," and that his plan was "to make Egypt so strong and pros-

10 Ahmad Shafiq, *Mudhakkirati fi Nisf Qarn* [My Memoirs over a half Century] (Cairo, 1936), Vol. ii, Part i, p. 17. The memoirs of this Egyptian official, personal secretary to Abbas, are a prime source of information for the Egyptian side of the case.

11 France, Ministère des Affaires Étrangères, *Documents Diplomatiques Français*, Série i, 1892-93, Vol. x, Reverseaux to Develle, Nos. 83, 85, and 93, January 12 to January 14, 1893.

perous materially that one shall only have to thank the English for their help, now not necessary."[12]

In the first few months of his reign, however, Abbas and the British got along well together. Cromer wrote to Foreign Minister Salisbury in February, 1892:

> I see that the young Khedive is going to be very Egyptian, by which I mean, not so much anti-European—and certainly not anti-English—as anti-Turk, anti-Syrian etc. . . . By giving my French and Russian colleagues plenty of rope they are rapidly hanging themselves, so far as the good graces of the Khedive are concerned. They offer advice to him, they try and humiliate him in little matters of etiquette and interfere with appointments in his household, etc., all of which he resents. I am taking up the line of non-interference in all small things, and waiting to be asked my advice rather than proffering it. I feel convinced that by this means I shall soon have him completely in my pocket without his knowing it or feeling the yoke.[13]

The first crisis of his reign bore out Cromer's confidence, for Abbas sided with the British. He resisted the attempt of the Ottoman Sultan to deprive Egypt of old garrisoning rights on the Sinai peninsula. The firm stand taken by Cromer and Abbas forced the Sultan to reaffirm Egypt's authority in this territory.[14] Not much later, the

[12] France, Ministère des Affaires Étrangères, *Documents Diplomatiques Français*, Série i, 1891-92, Vol. iv, Decrais to Ribot, No. 185, February 5, 1892.

[13] Baring to Salisbury, No. 174, February 21, 1892, Cromer Papers, PRO, FO 633/6.

[14] Cromer's letter to Salisbury at the conclusion of the crisis is a revealing document. It was meant to show Salisbury that Cromer and the Khedive were working well together. But it clearly demonstrates how badly Cromer misjudged the potential of Abbas as a leader in Egypt and how he tended to treat the Khedive—with scant regard for Abbas's position as ruler of Egypt: "The position here during the last week or two, has, in fact, been

young Khedive called in the Turkish representative to Egypt, Mukhtar, and criticized him publicly for interfering in Egyptian politics. When Cromer left for his summer vacation in 1892, he could very easily have congratulated himself on the ease with which the transition from Tawfiq to Abbas was being effected.

By the time Cromer returned from England in the fall the situation had changed drastically. The British officials in Egypt were vehement in their denunciations of Abbas for having interfered with their programs. Blunt wrote that "there were elements here of a stronger opposition to the English regime than was the case under Tawfiq."[15] One of the British officials observed during the summer, while Cromer was still on vacation, that the British were being obstructed at every turn and that "the cry is for Lord Cromer's return, and I dare say he will soon put things right."[16] Blunt attributed the change in Abbas's attitude to the influence of Reverseaux and the Turkish representative, Mukhtar. Whatever the explanation, Abbas was beginning to solidify the disparate elements of discontent and nationalism behind him. Ali Yusuf's paper, *al-Muayyad*, and *al-Ustadh* of al-Nadim

---

rather delicate. First, my poor little Khedive was bandied about like a shuttlecock between rival interests, but he behaved well. . . . The Khedive is much too European to obtain any real hold over the ultra-Mohammedan part of the population. . . . All these diplomatic interests have naturally pushed me to the front, but I hope soon to be able to retire somewhat from the public gaze, and when we get into smoother waters, I shall be able to take in hand the education of the young Khedive. I cannot make him a Mohammedan, but I shall try to make him appear as if he was one. As it is, he resembles a very gentlemanlike and healthily-minded boy fresh from Eton or Harrow—not at all devoid of intelligence, but a good deal bored with el-Azhar, Sheikhs, Ramazan feasts, etc. I really wish he was not quite so civilized." Baring to Salisbury, No. 177, April 15, 1892, Cromer Papers, PRO, FO 633/6.

[15] Blunt, *My Diaries*, I, 85.
[16] Hollings, *Life of Scott-Moncrieff*, p. 270.

were loud in their praise of the new ruler. The moderate, Muhammad Abduh, saw in Abbas a liberal sovereign whose patronage could easily be decisive in the reform of Islamic institutions in Egypt. Muhammad Abduh had had little success in winning the support of Tawfiq. A firm friendship with Abbas seemed in the offing, and Abduh began to draw up schemes for the reform of al-Azhar.[17] The young, Westernized nationalists found much that was appealing in Abbas' resistance to British rule and his interest in the government educational system.[18] They looked eagerly toward the palace for guidance. Moreover, a court party, disgruntled by increasing British dominance of high administrative positions, looked to Abbas to save it from extinction. Advisers close to Abbas at court were given positions in his private cabinet. The men who wielded the most power in the private cabinet were Rouiller, head of the European section, and Tigrane, an Armenian minister. The latter, although a keen advocate of modernization, was opposed to British influence in Egypt. Abbas tended to work through his special cabinet, rather than the regular ministers, a fact resented bitterly by the British and by the regular Egyptian ministers.

At first, Cromer disdained the threat. He had weathered a number of crises previously, he reasoned, and he now found it difficult to believe that a lad of eighteen could upset the mechanism of British rule. In November, 1892 he wrote Salisbury that the Khedive "had been foolish about a number of small things, but he is so

[17] Rashid Rida, *Tarikh al-Ustadh al-Imam al-Shaykh Muhammad Abduh*, I, 426, 494, and 569 and Ahmad Shafiq, *Mudhakkirati fi Nisf Qarn* [Memoirs], Vol. II, Part I, p. 185.

[18] Abbas toured the government schools in November, 1892, criticizing the system for inadequate instruction in Arabic. On his visit to the Law School a poem was presented in his honor by Mustafa Kamil. Ahmad Shafiq, *Mudhakkirati fi Nisf Qarn* [Memoirs], Vol. II, Part I, p. 50.

young and inexperienced that he ought not to be
judged too harshly. I lectured him in plain but very
unfriendly terms, and I do not anticipate that for the time
being I shall have much difficulty with him."[19] Blunt
cautioned Cromer that the Khedive resented being treated as an inferior and being lectured to by Cromer as
if he were "a schoolboy." He added that "the Khedive
would not bear driving with any but a very light rein";
but the British Consul-General paid little heed to the
advice.[20] By the end of the year, however, Cromer began to realize how serious the situation had become. The
intrigues against British officials continued to grow;
Cromer's lectures to Abbas and his advisers had little
effect. Cromer's letter of January 13, 1893 to the new
Foreign Minister, Rosebery, showed his new-found concern. "The young Khedive," he wrote, "is evidently going
to give a great deal of trouble. He is an extremely foolish
youth. It is difficult to know how to deal with him."
And Cromer closed his correspondence with ominous
words: "I think he will have to receive a sharp lesson
sooner or later and the sooner the better. The difficulty
consists in finding the proper occasion for giving him
a lesson and the proper manner of giving it to him. . . . If
the youth gets his head up in the air and thinks he can
do just as he pleases, things in general will go wrong
here."[21]

The measures that the Egyptians protested against
most bitterly were connected with the extension of
British influence over previously independent branches
of the Egyptian administration. About 1890, the British began to move into the Ministries of Justice and

[19] Cromer to Rosebery, No. 178, November 12, 1892, Cromer
Papers, PRO, FO 633/6.
[20] Blunt, My Diaries, I, 64. Cromer's reply to Blunt was that it
was "necessary to treat Orientals firmly."
[21] Cromer to Rosebery, No. 180, January 13, 1893, Cromer
Papers, PRO, FO 633/6.

the Interior, previously Egyptian domains. The justification given was that these branches of the administration were not keeping pace with other branches. It was also argued that their backwardness jeopardized reforms introduced into the rest of the administration. The failure to attain the necessary level of public security, the British contended, threatened the general economic development of the country, undermined public works projects, and financial stability. Egyptians were not inclined to accept such arguments, casting reflections, as they did, on their own administrative abilities. They tended to see the growth of British influence as part of a conspiracy to deprive Egyptians of all power, to make Egypt into a British colony, and to exploit the wealth of the country for British purposes.

The impulse for the extension of authority seems to have stemmed primarily from the British bureaucracy in Egypt. Its members were anxious to secure administrative efficiency, to remove what they regarded as defects in the existing system. They viewed Egypt basically as an administrative problem, not as an imperial question subject to other considerations. These men put British officials like Cromer under increasing pressure to allow them to go ahead with their reform programs. It is not surprising that it was during Cromer's summer vacation in 1892 that some British officials attempted to assume far-reaching powers in Egypt.[22] Other groups played their part in the extension of British authority in Egypt by supporting the modernizing efforts of the British officials. Joseph Chamberlain's criticisms of the judicial and police systems undoubtedly provided an incentive to the British. Foreign commercial com-

[22] This fact is attested by three British officials. Gorst to Milner, February 3, 1893, Milner Papers, Box 10; Wingate to Milner, January 18, 1893, Milner Papers, Box 10; and Add MSS 48950 D'Abernon Papers, British Museum.

munities, particularly the British community, were rapidly increasing in size and power. Capital was once again being attracted to Egypt.

Bitter power struggles occurred behind the scenes from 1890 to 1893, as the British moved to control the Ministries of Justice and the Interior. The appointment of Scott resulted ultimately in the resignation of the Minister of Justice and, following him, the Egyptian Prime Minister, Riyad Pasha. In 1891 a young aspiring British army officer serving in the Egyptian army, Herbert Kitchener, was made responsible for reorganizing the Egyptian police system. Egyptians in the government rightly interpreted his appointment as an opening salvo in a campaign to control the Ministry of the Interior. While unable to block the appointment, they tried to restrict Kitchener's influence. Egyptian ministers carefully watched the British and resisted further attempts to extend influence in the Interior Ministry. The growing Anglicization of the administration aroused discontent, not only among Egyptian officials, but also among journalists, students, and other nationalist elements. It was, in fact, an overt step to increase British power in the Ministry of the Interior that precipitated direct opposition toward the end of 1892.

*

While the Conservatives were in power, the Egyptian question was quietly and gradually withdrawn from the international scene. They had supported the increasing British domination of the Egyptian administration. But the question persisted whether the Liberal party would give the same firm support to British administrators in Egypt. Thus, the third and final factor shaping the events of 1893 and 1894 was the campaign and election of the Liberals in 1892. The fall recess of the Parliament in 1891, with elections set for the next year, was a time of campaigning. Although the campaign centered on domestic issues and Irish home rule, both Gladstone and John Morley of the Liberal party made statements about the burdensome occupation of Egypt. Morley called on the Foreign Minister to display "the courage to point out that England in the present system of indefinite occupation in Egypt is a vulnerable England—England in constant risk of being drawn into the vortex of continental war"; while Gladstone exhorted "Lord Salisbury to make an effort to relieve us from that burdensome and embarrassing occupation of Egypt, which so long as it lasts, rely upon it, must be a cause of weakness and a source of embarrassment."[23] These were really minor remarks when viewed in the context of the general campaign, but they were taken up excitedly by the press in France and Egypt, where the question was raised whether the Liberals, if elected, would evacuate Egypt.[24]

The French *chargé d'affaires* at London thought he saw a movement of public opinion in favor of evacuating Egypt and coming to terms with France.[25] Not even the disclaimers by Gladstone or Morley, nor the speech of Salisbury affirming England's continuing interest in Egypt, could remove the feeling among many that the

[23] The remarks are printed in *Hansard's Parliamentary Debates*, 4th Series, 1892, Vol. I, Columns 222-226.

[24] Cromer was disturbed by the reaction of the Egyptian press to the speeches of Gladstone and Morley: "They have attracted a great deal of attention, more especially in the towns. . . . The local situation is not all I could wish. All the talk about evacuation has unsettled people's minds. The French press and (which is more important) the vernacular press inspired by the French and written by gallicized Syrians is extremely violent, more so than at almost any previous period." Baring to Salisbury, Nos. 171 and 172, October 25, 1891 and December 11, 1891, PRO, FO 633/6, The Cromer Papers.

[25] France, Ministère des Affaires Étrangères, *Documents Diplomatiques Français*, Série I, 1892-93, Vol. IX, D'Estournelles de Constant to Ribot, No. 27, October 3, 1891.

Liberals would finally fulfill their original pledges to withdraw if they were elected.

The election was held in July, 1892. Gladstone had hoped for a majority of 80 or 100; the Liberals had won by only 40. There was general pessimism in the party, for the Liberals were committed to pass a Home Rule bill and yet knew that the bill would be defeated in the House of Lords. When the cabinet was constituted, Lord Rosebery was named Foreign Minister. This was a setback for the French and the Egyptian nationalists. Rosebery was known for his Francophobia and for his desire to maintain the policies of Lord Salisbury. It was even rumored that he had agreed to take office only on the implicit understanding that there would be no evacuation of Egypt.[26] Nevertheless, Gladstone and Morley were equally as well known for their sympathies toward France and their desire to terminate the occupation of Egypt. Waddington, the French ambassador at London, approached Gladstone with the suggestion of resuming Egyptian negotiations.[27]

Apparently, certain Egyptians were persuaded that resistance to British rule in Egypt might convince the Liberal government to be rid of the obligations and problems of governing Egypt. The Egyptian crisis of 1893 was an abrupt crisis, played mainly behind the scenes, lasting little more than a week. On January 15, 1893 Abbas, without previous consultation with Cromer, shuffled his cabinet and replaced his Prime Minister, Mustafa Fahmi, with Husayn Fakhri, a well-known Anglophobe, who had resigned his position at the Ministry of Justice in 1891 in protest over increasing British influence. The Khedive replaced Mustafa Fahmi because he regarded

[26] Rosebery's power in the cabinet is discussed in Robinson and Gallagher, *Africa and the Victorians*, pp. 320-21.

[27] France, Ministère des Affaires Étrangères, *Documents Diplomatiques Français*, 1884-93, Vol. CIX, Reverseaux to Develle, No. 434, January 14, 1893.

him as a puppet of the British, ineffectual in resisting the growth of British influence. The crisis, in fact, was touched off when the attention of the Khedive was called to a circular issued by an English official in the Ministry of the Interior, ordering the provincial officials to address their correspondence to the English Director of the Police instead of the Egyptian Minister. To Abbas, this step seemed to be clear proof that the British were moving to take over the Ministry of the Interior. Abbas held Fahmi responsible for this action; he hoped to find in Husayn Fakhri a minister unafraid to resist the spread of British influence. Also, the Khedive was under the impression that he was free to change his own ministers. He had had a previous dispute with Cromer over the removal of the Prime Minister, and Cromer had led him to believe that he was at liberty to choose a new prime minister so long as he was a Muslim.[28]

Cromer was informed of the change by the Khedive's secretary. He reacted quickly to the situation. After dispatching a telegram to London, condemning the action of Abbas in the strongest terms, he met with Abbas and obtained from him a promise that he would not announce the changes until Cromer had had a chance to consult the British government in London. Cromer's argument was that Abbas had overstepped his authority in removing the Prime Minister without seeking the advice of the British; Abbas contended that as Khedive he had the power to dismiss and appoint ministers, and furthermore that Cromer had led him to believe he was free to select a new prime minister on the condition that he be a Muslim. Cromer's telegram caused a furor in the cabinet in London. An additional telegram, sent after Abbas had refused to back down, and suggesting that British

[28] This view is borne out by Cromer himself in his book, *Abbas II*, p. 19 and by Ahmad Shafiq, *Mudhakkirati fi Nisf Qarn* [Memoirs], Vol. II, Part I, p. 57.

troops seize the telegraph offices and occupy all the government offices until the dispute was solved, alarmed the British ministers even more. No one in the cabinet was willing to sanction such aggressive action. Rosebery said that Cromer's suggested measures reminded him of Napoleon's *coup d'état* of December 2nd, 1851.[29] But the cabinet officials agreed to support Cromer in not approving Abbas's change of ministers. No doubt all were relieved, therefore, when a compromise formula was reached in Cairo. The Khedive's nominee, Husayn Fakhri, was to be dismissed, but the Khedive was not compelled to take Mustafa Fahmi back. Instead, Riyad was named Prime Minister. Of greater importance, as far as Cromer was concerned, Abbas made a formal promise to follow the advice of the British in all important matters.

If the furor in the cabinet over these telegrams seemed great, it was as nothing compared with the home reaction to Cromer's request for additional British troops on January 19, 1893. Cromer's reason for demanding troops after the resolution of the ministerial dispute was that the crisis had agitated the population against British rule. His telegram to the Foreign Office was once again couched in the strongest terms against the Khedive, and he argued that he could not be responsible for public safety if the British garrison was not strengthened. Gladstone told a fellow cabinet colleague that "my life is a perfect burden to me. I would as soon set a torch to Westminster Abbey as send troops to Egypt."[30] The opposition to Cromer's policy was so strong that Foreign Minister Rosebery telegraphed Cromer: "I can only answer your private telegram in these words:—There is a cabinet [meeting] on Monday, and if you do not receive

[29] Marquess of Crewe, *Lord Rosebery* (New York, 1931), p. 338.
[30] Philip Magnus, *Gladstone, A Biography* (London, 1954), p. 408.

the powers you ask on Monday evening, the Foreign Office will have passed into other hands." Cromer replied: "If you should unfortunately leave the Foreign Office, I shall follow your example in my smaller sphere."[31] But Rosebery carried the day, and additional troops were dispatched to Egypt.

Rosebery had supported Cromer throughout this affair, but at its conclusion he wrote the British Consul-General informing him of his dissatisfaction with Cromer's handling of the dispute. He cautioned Cromer to use less violent language and to deal with the situation at hand in his correspondence. The Foreign Minister also urged Cromer to show more patience in dealing with a young Khedive who felt the inferiority of his position so acutely. The suggestion of forcibly seizing government offices, Rosebery thought, should have been reserved "as a fifth act, and not as a second." Many of Rosebery's feelings are expressed in a long dispatch he sent Cromer January 23, 1893:

> I know you will not mind my saying frankly that your telegrams would have helped me more if they had been somewhat differently framed and had kept the question of present necessities more distinct from that of future policy. Had you telegraphed on Thursday your opinion and that of General Walker that you could not answer for order unless garrison was increased, you must have had assurance of reinforcements that day. There were, however, passages in your telegrams which the cabinet took as indicating that you wanted troops mainly, if not entirely, for the purpose of reducing the Khedive to immediate and complete subserviency. Do not disdain the suavity so

[31] Rosebery to Cromer, No. 283, January 21, 1893 and Cromer to Rosebery, No. 284, January 22, 1893, Cromer Papers, PRO, FO 633/7.

expedient in dealing with a rash youth, both sore and headstrong.[32]

Although the compromise proved advantageous to Cromer, Abbas emerged as the hero of the Egyptian nationalists. As Rosebery noted in his diary, "the Khedive gave in, but snake scotched, not killed."[33] Wherever the Khedive went, he was hailed for his courage in opposing the British. He was given a standing ovation when he attended the opera just a few days after the crisis; his tour of the provinces in the summer of 1893 was a triumphal march. Not surprisingly, the animosity between the British and the Egyptians supporting the Khedive continued to mount. In the debate on the budget, Egypt's Legislative Council, not known previously for its opposition to the British, drafted a long list of criticisms of British policy. Cromer began to feel once again that the Khedive must be given "a sharp lesson." The supporters of the occupation, he argued, were "calling out for a sign, by which many—the natives especially —mean a very manifest assertion of strength after the oriental fashion."[34] As Cromer observed in his book, *Abbas II*, "I determined to choose my own battle-ground in the struggle which was obviously impending. It was necessary that the quarrel would be brought to a head over an issue which would, on the one hand, be comprehensible to the British public, and on the other hand, would afford no justifiable grounds for the intervention of foreign powers."[35]

Cromer had not long to wait for the opportune moment. Rumors had been circulating that the nationalists

[32] Rosebery to Cromer, No. 287, January 23, 1893, Cromer Papers, PRO, FO 633/7.
[33] Crewe, *Lord Rosebery*, p. 338.
[34] Cromer to Rosebery, No. 197, December 25, 1893, Cromer Papers, PRO, FO 633/6.
[35] Cromer, *Abbas II*, p. 50.

and Abbas were trying to build up a following in the Egyptian army. A confidential report indicated that Mahir Pasha, the new Minister of War, had instructions to ferret out the pro-English officers and advance the anti-English officers.[36] The Egyptian army was an organization in which the British would countenance no disloyalty; it was regarded by them as the one Egyptian body capable of posing a threat to the occupation if it became a center of revolutionary sentiment, especially as it was much larger than the British army of occupation. Compounding the situation was the fact that Herbert Kitchener had just been appointed Commanding-General (*Sirdar*) of the Egyptian army. Kitchener was insatiably ambitious, sensitive to all criticism, shy, reserved, and painfully aware that he was disliked by many of his officers, Egyptian and British alike. It was not surprising, then, that he was not happy to learn that the Khedive was anxious to inspect the Egyptian army battalions in Upper Egypt. Nevertheless, the visit was scheduled for mid-January, 1894, just one year after the previous crisis.

The Khedive's inspection of the army, as might have been expected, soon degenerated into a frightful row between Kitchener and him, which is not, however, without its moments of humor and pathos. Unfortunately, it is probably impossible to know the true details of the crisis, since there are two accounts, one given by Kitchener and corroborated by the other English officers, and the other by Abbas and his aides.[37] In any

[36] Cromer to Rosebery, No. 182, October 28, 1893, PRO, FO 78/4516. One of the British officers, Reginald Wingate, also mentioned that Mahir had organized an Officers Patriotic Society in Cairo which was in constant communication with the officers in Upper Egypt. Cromer to Rosebery, No. 20, January 28, 1894, PRO, FO 78/4574.

[37] The following account is pieced together from two sources: (1) Kitchener's dispatch containing the diary kept by Reginald Wingate, one of the British officers, both contained in Cromer's

case, Abbas arrived at Aswan on January 13, 1894, accompanied by his Minister of War, Mahir, and other aides. He reviewed one of the battalions and complained of the way the soldiers held their rifles and also of the differences in their heights. After observing other military exercises, he visited the military hospital. In conversation with the British officers, he continued to make disparaging remarks about the troops. During the hospital trip he also criticized the hospital interpreter for his pronunciation of Arabic, remarking that "his Arabic resembled that of an English officer." On leaving, he expressed himself satisfied, but later, upon receiving the report of his personal physician who had accompanied him on the tour, he retracted his earlier statement and called the British officer in charge of the hospital "incompetent." At subsequent reviews Abbas repeatedly criticized the British soldiers and praised the Egyptian-officered companies. These statements convinced the British officers of Abbas's intentions.

The climax came on January 19th, at Wadi Halfa, a garrison station on the border between Egypt and the Sudan. A Sudanese battalion was marched past the Khedive's reviewing stand, but the band played fast and the march was hurried. The Khedive again made disparaging remarks. Later, after Kitchener himself took the battalion for a special drill, Abbas singled out English officers for special criticism. At the completion of the review Abbas remarked to Kitchener: "To tell you the truth, Kitchener Pasha, I consider it is disgraceful for Egypt to be served by such an army." Kitchener immediately replied: "I beg then to tender Your Highness my resignation." Abbas seemed to be much taken

letter to Rosebery, No. 20, January 28, 1894, PRO, FO 78/4574; and (2) the description by Ahmad Shafiq, who accompanied Abbas, in *Mudhakkirati fi Nisf Qarn* [Memoirs], Vol. II, Part I, pp. 120-31.

aback. He altered his tone, saying to Kitchener, "Why do you take it in that way Kitchener Pasha?" Kitchener replied, "Your Highness I am not in the least angry, but in resigning, I consider I am doing my duty." Abbas then said that the remarks had not been directed against the entire army and that he was quite satisfied with the present officers. Taking Kitchener's hand in his own he begged Kitchener to consider the incident closed.

After leaving Abbas, Kitchener telegraphed Cromer, described the differences between the Khedive and himself, and then informed Cromer he had threatened the Khedive with resignation, but "had given Abbas to understand that he would not persist in his resignation." This was the incident Cromer had been waiting for. Immediately, he dispatched a telegram to Lord Rosebery. There was no indecision this time in London, as the cabinet was not in session, and Lord Rosebery gave Cromer authority to demand the dismissal of Mahir, the Minister of War, and the promulgation of a general order, expressing satisfaction with the army, especially the British officers.

While Cromer was conducting his correspondence with Rosebery, Kitchener made one last effort to effect a compromise with the Khedive. In a private conversation he asked Abbas to modify his position and express satisfaction with the army, but Abbas replied: "I cannot, Kitchener Pasha, do anything to modify what I said at Halfa. I think I was acting within my rights." Kitchener then replied: "I am afraid, Your Highness, that under these circumstances I shall not be able to restore the state of affairs at Halfa to what it was before." He said nothing, however, about his communications with Lord Cromer.[38] Following the interview, Abbas and his party

[38] There are more copious extracts from Wingate's diary in Philip Magnus's biography, *Kitchener, Portrait of an Imperialist* (New York, 1959), pp. 83-88. Magnus ascribes much of the

began their journey by yacht down the Nile to Cairo. As one of his advisers remarked, they talked at length about the dispute with Kitchener, but all regarded the incident as closed. It was with great surprise, therefore, that they received a message from Riyad while on their way to Cairo, informing them of Cromer's demands. Abbas's first inclination was to reject these demands, but Riyad prevailed upon him, arguing that Cromer would be supported at home and that the French were not willing to intervene in the dispute.[39] Shortly thereafter, Abbas dismissed Mahir and issued a public order, praising the army and its British officers.

It is difficult to gauge the motives of Abbas in these two disputes. No doubt the British exaggerated the crises, as Abbas claimed. Also, beyond doubt, Abbas had no definite program for forcing the British out of Egypt, as Cromer seemed to imply occasionally. Many of his actions stemmed from personal pique. He resented the inferior status accorded him so often by Cromer and other British officials, and struck out rather wildly in an effort to assert his authority. He also wanted to stand well

responsibility for the incident to Kitchener, whom he regards as awkward and stiff in his dealings with Abbas and unwilling to accept the olive branch extended by the Khedive after Kitchener threatened to resign. Magnus's interpretation overlooks the fact that the British were alarmed about nationalist feelings in the army and, more important, that Cromer was anxious to find an incident through which he could humiliate the Khedive.

[39] The French were by this time thoroughly disgusted with the Khedive. They had hoped that Abbas might oppose British influence in a more subtle fashion, and they feared that his bold actions might provide the British with a pretext for increasing their control over Egypt. The dispatch from Egypt describing the dispute between Kitchener and Abbas bore the following marginal comments of the Ministry of Foreign Affairs: "This is useless and justifies the advice of moderation and reserve which we have always given to the Khedive." France, Ministère des Affaires Étrangères, *Documents Diplomatiques Français*, Série I, 1894-95, Vol. XI, Reverseaux to Casimir-Périer, No. 22, January 24, 1894.

with the nationalists and critics of the British occupation, and their minimum desire was to oppose the growth of British influence which was gradually turning Egypt into a British colony. Abbas could cooperate with them without hesitation, for British dominance of the administration was rendering him a mere figurehead. Perhaps he hoped to make a disturbance for the British in Egypt, particularly while the Liberals were in power, and to raise the Egyptian question once again to the international scene.

Abbas's advisers served him poorly, and must share a full measure of responsibility for the incidents. They claimed to know how the French and the Turks would react if a crisis developed, and many thought the Liberals meant to evacuate Egypt. These advisers tried to direct the Khedive's undisguised, but unchanneled, hostility toward the British to their own ends; they spurred him on to actions without explaining the consequences that were likely to develop. Abbas, the nationalists, and the advisers sadly misjudged almost all the factors. They underestimated the commitment of the Liberal party, not just to remain in Egypt, but to support the growth of British influence in all branches of the administration. They drastically overestimated the influence of France and bitterly chided the French for their failure to support the Khedive more forcefully. The French were in favor of obstruction to British rule, but they did not want a dispute *trop éclatant*, which might give the British a convenient pretext to strengthen their hold on Egypt. Abbas's most egregious blunder was the dispute with Kitchener. Even before he left Cairo, he was cautioned by some of his advisers not to raise the military question because it was a particularly sensitive matter with the British.[40] In disregarding the advice, he seemed to forget

[40] Ahmad Shafiq, *Mudhakkirati fi Nisf Qarn* [Memoirs], Vol. II, Part I, p. 121.

that Cromer was lying in ambush for him. He also failed to realize that Kitchener was new to his position, insecure, and unreceptive to criticism. Like the nationalist movement Abbas represented, his goals were ill-defined. His bearing was always courageous, but his actions were not always the wisest.

The Khedive's foolhardy action played into the hands of Cromer. The crises were largely Cromer's doing, for on each occasion, he was waiting for an incident which he could blow up into a major crisis in order to check the growing popularity of the Khedive. Almost the entire British community in Egypt felt that he handled Abbas too severely. Had he been more tactful in his treatment of the young ruler he might have brought him to realize his proper role in the British occupation without any major disturbances. After the crisis of January, 1893, Cromer bided his time for an opportunity to humiliate Abbas. Clearly, the British Consul-General exaggerated the threat to the Egyptian army from the Khedive's actions. As some English officials indicated, most of the army, including many British officers, were unaware of the dispute between Abbas and Kitchener until they read about it in the papers three days later.[41]

*

These two crises, short and without violence, nevertheless left a deep impression on the relations between Great Britain and Egypt. They confirmed what everyone had suspected: that the Liberal party was not contemplating evacuating Egypt according to its earlier pledges. Gladstone's speech in the House of Commons on May 1, 1893 was all the proof needed to indicate that the Liberals, like the Conservatives, intended to set no date for the evacuation of Egypt. The question of immediate evacuation was never again raised in such an acute

[41] Blunt, *My Diaries*, i, 134.

form before the First World War. To be sure, the radical wing of the Liberal party continued to call attention to Egyptian affairs. But more often they raised questions about the administrative policies adopted by the British in Egypt, rather than the need for withdrawing British troops.

In the midst of the crises Cromer warned the Foreign Office that the old system of undefined and concealed British authority could not persist. He realized that nationalist feelings and the growth of British influence in the government would force the British to the fore in governing Egypt. He suggested a clearer statement of Britain's intentions to remain in Egypt, with a clarification of the increased powers to be wielded by the British. Rosebery opposed such a step and argued that in the present state of English party politics the old system must be maintained. "My own view," he stated, "is that we must attempt to go on as before, but with ten-fold vigilance."[42] Although no external changes were made, Cromer's estimate proved more realistic than Rosebery's. In actual practice, the old system of shared authority and indirect rule came to an end. British powers were increased and introduced into almost every branch of the administration.

The change in British power was best represented in the latter part of Nubar Pasha's career. Nubar came from a well-known Armenian family in Egypt. He had become a leading minister during Ismail's reign and was responsible for the creation of the Mixed Tribunals. He

[42] Rosebery to Cromer, No. 121, January 27, 1893, Cromer Papers, PRO, FO 633/7. Cromer had written on January 21, 1893 to Rosebery (No. 282): "What I particularly wish to impress on you is that the system under which Egypt has been governed for the last ten years has broken down. It was always very artificial and unsatisfactory, and the wonder is that it lasted so long. . . . You will have to choose between going forward or backwards." Cromer Papers, PRO, FO 633/7.

[*174*]

held office as Prime Minister from 1884 to 1888 and from 1894 to 1895. Known for his Western and British proclivities and much criticized for them by Egyptian nationalist historians, he is reported to have said: "If the British withdraw, I shall leave Egypt with the last battalion."[43] Yet these critics have surely done an injustice to Nubar by describing him as a puppet of British rule. Nubar was patently no Egyptian nationalist; representing a different class in society, he stood to lose a great deal if nationalism should engulf Egypt. As a faithful representative of his class of alien (Turkish, Circassian, and Armenian) landholders and administrators, Nubar used British influence to counterbalance that of Egyptian nationalism. At the same time, he resisted the movement to make British influence dominant. He opposed Clifford Lloyd and forced his resignation. Although in power when a new British adviser was appointed in the Ministry of the Interior in 1894, Nubar hoped to limit his influence. Two other Egyptian ministers, Riyad and Sharif, also roughly represented the same class and the same point of view. Sharif, the most avowedly opposed to the occupation, resigned and did not return to power when the British forced Egypt to withdraw from the Sudan in 1884. Riyad served from 1888 to 1891. Unlike constitutionalist Sharif, he believed in resisting the growth of British influence and maintaining autocracy in Egypt. But like Sharif, he had some appeal among the nationalist groups. The resignation of Nubar in 1895 spelled the end of independent authority exercised by these groups. Nubar was succeeded by Mustafa Fahmi, a well-meaning but ineffectual minister of Turkish origins, and a weak puppet of the British. He had, in fact, been the Minister of Foreign Affairs during the Arabi revolt, not because of his nationalist leanings but because he could be trusted not to oppose the

[43] Cromer, *Modern Egypt*, II, 339.

will of the majority. He was to rule as Prime Minister (and advocate of British interests) from 1895 to 1908.[44]

The crises established the British attitude toward the nationalist movement. They saw the nationalists as embittered critics of British rule, as a tiny minority of half-Westernized intellectuals quite unrepresentative of the country. The British were therefore unwilling to cooperate with them or to put individuals of this movement, no matter how moderate, in responsible executive positions. As it became clear that the occupation would not be popular with all elements of the population, there was increasing pressure on the British to resort to coercive and autocratic measures to safeguard their position. The nationalist attitude also hardened toward the British. Men like Muhammad Abduh remained convinced of the need to cooperate with the British. Others were not so optimistic; they felt that the British would never work for Egyptian goals and would never give Egypt its independence unless opposed by the Egyptians themselves. Moreover, a great deal of nationalist popularity among the people rested on the anti-British, anti-Christian appeal of the nationalists who were hesitant to sacrifice the dynamism of their xenophobic appeal for minor, or even moderate, concessions. The strength of their opposition to British rule made compromise seem like defeat to the followers.

In the decade before the crises, Cromer had hoped to associate popular Egyptian leaders with the administration. While governing through the traditional alien or Turkish aristocracy, he was conscious that the majority of the Egyptian population was unrepresented in the government. He was aware that the Arabi revolt had been directed against these Turkish rulers. Though the Arabi movement had been crushed, Egyptians still held grievances against their rulers. It had therefore been Cromer's intention to gradually introduce into the government "an

[44] Al-Rafii, *al-Thawrah al-Arabiyah* [The Arabi Revolt], p. 204.

Egyptian element." He had tried to persuade Tawfiq just before his death to appoint an Egyptian minister to his cabinet.[45] Cromer was particularly interested in this reform, for he believed that if the British were compelled to evacuate Egypt, stability would best be secured if the people felt that some of their interests were represented in the government. The crises of 1893 and 1894 ended this experiment abruptly. Cromer was willing to sponsor an Egyptian element in the government only so long as he believed that it would be sympathetic to the British. His experience with the nationalists turned him away from them; he came to fear popular Egyptian leaders, for he invariably saw them as opponents of the British occupation, and he became generally unwilling to trust them with political power. It was not until the last year of Cromer's administration that the British were to experiment again with the idea of adding a popular Egyptian figure to the government.

The nationalistic disturbances revealed the opposition to the British. They also forced upon the British a realization that force, as well as persuasion, would be required to maintain British rule. This new-found interest in coercion as a technique for maintaining British rule was reflected in certain changes in Cromer's attitude toward the occupation. He believed more firmly than before that "Orientals" exploited weakness and understood only superior force. He was convinced that Abbas and the nationalists had questioned British authority in Egypt as a test of strength, thinking the British administrators would not be supported in London. According-

[45] Cromer was never optimistic about appointing Egyptians as ministers. In a letter to Salisbury, where he mentioned that he had tried to persuade Tawfiq to introduce "a really Egyptian element into the cabinet," he was forced to admit that he had not pressed the subject, as he "had no individual in mind whose nomination I should have cared to recommend." Baring to Salisbury, No. 118, May 15, 1891, PRO, FO 78/4385.

ly, Cromer did all he could to keep the image of superior British strength before the Egyptians. The birthday of the British sovereign was the occasion for a great military display in Cairo, reviewed by Cromer and attended by Egyptian officials. Cromer demanded from the Egyptians scrupulous respect for British officials. Whenever there was a serious nationalist attack on British authority, he increased the size of the British garrison in Egypt. The justification he gave Parliament was that the security of Egypt was endangered; the real reason was to show the Egyptian populace that the British could meet any challenge with renewed vigor. His technique for dealing with Abbas was to keep him in a constant state of fear that he would lose his throne if he provoked any further serious disturbances. As Cromer indicated in a letter to the British Foreign Minister, the Khedive was becoming "less dangerous" because "by judicious treatment, he can be frightened into behaving well to all outward appearances."[46]

The crises had begun partly over increasing British dominance of the Egyptian administration. The British had won, and their plans for the development of Egypt continued to go forward. But the tone and pace of modernization in Egypt was now altered. The fond hope of the British that they might free themselves from dependence on the old ruling aristocracy and rule Egypt through popular leaders had been shattered. The British had to continue to gear their programs of change to the class most opposed to it. By the turn of the century the Westernized nationalists were attacking the British primarily because they were not modernizing the country rapidly enough. Moreover, the British became increasingly concerned with the security of their rule. Their programs of modernization were evaluated in terms of their

[46] Cromer to Kimberley, No. 232, February 9, 1895, Cromer Papers, PRO, FO 633/6.

effect upon Egyptian stability. English officials grew more unreceptive to criticism, more autocratic and quicker to react to any movement that seemed to constitute a threat to their authority.

If the first dispute with the British had enhanced the reputation of Abbas, the second drastically weakened his influence. He was no longer able to oppose the British openly, for fear of losing his throne. At the same time, the disparate elements of the nationalist movement began to pull apart. Al-Nadim was already in exile. The moderates, like Muhammad Abduh, felt that the question of evacuation should be postponed to a more opportune time and that Egyptians should concentrate their energies on domestic reform.[47] Secretly Abbas aided the more radical nationalists. He always held an influential position in the nationalist movement, with access to great wealth which he showered on his friends and held back from his enemies. Abbas was a consummate intriguer, but he was never again to hold the attention of the nationalists, and Egypt in general, as he did in 1893 and 1894.

[47] Muhammad Abduh and Abbas quarreled over the use of *waqf* (religious endowment) funds and eventually became bitter enemies. Rashid Rida, *Tarikh al-Ustadh al-Imam al-Shaykh Muhammad Abduh*, i, 497.

CHAPTER VI

ADMINISTRATIVE PROGRESS, 1895-1907: THE BUREAUCRACY

SINCE THE British had promised a hasty evacuation of Egypt, their avowed intention was to restrict the number of foreign, and especially British, officials employed by the Egyptian government. In fact, Baring indicated in a letter to Granville in 1883 that he was quite prepared to sacrifice administrative efficiency by using less well-trained Egyptians rather than bringing in a host of European specialists.[1] Cromer estimated ten years later that the Egyptian government was employing 1,157 Europeans, almost half of whom were part of the international administrations like the *Caisse* and the Mixed Railway Board. In the Egyptian administration 33 percent of the Europeans were English and 15 percent were French. The Europeans, of course, commanded some of the best governmental salaries, but there had been no significant increase in the number of foreign officials. The number of British officials in the civil administration had only risen from 170 to 250.[2] Most of the top British officials were hand-picked by Cromer.

The crises of 1892-1894 proved to be a turning point in the administrative life of Egypt, for in their aftermath came the influx of English officials. From 1890 to 1895

[1] Baring to Granville, September 27, 1883, Granville Papers, PRO 30/29/161.

[2] For comparative purposes these figures leave a great deal to be desired, since some of the estimates include foreign protégés and others do not. There were additional difficulties in determining what agencies to consider as part of the Egyptian bureaucracy. The estimates made in this paragraph were compiled from official British reports. Cookson to Granville, March 13, 1882, *HCSP*, Egypt No. 4 (1882), Vol. LXXXII, c. 3188 and Cromer to Rosebery, No. 66, April 2, 1893, PRO, FO 78/4514.

the British increased their influence over the Ministries of Justice and the Interior. The number of officials in other branches of the administration also rose significantly. Cromer's Annual Report of 1906 showed that there were marked increases in the number of European officials employed in all the departments. The Justice and Interior Ministries nearly doubled the number of their European officials.[3] The Milner Commission of 1920, sent out to study the causes of the nationalist disturbances of 1919, reported that Egyptians occupied less than one-fourth of the higher posts in the government bureaucracy. The Commission also discovered that since 1905 the percentage of Egyptians in all posts had increased from 45 to 51 but in higher posts it had declined from 28 to 23. The proportion of the British in such posts had increased from 42 to 59.[4] By World War I the British had established a dominant position in every ministry and department except those relating to the religious life of the country, such as the Department of Waqfs. The Ministries of Finance, Public Works, the Interior, Education, and Public Health all had English inspectors and, in some cases, sub-inspectors who supervised the domestic affairs of the country.

The burgeoning of English officialdom in Egypt ran counter to the avowed aims of the occupation, for the British had repeatedly stressed that their goal in Egypt was to prepare the country to govern itself. Cromer had laid down the principle that the number of Europeans employed in the Egyptian administration should be limited, so that Egyptians might be given training in the government. There was a gradual alteration in this thinking as the occupation began to assume more permanence.

[3] The same difficulties mentioned in footnote 2 were encountered in the use of these statistics. Cromer, Annual Report for 1906, No. 31, PRO, FO 371/247.

[4] Quoted in Morroe Berger, *Bureaucracy and Society in Modern Egypt* (Princeton, 1957), p. 32.

Leading British officials, although never repudiating the promises of ultimate evacuation, came to think that this event would occur in the distant future. Cromer's book, *Modern Egypt,* and other essays written by him after he left Egypt, make it clear that he did not anticipate Egyptian autonomy for a great many years. There was, therefore, less pressure on the British administration to give administrative experience to Egyptian officials.

Even while the pressure to prepare Egypt for immediate independence was lessening, new administrative needs were arising. Having attained financial solvency, the government was in a position to undertake more extensive reform programs. Attention was directed to further hydraulic projects—agriculture, sanitation, and a variety of others. British officials already in the administration pressed for additional European personnel to carry out these programs. As Cromer wrote in *Modern Egypt*: "When once the full tide of prosperity set in, demands arose on all sides for the employment of agents possessing technical knowledge of all sorts. European lawyers were required to deal with the numerous legal questions which arose and in which a knowledge of Europeans and their laws was indispensable. Hydraulic engineers were required to deal with irrigation questions; medical men to look after hospitals and the sanitary condition of the country. . . . All these demands fell suddenly on a country almost wholly unprepared to meet them."[5] In many cases it was impossible to find Egyptians with the required technical training, for the Egyptian educational system was not producing men capable of undertaking some of these complicated administrative and scientific functions. The technical branches of the Ministry of Public Works, and the Departments of Agriculture and Public Health were staffed almost entirely by English and European personnel at the higher, technical levels.

[5] Cromer, *Modern Egypt,* II, 297.

Moreover, the British also reserved top executive positions for their own men, arguing that the Egyptians did not yet have the requisite administrative skills.[6] The pressure for administrative efficiency was not engendered entirely within the ranks of British officialdom. Foreign communities in Egypt, especially the merchant groups, were eager for the modernization of the country. Interested observers in England and Europe also kept up a barrage of demands for the reform of the Egyptian administration and economy. Even articulate Egyptians called for modernizing programs, perhaps little aware that some of the reforms they demanded would require an increase in the foreign personnel in Egypt.

There can be no question, however, that Egyptians were discriminated against in top administrative positions. Few Egyptians were given opportunities to work at levels commensurate with their educational attainments where they possessed them. Although Egypt had a School of Engineering, there were very few Egyptian hydraulic engineers who held top administrative positions. (One exception was Ismail Sirry, an engineer trained in the School of Engineering, who eventually became a quite good Minister of Public Works.)[7] Also, promotions in the civil service among Egyptians tended to favor the most submissive and obedient, discriminating against the imaginative and resourceful. Those with capabilities, zeal, and ideas were commonly passed over. Muhammad Abduh said of the British practice: "Its principal fault lies in the unsatisfactory choice of its officials. As a rule one thing alone is exacted in a candidate and that is that he should possess a nature entirely passive. A man in the smallest degree independent will not

---

[6] In Cromer's last Annual Report in *HCSP*, Egypt No. 1 (1907), Vol. o, cd. 3394.

[7] There is a biographical sketch in Muhammad Mujahid Zaki, *al-Alam al-Sharqiyah* [The Great Men of the East] (Cairo, 1949), I, 63.

be admitted or, if by mistake he should be, he will not remain long."[8]

Although British influence reached large proportions in the administration, the Egyptian administrative structure was permitted to remain intact. Provincial and local organizations were not dissolved. The British ruled Egypt through, or more precisely, behind, the Egyptian governmental apparatus. On the lower levels were the inspectors and sub-inspectors and above them the advisers to the ministries themselves. The British officials, theoretically only advisers and inspectors, exercised decisive control when they desired. Thus, there was a constant tension between Egyptian officers and English advisers at all levels of the administration.

The most significant step in the direction of increasing British control over the administration occurred in 1894-1895, when the British extended their influence in the Ministry of the Interior. Except for a short period when Clifford Lloyd was in the country, the British had allowed the central agency of the Ministry to operate in a relatively autonomous fashion.[9] Nubar Pasha had sedulously removed all traces of British influence at the central office of the Ministry and reduced the control of the British over the police, a branch organization of the same ministry.

The need to establish English predominance over the Interior Ministry was great, especially since general domestic insecurity disrupted the economic development of the country and was one of the most criticized aspects of British rule. The first efforts by the British came in 1891 when Colonel Herbert Kitchener was appointed Inspector-General of the Egyptian police and began to initiate reforms there. In 1894 Nubar was finally forced

[8] Quoted in A. B. de Guerville, *New Egypt* (London, 1905), p. 161.
[9] See above pp. 70-73.

to allow the British to establish an adviser at the Ministry of the Interior. Eldon Gorst, who was appointed, wrote in 1894 that "on looking around I perceived that the one thing yet left to be taken seriously in hand by England was the Ministry of the Interior. The police, run on stiff military lines by a series of incapable chiefs, was the one English failure. The rest of the local administration had hardly been touched at all."[10] Gorst led a campaign to tighten up local administration. The most far-reaching of his reforms was the creation of an English inspectorate at the Ministry, responsible for supervising local and provincial officials and securing the observation and enforcement of decrees and proposals sent out from Cairo. The English inspectors of the Ministry of the Interior, like those attached to the Ministry of Public Works, were to become a power in the internal life of the country. They involved themselves in all security and administrative problems on the village level. Although they were only advisers, they clearly could make their influence felt, since they had the support of the English adviser at the Ministry of the Interior. They were not nearly so well received as the irrigation inspectors whose superior technical skills were often recognized. The presence of the Interior Ministry inspectors aroused considerable opposition on the part of local and provincial Egyptian administrators. The *mudirs* and the *mamurs*, whose authority they were usurping, were particularly antagonistic to them.[11]

As might have been expected, there was no formal system for recruiting English and other non-Egyptian personnel to the Egyptian civil service in the early years of the occupation. Egypt was not a British colony and

---

[10] Gorst Papers, Autobiographical Notes, I.

[11] The best description of the duties and powers of the English inspector may be found in Thomas Russell, *Egyptian Service, 1902-1946* (London, 1949).

its personnel were not recruited by competitive examination, as was the case for India and certain other colonies. Many of the first British administrators were sent out from India on loan and expected to return as soon as they had discharged their responsibilities or Egypt had obtained its independence. Almost the entire irrigation staff in the first decade of British rule was drawn from India; many of them stayed on in Egypt on a regular basis. A large percentage of the financial experts sent to Egypt in these early years came from India, as did a certain number of individuals in the Ministry of Justice and in the Police Department. As time passed, although recruitment was not regularized, an increasing number of persons without previous colonial experience were drawn straight from the major English universities—Cambridge, Oxford, the University of London, and Trinity College in Dublin.

Individual Egyptian departments theoretically recruited their own English personnel, although the usual practice in this period was for the Education Department to do the lion's share of the recruiting. In the 1890's young men were brought out to teach English and other European subjects in the Egyptian primary and secondary schools. After an apprenticeship of a few years in the education system, they were moved into other branches of the administration, especially the Ministries of Finance and the Interior. This system enabled new men to acquire a certain amount of experience in the country—especially its language and customs—before moving into more demanding posts. It provided indispensable training for men who had to go out into the provinces as inspectors of the Ministry of the Interior, who had to cope with local problems and get along with Egyptian officials. On the other hand, this arrangement had an injurious effect on the educational system, for no one took his apprentice work seriously, and looked on his job merely as a jumping-off point for more prestigious work. The technical experts, especially those in the irrigation, agriculture, and public health departments, were recruited by their own departments and did not go through this apprentice training.[12]

In 1902 the system for recruiting foreign personnel for the Egyptian civil service was changed. The chief reason for the reform was the acquisition of the Sudan and the desire to obtain first-rate men for the then-forming Sudanese civil service. As the Sudan was under the control of Egypt, the new recruiting system was to be applied to both countries. Drafted by Reginald Wingate, the Governor-General of the Sudan, and Eldon Gorst, Egypt's financial adviser, the new regulation stipulated that vacancies in the nontechnical branches of the administration were to be advertised in the major English and Irish universities. Applications from the graduates or prospective graduates of these schools were to be received and judged by a board composed of high-ranking British officials serving at the time either in Egypt or the Sudan. There was to be no competitive examination for positions, but those candidates judged most suitable by the board were to be interviewed in London. The board would then select the men for the vacant positions. The successful candidates were required to enroll either at Cambridge or Oxford for a year of training in Arabic before going out to Egypt or the Sudan. Although theoretically the applicants could choose to serve either in Egypt or the Sudan, in many cases that decision was made for them by the British staff in Egypt. There the new men served in subordinate positions, generally at the Ministry of the Interior, or Finance, as sub-inspectors, for a year of probation. At the end of this time, if their work was acceptable and they were able to pass fairly simple

[12] This system is described in Humphrey Bowman, *Middle East Window* (London, 1942), p. 38.

examinations in the reading and writing of Arabic, their appointments became permanent, and they were irremovable except for ill health, misconduct, or suppression of post. The salary scale established by the new regulations was a minimum beginning salary of £E240 per year, excellent prospects of a salary of 400 to 600 after six or seven years, and salaries of 800 to 1500 for the most talented individuals.[13]

The intention of the reformed system was to enable Egypt and the Sudan to recruit highly qualified young Englishmen and give them preliminary training in the language and customs of the country before they came out to the East. A common criticism of the British administrative staff before this time was that only a small percentage of the British officials had a working knowledge of the language.

The preliminary training at Oxford and Cambridge could have given the candidates a real start in their learning of Arabic, but it appears that such was not the case. Arabic instruction at Cambridge and Oxford proved of very little worth. Although the courses were given by noted Orientalists and Arabic scholars, Margoliouth at Oxford and Edward G. Brown at Cambridge, in conjunction with Arab *shaykhs*, the emphasis of the course was on classical Arabic. The books to be read were a fully-vocalized chrestomathy of Arabic prose selections compiled by Père Cheikho, the first volume of *A Thousand and One Nights*, material from al-Fakhri, and some other selections from classical Arabic. "L'Arabe Moderne etudié dans les Journaux et les Pieces Officieles" was only recommended for purchase and study. Furthermore, "the selected candidates [are] not recommended to devote much attention to the vernacular until they arrive in Egypt and know in what district their work will

[13] This information is to be found in PRO, FO 371/67 file 27092.

be."[14] According to one official, "Margoliouth's teaching seems to be quite useless and I do not think the *shaykh* at Oxford is doing his duty."[15]

The in-service training in Arabic was also disappointing; the standards were low, the examinations so insignificant that no one was known to have been dismissed from the service for having failed. The ideal of creating and maintaining a corps of British officials fluent in the language of the country was never realized. Officials who spent long periods in the provinces, like the inspectors of the various departments, learned to speak the colloquial Arabic, but only a handful of officials ever learned how to read and write Arabic.

The new regulations for recruitment, in practice, applied only to recruits for the Ministries of Finance and the Interior. The other departments, including Education, recruited their personnel by themselves, on the grounds that as technical branches of the administration they had to apply their own standards of selection. Certain of these departments had their own language requirements and examinations for foreign personnel. Inspectors in the irrigation service and the teachers in the Department of Education had to pass language tests, but according to one official they were "embarrassingly easy." Irrigation inspectors were required to read simple canal regulations while the teachers in the Department of Education had to translate departmental regulations. The more specialized technical experts were not required to master the language. One of these men stated:

Soon after my arrival in Egypt I considered whether I should take up the serious study of Arabic, including the written language, and came to the conclusion that

[14] *Ibid.*
[15] Bonham Carter to Wingate, January 1, 1906, Wingate Papers, 278/1.

as I was in a scientific job it was more important to spend the time which I had to spare on keeping abreast of the developments in my own subject rather than becoming an Arabic scholar. However, like most British officials, technical or administrative, I acquired a good enough knowledge of the Arabic spoken by simple uneducated people to enable me to direct work and for ordinary purposes, and often in my early years spoke little else for weeks at a time. As all educated Egyptians spoke and read English or French or both, discussions on more learned subjects were easily carried on in one of these than in Arabic. Moreover, most Egyptians preferred to talk English on such occasions. It was unnecessary therefore for me to study the intricacies of the classical language which many officials were compelled by their work to do.[16]

The British administrators in Egypt, thus, were amateurs in government; they had only a modicum of training in the history and the cultures of the peoples they ruled. The year of training at Oxford and Cambridge concentrated on language, which was pitched at a level too difficult for most to handle; virtually no training was given in the culture, customs, history, and institutions of Egypt either before and after the posting of the candidates to the area. These men, however, were drawn from the upper classes of English society—classes accustomed to ruling over others and to being obeyed. And they transferred their expertise in ruling to their imperial possessions. What they undoubtedly lacked in an understanding of alien peoples, they partially made good in a belief in themselves and in their capacity to rule others.

The 1902 regulations brought an end to the old system of channeling new personnel through the Department of Education. This change was beneficial to the

[16] Letter from Harold Hurst, June 26, 1965.

Education Department, but had just the opposite effect on the other departments. Young, relatively inexperienced Englishmen were brought out to Egypt and sent into the provinces as inspectors and sub-inspectors for the Ministries of Finance and the Interior. They were brought immediately into contact with Egyptian provincial officials, many of whom were men with many years of administrative experience. The young inspectors, of course, expected to supervise the provincial and local administrators and to have their advice followed. Not unexpectedly, there was friction between the British and Egyptian officials on numerous occasions, and resentment against the powers wielded by these young men.[17]

The largest percentage of young men recruited by the new system preferred the Sudan over Egypt, as the Sudanese civil service was an elite corps with great prestige. The Sudan, thus, had the pick of the young applicants. Egypt did not suffer noticeably from the operation of the system, however, for there were special requirements for service in the Sudan. Because of the exacting climatic and geographical conditions, the Sudanese civil service favored men who could bear the heat and the separation from settled life.[18] Egypt obtained those who were not suitable on these grounds, many of whom were far better qualified for the administrative and technical duties required of them in Egypt. The Egyptian and Sudanese appointees had acquired, for the most part, the best education that Great Britain could offer. All were university graduates, the overwhelming majority from England's leading institutions. The caliber of training was especially high in the technical branches of the administration, where one former official from this period estimated that in one of the technical branches, of the senior

[17] The operation of this system is severely criticized by a British official in Coles, *Reflections and Recollections*, p. 170.
[18] H. C. Jackson, *Sudan Days and Ways* (London, 1954), p. 16.

[*191*]

staff between 1904 and 1914 at least two-thirds were honor graduates of British universities and nine had taken first class honors.[19]

Egypt and the Sudan probably drew more men from the upper classes of English society than most other overseas possessions. Egyptian colonial service was particularly attractive to upper segments of the middle class and to sons of professional men. Although there are no statistics on the subject, sons of the clergy, business men, and the smaller landed gentry appear frequently in the biographical notices of the British officials in Egypt. In India and other colonial services competitive examinations were utilized in the selection of personnel, with the result that positions were open to well qualified individuals from any segment of society. Universities were still very much the preserve of the established groups. Egyptian and Sudanese officials, without the levelling influence of competitive examinations, were drawn almost exclusively from the upper classes, special attention being paid to a man's antecedents in the interviewing sessions. The predominance of this group undoubtedly left its imprint on British rule in Egypt and the Sudan in the form of exclusiveness, a certain amount of racial arrogance, a feeling of *noblesse oblige* for the less fortunate classes, a pride in accomplishments, and a sense of duty. One of the most perceptive statements of this set of characteristics, viewed in another part of the world, is contained in the autobiographical notes of Leonard Woolf, who served in Ceylon and characterized himself as "a very innocent, unconscious imperialist, . . . an anti-imperialist who enjoyed the fleshpots of imperialism." Woolf describes the clannishness of the British officials, their studied isolation from the rest of the population, their sense of superiority. They all enjoyed the feeling of ex-

[19] Letter from Harold Hurst, July 28, 1962.

[*192*]

hilaration and power which came with their wide sphere of authority over the local population.[20]

In Egypt there can be no question that English exclusiveness was carried to great extremes and was bitterly resented by the Egyptian populace. The British officials rarely associated with the Egyptians on a social basis. Some senior officials even lectured the young English recruits on the proper social conduct in Egypt, one of the basic principles being that the English were not expected to associate with Egyptians outside of work. In secondary schools there were separate commons rooms for the Egyptian and the English lecturers.[21] British exclusiveness was virtually enshrined in its two social and sports clubs—the Gezira and Turf clubs. Founded in the early years of the occupation for the social life and relations of British officialdom, they were almost completely barred to the Egyptian population before the outbreak of the First World War. No Egyptian obtained membership in either of them in this period; additionally, it was regarded as being extremely bad taste for a British member to bring an Egyptian into the club as a guest. These two clubs were to become objects of envy and hatred for the Egyptian population.[22]

Coupled with British exclusiveness was arrogance and a feeling of racial superiority. The British regarded the Egyptians as inferior and backward people, to be treated as children. In private conversation they referred to the Egyptians as "Gyppies" and after World War I as "wogs." Another example of the arrogance of the British administrators is related by a British official in the Department of Education. He was called to the room of the English adviser of the Department, to discover

[20] Leonard Woolf, *Growing, An Autobiography of the Years, 1904-1911* (New York, 1961).
[21] Bowman, *Middle East Window*, p. 40.
[22] Cecil Alport, *One Hour of Justice* (London, 1946), p. 52.

[*193*]

three senior officials there: an Englishman, a Frenchman, and an Egyptian. He timidly approached the table where the adviser was sitting until the latter turned to him and exclaimed, "You come into the room like a native." This was said in front of one of the high ranking Egyptian government officials.[23]

Racism was part of the late nineteenth-century European experience, its intellectual justification being found in the popular Darwinian theories of the age. It was on the lips of articulate members of this generation and was used to corroborate, at times, the most contradictory ideas and policies. But, at the same time, this doctrine, transported and developed to a high degree in the colonial world, was an effective technique of rule. Throughout the colonial world, England and other European countries had undertaken the task of governing large numbers of peoples with their own limited populations and resources. They had superior military technology at their disposal, but they would have had difficulty suppressing spontaneous uprisings of large segments of the population. In Egypt the British army of occupation was often less than 5,000 men. British officialdom was small before the outbreak of the First World War, while the British community in Egypt was not large; nor was the rest of the European population which, in any case, could never have been relied upon to support the British. The Egyptian population was close to 15 million. One method by which the British were able to control this population was that of extolling their own racial superiority, maintaining their isolation from the Egyptians, and treating the Egyptians as kindly, but inferior peoples. This attitude instilled fear and respect in the populace, so long used to having an alien minority rule by many of the same techniques. When supplemented with force or the

[23] Bowman, *Middle East Window*, p. 43.

threat of it and coupled with genuine efforts to bring material and other benefits to the subject peoples, this technique enabled the British to maintain order with a minimum of drain on their military establishment.

Cromer was a grand exponent of this system of rule. He isolated himself from the Egyptian population, almost in the manner of an oriental despot. At the same time, he maintained his prestige and that of his country in his periodic appearances before the people. Whenever he moved around the city, he travelled in a carriage with coachmen running before the carriage shouting make way for "the lord" as Cromer was called by the Egyptians. On ceremonial occasions like the Queen's birthday, the British armed forces were put on display at full strength and reviewed by leading members of the British and Egyptian communities.[24] Cromer was, unknowingly, a master psychologist of this imperial relationship, striking fear and at the same time instilling respect in the subject peoples. This was done by establishing the image of the superiority—both military and moral—of the British and by punishing all efforts to challenge this position.

There were, however, pitfalls in this technique of rule. The isolation and arrogant racism of the British overlords offended the Egyptian populace and lent special bitterness to the attacks on the regime. Moreover, and more important, the enforced isolation of the British kept them out of touch with the Egyptian populace. They were unable to acquire accurate knowledge of the feelings of the Egyptian people, in order to fit their policies to these realities. In the nationalist period they were at a great disadvantage in determining effective policies because of their ignorance of this movement. When, in addition, segments of the Egyptian population

[24] Abd al-Rahman al-Rafii, *Mustafa Kamil* (Cairo, 1950), p. 181.

realized that the British had neither the desire nor the overall military strength to enforce policies if challenged—that is, that their system of rule was a technique to keep the ruled from challenging the authority of the ruling power—then the position of the British became even more difficult. The only way, under these circumstances, that the British could sustain their position was to make actual the threat of force—a practice condemned by a large segment of British society at home.

✿

A question that seems to have intrigued historians is the type of Europeans who went out to the colonies, and their reasons for going. Nineteenth-century observers had their own rude theories when they remarked that the colonies were a vast system of outdoor relief for the upper classes, the assumption being that the colonies attracted the most ineffectual members, those unable to find a place for themselves within English society at home. This interpretation has persisted.

Two recent studies have presented even more suggestive ideas. D. O. Mannoni, in his *Prospero and Caliban*, argues that colonial officials were generally individuals who found satisfaction in the dependency relationship between absolute ruler and ruled, developed in the colonial world. Most commonly, these were men who had not resolved conflicts in their upbringing, who had, to use the author's term, "infantile complexes," the expression of which could be given more fully within the colonial world.[25] And according to Hannah Arendt, in her work, *The Origins of Totalitarianism*, the colonial administrators of the late nineteenth century were men who refused to give up their boyhood ideals as they grew up in a rapidly changing European society. Unable to

[25] Dominique O. Mannoni, *Prospero and Caliban: The Psychology of Colonization* (New York, 1956).

realize these ideals in their own societies, and also the most dangerous and idealistic element in European society, they fled to the non-European world where they "preserved and infantilized Western moral standards."[26]

A cursory glance at the careers of English officials in Egypt would quickly reveal the difficulties in generalizing about these men. They seemed to have gone to Egypt for the greatest variety of reasons. Scott-Moncrieff, Garstin, and the other hydraulic engineers had greater opportunities to practice their skills, and could acquire greater professional reputations for themselves in Egypt, with its vast hydraulic problems, than they could in England. There seem to be indications that Cromer chose a colonial career because of his disillusionment with the trends in English society and because of his desire to preserve his boyhood ideals. It should be remembered, however, that colonial service, especially in Egypt, could be used as a stepping-stone for good positions in England and certainly for recognition by the English public. Cromer and Kitchener, for instance, rose to the peerage in recognition of their work in Egypt and the Sudan. Countless others were knighted for their accomplishments. The doors of opportunity within English society were, in fact, opened to the most successful administrators. Cromer was offered the Foreign Office; Kitchener became Secretary of War in 1914, and Gorst moved from a top administrative position in Egypt into the Foreign Office and then back to Egypt as Cromer's successor. Other men, not so talented or ambitious as Cromer, Gorst, and Kitchener, did not expect to attain responsible and powerful positions at home. Colonial service presented great opportunities to them and held out the prospect of carving out spheres of power and prestige and developing their talents fully.

[26] Hannah Arendt, *The Origins of Totalitarianism* (New York, 1958), p. 211.

[*197*]

It is of considerable value to trace the Egyptian careers of three English officials here—Alfred (later Lord) Milner, Harry Boyle, and Thomas Russell. These careers reveal many of the basic reasons for Englishmen selecting colonial service in this period. The common themes running through the careers of these officials were the attraction of power, the desire to exercise it in an unfettered form, the search for fulfillment of one's talents in a different setting, and the disillusionment with certain aspects of English society. Although there is not enough psychological evidence for a detailed analysis of personalities, the decisions of these three men do lend credence to some of the ideas put forth by Mannoni and Hannah Arendt.

Milner, born of a modest family, was destined by training and inclination for a career in politics. He went to Balliol College, Oxford, where he was recognized by his fellow students as a potential political leader. Having served as private secretary to G. J. Goschen, he accepted a position as director-general of accounts in the Egyptian Ministry of Finance in 1889. Milner was a top official in the Ministry from 1889 to 1892, when he resigned his position and returned to England. Milner made his decision to go to Egypt because he believed that Egypt was very much to the fore in colonial affairs, so much so that a person of ability could enhance his reputation through his work there. The second major contributory factor was that he had no love for English party politics, with their red tape, enervating bureaucratic conformism, and dominance of party over individual. Milner had a great desire to be free to do as he liked. He wrote to a friend: "So far, I have realized the idea with which I started, of going somewhere where good work was being done by Englishmen, unhampered or little hampered by the blighting influence of home politics." He constantly affirmed that in the colonies "the individual counts for more."[27] Milner was, in fact, ambivalent about the colonial service. He enjoyed the power that came from being a top man in a powerful bureaucracy, not bound by the rules and conventions of English society. Yet he saw his ultimate place in England, and he used his successes in the colonial world to enhance his reputation and his career possibilities at home. Actually it was his hope that he and other like-minded men might eventually carry out reforms in English society, the essence of which would be to release the individual from the formalism and conventions of party politics, thus enabling him to operate with virtually as much freedom as he did in the colonial world. Milner was attracted to the colonial world by the opportunities to exercise power, to act freely, and by the feeling that such opportunities were then denied to him in England.

Harry Boyle's reasons for going to Egypt were quite different from those of Alfred Milner. With a lazy streak and a self-effacing personality, Boyle did not have the educational background of his English contemporaries. He had entered the foreign service and might well have looked forward to an uneventful career in minor posts. His saving grace, however, was his extraordinary linguistic ability. Through his own exertions he had passed a difficult examination for the Levant Consular service and had entered the School for Student Interpreters in Turkey. After two years of training he had a knowledge of Turkish, Persian, a fair amount of modern Greek, and some Arabic. After having served at Constantinople for a short period of time, he was sent to Cairo in the 1880's. There he became the eyes and ears of Lord Cromer, who, not knowing Arabic or much Turkish, was completely dependent on men like Boyle for information about the attitudes of the Egyptian population. In the

[27] Milner to Henry Brebaugh, January 10, 1897, The Milner Papers, Box 7.

[*199*]

1890's the post of Oriental Secretary was created for Boyle, who thereby became the power behind the throne, especially in the later years of Cromer's administration when information about the nationalist movement was so desperately required. It is clear that he revelled in the power he exercised in Cairo and the special position of honor accorded to him by the British staff. Yet he had no desire—unlike Milner—for higher positions. He never advertised himself to the outside world; he was secretive and enjoyed exercising power behind the scenes without proper recognition. In a letter to his mother explaining the absence of his name from among those taking part in official functions, he wrote: "Even if I am there, I always omit my own name from lists, as I inherit the fine old gentlemanly plan from my father of not putting myself forward, and the Lord's [Cromer's] school has gone still further in this direction. Blow semblance of power. I like reality and you don't often get the two together."[28] In England Boyle's unusual talents and energies could hardly have been utilized to the extent they were in Egypt.

The career of Thomas Russell can be traced in more detail, not only for the career decision, but also because of the insight it gives into the Egyptian civil service. Russell came from old aristocratic stock. After graduating from Trinity College, Cambridge, he successfully applied for service in Egypt in 1901, selecting Egypt primarily because of his cousin, Percy Machell, then adviser to the Ministry of the Interior and because, as a young, energetic, and athletic man, he would be able to live the kind of outdoor life he wanted. In Egypt he felt freer to express and develop all facets of his personality than in English society. As a devoted sportsman, he was at-

[28] Clara Boyle, *A Servant of the Empire: A Memoir of Harry Boyle* (London, 1938), p. xix.

[*200*]

tracted to Egypt because of the possibilities for hunting and for life outside of the city. The colonial service was often composed of a large number of young men escaping from complex, industrial European society into a rural environment. After a year of Arabic in England, Russell was appointed to the Ministry of the Interior and assigned to a coast guard unit just outside Alexandria. There he lived as the only Englishman among a group of Egyptians, most of whom spoke no English. The reason for this arrangement was to force the young recruit to acquire a fluency in colloquial Arabic. After several months' stay in the coast guard unit, Russell was made a sub-inspector at the Ministry of the Interior; during the next few months he worked in various Egyptian provinces, acquiring a knowledge of Egypt's domestic life and a familiarity with the different conditions in each of the provinces. Finally he was given a permanent post as a sub-inspector in Upper Egypt. The British administration encouraged inspectors to spend their time in the provinces by increasing their pay for each day outside of Cairo. The ordinary inspector like Russell was in the habit of residing in the provinces about 25 or 26 days every month and spending the remaining few days in Cairo. There were also pay incentives for demonstrating a mastery of Arabic, and Russell managed to increase his pay regularly by passing examinations in Arabic. Russell's advancement in the service was rapid; he moved from sub-inspector to inspector, then to sub-commandant of the Alexandrian police and finally in 1918 he was made commandant of the Cairo police.[29]

[29] The information on Sir Thomas Russell was compiled from his autobiography, *Egyptian Service, 1902-1946* and from a collection of letters he wrote to his father during this period. The latter are invaluable for a description of the duties of the English inspectorate of the Ministry of the Interior and a portrait of daily life in the country, as seen by the English observer.

For Egyptians the most coveted positions in society were to be found in the Egyptian bureaucracy. Parents sent their sons to the primary and secondary schools so that they might qualify for admission into it. Ever since Muhammad Ali had developed and professionalized the civil service and employed Egyptians on a large scale, Egyptian families had guided their sons into it. Although it did not pay handsome salaries at the lower levels, Egyptians preferred the relative security of an administrative position to the uncertainty of striking out on their own and attempting to make a living in private occupations. Egypt was a society run by the government; little was done privately, and consequently the Egyptian government did, in fact, employ large numbers. Its uppermost levels paid well in comparison with employment in private life. Even graduates of the Schools of Law and Medicine sought safe, less demanding positions in the government, over private practice with its risks and yet its opportunities for high income. Egyptian novelists from this period and from a slightly later period confirm this trend.

The Egyptian civil service, like most civil services, had a tendency to produce conservative and obedient personnel. Advancements commonly went to those who demonstrated complete acceptance of the system. Economic incentives to conform were great, since bureaucrats were especially anxious to leave poorly paid subordinate positions and felt they could do so only by an absolute adherence to the system. The British were disinclined to alter the mentality of the government bureaucracy, even if they could, because it proved an ideal instrument through which to implement their own policies in Egypt. The majority of civil service members were clerks and holders of the primary certificate. The recipients of secondary certificates were usually found in the higher positions, although in the 1880's it was not uncommon for primary-certificate holders to attain higher positions. The Law School tended to feed its graduates into the Ministry of Justice, less so into the provincial administration as *mudirs* and *mamurs*. Graduates of the Medical School and the School of Engineering staffed some of the higher administrative positions in the Ministry of Public Works and the Department of Public Health. Offices of the greatest power and responsibility in these and other branches of the government, particularly in the inspectorate of each department, were almost entirely reserved, however, for British officials.

At the beginning of the occupation the British were quick to note that the civil service was much larger than it needed to be—unwieldy—and very expensive. Such had been the case throughout the nineteenth century, but the bureaucracy's growth had been quickened in the troubled years leading up to the Arabi revolt. In a three-year period before the occupation, more than 598 new administrative positions had been created.[30] It was quite apparent that the same amount of government work could easily have been performed by a vastly reduced corps of officials. Nevertheless, the British were conscious that wholesale dismissals of excess officials would create grievances and discontent among the Egyptian populace. It was decided not to enforce such radical measures. Instead, a financial committee, headed by the adviser to the Ministry of Finance, Edgar Vincent, was empowered to supervise all new appointments.[31] From 1883 to 1888 the number of new appointments of the civil service was cut by one-third. In succeeding years, some of the departments, most noticeably the Department of Public Health, made large strides in ridding the government of

[30] Percival G. Elgood, *The Transit of Egypt* (London, 1928), p. 19.
[31] Baring to Salisbury, No. 8, April 12, 1889, *HCSP*, Egypt No. 4 (1889), Vol. LXXXVII, c. 5718.

incompetent and functionless officials.[32] The British, however, never did reduce the size of the civil service to a reasonable relationship with its duties. In 1914 it was essentially what it had been in 1880, a large, unwieldy body of undertrained individuals, poorly paid, discharging functions which could easily have been handled by a much smaller number.

Although the size of the civil service was not limited drastically, the British did attempt to define entrance requirements more sharply. In 1892 the administration was divided into upper and lower levels. Although limited opportunities did exist for movement from the lower to the upper ranks, basically the lower ranks were staffed by graduates of the primary schools and the upper ranks by graduates of the secondary schools.[33] The division of the government bureaucracy was made firmer by a ruling at the turn of the century that holders of the primary certificate, no matter what positions they attained, could not receive a salary in excess of £E11 a month.[34] This reform, enacted to improve the caliber of the civil servants by forcing parents to send their children on to secondary schools, discriminated against talented young men who had been able to acquire only primary certificates. It tended to make the civil service even more formal and rigid, and to discount individual initiative. There were many individuals in this category, for education was not free; in fact, it was quite expensive by Egyptian standards, and many families could not afford to educate their sons beyond the primary-school level.

[32] Égypte, *Bulletin des Lois et Décrets*, 1887, p. 95.
[33] Lord Cromer, Annual Report for 1892, *HCSP*, Egypt No. 3 (1893), Vol. cxi, c. 6957.
[34] The decree is given in the Departmental Orders of the Department of Public Health, No. 60, 1911. These orders are to be found in the archives of the Egyptian Department of Public Health.

Since the reign of Muhammad Ali the education system had been regarded as the supplier of the government bureaucracy. Reforms by the British strengthened and formalized the close relationship between education and the government. Holders of certificates automatically qualified as applicants for positions in the civil service. Although there was no reason why graduates could not seek employment in the private sphere, the ease with which they could move into the civil service made the step a rather natural one.

Although receipt of a degree from a primary or a secondary school qualified a person for employment in the civil service, appointments depended upon the individual requirements of the departments. There were no universal standards for selecting civil servants. Some of the departments used examinations; others used a general exam drawn up by the Department of Education, and quite a number did not give any examination. As late as 1914 two departments had not laid down a definite scheme for the recruitment of personnel.[35]

The department that attracted the most talented young men was the Ministry of Justice, as it was the obvious source of employment for a large percentage of the graduates of the Law School, the best higher education institution in Egypt. The Justice Ministry employed these men mainly in the office of the Parquet, for the investigation of crime or the presentation of the government's case in the law courts. Although it obtained the best recruits, its pay scale was quite low, a factor causing a great deal of discontent. It is not surprising, then, that in the lower ranks of the Ministry the nationalist movement had a large following. The government attempted to attract qualified men from the Law School into the Ministry of the Interior to serve as *mamurs* and, if they

[35] This material comes from a report made by Henry Higgs, Inspector-General, on April 8, 1914, Wingate Papers, Box 157/2.

proved successful, as *mudirs*. This campaign failed, however, because graduates of the Law School preferred to engage in work more in keeping with their educational experience. The caliber of administrators of the Ministry of the Interior, consequently, was not nearly so high as that of the Ministry of Justice.[36]

＊

Before the British came to assume positions of predominance in the Ministry of the Interior, provincial and local administrators were allowed to operate more or less without British guidance. They remained essentially what they had been before the occupation. The *mudirs*, or governors of the provinces, and the *mamurs* of the districts were the immediate representatives of the Ministry of the Interior, transmitting its decrees and regulations to the local levels and responsible to the central administration for the security of their areas. At the village level, the *shaykh al-bilad* or the *umdah*, known in the English parlance of the day as the village headman or the village mayor, was the chief administrator, the connecting link between the central government and the village. He was aided in turn by other *shaykhs*, or administrative chiefs for the different sections of the village. For the purpose of maintaining village security the *shaykh al-bilad* recruited village policemen (*ghaffirs*). The *umdah* and *shaykhs* were traditionally recruited from the wealthiest and most influential village families.

Following their assumption of control over the Interior Ministry in 1895, the British inaugurated a campaign to reform village administration.[37] This effort stemmed from a general drive carried out by the British in this period

[36] Coles, *Reflections and Recollections*, p. 166.
[37] A detailed description of these reforms may be found in Lord Cromer, Annual Report for 1895, *HCSP*, Egypt No. 1 (1896), Vol. xcvii, c. 7978.

to reduce crime in the provinces. Kitchener, of the police administration, fostered a reform of the *ghaffirs*, the effect of which was to halve their numbers while increasing their pay. The hope was that more responsible citizens of the community would be attracted to undertake this work.[38] Gorst, at the Ministry of the Interior, introduced a scheme for associating the village communities and the Ministry in the selection of the *umdah*. It also regulated the powers of the *umdah* and the *shaykhs*, conferring judicial powers on the *umdah*. Periodically, new efforts were made to improve local administration, commonly spurred on by sharp increases in crimes of violence in the countryside. The most energetic program was that carried out in 1911, in which village *ghaffirs* were brought by the central government to provincial centers, given military training, and then equipped with light arms.[39] The import of the program in the villages was to render amateur officials there capable of discharging the increasingly complex and demanding functions of a modernizing state. The government could not afford financially to create and establish a professional bureaucracy. It had to make the best of what already existed; therefore, it attempted to ensure at least minimum standards of performance by giving some training to the amateur staffs and by paying larger salaries, thereby attracting more responsible individuals.

The problems of trying to adapt the traditional local administration to the more demanding requirements of Egypt under the occupation can be seen by examining the changing role and status of the *umdah* and the village barber. The *umdah*, throughout the first half of the nineteenth century had been responsible for preserving secu-

[38] Lord Cromer, Annual Report for 1896, *HCSP*, Egypt No. 2 (1897), Vol. cii, c. 8382.
[39] Lord Kitchener, Annual Report for 1911, *HCSP*, Egypt No. 1 (1912), Vol. cxxi, cd. 6149.

rity in the villages—collecting taxes, redistributing land, and calling out the *corvée*. His authority and respect rested in part on a leading-families tradition. It was also strengthened by his being able to mete out harsh, even arbitrary, punishment against those who threatened his position.

As Egyptian life began to change, so the role of the *umdah* changed. Many of the traditional responsibilities were taken out of his hands. The institution of forced labor was progressively abolished; even when in use after 1880, its recruitment was undertaken by the central government. Land was coming under a system of private property, thereby forcing the *umdah* to give up his power of redistributing the land periodically. Tax collection and recruitment for the army were taken over directly by the Ministries of War and Finance. At the same time, new responsibilities were added, such as enforcing sanitary regulations within the village or helping with the census counts, both duties clearly the result of new functions being performed by the state. Traditional duties—adjudication and maintaining security in the village—although still in the hands of the *umdah*, had to be discharged in a more precise fashion than previously. The right to try cases, for instance, was retained as part of the administrative duties of the *umdah* during the occupation and defined more rigidly. *Umdahs* were permitted to handle minor civil and criminal cases. In every area in which the *umdah* exercised power he was subject to constant surveillance by inspectors of the Ministries of the Interior, Finance, Justice, and Public Works. Violations of responsibilities were criminal offenses and could be punished severely. In sum, many old responsibilities were taken out of the *umdah's* hands; others remained and new ones were added, but the functions of the office were far more demanding than those of the past; they brought the *umdah* squarely into contact with numerous officials of the central government.[40]

Striking changes were also occurring in the sources of the *umdah's* power. In earlier periods, these sources had come from his traditional prestigious position within the community. Now, because of new tasks and because of the increased role of the centralized bureaucracy in the operation of the village community, more authority derived from the central government. The government played a role in the selection of the *umdah*, placing some emphasis on qualities of merit as well as birth. While it was not usually able to reward officeholders for their efficient discharge of duties, it could punish for failures. These changes tended to alter the traditional relationship of *umdah* to community, making him more an agent of the central government than a representative of the village and an extension of the family system.

The office of the *umdah* had been much sought after in the first half of the nineteenth century. As an administrative officer of the central government, the *umdah* was able to wield enormous power over his village community. This office continued to be an important one during the occupation, a cause of bitter strife among leading families competing for this position of power. Yet the administrative changes wrought by the British tended to diminish the prestige and influence of the office. The most far-reaching changes were those that deprived the *umdah* of traditional sources of revenue. In the first half of the century the *umdah* because of his control over the *corvée*, military recruiting, redistribution of land, and collection of the land tax, had been able to derive large profits from bribes. These functions were either taken

[40] See the article by Gabriel Baer, "The Village Shaykh in Modern Egypt (1800-1950)" *Scripta Hierosolymitana, Studies in Islamic History and Civilization*, Uriel Heyd, ed. (Jerusalem, 1961), IX, 121-53.

out of his hands entirely or were subject to more rigorous control from the central government, so that he ran risks of being caught if he attempted to take bribes from villagers. Under the new regulations the *umdah* was required to undertake more extensive responsibilities in certain areas, notably public health, security, and justice, and his performance was checked by an inspection system, breaches to be punished by commissions of discipline. Thus, the *umdah* still had fairly onerous duties but did not enjoy the rewards that traditionally went with the office. The remuneration provided by the government was not substantial. The *umdah* and members of his family were exempt from military service, or more precisely from the *rachat militaire,* an exemption all the wealthy paid for. Also, he did not have to pay land tax on five acres of his land.[41] The *umdah's* powers became so severely regulated by the government that the villagers were often able to flout his authority, even threaten his life, with the knowledge that he could not employ his former arbitrary powers. By the beginning of World War I the British recognized one of their problems as that of protecting the weakened *umdah* against his own villagers and rebuilding the prestige of the office. As one British official wrote: "The *umdah* has come to need protection. He is the servant of all and master of none, not even of his own home."[42]

The role of the sanitary barber in Egyptian society during the occupation is another clear example of efforts made to utilize traditional and amateur officials for more extensive and exacting functions. In traditional Egyptian society the sanitary barber played an important, if not always successful, role in whatever attempts were

[41] Lord Cromer, Annual Report for 1902, *HCSP*, Egypt No. 1 (1903), Vol. LXXXVII, cd. 1529.
[42] Lord Cromer, Annual Report for 1905, *HCSP*, Egypt No. 1 (1906), Vol. CXXXVII, cd. 2817.

made to preserve the health of the village community. With only apprentice training, he undertook to perform circumcisions and operations on the eye, to diagnose diseases and prescribe remedies. One of the European doctors, who served under Muhammad Ali, said of the barbers that they "had neither a sufficient preliminary education nor the means for studying the art which they practice because they have neither schools, nor libraries, and because they never engage in anatomical research. These men have no scientific notions, and they are guided only by the experience which they are able to acquire in a rather long practice."[43] In many cases, the remedies they prescribed for the cure of sickness had the contrary effect. Under Muhammad Ali and Ismail various programs were carried out to regulate the activities of the barbers and make them useful agents for the protection of the country's health. The most effective of these programs was one undertaken by Clot Bey in the reign of Muhammad Ali, to give barbers training in vaccinating against smallpox at provincial health centers. By 1882 the barbers were expected to state deaths, register births, vaccinate, and "assure the steady progress of the service."[44] In spite of their inadequacies they were clearly Egypt's only grassroots protection against disease.

The British studied plans to establish professional medical technicians in the villages, which were always rejected because of the expense and insufficiency of personnel. Rather, further efforts were made to give the barbers a modicum of training and to regulate their duties stringently. In 1893 barbers were required to take a three-week training course at a provincial hospital

[43] A. B. Clot Bey, *Aperçu Général sur l'Égypte* (Paris, 1840), II, 386.

[44] Salim to Khairy, No. 230, March 30, 1881, Egyptian Department of Public Health, copy letters, 4215, Egyptian Archives at the Citadel, Cairo.

and to pass an examination at the end of the course, in order to qualify for state registration.[45] Barbers were brought to the provincial hospitals, given a course in practical and rudimentary personal cleanliness, first aid, recognition of certain infectious diseases, and ophthalmology. After taking an exam for state certification, they were sent back to the provinces with a dispensary kit with which to perform minor operations and to prescribe certain cures for common and easily recognized ailments.[46] It was hoped that the barber, as the village health official, might discharge minor responsibilities with relative efficiency, and confine himself to these activities; the major tasks assigned the barbers were vaccination against smallpox, circumcision, and—most important— notification of the department's central inspectorate of any unusual increase in the death rate. This last duty was designed to alert the Department of Public Health against the possible outbreak and spread of infectious diseases, by calling their attention to any abnormal changes in the death rate in village communities.[47]

In actual practice, the sanitary barbers worked out about as well as the *umdahs*. Many of them reverted to their old ways and undertook tasks for which they were wholly unprepared. The rural populace, not educated enough nor wealthy enough to seek the assistance of the more qualified barbers, sought out cheaper, unqualified men. Quite a number of these uncertified barbers were able to carry on practices. Moreover, almost the entire local administration, from barber to *umdah*, balked at notifying the central government of unusual increases in the death rate, because they, along with the entire vil-

[45] Department of Public Health Archives, Departmental Orders, No. 61, April 11, 1893.

[46] Department of Public Health, *Annual Report*, 1911, p. 6.

[47] Department of Public Health Archives, Departmental Orders, No. 37, March 30, 1895.

lage, dreaded government interference. And the central inspectorate was not nearly large enough to ferret out and curb the repeated violations of the rules.[48]

[48] For an instructive survey of rural health practices and the role of the barber, see Muhammad Fakhr al-Din al-Subki, *Mudhakkirat Tabib fi al-Aryaf* [Memoirs of a Rural Doctor] (Cairo, 1946), which covers a period slightly later than that of the occupation.

CHAPTER VII

ADMINISTRATIVE PROGRESS, 1895-1907: AGRICULTURE AND IRRIGATION

THE DECADE 1895 to 1905 was a period of increasing prosperity in Egypt. Government revenues grew steadily. The financial position of the government was given a boost by the Anglo-French Accord of 1904, which gave the British a hitherto unknown financial and political freedom in Egypt.[1] According to this agreement, which was part of a larger reconciliation of issues between the English and the French, the French agreed that they would not obstruct British rule in Egypt by asking that the British fix a time limit on the occupation. Modifications were also made in the financial arrangements pertaining to Egypt. The mixed administrations, such as the railroads, the port of Alexandria, and the telegraphs, were abolished and brought under the direct control of the Egyptian government. The *Caisse de la Dette* was shorn of a great deal of its enormous power, by becoming only a receiver of payments on the debt. The land tax was now substituted for the different sources of revenue formerly set aside for the debt. Any surplus, after a reserve fund of £E1,800,000 had accumulated in the hands of the *Caisse*, was completely at the disposal of the government and could be employed for any purpose.[2]

In the late 1880's the foreign powers had negotiated basic changes in the interest rate on the Egyptian debt. Money saved by these changes in the interest rate had,

[1] Cromer, *Modern Egypt*, II, 388-93.
[2] *Journal Officiel*, December 1, 1904.

however, lain idle because the French and English governments could not agree how to spend it. According to the agreement of 1904, these conversion economies, totalling £E6,000,000, were turned over to the Egyptian government unconditionally.[3] The 1904 Accord was indeed a great turning point in the British occupation, as it gave the British considerable financial freedom, a more secure international position in Egypt, and a termination of official French opposition to British rule.

Two factors, however, continued to hamper the financial position of the Egyptian government, and consequently the amounts of money it could expend on reform programs. The first was the restriction on the amount of money the Egyptian government could borrow. In the reign of Ismail Egypt had finally won the right to borrow money without obtaining the consent of the Ottoman Sultan; but following the financial crises of the latter years of Ismail's rule, the Sultan had withdrawn this power from the Egyptian government. During the occupation Egypt was forbidden to borrow in excess of £E1 million without first engaging in protracted negotiations with the Ottoman Empire to obtain its consent. Since this procedure was not feasible (for the Ottomans could find a variety of reasons for withholding consent), the Egyptian government was thrown back on its own resources. Although this restriction did not keep Egypt from obtaining foreign capital, particularly in the form of private investment, the government itself was unable to borrow for its own capital expenditures. Thus, the Egyptian government was compelled to employ tax money for remunerative projects which otherwise would have been financed by foreign loans. Its budgetary expenditures were framed in the most conserv-

[3] Cromer to Lansdowne, No. 135, December 25, 1904, PRO, FO 78/5367.

ative fashion so that surpluses might be utilized as capital expenditure.[4]

The second factor impeding the financial development of the country was the Sudan. The defense of its frontier against hostile Mahdist forces was expensive to the Egyptian government. To Cromer and other British officials, there was never any doubt that Egypt would at some date have to reconquer the Sudan, since it was absolutely essential that no other European power hold the upper regions of the Nile from which it could threaten Egypt's water supply. At the same time, Cromer did not want Egypt to embark upon the reconquest until, having set its own finances in order, it could afford such an undertaking.

The decision to reconquer the Sudan, however, was forced on the Egyptian government before such a state had been attained in Egypt. In 1896 Italian troops which held part of East Africa were defeated by Mahdist forces at Kassala, and called upon the British to send a relief expedition. The Foreign Office at London, aware of French designs on the Upper Nile and the interests of other powers in this area, decided that the time was ripe to extend the influence of Egypt into the Sudan. Cromer, caught by surprise, bitterly resented this decision. At that time, he was planning for the construction of the Aswan Dam, an expensive undertaking, and had received assurances from the Foreign Office in 1895 that the Sudan expedition was not contemplated in the near future.[5] His pleas that the English government should bear a large part of the expense, or should help to release Egypt from some of its onerous international financial obligations, fell on deaf ears. Prime Minister Salis-

[4] The financial policies of the Egyptian government are discussed by Cromer in his Annual Report of 1906, *HCSP*, Egypt No. 1 (1907), Vol. c, cd. 3394.

[5] Rodd, *Social and Diplomatic Memories*, II, 86-87.

bury informed Cromer that the expedition would probably not be supported in England if British financial help were required.[6]

The reconquest of the Sudan was almost entirely financed by the Egyptian government and was undertaken for the most part by Egyptian troops commanded by British officers. The British army of occupation was strengthened during this period in order to release Egyptian troops for service in the Sudan, while Indian troops were brought to Egypt to hold the Eastern Sudan, thus releasing more Egyptian troops. The additional expense of the English and Indian troops was borne by the Egyptian government, in keeping with the financial arrangements between Egypt and Great Britain. England's contribution to an undertaking it considered vital was limited to a grant of £E800,000 and the dispatching of some English troops for action in the Sudan at the height of the campaign in 1898.

Once the Mahdists had been defeated and the French threat on the Nile repulsed, the Sudan was placed under the joint authority of Egypt and England in the Anglo-Egyptian condominium.[7] According to this arrangement, England and Egypt were jointly responsible for the pacification and administration of the Sudan. The British themselves were not prepared to assume full authority over the Sudan for financial reasons and because of prior Egyptian claims. At the same time, they elected not to treat the Sudan purely as an Egyptian conquest, because this would have entailed applying Egypt's international obligations, both financial and legal, to the Sudan. So it was decided to place the Sudan under dual Anglo-Egyptian authority. In practice, Egypt supplied

[6] Salisbury to Cromer, April 16, 1896, Cromer Papers, PRO, FO 633/7.

[7] Cromer to Salisbury, Nos. 14 and 15, January 2 and January 28, 1899, PRO, FO 78/5022.

the money for the administration of the Sudan while the British held the positions of authority and determined policies.

From 1898 until the First World War, Egypt turned over to the Sudan, unable to balance its own budget, large sums of money for its administrative development. Part of this money was appropriated to the Sudan as capital expenditure and was repaid later at a regular rate of interest. But a great deal of the money was given as an outright subsidy, without repayment, on the tenuous justification that since the pacification and development of the Sudan contributed to the welfare of Egypt, the Egyptian government could not begrudge money spent on it. Cromer, his successors, and the Governor-General of the Sudan, Reginald Wingate, were opposed to this policy which they felt worked to the detriment of Egypt, and they became increasingly resentful at being compelled to enforce it in the face of mounting criticism in Egypt.[8] They were especially bitter at the unwillingness of the British government to shoulder more of the military and financial burdens in the Sudan. While supplying men for leading administrative positions, the government refused to underwrite loans for the development of the Sudan and contributed a paltry number of troops to the joint military force located there. Nationalist critics of British rule were incensed by the arrangements of the condominium, for they saw desperately needed money siphoned off into the Sudan. They also recognized the sham of a condominium that was obviously dominated by the British.

It is difficult to obtain statistics on the amount of Egyptian money expended in the Sudan, for the British were reluctant to publish figures, and juggled those that *were* released. The Annual Report of 1909 does give a

[8] File 30903, memorandum by Gorst on the Sudan, August 19, 1908, PRO, FO 371/452.

general idea of the amount of money allotted to the Sudan up to this point. Financial appropriations continued

Egyptian Money Spent on the Sudan from 1899 to 1908[9]

	Advancements for capital expenditures	3 percent of capital exp.	annual subsidy
1899			£E439,800
1900			457,700
1901	£E121,000		417,000
1902	143,000	£E3,630	390,000
1903	129,000	7,920	380,000
1904	622,000	11,790	380,000
1905	750,000	30,450	380,000
1906	699,000	52,950	380,000
1907	922,000	73,920	380,000
1908	638,000	101,580	380,000
	£E4,024,000	£E282,240	£E3,994,500

Grand Total £E8,400,740

until the outbreak of World War I. They were one of the major reasons for the steady depletion of Egypt's large reserve fund, which had totalled over £E11,000,000 just after the financial accord of 1904.[10]

Agriculture and hydraulics derived the benefit of Egypt's increased prosperity. The motivations for the continuance of reforms in this area were much the same as they had been at the outset of the occupation, namely the British desire to ensure the financial stability and prosperity of the country. To these motivations, however, were now added the pressures from a variety of private, interested economic groups. Foreign financiers, again attracted to Egypt after financial solvency had been attained, saw immense areas of investment, both in the large-scale hydraulic undertakings planned by the British and in the expansion of Egyptian agriculture.

[9] Gorst, Annual Report for 1909, HCSP, Egypt No. 1 (1910), Vol. xci, cd. 672.
[10] Gorst, Annual Report for 1910, HCSP, Egypt No. 1 (1911), Vol. ciii, cd. 5633.

English textile manufacturers were eager to reap the benefits from an extension of cotton cultivation.

By 1890, at the time of the repair of the barrage, hydraulic engineers were aware that additional supplies of irrigation water would be needed. Scott-Moncrieff deputed William Willcocks, to study the various areas in Upper Egypt, to determine where a large water-storage dam could be constructed. After a survey, Willcocks, in his report, "Perennial Irrigation and Flood Protection," published in 1894, argued that the best site for a dam was at Aswan. The advantage of the site was that the bed was wide and divided into various channels. The water could be diverted from one channel to another, enabling engineers to lay the foundations of the dam in the dry. Also, a broad dike of hard syenite granite crossed the Nile Valley at Aswan, forming the first cataract. This rock would provide a solid base on which to build the dam. Willcocks' plans called for a dam capable of storing 85 billion cubic feet of water. The dam was intended to provide summer irrigation water and at the same time not to interrupt the flow of the winter flood waters. It would, therefore, have to be designed to pass flood waters through it and then to store water during the low Nile summer season. The increased water supply would ensure the cotton crop of Lower Egypt, permit the reclamation of more land in the delta, and enable the government to convert large tracts of land in Middle and Upper Egypt to perennial irrigation. Most of Upper and Middle Egypt, except those areas irrigated by the Ibrahimiyah canal, still used the basin system of irrigation and did not raise summer crops.[11]

The major engineering problem faced in preparing

[11] There are numerous sources for the study of the Aswan Dam. Much of the material here is drawn from an article by William Willcocks, "Irrigation in the Nile Valley and its Future," *International Engineering Congress*, Glasgow, 1901.

plans for the Aswan Dam was that of designing its sliding gates so that they would be large enough to pass the enormous quantities of flood waters through them. The engineers did not want to store the flood waters because they brought sedimentation to the Egyptian soil and because the engineers feared that if these waters were stored, the sedimentation would be precipitated out of the water, fall at the base of the dam, and eventually cause it to silt up. Willcocks was sent to Europe to investigate the various irrigation gates in use there. He found one that ideally suited Egypt's needs. Sliding gates designed by F. M. Stoney for the Manchester Ship Canal, fitted the conditions in Egypt. The dam was to have 180 sluiceways spaced along it, a number of which were to be 23 feet high and 6½ feet wide. When the reservoir was full, the total thrust of the water on a single gate would be one to two hundred tons.[12]

Willcocks' report engendered furious controversy in Europe (on the same order but far more intense than the objections of the 1960's to Egypt's new high dam at Aswan which will submerge many of Egypt's archeological treasures). The dam projected by Willcocks would have submerged Philae Island and one of Egypt's most spectacular archeological treasures, Philae Temple. The controversy was carried in Europe's leading newspapers and periodicals, with European archeologists almost unanimously opposed to the dam. Although engineers argued that Egypt's present needs were more compelling than the preservation of its ancient monuments, the Egyptian government was hesitant to support this expert opinion in the face of such adverse criticism. "For once and only once, I fear, since we occupied Egypt in 1882," wrote Scott-Moncrieff, "was educated opinion in England and France at one. Both insisted that Philae should not

[12] Herbert Addison, *Sun and Shadow at Aswan* (London, 1959), p. 36.

be drowned."[13] In order to obtain the advice of outside observers, Scott-Moncrieff established an international commission, composed of a French, an English, and an Italian engineer, but their work did not lead to a successful resolution of the problems. In the midst of all these difficulties Egypt embarked upon the Sudan campaign, and Cromer feared that funds could not be found for the construction of the dam.

Brushing aside these difficulties, however, Cromer decided in 1898 to give his approval to the project. One of the major reasons was his realization that Egypt would have to increase its revenues if it was to finance the development of the Sudan.[14] As a concession to foreign critics the hydraulic engineers reluctantly agreed to reduce the size of the dam so that Philae Temple would not be totally submerged. They also engaged to take pictures of the antiquities to be submerged and to protect some of the more outstanding monuments against the water. The reduced dam would store 35 billion feet of water, less than half of the original capacity, but would still allow for the introduction of perennial irrigation into large areas of Upper and Middle Egypt.

The problem of financing the dam proved serious, but the resourceful Cromer devised a plan for its solution. Unable to borrow because of Egypt's financial arrangements, and unable to obtain all the necessary funds from the reserve fund of the *Caisse*, Cromer obtained money from one of Europe's great financiers, Ernest Cassel, on the stipulation that the loan was to be paid back over 30 years. Aird and Company, an English construction firm, undertook to build the dam. The dam was begun in 1898 and completed in 1902. Although the engineers

[13] Scott-Moncrieff, "On the Nile," *Proceedings of the Royal Institution of Great Britain*, 1895, Vol. xiv, 417.

[14] Cromer to Salisbury, No. 286, November 12, 1897, Cromer Papers, PRO, FO 633/6.

had estimated that the construction would cost £E2,-000,000, the total cost came to £E3,500,000.[15]

The dam immediately proved its value to Egypt. The flood of 1905 was extremely low, and it was feared that the summer supply would prove insufficient. The dam was put into use and the irrigation waters were distributed throughout Egypt without difficulty.[16] The decline in the amount of *sharaki* land, i.e., regularly arable and taxable land not cultivated because of a lack of water, also attested to the importance of the dam. The lands in Upper and Middle Egypt were prepared for perennial irrigation by the introduction of the necessary weirs and subsidiary canals by 1910.

Scarcely had the dam been completed before demands for its heightening were heard. According to Egypt's hydraulic expert at this time, William Garstin, the dam at its present height provided only one-quarter of Egypt's summer irrigation requirements. Heightening by seven meters would more than double its storage capacity and would ensure the delta region of all its irrigation needs.[17] The new construction would have to be placed on top of the old and British engineers feared that the masonry of the two structures, with different thermal rates, would expand and contract at differing rates. A stroke of engineering genius was devised by Benjamin Baker. The new masonry of the dam was kept separate from the rest of the dam by means of iron rods inserted into the sloping face of the existing dam until its thermal rate of expansion was the same as that of the rest. These rods gave temporary support to the new layer of masonry, leaving an intervening space of about six inches to be filled in

[15] Cromer, Annual Report for 1903, *HCSP*, Egypt No. 1 (1904), Vol. cxi, cd. 1951.

[16] Cromer, Annual Report for 1905, *HCSP*, Egypt No. 1 (1906), Vol. cxxxvii, cd. 2817.

[17] Note by Garstin on the Egyptian water supply, *HCSP*, Egypt No. 2 (1907), Vol. c, cd. 3397.

with graded broken stone. After this matter had solidified, the two constructions were amalgamated.[18] The heightening of the dam was carried out from 1907 to 1912, with a second heightening in the 1930's.

The conquest of the Sudan opened up further opportunities for harnessing the Nile. In 1902 William Garstin made a hydrological trip up the Nile. His report was a pathfinding study by an expert engineer, the first of its kind for the upper regions of the Nile, and laid the foundations for the further development of the Nile.[19] Garstin was keenly interested in learning more about the two major branches of the Nile, the White Nile with its headwaters in the Central Lakes region and the Blue Nile flowing from the hills of Ethiopia. His investigations immensely increased Egypt's knowledge of the behavior of the Nile, showing in great detail, for instance, that it was the swollen Blue Nile that produced flood conditions in Egypt, the White Nile maintaining a fairly steady flow throughout the year. These findings also revealed that the marshes and mass of vegetation in the upper regions of the White Nile, known as the Sudd, blocked the flow of the Nile in this area and were responsible for the loss of a considerable amount of water through evaporation. Garstin put forward recommendations for the further development of the Nile, recommendations that were to be adhered to carefully throughout the next two decades. The major suggestions were that the waters of the White Nile should be utilized for Egypt and those of the Blue Nile, when it was not in flood, for the Sudan. The first projects on the Upper Nile, he felt, would be clearing operations in the Sudd, then a barrage across the Blue Nile. Garstin recommended that the greatest emphasis in these years, while the Sudan was still financially dependent on Egypt, should be devoted to Egypt's

[18] Addison, *Sun and Shadow at Aswan*, pp. 63-64.
[19] *HCSP*, Egypt No. 2 (1904), Vol. cxi, cd. 2165.

irrigation needs in the Upper Nile. The Sudan's irrigation staff was to be limited to £E24,000.[20]

The reconquest of the Sudan also permitted the Egyptian hydraulic service to obtain more accurate information about the amounts of water that would reach Egypt from the upper regions of the Blue and White Niles throughout the year. Gauges were established along both the Blue and White Nile from their sources to Egypt. Readings in the upper regions of the Nile enabled the irrigation service to predict the amount of water available in Egypt before it arrived and to make the necessary adjustments in the distribution of this water throughout the country. When Kitchener was appointed Consul-General in 1911, he took a special interest in the irrigation problem. The transfer of a number of men from the survey department into the irrigation service, including physicists like Harold Hurst, who had statistical knowledge about Nile floods, enabled the irrigation service to make more accurate calculations on the future behavior of the Nile. The general approach was to obtain as much statistical information on the behavior of the Nile as possible, not only from the gauge readings but also from the previous records of the Nile. On the basis of this information the irrigation service could predict with relatively high accuracy the quantities of water available for Egyptian irrigation throughout the year. Then, through the rotation of water in the irrigation canals, restrictions against growing crops that consumed large quantities of water other than cotton, and other techniques the available water could be distributed so that the crops most profitable to Egypt would be grown in maximum quantities.[21]

[20] The major lines of this report were reaffirmed in an equally famous study of the Nile, published by the Egyptian government in 1920.

[21] Harold Hurst, *The Nile, passim.*

The cultivation of cotton increased during these years. By 1912 cotton accounted for 80.1 percent of Egyptian exports in comparison with the figure of 66.6 percent in 1884. Cotton came to occupy such a large part of the agricultural life of the country that grain products, which made up 25.8 percent of Egyptian exports in 1884, accounted for only 15.5 percent in 1912.[22] With an increasing population, the country lost its self-sufficiency in grain production, and was compelled to import a considerable amount of foodstuffs. The introduction of perennial irrigation into Middle and Upper Egypt enabled cotton to be grown in these areas. The total revenue derived from the sale of cotton throughout the occupation grew despite variations in prices.

Cotton Cultivation[23]

Year	Cultivated Area (*feddans*)	Crop (*qantars*)	Middle Price	Total Value
1885		3,629,000	£E3.00	£E12,808,000
1890		4,159,000	2.27	11,107,000
1895	998,000	5,276,000	2.24	13,426,000
1900	1,230,000	5,435,000	2.76	17,503,000
1905	1,567,000	5,960,000	3.20	21,704,000
1910	1,643,000	7,505,000	4.13	35,667,000

Egyptian cotton, because of its strength, uniformity of fiber, length, elasticity, and fineness, was recognized as one of the highest quality cottons on the world market. The various strains of Egyptian cotton ranked with the Sea Island cotton, produced in the United States, and sold at the highest prices.[24] These quality cottons were

[22] Myer Ornstein, "Cotton Notes," *Cairo Scientific Journal*, 1914, pp. 17-22. Ornstein analyzed the trade statistics for these years and showed that while grains and other commodities fell off in export value relative to cotton, the actual revenue realized from these exports did, in fact, increase during the occupation.

[23] Egypt, Ministry of Public Works, *Irrigation Service*, p. 89.

[24] G. P. Foaden, "Notes on the Botany of Cotton," *Journal of the Khedivial Agricultural Society*, 1899, pp. 49-67.

used primarily where high resistance cotton was required. Lower grade cottons were not produced in Egypt, but were grown mainly in the United States and India. From the time of the development of the high grade cotton in Egypt in the reign of Muhammad Ali, various strains of this type of cotton appeared, one replacing the other as the quality of the strain declined. During the occupation the most widely cultivated strains were *Mit Afif* and *Ashmouni*, the latter being grown extensively in Upper Egypt. In the decade before the First World War new strains of cotton with special features were developed; the most popular were *Abyad, Gallini,* and *Abbasi*—the last a high-quality white cotton, in contrast to the other brown Egyptian cottons, competitor with the white Sea Island cotton produced in the United States.[25]

Cotton yields, according to admittedly questionable statistics, had been on the rise from the end of Ismail's reign until the mid-1890's. These yields, however, began to fall steadily from then until World War I. Inadequate statistics notwithstanding, the decline of cotton yields indicated by the Ministry of Public Works cannot be refuted. The more controlled statistics of the government state farms further corroborated these findings, showing that even on the well irrigated and scientifically farmed lands of the government there was an alarming decline.

Cotton Yield 1895-1906[26]

Years	Average Yield Per *Feddan*
1895-1897	5.55 *qantars*
1898-1900	5.01
1901-1903	4.85
1904-1906	4.29

[25] Lawrence Balls, *The Cotton Plant in Egypt* (London, 1912), p. 5.

[26] Gorst, Annual Report for 1907, *HCSP,* Egypt No. 1 (1908), Vol. cxxv, cd. 3966.

These quite unexpected results proved to be the most serious agricultural problem faced by the Egyptian government in the decade preceding the First World War. A group of first-rate scientists was brought to Egypt in connection with this problem, one of whom, Lawrence Balls, laid the foundations for later research on cotton. The scientific investigations carried out in this period ranged over a great variety of subjects, but most were closely related to the general decline of cotton yields. Part of the decline was explained simply by the fact that new lands being brought under cultivation on the fringe of the best land did not allow for the customary high crop yields. Other contributory but secondary causes were the regular distribution of inferior grades of seed, attacks by cotton pests such as the cotton worm and the bollworm, and overplanting of cotton with consequent depletion of the soil. By means of experiments carried out in the first decade of the twentieth century, Balls isolated what he and many other subsequent researchers considered to be the major factors: excessive irrigation and inadequate drainage of the soil; both caused large quantities of water to remain on the soil and produced a rising of the water table. When this water reached the surface it left salt deposits, making cultivation nearly impossible. In other areas high sub-soil water, which was brought into contact with the roots of the cotton plant, affected the crop yields of the cotton plant. Balls' findings placed a primary emphasis upon controlled watering of the crop and rapid removal of water through drainage canals, once it had been used.[27]

In the period 1900 to 1914, steps were taken to bring the problem of declining cotton yields under control. The government undertook a campaign to convince cultivators of the harmful effects of cultivating cotton more

[27] Egypt, Department of Agriculture, *Preliminary Report on Field Experiments*, 1912, pp. 3-4.

than once every three years. According to a report published in 1911 cotton yields were considerably higher if cotton was planted once every three years and followed bersim in the crop rotation.[28] Cotton was to be raised only after the soil had been reinvigorated by other crops. Cultivators were also encouraged to employ manures on the soil. Although the *fellahin* had used homemade manures to enhance crop yields, the first chemical fertilizers imported from Europe, were not employed until the turn of the century. But from that time they were used increasingly in Egypt, with the large and wealthy proprietors leading the way. The government also undertook to ensure the distribution of superior grades of seed at cheap prices to the *fellahin*. It took high-quality seeds from its state farms and distributed them to farmers throughout the country. Small landowners, who usually purchased inferior grades of seed from village merchants and money-lenders, were encouraged to accept government seed, arranging for the payment of the seed at the time government taxes were collected. Campaigns were also begun to stamp out the cotton worm and the bollworm. Finally, drainage projects and controls on the amounts of water that reached the soil were designed to lower the sub-soil water level. Although all of these plans were put into effect before 1914, it was not until after World War I that crop yields slowed in their decline.[29]

The problems encountered in cotton production and in other areas of Egyptian agricultural life convinced the government of the need to increase its agricultural, as distinct from its hydraulic, personnel. Prior to the turn of the century nearly all of Egypt's agricultural needs were handled by hydraulic engineers, with an understandable neglect of agricultural requirements. In 1898 lead-

[28] *Agricultural Journal of Egypt*, 1911, p. 33.
[29] Kitchener, Annual Report for 1911, *HCSP*, Egypt No. 1 (1912), Vol. cxxi, cd. 6149.

ing Egyptian landlords formed an Agricultural Society, a private group, to undertake with its own personnel and funds research and technical programs in agriculture.[30] The government helped to support the meager budget of the Society with subsidies, but tried to resist the mounting pressure, as agricultural difficulties increased, to create a government department of agriculture. *Laissez-faire* attitudes predisposed the British to favor private initiative over governmental interference for the solution of these problems. Finally in 1910, the British succumbed to the pressures by agreeing to bring an agricultural adviser to Egypt, an expert in the cultivation of cotton and later by creating an agriculture department.[31] The Agriculture Department soon assembled a solid core of research workers. Although these men were not able to conduct basic research in a large number of areas, they did investigate problems of special importance to Egypt and attempt to adapt the discoveries of European science for Egyptian use.

At the time, and in subsequent years, the critics of the occupation have charged the British with attempting to convert Egypt into a cotton farm for the factories of Lancashire. To be sure, cotton did become more of the primary source of wealth and export during the occupation. And there can be no doubt about the constant interest of the Lancashire industrialists in both Egypt and the Sudan as cotton-growing areas. But, in truth, the percentage of land planted with cotton in proportion to the total of cultivated land did not alter as radically as one might have imagined. The percentage planted in cotton doubled between 1879 and 1913, but that on which maize (corn) was grown also increased rapidly. Wheat, beans, and barley declined, but the actual amount of land plant-

[30] *Journal of the Khedivial Agricultural Society*, 1899, p. 1.
[31] Gorst to Nicholson, file 47209, December 24, 1910, PRO, FO 371/895.

ed in these crops did not drop appreciably. Bersim remained about the same. The significant shifts occurred

Distribution of Crops in Egypt[32]

Crop	1879 (feddans)	Per-centage	1899	Per-centage	1913	Per-centage
cotton	495,707	11.5	1,153,307	16.4	1,723,094	22.4
maize	601,217	14.0	1,559,659	22.4	1,852,760	24.0
rice	40,891	0.9	217,426	3.1	242,367	3.1
wheat	890,699	20.6	1,214,052	17.6	1,305,577	16.9
beans	616,317	14.1	637,752	9.1	478,187	6.2
barley	490,565	11.5	536,416	7.6	369,159	4.8
sugarcane	45,999	1.1	86,529	1.2	48,468	0.6
bersim, vegetables and others	1,133,400	26.3	1,600,570	22.8	1,672,800	23.0
Total	4,314,855		7,032,711		7,712,412	

in the export patterns of Egypt, with cotton supplanting all other products, and with certain grains ceasing to be exported—even being imported—between 1900 and 1914.

The reason for the changes in exports was closely related to the growth of the population, which rose from an estimated 9,715,000 in 1897 to 12,751,000 in 1917. The population could have been fed without the import of grain only by limiting the cultivation of cotton, but this would have meant a reduction in the total amount of wealth produced on the land and a general lowering of standards of living. The Agricultural Department, with its limited research facilities, did not experiment extensively on the suitability of new crops in Egypt. Also, it must be admitted that cotton was, and has continued to be, the best money crop in Egypt. Experiments in the cultivation of other export crops, such as rice and sugar, did not give promising results. Rice consumed far too

[32] Taken from A. E. Crouchley, *The Economic Development of Modern Egypt* (New York, 1937), p. 164.

much irrigation water and was suited only to the marsh lands of the delta. Although sugar cultivation expanded intermittently in Upper Egypt, it could not compete with the superior cash-producing ability of cotton. The real problem in agricultural spheres was not that cotton was grown to the exclusion of other wealth-producing crops, but that the cotton crop tied the Egyptian economy to a fluctuating world market, over which Egypt, as a large producer but not as the largest producer of cotton, had only a slight influence. When prices were high, Egyptian cultivators realized substantial profits. But a dip in prices cut these profits, often bringing many peasant cultivators to the verge of bankruptcy, particularly the small land-holders, profligate by habit and ignorant of the workings of the world market. Purely by chance in the late 1880's and the early 1890's, cotton prices on the world market were declining, while cotton yields were rising. Conversely, while market prices were ascending to new heights in the two decades before World War I, cotton yields were diminishing.[33] The Egyptian government, operating mainly on its *laissez-faire* philosophy, did not endeavor to stabilize cotton prices paid to cultivators, much as was done throughout the twentieth-century colonial world by the creation of marketing boards.

❋

The agricultural and hydraulic developments of the British occupation wrought vast changes in rural Egypt and in the daily lives of the peasants. Perennial irrigation, supplanting the old basin system, meant that water no longer remained on the fields for a month of the year, but was carried to the fields in large irrigation canals and applied to the land as needed. This change, in turn, made it no longer necessary for the houses of villages to

[33] Gorst, Annual Report for 1909, *HCSP*, Egypt No. 1 (1910), Vol. cxii, cd. 5121.

be huddled together in elevated patches of land solely for protection from flood waters. Rather, it became possible to build homes and small villages on low-lying land, quite close to the arable fields.[34] Peasants now had to farm throughout the year without interruption. They had to master new problems created by the system of perennial irrigation: crop rotation, fertilizing, the proper watering and drainage of the soil.

The cultivation of cotton produced an immense transformation in the life of the Egyptian peasantry. Before the introduction of perennial irrigation and the cultivation of cash crops, the farming requirements of grain crops had been relatively simple. Cotton, however, was a demanding crop; its cultivation required more precise knowledge and care than the peasantry had been used to giving to farming. Before cultivation, the soil had to be prepared with great attention. It was ploughed; then, after the first watering, it was divided into ridges into which the cotton seeds were planted with a precise spacing. Subsequent waterings were required at regular intervals and with fixed quantities of water, for irregular irrigation affected the growth rate of the plant and its yield. The peasant had to keep close watch on his field during the growing season, at first to eliminate inferior cotton plants and replant in their places, and throughout to guard against cotton pests. When pests were discovered, the peasant, with the assistance of the government, was expected to eradicate the pests without destroying the cotton plants. Cotton cultivation imposed upon the peasantry a vast new set of work routines, a peasantry that was, however, able to adapt to the new requirements with only a fair degree of success. The declining crop yields revealed that many peasants grew cotton more frequently than was advantageous, that

[34] Jean Lozach and G. Hug, *L'Habitat Rural en Égypte* (Cairo, 1930), *passim.*

they failed to notify the government of the outbreak of attacks on the plants, used inferior grades of seeds, and watered their crops more often than required. The larger estates, on which approximately 70 percent of Egypt's cotton was grown, had considerably more success, for here peasant cultivators followed the directives laid down by the large landholder or his farm manager.[35]

New developments in agriculture brought an increase in the mechanization of Egyptian agriculture. More steam pumps were employed to raise water, especially on the large estates, in place of the traditional instruments: the *Shaduf, Sakis,* and Archimedean screw. On scientifically farmed state lands a host of farm machinery was used, from seed drills to reapers and threshers. More commonly, the traditional instruments of the *fellahin*—the hoe, plough, and winnowing machine—were improved. Nevertheless, Egyptian farming continued to be performed by means of *petite culture,* that is, by means of small plot farming, intensive use of manpower with a consequent small use of farm machinery. Even on large estates the most common system was to use a large number of tenant farmers to cultivate the soil with their time-honored farming implements. Some of the government farms were cultivated by modern farming machinery and with as little manpower as possible, much as farming was done in parts of Europe and the United States. But these large, scientifically farmed estates were run at a loss to the government and were justified only because they were agricultural experiment centers. In 1914 a British agricultural specialist, after studying conditions in Egypt, came to the conclusion that "the policy of direct [state] farming of large scattered estates in a high state of cultivation is condemned both by reason and by experience. . . . There can be no reasonable doubt that

[35] *Agricultural Journal of Egypt,* 1911, pp. 29-38.

petite culture will maximize the output of the soil and add to what may be called the national dividend, will support a larger population, will be of greater permanent benefit to the soil, and while lessening the administrative burden on the shoulders of the government will yield a larger net return to the treasury."[36]

Another disturbing problem confronting the British in the realm of agriculture was that of peasant indebtedness, leading to the expropriation of the peasant's land by moneylenders. In pre-nineteenth-century Egyptian society this problem did not exist in such an acute form. Although the moneylender played an important role in making capital available to the villagers, the land, communally-shared rather than privately owned, could not be given to the moneylender as security for a loan. It was held that the moneylender took great risks when lending and therefore was justified in charging extremely high rates of interest. This situation was altered with the growth of the system of private property and the establishment of modern courts in the nineteenth century. The creation of the Mixed Tribunals in 1875 proved a great boon for the moneylenders, many of whom were foreign subjects; for the purpose of recovering debts, they could now carry their cases to the courts and expropriate land for nonpayment. Actually most moneylenders preferred to "nurse" debtors along, turning them into a kind of bonded servant or tenant farmer. The *fellahin* continued to rely on the moneylenders for their capital needs, using the money for a variety of purposes, some quite necessary, such as the purchase of tools and seeds; others such as social life and personal prestige, were not so, at least in the eyes of the British. These latter uses included borrowing money for lavish feasts and ceremonies on important moments

[36] Report on the State Domains by Henry Higgs, Inspector-General, March 2, 1913, Wingate Papers, Box 179/8.

in the life of the family: births, deaths, weddings, circumcisions; but most important, for the purchase of additional pieces of land. Land was, in fact, the most highly valued object in Egyptian peasant communities, a mark of great prestige; peasants were willing to risk their futures to acquire an object which would increase their standing in the community.[37]

Dufferin was aware of the problem of peasant indebtedness when he wrote his report on Egypt; he regarded indebtedness as a major threat to the stability and tranquility of the population.[38] Cromer recognized the seriousness of the issue, but for a long time he treated the problem as insoluble: "As to indebtedness of the *fellahin*, the question whether from the political or economic point of view is one of the first importance. I doubt whether anything short of taking away an absolute right of property in the soil and giving the *fellah* a life interest only will prevent the accrual of a large expropriated peasantry."[39] During this period he attempted to show in his official reports that indebtedness was much more widespread among wealthy landowners than among the small landholders. This position was apparently inaccurate, as the British themselves came to realize in the 1890's.[40] The traditional practice was for the *fellahin* to borrow money at incredibly high rates of interest—20 to 30 percent—from village moneylenders; then, when unable to make payments, to come to some arrangement with the moneylenders, by which the *fellahin* became tenant farmers for their creditors.

Cromer realized early that the basic problem was the

[37] Hamed Ammar, *Growing up in an Egyptian Village* (London, 1954), p. 21.

[38] Dufferin to Granville, No. 71, February 6, 1883, Granville Papers, PRO 30/29/287/10.

[39] Baring to Granville, September 27, 1883, Granville Papers, PRO 30/29/161.

[40] Lord Cromer, Annual Reports from 1900 to 1906, *HCSP*.

peasants' need for capital, and that the only way in which they could be aided would be to make available an alternate, cheaper source of capital. For many years he believed that no such supply could be established, primarily because of the extravagance of the peasants, the difficulty of collecting interest, and—where defaulting occurred—of expropriating the land and reselling it. In the early years of the occupation some agricultural capital was supplied by the *Credit Foncier,* a French-supported agricultural bank which at its inception had floated small loans to the *fellahin,* but at such a loss that it had established £E300 as its minimum loan.

In 1895 Cromer was finally persuaded to use government funds on an experimental basis for small loans to peasants. The British considered the experiment successful, and a privately endowed, but government-supported, National Bank assumed responsibility for agricultural loans in 1898.[41] By 1902 the operations of the National Bank had grown so large that a separate Agricultural Bank was created with £E2,500,000 capitalization. Its loans were divided into two categories: those for less than £E20, secured by the borrower's note of hand; and those not exceeding £E500, secured by a first mortgage on land. Loans were to be negotiated by government agents whose payment was to be 1 percent of the interest rate.[42] The interest on loans was fixed at 9 percent with interest and principal being collected by tax collecting agents at the same time that taxes were collected. The first years of the Agricultural Bank proved to be most successful; the much-feared defaulting on payments did not materialize and the Bank increased its outlays to small proprietors. The Bank loaned over £E3,000,000 in the decade 1900 to 1910, a substantial capital influx

[41] Cromer, Annual Report for 1898, *HCSP,* Egypt No. 3 (1899), Vol. cxii, c. 9231.

[42] Gorst to Grey, March 20, 1909, PRO, FO 368/284.

into rural areas, but the vast majority of these loans were between £E20 and £E50, and were well beyond the reach of the small landholders in whose interest the Bank had theoretically been formed. In 1903, for example, only 759 persons received loans of £E1 and under and only 5,963 got loans of £E1 to £E5, while 53,481 owners received loans from £E20 to £E50. It is to be doubted that the small landowner could afford to borrow between £E20 and £E50.[43] The recipients of the loans, therefore, were owners of medium and large estates. In spite of this imbalance in the granting of loans, Egypt was at this time enjoying unprecedented financial and economic prosperity. Money was readily available for all kinds of loans, and a large part of the money on loan from the Agricultural Bank was used to liquidate debts to village moneylenders. In 1906 and 1907 the Egyptian economy faltered; credit facilities were reduced, and the Agricultural Bank began to experience difficulties in collecting outstanding debts. By 1909 the situation had become so bad that arrears represented 17 percent of the annuity for new loans, whereas they had been only 3 percent in 1904.[44] The reasons for the failure of the Agricultural Bank were by this time quite clear. Without a staff to investigate the resources of the loan applicants and the purposes for which loans were being contracted, the government had no security on its outlays. The one percent profit paid to officials who negotiated the loans was a positive incentive to pursue an extravagant policy. Without doubt, a large portion of the money floated by the Agricultural Bank was used to pay off previous debts to village moneylenders, with only a small proportion being used to develop the land. Moreover, the recourse

[43] Cromer, Annual Report for 1903, *HCSP*, Egypt No. 1 (1904), Vol. cxi, cd. 1951.

[44] Gorst, Annual Report for 1909, *HCSP*, Egypt No. 1 (1910), Vol. cxii, cd. 5121.

the government had for default of payment was quite inadequate. Expropriation of *fellahin* land entailed costly legal proceedings, and left the government with land which it either had to sell or lease.

When Kitchener was appointed Consul-General in 1911 he quickly adopted a completely different approach to the problem of indebtedness. As part of a general law designed to facilitate the whole procedure of expropriating the land of debtors, Kitchener passed the famous Five *Feddans* Law. According to this law, which was inspired by the Punjab Land Alienation Act passed in India in the early twentieth century, peasants owning five *feddans* of land or less could not have their land, houses, or equipment expropriated.[45] The law was designed to protect and win the favor of small landholders in Egypt, by removing one of their greatest sources of discontent. The project aroused criticism from almost all of the influential groups in Egypt. Cromer, no longer on the scene, heartily opposed on the grounds that the law was unenforcible without a large staff of inspectors. The Agricultural Bank was the most bitter critic, as its owners feared that the law would virtually put it out of business since it would no longer be in a position to make loans to small landowners.[46] Other groups, including many of the small landholders, argued that the peasantry would no longer have access to sorely needed capital at legal, low rates of interest; that they would turn again to the village moneylenders; and that, while not having their holdings expropriated outright, would still become virtually bonded servants of these moneylenders.

The outbreak of World War I interrupted the operation of the law before it could be evaluated accurately.

[45] Text of the Five *Feddans* Law is to be found in KK 1, Kitchener Papers, PRO 30/57/42.

[46] Cheetham to Grey, No. 106, September 21, 1912, PRO, FO 407/76.

The evidence both from this period and after the war, while the law was still in force, seemed to suggest that the criticisms of Kitchener's scheme were well founded. The law was unenforcible in the majority of cases, as Cromer had predicted. The purpose of the Agricultural Bank had been undercut by the new law, and the Bank gradually passed out of existence. Moreover, various devices of the moneylenders, short of outright expropriation, deprived the peasants of real control over their land. What was needed was a change in peasant mentality and habits: an end to extravagance and fatalism. Another attempt at providing a cheap supply of capital was not to be forthcoming until agricultural cooperatives were created after World War I and the government once again undertook to make small loans.[47]

Throughout the nineteenth century—until the British occupation—there had been a tendency in Egypt toward the growth of large estates in the hands of the wealthy, with the royal families as the greatest beneficiaries. This development had occurred partly as a result of conscious policy by the ruling class, desirous of obtaining ownership of the land, and partly as a result of social and economic changes in this century—that is, the break-up of village solidarity, the creation of private property, and the establishment of the Mixed Tribunals. Accompanying all of this was the decrease of the size of plots held by the mass of the population and the increase of the number of tenant farmers.

The British indicated their opposition to the situation. They felt a natural sympathy for the *fellahin*; they feared a discontented peasantry as a threat to their position in Egypt. The desire of many British officials was to create a class of small peasant proprietors, contented with, and supporters of, British rule. In order to create

[47] M. A. Rifaat, *The Monetary System of Egypt* (London, 1935), p. 152.

this class, however, the British would have had to oppose the existing trend toward the accumulation of land in the hands of the few, and would have had to see that the holdings of the smaller proprietors were adequately protected. The schemes to reduce peasant indebtedness and to prevent the expropriation of peasant land were, in fact, steps in this direction. Nevertheless, the British were not able to break the prevailing trend. During 30 years of occupation there was the continued growth of larger estates, the continued impoverishment of the small peasantry by the reduction of landholdings, and the loss of proprietary rights. Statistics here are trustworthy only as general indicators, but they clearly show that the vast majority of Egyptian landowners owned

Distribution of Land in 1900[48]

Area	Europeans		Egyptians	
	Number	*Feddans*	Number	*Feddans*
below 5 feddans	2,416	4,877	758,891	1,108,534
5 to 10	792	5,892	79,979	554,303
10 to 20	717	10,724	38,993	540,056
20 to 30	372	9,224	11,895	292,110
30 to 50	467	18,337	8,523	326,428
above 50	1,553	537,095	10,386	1,706,478
	6,347	586,149	908,067	4,527,903

Distribution of Land in 1913

Area	Number	*Feddans*	Number	*Feddans*
below 5 feddans	4,054	6,527	1,407,104	1,412,432
5 to 10	824	5,963	75,513	522,743
10 to 20	601	8,083	36,022	496,661
20 to 30	345	8,541	10,810	262,844
30 to 50	381	15,133	8,008	312,845
above 50	1,586	657,833	10,972	1,762,725
	7,791	702,833	1,548,519	4,770,250

[48] Tables drawn from Égypte, Ministère des Finances, Departement de la Statistique Générale, *Annuaire Statistique de l'Égypte*, 1914, p. 320.

less than five *feddans* that this group was on the increase, and that a relatively small group of wealthy European and Egyptian landowners held most of the land in Egypt. Between 1900 and 1913 the number of landowners holding less than five *feddans* nearly doubled, but the amount of land held by this group increased only by approximately 25 percent. The average size of the holding among these small landowners fell from 1.5 *feddans* to 1.0. At the same time the number of large and medium landholders (50 *feddans* and above) and the amount of land held remained fairly static.

There were four basic causes for the inability of the British to realize their goals: the *laissez-faire* attitudes of the British; the influence of foreign elements and the established classes in Egypt; financial and political pressures on the government; and the steady growth of the population.

In the first place, the British had a basic belief in the sanctity of private property. They believed in the free operation of a market economy, in the right of the individual to buy and to dispose of property freely. In fact, the British abolished some of the remaining restrictions against holding private property. They felt that one of the important duties of the state was to secure and defend private property. For this reason, therefore, they could hardly have espoused the idea that the state had the right to limit the size of estates or to attempt to take land from large landowners in order to redistribute it among the peasantry. This kind of action would constitute, in the minds of British officials, an overstepping of the legitimate powers of the government, a violation of the principles of limited government and *laissez-faire*.

Although the government was not prepared to undertake radical redistribution of the land, it did play an important role in the distribution of state land among private owners. The government was, in fact, one of the largest landowners in the country, especially after Ismail had been compelled to turn over large portions of his private land to the state in the last years of his reign. The government was also engaged in bringing new land into cultivation through reclamation and other hydraulic projects. Since it had no desire to retain proprietary rights over all this land, it was in the position to distribute the land to private landowners. The decisive reason that more of the land sold by the government did not reach the hands of the small landowners was related to financial and political pressures. First, a large proportion of government land was pledged to the payment of the debt—specifically, the *domains* and *daira* estates of the government, lands once held as private property by Ismail but mortgaged by him for loans. As a result of the mortgage, mixed, international administrations were created to represent the interests of European financiers, and it was only in agreement with these mixed administrations that the Egyptian government could carry out any policies on these lands. The Egyptian government favored the sale of lands to private landowners as a means of decreasing the debt, and also of getting the lands into the hands of cultivators. It hoped to break up the estates into small plots and sell them to the *fellahin* at favorable rates. The international commissioners opposed this plan on the grounds that it did not provide sufficient guarantees for repayment of the debt. Instead, at their behest, a policy was adopted of selling the land by auction in relatively large strips, an effective means of ensuring that sales prices would be high enough to extinguish the debt in a relatively short period of time. In the first years of sales, in fact, the lands were so large that there were few sales, and the commission was compelled to redivide the estates in order to attract more buyers. Even so, most estates were considerably larger than any of the small landowners could ever hope to purchase. The average lot sold was reported to have been between 30 and 40 *feddans,* quite large figures by Egyptian standards.[49] In 1892, for instance, while several plots of less than five *feddans* were sold, others of 2,897 *feddans,* 1,246 *feddans,* and 137 *feddans* were sold to such rich landowners as Tigrane Pasha, Boghos Nubar, and others.[50] Although the Egyptian government was predisposed to getting these lands into the hands of small landowners, it did not always cavil at the conservative policies of the commissioners. In 1898 it came to an agreement with a financial group which undertook to sell the remaining *daira* estates at a 20 percent profit and to split the profits of sale with the government.[51] Such engagements did not ensure the distribution of land to the *fellahin.*

In spite of its complaints against foreign commissioners the Egyptian government employed much the same policy as the international commissions had done with the *domains* and *daira* estates; that is, in the distribution of its own land, it sold large plots of land by auction at extremely high prices. It was the policy of the Egyptian government to sell land potentially cultivable to private land companies, many of them European, who undertook first to reclaim the soil and put in secondary irrigation works, then to sell the land to private individuals. The reason for this policy was that the *fellahin* could not be entrusted with making the land cultivable and the government, because of financial pressures, preferred in most cases to have private land companies do this work.[52] These companies, of course, sold the land to make a profit. They therefore kept it in relatively large

[49] Egypt, Domains Commission, *Rapport,* 1893, p. 145.

[50] *Ibid.,* 1892, p. 95.

[51] Cromer, Annual Report for 1902, *HCSP,* Egypt No. 1 (1903), Vol. LXXXVII, cd. 1529.

[52] Cromer, Annual Report for 1906, *HCSP,* Egypt No. 1 (1907), Vol. c, cd. 3394.

blocks, sold it by means of auction, and did little to ensure that the land was turned over to small landowners.
Even when the government possessed reclaimed and
cultivable land, it was under enormous pressures to distribute this land to the wealthy. Throughout the 1880's,
while the Egyptian government was trying to stave off
bankruptcy, it exchanged plots of government land for
pension payments. Many of these, undoubtedly, were later
sold to wealthy landowners, as few pensioners would
have wanted to cultivate the soil. On other occasions the
government exchanged land to settle financial obligations—to the Behera Land Company, for instance, in exchange for the cancellation of an expensive contract for
the irrigation of parts of Lower Egypt and then to a
group of English financiers for a timely loan during
the Sudan campaign.

It was not until Lord Kitchener's administration that
a truly concerted effort was made to place land at the
disposal of the peasantry. By this time both the *daira*
and *domains* loans had been extinguished, and all government land had been brought under a single government
administration which had unfettered control over this
land. Kitchener put into operation a scheme calling for
the sale of small plots of land, customarily five *feddans*
at cost—not at auction prices—only to *fellahin* who actually lived on the land and had cultivated it over the years.
The program was so limited, however, that it had little
effect upon the structure of rural society.[53]

The reasons for the rapid growth of the number and
the percentage of landowners holding less than five *feddans* are not hard to find. They stemmed from an increase
in population, subdivision of the land in accordance with
the Muslim law of inheritance, and the lack of economic
opportunity outside the agrarian sphere. A *feddan* or

[53] Marshall, *Egyptian Enigma*, p. 200.

less of land did not suffice to support a family. Therefore, a common practice among small landholders was
that of working on larger estates as tenant farmers or
itinerant laborers for the purpose of augmenting income.
Another large percentage of the peasants were not proprietors at all, but worked on other estates as tenants and
itinerant laborers.[54] The British, therefore, did not alter
the prevailing patterns of land distribution in Egypt.
Working in political alliance with the established classes,
they were not prepared to undermine the economic
status of these classes by radical land distribution programs.

The right of private property was firmly established
in Egypt during the reigns of Said and Ismail. According to the law of 1858, in the reign of Said, a person
who had held a certain plot of *kharaj* land for five con-
secutive years, tilled it, and paid its taxes acquired ir-
revocable ownership of it. The next important step was
the *Mukabala* Law of 1871. Designed as a financial expedient by the hard pressed Ismail, it guaranteed complete
freedom of private property to any owner who paid six
years' taxes in advance.[55] By the time of the British occupation all the land, *kharaj* and *ushr* alike, was treated
as private property, except for that portion of *kharaj*
land on which the *Mukabala* had not been paid. By the
law of 1891 this remaining legal distinction between
kharaj and *ushr* was abolished. Nevertheless, there were
still vast inequalities in taxation between *kharaj* and *ushr*
land, as investigations had disclosed. The British felt,
however, that there should be no fundamental changes in
tax burdens until a survey of lands had been completed.
The last survey had been done under Ismail; since then,

[54] Cartwright, "Notes on Rent, Labor, and Joint Ownership in
Egyptian Agriculture," *Cairo Scientific Journal*, 1910, pp. 29-37.
[55] Gabriel Baer, *A History of Landownership in Modern Egypt,
1800-1950* (New York, 1962), pp. 7-12.

with continual changes in Egypt's hydraulic system and the size of individual holdings, the value of the land had changed considerably.[56]

In 1892 the government undertook a survey of government lands to determine which of these were being farmed illegally by Egyptian peasants. The survey was extended to a revenue survey in 1895, then a few years later into what constituted a cadastral or proprietary survey. The government decided that the total amount of taxation was not to be reduced, but that the tax burdens were to be equalized, with taxes on formerly *kharaj* land to be reduced and those on *ushr* increased. The revenue survey of 1896 and 1897 established the rental values of the land and set the land tax at approximately 30 percent of the rental value. The readjustment of the tax had to be delayed, however, until a more exact cadastral survey had determined the value of individual holdings. The survey carried out from 1899 to 1907, two provinces at a time, was the basis for the new tax schedules, which went into effect shortly after the completion of the survey.[57]

One of the most significant developments in rural Egypt during the nineteenth century was the dissolution of the village community.[58] The breakdown in the communal village system is seen most clearly in the substitution of private property right for communal right. Yet private property was not fully guaranteed against all threats unless properly registered by the government, and through such records protected against encroachment. Records could only be maintained by a government

[56] H. G. Lyons, *The Cadastral Survey of Egypt, 1892-1907* (Cairo, 1908), p. 2.

[57] A. T. McKillop, *Note on the Readjustment of the Land Tax in Egypt, 1895-1907* (Cairo, 1907).

[58] See Gabriel Baer, "The Dissolution of the Egyptian Village Community," *Die Welt des Islams*, 1959, pp. 56-70.

cadastral survey of proprietary rights, and the careful re-
cording of all subsequent changes in ownership was particularly pressing in Egypt where the usurping of land
was a common practice. The cadastral survey was only
in a general way a proprietary survey; it was basically a
revenue survey, since it attempted to determine the oc-
cupiers of the land rather than its owners. But because
occupancy and ownership of the land were roughly similar, it could serve as the basis for a proprietary survey.
The survey, however, had to be maintained through the
registration of changes in ownership if proprietary rights
were to be guaranteed by law. As the observations of a
land registration commission set up after World War I
indicated, the changes in ownership were not regularly
registered. Therefore, it was not surprising that in only a
fraction of the cases observed by the land registration
commission did the government proprietary records conform with actual situations as they existed some 20 or
more years after the survey had been conducted. If
sons succeeded a father and subdivided the land, the
common practice was not to notify the authorities of the
change, but for the sons to collect and pay a single tax
when it was due. The cadastral survey carried out in the
1920's was considered to be more effective, and landowners were said to have registered changes in
ownership with greater care. Nevertheless, although private property was the prevailing form of occupancy during the occupation, communal practices, especially within a single kinship group, were quite widespread. So
long as the taxes shown in the records were paid, the
government did not question the way in which the land
was divided and worked.[59]

[59] Egypt, Ministry of Public Works, *Reports on Registration of
Title*, Paper v.

CHAPTER VIII

THE NATIONALISTS AND
LORD CROMER, 1895-1907

THE BRITISH occupation proved fertile soil for the development of Egypt's intellectual life. The period immediately following the crushing of the Arabi revolt and the exiling of its leaders was barren, but in the two decades prior to the outbreak of the First World War Egyptian culture flourished. Arabic newspapers regained their position of predominance. *Al-Ahram,* founded in 1875, *al-Muqattam* (1889), *al-Muayyad* (1889), and *al-Liwa* (1900), were the leading Arabic papers of the day. *Al-Liwa,* the nationalist paper of Mustafa Kamil, was estimated to have a circulation of 10,000 during its best years at the turn of the century. There were other more specialized publications. *Al-Muqtataf,* published by the editors of *al-Muqattam,* was one of the truly great and path-finding scientific periodicals in the Arab world. Its science and social science articles, many of them translations from leading European journals, were followed by a sophisticated audience throughout the Middle East. It was through *al-Muqtataf* that the Arab world was given an introduction to the writings of Charles Darwin, Nietzsche, Comte, Freud, and other leading European thinkers. The editors of *al-Muqattam* and *al-Muqtataf,* three Syrian Christians who had been educated at the Syrian Protestant College before migrating to Egypt, were famous for their concise, direct, "telegraphic" style. *Al-Manar,* founded in 1898 by Rashid Rida, a disciple of Muhammad Abduh, was a journal for the discussion of Islamic subjects; while Jurji Zaydan, a Syrian Christian, established an Arabic literary periodical, *al-Hilal,* for reviving interest in the culture and literature of the Arabs. All

[249]

of these periodicals and newspapers did a great deal to familiarize educated Egyptians with the thought and events of the Western world.

Among the most significant intellectual trends was the development of Western literary forms. The poetry of Ahmad Shawqi and Hafiz Ibrahim, Egypt's leading poets, although more traditional than other literary expressions, was used to express many of the political feelings of the community. The short story attained a great vogue at a time when so much literary work was published in short articles in newspapers. Short stories of Muhammad Taymur, for instance, revealed unmistakable influences of French literature. The most far-reaching developments were in the field of the novel. While the novel did not attain great popularity until the writings of Taha Husayn, Tawfiq al-Hakim and others after World War I, its foundations were laid in this period. One of the first novels to be written in Egypt, the *Hadith Isa ibn Hisham*, byMuhammad al-Muwaylihi, made a critical social survey of Egypt. One of Egypt's greatest novels, *Zaynab*, by Muhammad Husayn Haykal, a story centered around rural Egypt and the life of a young peasant girl, was written just before the War. Conceived and written almost entirely in France, it almost was not published, since the author had second thoughts about its publication in Egypt, fearing public reaction to the form and ideas presented.[1]

All of this literary work showed most clearly the impress of Western literature. The novel was a completely new art form to the Egyptians. Literature was employed as a medium of social criticism rather than purely as an aesthetic and artistic exercise. There was a new concern for the heretofore neglected or repressed aspects of Egyptian life: the peasantry, rural life, the position of

[1] Muhammad Husayn Haykal, *Zaynab* [A Girl's Home] (Cairo, 1914), p. 3.

women in Egyptian society, and love between the sexes. All of these themes were graphically represented in Husayn Haykal's novel, *Zaynab*, and have continued to inform Egyptian literature in the twentieth century.

The transformation of the language was startling. In the *Hadith Isa ibn Hisham*, al-Muwaylihi still employed the traditional flowery style with rhyming prose, but in Tawfiq al-Hakim's widely read novel, *Awdah al-Ruh*, published after the First World War, the language was simple, direct, yet eloquent. The colloquial was used by the novel's characters to give added force and realism. Language was gradually coming to be regarded as a tool for conveying ideas and feelings to the entire literate population, rather than as a device with which professional litterateurs regaled each other by means of subtle and elaborate expressions. Thus, Western literature had a liberating influence on Egyptian writing, tearing down the formal rules which once governed writing, encouraging the writer to express his own deepest feelings, and enabling him to direct his thought to problems of contemporary importance.[2]

In the 1870's, during the transformation of Egypt, Khedive Ismail Pasha had proclaimed that Egypt was now a part of Europe. There was undeniable evidence for this assertion, since the Egyptian economy was tied to Europe through the export of cotton, the Suez Canal linked Europe and the Far East, and Egypt's attempt to emulate the West had been proceeding apace for more than half a century. Yet Ismail's claim would apply more fully to the last two decades of the British occupation than to the earlier period. During Ismail's reign educated Egyptians had only limited access and exposure to the West. Many Egyptian intellectuals had not

[2] There is a comparison of these two works in Salah al-Din Dhuhni, *Misr bain al-Ihtilal wa-l-Thawrah* [Egypt between Occupation and Revolution] (Cairo, 1939).

travelled in Europe; some of them did not know a European language. The number of books and articles written in Arabic about Europe, either as translations of European works or as commentaries on Europe, was not sufficient to give a well-rounded view of the West. It is not surprising, therefore, that the leading intellectuals of this period saw the West mainly as a materialistic civilization, technologically and militarily superior to the East, and a constant threat.

During the British occupation the avenues of access to the West were substantially increased. It was commonplace for the educated to learn European languages, as they were emphasized in the government schools. Indeed, Muhammad Abduh, who had been educated in traditional Islamic schools and had learned French only by sheer dint of his own efforts later in his career, felt that no scholar could claim to be serving his country if he did not master a European language.[3] By this time, also, most talented young Egyptians received some opportunity to study and travel in Europe and to obtain first-hand information about the Western world; memoirs of the period reveal the extraordinary impact first visits to Europe had on these young men.[4] Even for those who had not travelled in Europe and did not know a European language, there was considerably more European literature available in translation. *Al-Hilal* and *al-Muqtataf* were noted for their numerous translations from European scientific and literary works. Through translations educated Egyptians were made familiar with the writings of Marx, Nietzsche, the Russian novelists, the Fabians, Comte, the English utilitarians, Darwin and many others, as well as the thought of the French Enlightenment: Voltaire, Rousseau, Condillac, which had

[3] Uthman Amin, *Muhammad Abduh*, p. 109.
[4] Salamah Musa's *Tarbiyah* [The Education of Salamah Musa] is quite good, and is representative of this phenomenon.

dominated the field of translation before the British. One of the most prolific translators, Fathi Zaghlul, put the burgeoning legal profession in his debt by translating some of the crucial European works on law. He was responsible for the translation of Bentham's *Principles of Legislation,* and the works of Gusteve le Bon and others.[5]

But the increased exposure to the West, while bringing a better understanding of its civilization, did not necessarily alter some of the basic attitudes of Egyptian intellectuals. They still felt alienated and hostile to the West, which was regarded as a political conqueror and a threat to the existence of other civilizations. They had experienced the sting of political defeat and subjugation at the hands of an alien people who, unlike the Turks, their previous conquerors, belonged to a different religion. The repeated criticism of their religion and their mores by European intellectuals left them resentful and defensive, often so antagonistic to the West as to warp their understanding of it. In their humbled state, they continued to see the West largely in terms of its greater power; they were still overawed by the West's military and technological superiority. But by the time of the British occupation they were aware that the West's military strength was only an external manifestation of deeper sources of power. Fathi Zaghlul's translation of Edmond Demolin's work, *À quoi tient la superiorité des Anglo-Saxons,* was indicative of the search for the roots of this strength in Western society. To many Egyptians the real bases of power were the democratic institutions of the West and its solidified nationalistic feelings. Their overriding desire was to ferret out these sources of strength, embrace them, and then turn them on the West. The numerous critiques

[5] For the period before the British occupation see Ibrahim Abu-Lughod, *Arab Rediscovery of Europe: A Study in Cultural Encounters* (Princeton, 1963).

of despotism in Egyptian literature, it may be safely argued, stemmed from the feeling that this form of government was the chief source of weakness in the East.

Yet the view of some intellectuals of this period was not entirely distorted by their admiration and fear of the power of the West. They were also attracted to Europe because of its liberalism, democratic institutions, humanitarianism, and egalitarianism. They saw Europe as a civilization of deep spiritual values, promoting a more satisfactory life than did traditional Egyptian society. They felt that European society, through its promise of a more abundant life for all, was to be seen as a model for all other societies. Some Egyptian intellectuals carried their open and sympathetic attitude toward the West to the point of trying to identify Egypt with Europe. They argued that Egypt had always been part of a greater Mediterranean civilization which had included Europe as well as the Near East, that during the Pharaonic age and later the Islamic, Egypt and the rest of the East had fertilized Europe. Now, while Europe was at the peak of its power, it was reinvigorating the countries of the eastern Mediterranean. Later, in the 1920's and 1930's, Taha Husayn was one of the keenest exponents of this thesis. He contended that Egypt was reclaiming its rightful place in the age-old Mediterranean civilization by an espousal of the basic features of Western civilization.[6] Two of the most influential intellectuals of the pre-World War I era, Ahmad Lutfi and Qasim Amin, held similar views. Qasim Amin's justifiably controversial book, *al-Marah al-Jadidah*, contained trenchant attacks on the backwardness of Egyptian mores and institutions, particularly traditional Egyptian attitudes toward women, in comparison with the more humanitarian and liberal attitudes of the Western world. In his analysis of Islamic civilization, Qasim

[6] Pierre Cachia, *Taha Husayn* (London, 1956).

Amin pointed out that its foundations were laid in a pre-scientific era and therefore were encrusted with practices detrimental to the well-being of society. For him, and for those of like mind, Europe, far from being an enemy to be resisted, should be seen as a civilization that had developed a superior organization of society and had enhanced the general well-being of its individual members. Europe was to be imitated, in Qasim Amin's view, not merely in order to obtain political and economic independence, but also because the European way of life secured greater individual fulfillment and happiness.

Changes in attitudes toward the West, from Ismail's generation to the generation before World War I, are not to be explained, however, entirely by increased exposure to the West. They were also rooted in the practical exigencies of each period. Intellectuals during the reign of Ismail saw the problem as that of resisting the encroachments of the West on Egypt; they tended, therefore, to focus on the external manifestations of Western power. Moreover, they were still the representatives of the traditional order in society, having been trained in its institutions, and were not ready to admit that the West was superior to the East in anything except naked power. The later generation was spawned by the new, more modern educational institutions established in Egypt. Its thinkers represented a new professional group of lawyers, doctors, teachers, civil servants, and students, quite different from the older order of intellectuals. They felt an affinity for the prevailing economic doctrines of Europe, since these best represented their own interests. In particular, they favored the establishment of a liberal, constitutional regime in Egypt and a modified form of the *laissez-faire* economic system, both of which would ensure their political and economic predominance in Egypt. The professional class did not know how strongly Europe would oppose these goals; they believed, or perhaps wanted to believe, that Europe, because of its liberal and democratic tendencies, could be persuaded to establish autonomous governments in the East. The resistance they encountered from European imperial powers, then the disillusionment with Europe during and immediately following the First World War were to cause a profound change in these attitudes. Moreover, although the power of the professional classes was still unchallenged, the urban proletariat and the peasantry, as they began to make their influence felt, were to force this class to profoundly alter its intellectual attitudes.

Cultural attainments before the occupation were derived from the modernizing efforts of the nineteenth century. The creation of schools and the educational missions dispatched to Europe in the half century preceding the occupation had helped to produce a class of intellectuals in contact with the learning of the West. During the occupation the British reorganized Egypt's educational system and continued the practice of sending missions to Europe, although on a much reduced scale.

Egyptian-born artists, newspaper writers, pamphleteers, and novelists were principally educated in government schools. The British provided a relatively free atmosphere for the Egyptian intellectual. Although the Egyptian press was often bitterly critical of the British, Cromer did not attempt to suppress it. Freedom of expression in Egypt contrasted so sharply with the restrictions throughout the rest of the Ottoman Empire that quite a number of talented Arab and non-Arab subjects of the Empire emigrated to Egypt. Many of Egypt's most brilliant intellectuals were, in fact, immigrants from Syria. The editors of *al-Muqattam* and *al-Muqtataf* were Syrian Christians who came to Egypt in the 1880's. Jurji

Zaydan, another Syrian Christian, established his periodical, *al-Hilal*, in Egypt in 1892; while two of the most
influential Islamic thinkers of the age, al-Kawakibi, author
of *Tabai al-Istibdad,* and Rashid Rida, a disciple of
Muhammad Abduh and editor of *al-Manar,* were of
Syrian origin.

Islam was, of course, caught up in the intellectual current of the times. Many leading intellectuals, Muslim by
upbringing, attempted to adapt Islam to the new requirements of Egypt. Islam, however, was constantly thrown
on the defensive, attacked by modernizers within Egypt
and subjected to scathing criticism by skeptical, secular-
minded European thinkers. The leading Islamic reformer,
Muhammad Abduh, devoted a large part of his life to
attempting to show the compatibility between Islam and
the scientific, rational thought of the West. His major
theme was that Islam, the last and purest of the Near
Eastern religions, laid a great emphasis on reason as a
means of discovering truth. His disciple, Rashid Rida,
continued the reformist movement in the periodical,
al-Manar, where Islamic theology and ethics were
re-examined. A few Muslims—Qasim Amin, for instance—discussed Islam within a historical, relativist
perspective and argued that many of its teachings,
designed to meet specific problems of earlier times,
were no longer applicable to the changed circumstances of the modern Muslim world. To all of these reformers it was important that free inquiry be permitted,
that Islam not be treated as a hard and fast set of dogmas,
incapable of reinterpretation, and that Islam not act as
an impediment to scientific pursuit.

Muhammad Abduh, Rashid Rida, Qasim Amin, al-Kawakibi, the reforming and modernizing element in Islam,
were nevertheless in a minority among Muslim intellectuals. The tendency, especially in al-Azhar, was to view
Islamic ideas and doctrines even more rigidly than be-

fore. Muslim scholars, on the defensive because of repeated criticisms of Islam, reasserted its doctrines in the most literal form. Both Muhammad Abduh and Qasim Amin were under repeated attack from conservative religious forces. Muhammad Abduh was forced out of his position of influence in al-Azhar, while Qasim Amin's second book on women and Islam was greeted by strong criticism from the traditionalists. Nationalism, with its focus upon the secular nation-state, was difficult to reconcile with the religious loyalties between Muslims and the discrimination against non-Muslims required in Islam. Yet the most vigorous cultural activity was occurring among the secular-minded, secularly trained, young Egyptians. In spite of the efforts of Muhammad Abduh, the traditionally trained Islamic intellectuals became increasingly isolated from the major modernizing developments in Egypt.

*

Islam, the traditional intellectual system, now on the defensive against attacks from the West, withdrawn into a rigid, unadaptable, regressive ritualism, could no longer command the sympathies of most of the educated class, thereby creating a void in Egyptian society. Increasingly, nationalism came to fill this gap for the educated classes. It became an intellectual value system for them, and the educated directed to it much of the same emotional intensity that they had once felt for Islam. Ultimately, they used it in much the same fashion as Islam had once been used: to win the loyalties of the masses. Moreover, nationalism held out the promise of independence from the West, the end of an inferiority status, and the reassertion of Egypt's rightful place in the world.

The Egyptian nationalism of this period continued to be an elitist movement; like the nationalist movements in Germany and eastern Europe in the early nineteenth century, it was the work of the professional classes. Lawyers and students in the various, higher schools were the most strongly represented. Doctors, engineers, and government clerks were also to be found in the movement, though not to such an extent. Other classes were still excluded at this stage: the peasantry and the proletariat, because they were still unorganized; the merchant group, because it was almost entirely alien. The landlord class, Egypt's traditional ruling group, was tied by economic and political interests to the occupation, although when the nationalist movement became rather highly developed, some of its members made their peace with the nationalists. Since it was customary for the large landowners to send their sons to the government schools, many of the latter became nationalists. The military, vigorously watched by the British, could not assume a decisive role in politics.

Nationalism, then, was initiated in Egypt, as in many non-Western areas, by the professional classes. But how does one explain its rise? Is it to be seen as a reaction to British exploitation, and grievances against the British? Or is it to be explained as a natural development resulting from the closer integration of Egyptian society stemming from modernization? In part, the movement did stem from social, political, and economic grievances felt by the Egyptians. Socially, as we have already seen, the British treated the Egyptians as inferiors. Top administrative positions were reserved for the British, while they controlled almost entirely the economic development of Egypt. Racial discrimination against Egyptians added a special measure of bitterness to the nationalist movement. The modernization of Egypt, producing a closer integration and communication in Egyptian society, was an obvious, necessary prerequisite of nationalism— but not a sufficient cause. Of crucial importance was the image of the European nation-state, the promise of a more powerful and better organized way of life. Without this hope, this view of a superior political organization, the grievances felt by the Egyptians would surely have been borne as they always had been—by the populace. The prospect of a better future made the prevailing discrimination and subordination seem intolerable. Scholars have so often pointed out that revolutionary situations are not generated exclusively by oppression and grievances. More commonly, they arise in an atmosphere of optimism about the future, an atmosphere which makes whatever oppression may exist seem all the more unbearable. Such was the case in Egypt, where the newly emerging professional classes, informed of the content of European civilization, were spurred on by the concept, actively fostered by the left-wing in Europe, of national independence. The oppression in Egypt, while in many respects much less than that suffered under Ottoman rule, was deeply resented because it seemed to violate the kind of life Europe promised its peoples.

The growth of nationalist sentiment was closely related to the modernization of Egypt. The reforms in administration, education, and economics had helped to create the new professional class and had put them in touch with Europe. Cromer had hoped, rather pessimistically, that by controlling the pace of modernization in Egypt, particularly in the educational system, nationalism would not obtain a following; such was not to be the case. Members of the professional class, feeling the discrimination practiced by the British more acutely than any other segment of the Egyptian population, saw the nation-state organization as the key to power in Europe. They believed that the only way Egypt could reassert itself was through creating a similar nation-state in Egypt. To be sure, the nationalist movement had drawn heavily from the traditional classes during the Arabi revolt; support had come from Azhari *shaykhs*, the military, even large landowners. Such also occurred when nationalist feelings manifested themselves during the crises of 1893 and 1894. Traditionalists, Islamic reformers, and others cooperated with men trained in the new modernized educational institutions. But increasingly, the nationalist movement was dominated by the new groups, while the traditionalist elements—the Azhari-trained intellectuals, for instance —came to occupy a less exalted position in the movement.

Among the nationalists, particularly the leaders, the sense of personal grievance against the British occupation was strong. The most deeply felt grievance was the exclusion of Egyptians from top administrative positions. Indeed, many of the most ambitious graduates of the higher government schools, finding their advancement in the government bureaucracy blocked, turned to the nationalist movement as an outlet for their ambitions. The two leading nationalist figures, Mustafa Kamil and his successor, Muhammad Farid, were both destined for government service by their fathers. Each felt humiliation at the restrictions upon his potential advancement and a sense of frustration that Egyptian society under the British did not contain positions commensurate with the abilities of talented Egyptians. Denied the prestige, recognition, and fulfillment they wanted through the established career channels, these men pursued and, indeed, largely realized their goals outside the established order of society, and in conflict with this order. Mustafa Kamil never even entered the government bureaucracy, while Muhammad Farid resigned his position in the Ministry of Justice when his advancement was delayed. Both turned to careers of newspaper writing and political agitation.[7]

[7] Abd al-Rahman al-Rafii, *Muhammad Farid* (Cairo, 1948), p. 27.

As in France during the Enlightenment, so in Egypt was the salon the breeding ground of the nationalist movement. Following the Arabi revolt the spark of nationalist sentiment was almost extinguished. Sad Zaghlul mentioned that the Egyptians themselves were turning on the Arabists and probably did as much as the British to crush the movement. In fact, certain people wanted to exile Sad Zaghlul to the Sudan even after the courts had declared him innocent.[8] A low-keyed fervor was preserved, however, by a few of the leading figures of the day, who met from time to time to discuss the political affairs of Egypt. The most famous of the meeting places were those of Muhammad Sultan and Princess Nazli. At first, these salons were dominated by traditionally trained members of the old ruling class: Muhammad Sultan, former leader in the old Chamber of Deputies; Ali Mubarak, a minister in numerous ministries; Princess Nazli of the royal family; and, at times, Riyad Pasha, the erstwhile Egyptian Prime Minister.[9] Gradually, however, new men, graduates of the government schools and members of the professions, gained admittance to the salons. Mustafa Kamil, for instance, began to frequent the salons of Ali Mubarak and Princess Nazli and was brought into contact with the older generation of nationalists. He was reported to have been greatly influenced by his meeting with Abdullah al-Nadim, one of the leaders of the Arabi revolt at one of these salons.[10] The nationalist agitation still remained very much a movement of the upper and educated classes and had, as yet, barely touched the urban proletariat or the peasantry.

[8] Abbas Mahmud al-Aqqad, *Sad Zaghlul* (Cairo, 1936), p. 72.
[9] "Mudhakkirat al-Khidiwi Abbas" [Memoirs of Khedive Abbas], *al-Misr*, May 1951.
[10] Abd al-Latif Hamza, *Adab al-Maqalah* [Journalistic Articles], v, 68.

Abbas could hardly have expected to remain at the head of the nationalist movement for very long, since his position was such a tenuous one. The British could, if the occasion warranted, force his deposition as they and the French forced Ismail's. Gradually, the leadership of the movement passed to Mustafa Kamil. Abbas continued to aid the activities of Mustafa Kamil behind the scenes, by helping to finance his plans, for Abbas had considerable resources at his disposal. In addition to his civil list, he was able to obtain money through the sale of Khedivial orders and decorations. Also, as head of the still unregulated Ministry of Waqfs, he was able to transfer, sell, and trade lands at a substantial profit to himself. Much of this money Abbas lavished on himself and his mistresses, having retired to a life of pleasure. But because of his continued interest in the nationalist campaign, he also helped to finance some of its projects. Abbas apparently helped to underwrite Mustafa Kamil's trips to Europe, as well as the newspaper the latter created in 1900.[11]

Mustafa Kamil, a graduate of the Egyptian Law School and the French Law School in Egypt, was the leader of extremist nationalism in Egypt.[12] His goal was an autonomous Egypt that would remain an independent province of the Ottoman Empire. He attacked the British for having occupied Egypt on the pretext of restoring order and then exploiting its resources for their own uses. The British, he felt, had impaired the authority of the Khedive, had excluded Egyptians from top administrative positions, had deprived Egypt of its rightful possession of the Sudan, and were in the process of destroying Arabic as

[11] Abbas himself speaks of his activities along these lines in his memoirs, published in *al-Misr* in the latter half of 1951.

[12] The material on Mustafa Kamil is drawn largely from Abd al-Rahman al-Rafli, *Mustafa Kamil*; Abd al Latif Hamza, *Adab al-Maqalah* [Journalistic Articles], v; and Ahmad Rishad, *Mustafa Kamil* (Cairo, 1958).

the language of the educated classes. All this they had done, he argued, ostensibly for Egyptian welfare, but in truth seeking to solidify their position in the East, to maintain control of the Suez Canal, to exploit the agricultural resources of Egypt, and to deal a death blow to Islam, thereby further securing their position in India against Pan-Islamic feelings.

Mustafa Kamil's interpretation of the British occupation and the aims of the British in Egypt was a mixture of the modern and the traditional. Clearly, he was indebted to leftist European thinkers for his interpretation of imperialism as economically motivated, undertaken for the purpose of exploiting Egypt's resources. There was at the same time an appeal to traditionalist arguments in his emphasis on the anti-Muslim drives in European civilization. The overlapping of traditional Islamic and modern secular runs throughout the political propaganda of Mustafa Kamil. The French paper, *Le Temps,* contended that Mustafa Kamil had two faces, one for Egypt and the Ottoman Empire, and the other for Europe. "The first carries a *tarbouch* and directs the Pan-Islamic journal, *Liwa;* the other carries a hat and collaborates on *Figaro.*"[13] For Mustafa Kamil, it seems clear that the goal of political independence was decisive, and any means leading to this goal were legitimate. Within certain segments of Egyptian society, therefore, opposition to British rule and the goal of independence had to be couched in the religious idiom. There was almost no projection beyond the day of independence, an alarming failure to realize that his varying appeal might well arouse differing hopes about the future.

[13] *Le Temps,* August 22, 1906, quoted in Bertie to Grey, No. 326, file 29276, August 27, 1906, PRO, FO 371/67. For a more detailed discussion of Mustafa Kamil and Islam, see Fritz Steppat, "Nationalismus und Islam bei Mustafa Kamil," *Die Welt des Islams,* 1956, Vol. IV, No. 4.

It is, however, not surprising that Mustafa Kamil's appeal was contradictory and confusing, his political thinking imprecise. He was trying to define and to establish new concepts focusing on the nation-state, and many of these concepts clashed with traditionally-held attitudes. Islam had been the value system of both the masses and the upper classes in Egypt, but the modernization of Egypt, along with political defeat, had tended to discredit traditional Islam in the eyes of the educated classes. The political thinking of men like Mustafa Kamil may be seen as an attempt to establish a new value system acceptable to the disenchanted educated classes. It was to be expected that there would be an overlapping of traditional Islamic values and Western secular ideas. Other segments of the population still remained attached to Islam, and appeals to the masses had to be couched in the language they understood. The differing levels of political awareness and education in Egyptian society, intensified by modernization, helped to produce the strains in the political thinking of Mustafa Kamil who was trying to establish contact with various elements of the society.

Mustafa Kamil's strength lay not in his ideas, which were not new or even clearly defined, in many cases, but in his zeal, his domineering leadership, and his propagandist ability. He was a spell-binding orator and a powerful newspaper writer. He exacted complete obedience, almost reverence, from his followers, while his unbridled egoism and strength of personality brooked no opposition. For this reason, he tended to attract to his ranks a group of second-rate men. He threw all of his talents into the campaign for forcing the British out of Egypt. His social program, on the other hand, paled in comparison with those of many of his contemporaries, Ahmad Lutfi, and his successor, Muhammad Farid, for instance. The only radical program that he consistently supported was universal, free education for the Egyptian people; he made numerous attacks on what he regarded as the restrictive educational policy of the British. He was also active in establishing private, Egyptian schools and in organizing night classes for adults. To him, however, education had ulterior uses. He saw it as the most effective tool for promoting the unity of the Egyptian people, that is, for creating a sense of national solidarity which would enable the Egyptians to throw back the Europeans.[14] Although he occasionally called on Egyptians to develop the agricultural and industrial potential of the country, his interest in these reforms was lukewarm. On other social issues, he tended toward conservative views. *Al-Liwa*, his Arabic newspaper, adopted a critical attitude toward Qasim Amin's controversial works on the position of women in Islamic society.[15] He was a strong advocate of constitutional government in Egypt. But it seems clear that he favored only limited government intervention in the economic and social life of the country. The parliamentary regime that he advocated for Egypt would be dominated by the professional and established classes whose spokesman he was.

In the early years of his career Mustafa Kamil's nationalist agitation was directed at Europe, where he hoped to obtain support in realizing his goal of autonomy for Egypt. His efforts at this stage were largely devoted to presenting the Egyptian case to leading European politicians rather than to building up a large following in Egypt. For a long time, he was without a newspaper, a party organization, or any other means for reaching the Egyptian people. His appeal in Egypt was largely confined to students of the higher schools and to other professional men, in the hope that he might enlist more re-

[14] Abd al-Rahman al-Rafii, *Mustafa Kamil*, p. 139.
[15] Abd al-Latif Hamza, *Adab al-Maqalah* [Journalistic Articles], v, 198.

cruits for his propagandistic efforts in Europe or perhaps
demonstrate to Europe that he did command large fol-
lowings in Egypt. He and his followers presented their
cause in all the capitals of Europe, but their major focus
was on Paris, London, and Constantinople. In England
the bulk of Mustafa Kamil's campaign was devoted to
winning the support of the traditionally sympathetic left,
represented by such a figure as Henry Labouchere. The
left, in fact, received him well, but the mood of the times
was unfavorable to anti-imperialist sentiment. Mustafa
Kamil's two letters to William Gladstone after he had
stepped down as Prime Minister of the Liberal party, in
which Kamil reminded Gladstone of his previous
pledges to evacuate Egypt, fell on deaf ears. They enhanced the reputation of their author, but had no effect
on British policy in Egypt.[16] Mustafa Kamil also tried to
stand well with the Sultan, for he regarded the Ottoman
Empire as a bulwark against the British in Egypt. Like
so many other Egyptians, he feared the British would assume complete and unfettered control of Egypt if the Ottoman Empire were to collapse.[17]

His most vigorous campaign was carried out in France,
where the Egyptian nationalist cause found support from
both the right and the left in French politics, that is,
from the extreme imperialist party which resented British predominance in Egypt and from left-wing, anti-imperialist groups. Through his friendship with Juliette
Adam, a literary figure well-known in the political world,
he was introduced to many French politicians.[18] Juliette
Adam's periodical, *La Nouvelle Revue*, was available to
him; through it, he was able to present his case to the
French people. Etienne Deloncle, a leading poli-

[16] Abd al-Rahman al-Rafii, *Mustafa Kamil*, p. 62ff.
[17] Abd al-Latif Hamza, *Adab al Maqaluh* [Journalistic Articles],
v, 21.
[18] Juliette Adam, *Angleterre en Égypte* (Paris, 1922), p. 146.

tician in the colonial movement, who had always taken an interest in Egyptian affairs, was sympathetic. His relationship with politicians like Deloncle, however, was entirely an alliance of expediency, sustained by a common hatred of England.[19] All of these French groups, for quite different reasons, were anxious to see the British evacuate Egypt. During the 1890's Mustafa Kamil probably spent as much time in Europe trying to propagandize the Egyptian question, as he did in Egypt.

The nationalist hopes for support from France were dashed by the failure of the Marchand expedition of 1898 and the signing of the Anglo-French Accord of 1904. The French expedition, led by Captain Marchand, undertook to establish French predominance in the Upper Nile basin. The nationalists in Egypt were apprised of this venture; indeed, for a long time, they knew more about it than the British, and gave Marchand as much information as they could about the Mahdists in the Sudan.[20] Their expectations were high: they hoped that the French would be in a position to force the British out of Egypt. Marchand's capitulation to Kitchener at Fashoda, on the Upper Nile, came as a great blow, shattering the hopes of Mustafa Kamil for overt French political support. The Anglo-French Accord, in which the French recognized the position of England in Egypt, was quite anti-climactic. Even before the event it was clear that the French were no longer in a position to threaten the British in Egypt.

This emphasis on propagandizing the Egyptian cause in Europe seems, now, wildly naive; yet it had its own rationale. It was, in fact, necessary for two reasons: first, because Mustafa Kamil did not have the strength at home to challenge the British but could find influential

[19] Ahmad Shafiq, *Mudhakkirati* [Memoirs], Vol. II, Part I, p. 201.
[20] "Mudhakkirat Khidiwi Abbas" [Memoirs of Khedive Abbas], *al-Misri*, May 1951.

supporters in Europe where the Egyptian question was still of international importance; second, building a following at home was a dangerous venture for liberal nationalists like Mustafa Kamil. It would have meant, as it later did, going outside their own narrow group to increase their support. This broadening of the nationalist movement base implied concessions in Mustafa Kamil's political, social, and economic program to other groups, such as the urban proletariat. At this stage, the nationalists preferred to make a try at the easier way of obtaining independence.

The French surrender at Fashoda produced profound changes in the orientation of Egyptian nationalism and the techniques employed by the nationalists for realizing their goal of Egyptian autonomy. The immediate response was one of profound disillusionment, experienced by even the most zealous nationalists. Mustafa Kamil was deeply depressed by the turn of events, particularly by the resulting desertions from the ranks of the nationalists.[21] The nationalist leaders lost a great deal of support in Egypt. Especially significant was the cooling of the relationship between Mustafa Kamil and his patron, Khedive Abbas, who now made efforts to stand well with the British.[22]

Nationalist feelings, however, were too deeply ingrained among the educated segment of society to be eradicated by Fashoda. The nationalists, therefore, came to realize that Egypt must rely on its own resources to gain independence. The first step, it was felt, was to increase the support of the nationalist movement in Egypt; that is, to establish the nationalists' goal of independence with at least the professional classes, thereby obtaining a full measure of support from the most skilled and articulate class in Egyptian society. The campaigns in Eu-

[21] Abd al-Rahman al-Rafii, *Mustafa Kamil*, p. 124.
[22] *Ibid.*, p. 337.

rope did not cease, to be sure, for Mustafa Kamil continued to cultivate the friendship of the Sultan, to curry the favor of the English left, and to contribute to French periodicals and newspapers; but he and his friends now directed much of their propagandistic and organizing abilities to Egypt.[23] A political party had not yet been organized, but in 1900 Mustafa Kamil founded his nationalist newspaper, *al-Liwa*. Espousing extremist nationalist sentiments, this paper soon attained a wide circulation, reported to have been about 10,000. The nationalists also undertook to establish private schools for youths and night classes for adults, in which they spread their own political program. Their most effective public speakers were employed in large cities to stir up the feelings of the city dwellers. Other anti-British newspapers, *al-Ahram* and *al-Muayyad*, intensified their attacks on the British in response to the popularity of *al-Liwa*. These newspapers circulated freely in the large cities and were read avidly by students and by members of the professional classes. The only pro-British Arabic newspaper, *al-Muqattam*, was a poor match for these flamboyant, aggressive organs. The nationalist movement was still basically confined to the professional classes, but for the first time it was attempting to touch and organize this entire group.

*

The British had crushed the first manifestation of nationalist sentiment during the crises of 1893 and 1894. They undertook this severe policy primarily because the Khedive, who in the minds of the British threatened the entire machinery of British rule in Egypt, had placed himself at the center of the movement. Except for this the British had left the nationalist movement

[23] *Ibid.*, p. 125.

alone, regarding it with a mixture of tolerance and contempt; they made quite clear their lack of sympathy for the nationalists. The British did not associate with them, did not listen to them, and for a long period did not take nationalism seriously. Cromer did not mention the nationalist movement in his annual reports until the turn of the century, although by this time nationalism was a well established phenomenon.[24] Commenting on the nationalist press, Cromer wrote that he had never read in it "a single, accurate, well-argued or useful article on such matters as finance, education, or the working of the judicial system."[25] The contempt he felt for the nationalists is no more clearly stated than in an essay in which he characterized the Egyptian nationalist as no more than "a demoslemized Moslem and an invertebrate European" who was trying "to adapt garments whether of the political or industrial type, made on the banks of the Thames . . . to the unreceptive bodies of the inhabitants of Egypt."[26]

In reality, the British were inadequately informed about nationalist developments in Egypt. Their contacts with the Egyptian populace and their understanding of its needs had never been fully developed. Cromer intensified these tendencies by drawing his information about Egyptian attitudes from only a few trusted advisers. Although he had once taken great pride in his intimate knowledge of Egypt and his accessibility to all Egyptians, and had made an extensive fact-finding trip throughout Egypt in 1889, by the turn of the century Cromer was effectively isolated from the feelings of the

[24] Cromer, Annual Report for 1901, *HCSP*, Egypt No. 1 (1902), Vol. cxxx, cd. 1012.
[25] Cromer, Annual Report for 1906, *HCSP*, Egypt No. 1 (1907), Vol. c, cd. 3394.
[26] Cromer, *Modern Egypt*, ii, 228 and Cromer, *Political and Literary Essays*, p. 207.

Egyptian people.[27] During the 1890's he relied extensively on William Garstin, adviser to the Ministry of Public Works, whose information about the country was derived from his own inspectors. It is to be doubted that these irrigation engineers were well informed on Egyptian attitudes toward British rule. At the turn of the century, when nationalist agitation was becoming more intense, Cromer turned to his Oriental Secretary, Harry Boyle, for assistance. Although a marvellous linguist, Boyle's understanding of Egyptian affairs was undoubtedly distorted, since his contacts were almost exclusively with the old ruling classes and not the newly emerging nationalist element.[28] Moreover, he was so dedicated to Cromer that it is hard to believe that he would put to him an unpleasant opinion. On occasion, Cromer sought the advice of Egyptians directly, but his most common source was the editors of *al-Muqattam*, so compromised by their friendship with the British, that their opinion could hardly be regarded as independent and unbiased.[29]

The British lack of sympathy and understanding for the nationalist movement was largely a product of the British system of rule in Egypt. Because of severe limitations on the size of the military force they could support and the amount of money that could be spent in Egypt, they ruled by means of prestige, by the threat of force, by isolating themselves from the Egyptian populace, and by exaggerating their own power and superiority. They, therefore, were out of touch with the feelings

[27] Harry Boyle gives a description of Cromer's trip in 1889 in a letter to his mother, November 22, 1889, Boyle Papers. This material will presumably appear in Clara Boyle's forthcoming study of Harry Boyle.

[28] See, for instance, Boyle's letter to his mother, December 6, 1899, in the Boyle Papers.

[29] Cromer to Gorst, February 28, 1907, Grey Papers, General, Vol. 7.

of the Egyptian people. Moreover, the system of rule, as it operated in Egypt, had little place for the newly emerging classes. Power was channeled through the traditional ruling classes, and the traditional institutions were adapted to the new requirements of the country. The new, professional classes remained on the outside, unable to exercise power commensurate with their ambitions and incapable of establishing the modern institutions they desired. The relative tolerance of the British for the nationalists, mixed with contempt, was also related to a more practical and immediate problem: the British did not have the financial and military resources to suppress nationalist movements throughout their entire empire or to integrate the nationalists into their system of rule. The demands that these resources, in fact, be provided to troubled colonial areas, were invariably received coolly by Parliament, and especially by the left. Thus the British administrators had to do as well as they could with their limited resources, by trying to find bases of cooperation between the nationalists and themselves, or by cultivating divisive tendencies among the nationalists.

Cromer paid slight heed to the growing nationalist feeling until the very turn of the century; at this juncture he began to show concern. He was astonished that the embarrassment of the French at Fashoda and the signing of the Anglo-French Accord of 1904 had not seemed to stay the feelings against the British. The press was becoming more violent in its attacks; Mustafa Kamil was more open in denouncing the occupation. In his interpretation of the nationalist phenomenon Cromer still adhered to the notion that the nationalists had no fundamental grievances against the British. The movement, he felt, was led by self-seeking, insincere demagogues. While some of these leaders were secular-minded nationalists, the only way they could appeal to the mass of the population, Cromer argued, was by putting their demands in the language of Islam. The basic reasons for the growth of nationalism in Egypt, Cromer believed, were the divisions and attendant uncertainty of general British policy at London, an uncertainty the nationalists were quick to take advantage of. Recent developments in British politics—the growing anti-imperialist sentiment stemming from the Boer War and leftist attacks on the Conservative government—had led the Egyptian nationalists to believe that the British government at home was weakened, unsure of itself, and not prepared to enforce a strong policy throughout the empire. Nationalism, Cromer held, if it did not owe its existence to the leftist critics in British society, at least owed its immunity from counter assault to them. The critics, because of their strength in Parliament, made it difficult for the colonial administrators to take strong, forceful measures against the nationalists. According to Cromer, the nationalist movement was still only a thin veneer in Egyptian society. It had not yet penetrated the masses, but so long as the British in Egypt were restrained from dealing with it forcefully, it would continue to exist and to make its appeal to the untutored masses.[30]

Cromer's interpretation of nationalism was undoubtedly one-sided and distorted, but it is not to be dismissed out of hand. As so often observed, revolutionary circumstances are intensified by the lack of a clear-cut, counter policy on the part of rulers. The state of uncertainty about whether the British would have sufficient power to deal with nationalist agitators produced confusion and a loss of confidence in British rule. Faris Nimr, one of the editors of *al-Muqattam*, a pro-British Arabic news-

[30] Cromer presents this interpretation most clearly in his Annual Report for 1906, HCSP, Egypt No. 1 (1907), Vol. c, cd. 3394 and in a memorandum entitled "The Present Situation in Egypt" (September 1906) in file 41129, PRO, FO 371/68.

paper, wrote the following in 1910: "How I regret now that I have tied myself down to Egypt. I have invested every penny I have in it, and my children know nothing above it. I was carried away by the wonderful work done in Egypt by Lord Cromer and his men. I believed that that state of things would continue and that England would never allow anything of what we see these days. It was a great mistake on my part. I feel now very anxious for the future of my children, as the Egypt of today is the last place I would choose for them to live in."[31] As Cromer recognized, Egyptians, through long years of arbitrary and authoritarian rule, had a great respect for the power of the government. They were accustomed to being governed severely. A failure to dominate one's subjects was often interpreted as weakness. Any indication that the nationalists could defy the British might well result in an extraordinary increase in the following of the nationalists among a people with this deep respect for power. Leftist criticisms of imperial policy threatened to produce such a situation, Cromer believed, since they called into question the actuality of British power in the minds of the Egyptian population.

The attitude of Cromer and other British officials in Egypt was, in fact, a fairly typical reaction of colonial officials elsewhere to the challenge of nationalism. Denying the grievances of the nationalists and the sincerity of their motives, these officials argued that the movement had no real following in the country. It was kept alive, they felt, because an uninformed but ever watchful parliament would not permit colonial administrators to deal with it. Officials in Egypt, as elsewhere, regarded themselves as a specially informed group, disregarded by a distant, misinformed community whose interest they represented and even understood better than the com-

[31] Boyle to Cromer, April 30, 1910, PRO, FO 633/14, Cromer Papers.

munity did. Cromer increasingly came to think of himself less as the agent of the British Foreign Office and more as the ruler of Egypt, more deeply in touch with its problems than the home community. Cromer was forever talking about "the extreme difficulty of reconciling democratic government tinged with a high degree of sentimentalism at home with the requirements of an imperial policy abroad."[32] This feeling was held even more strongly by segments of the foreign business community in Egypt, in which economic interests quickened the sense of anxiety. Foreign business men tended to regard the Foreign Office and the British Parliament as hostile to their interests. They believed that the nationalist movement could be extinguished if it was given a sharp blow by the British, but that if the currently lenient and cautious policies were followed the nationalists would wax strong.

The colonial or settler mentality customarily springs from an identification of individuals with a foreign territory and is quickened by anxieties arising from threats to the settlers' positions. Men with similar vested interests band together; they regard both the native population which threatens their predominance and the home government as hostile. The home government comes under violent attack for its failure to support the interests of its nationals in a foreign territory. In somewhat modified form reactions of this kind developed in Egypt in the decade before World War I. The private British community, which had grown considerably over the years, possessed important commercial interests in Egypt. Its members included financiers who owned heavily capitalized land companies, or, like the Peel and Carver families, were cotton ginners and exporters. Many of these important families lived in Egypt permanently. Some of

[32] Memorandum by Lord Cromer on Egypt, 1906, file 41129, PRO, FO 371/68.

the most influential groups had, in fact, organized a British Chamber of Commerce in Alexandria, an openly avowed pressure group, which grew increasingly alarmed at the growth of the nationalist movement. Other foreign communities in Egypt with commercial interests, particularly the French, shared many of the same attitudes toward the nationalists. These groups greatly feared the nationalists' radical political programs as a danger to their privileged economic and political position. British officialdom reacted in much the same way. This similarity of attitudes was quite understandable since many of the British officials, including Lord Cromer, had been in Egypt since the beginning of the occupation. They identified themselves with the country and with its administration. It was said of Cromer and his wife, for instance, that "all the associations nearly of their married life are here [in Egypt]. They have built their own house and made their garden here after their own fancy."[33] Like settlers in foreign territories in which nationalism has developed, the British officials in Egypt felt themselves on the defensive as a result of the nationalist attacks. They came to regard themselves as a separate entity, attacked by part of the Egyptian populace and misunderstood by the British community at home.

*

The year 1906 was to prove one of the most decisive in the development of the nationalist movement in Egypt. It opened inauspiciously for the British in Egypt with the landslide election of the Liberal party in England. Although safe Liberal-imperialists occupied most of the major cabinet positions, with Sir Edward Grey at the Foreign Office, Cromer could well fear the strength of the left-Liberal and labor elements in Parliament. Indeed, a great many men with strong leftist leanings had

[33] Dawkins to Milner, August 16, 1896, Milner Papers, Box 13.

been elected to Parliament for the first time. Labor had its largest contingent. Cromer, who had already begun to feel out of step with the pace of English politics, especially with the retirement of Lord Salisbury, could remind himself of the last serious crisis with the nationalists, which had followed closely on the heels of the Liberal victory of 1892. If his interpretation of the nationalist movement were to prove right, he could expect the nationalists to intensify their attack on the occupation.

The first nationalist disturbance of 1906 occurred over an incident known as the Akaba crisis, which caught the British completely by surprise. In the early part of that year the Egyptian government became embroiled in a dispute with the Ottoman Empire over the Egyptian boundary in the Sinai peninsula. The peninsula had come to assume increasing importance to both powers at this time. The Turks, who were then building the Hijaz railway to Medina, were asserting a claim to a part of it. The Egyptian government claimed the territory as part of the *firman* of investiture of 1892, a claim the British firmly upheld because they did not want the Turks to occupy territory near the Suez Canal. The dispute proved a protracted one and was settled in favor of the British only after the cabinet in London had dispatched an ultimatum to the Sultan. Throughout the incident, nationalist papers had consistently supported the Ottoman Empire. Their position had come as a shock to Cromer, who felt that the British were acting in the interest of Egypt. The press attacks were vitriolic, the speeches were incendiary, and nearly all of them described the dispute as an attempt by the British to undermine the prestige of Islam by humiliating the Sultan. The incident strengthened Cromer's feeling that Egyptian nationalism was not nationalism, but Pan-Islamism in disguise. In his Annual Report for 1906, Cromer mentioned that because of the excited Islamic feelings Egypt was "within a measurable distance of such an outburst last spring."[34] In light of the disturbed state of affairs Cromer abruptly increased the size of the British garrison in Egypt.

There was some undeniable truth in Cromer's assertion that Egyptian nationalism was really Pan-Islamism. As indicated, nationalist leaders like Mustafa Kamil and Ali Yusuf often used religious appeals to galvanize their followers. In addition, throughout this period Egypt had been subjected to a considerable barrage of Pan-Islamic propaganda from the Ottoman Sultan, Abdul Hamid. The Egyptians had watched developments within the Ottoman Empire with great interest, especially the struggle between the Ottomans and the minority Christian groups, and had identified themselves with the Ottomans in their fight against Europe. While granting the existence of this sentiment, it must also be affirmed that the agitation accompanying the Eastern boundary dispute was as much a protest against British rule in Egypt as a sign of pro-Ottoman and pro-Islamic feeling in Egypt. Ahmad Lutfi interpreted the pro-Turkish feeling in Egypt during this crisis as being essentially anti-British sentiment.[35] There seems to be no reason to believe that the majority of Egyptians were anxious to see the creation of a greater Islamic empire. They were primarily desirous of establishing independence for Egypt within the protective shield of the Ottoman Empire. Thus, their agitation during the Akabah crisis was primarily a movement of protest against the British and a feeling of affinity for Ottoman resistance to a common enemy. It was one of the great mistakes of Lord Cromer to view the national-

[34] Cromer, Annual Report for 1906, HCSP, Egypt No. 1 (1907), Vol. c, cd. 3304.

[35] "Mudhakkirat Ahmad Lutfi" [Memoirs of Ahmad Lutfi], al-Musawwar, 1950.

ist movement in Egypt almost entirely as a recrudescence of traditional values, rather than a movement drawing inspiration from the West and led by men produced by Egypt's modern institutions.

Scarcely had the feelings over the Akabah crisis abated than the occupation was torn by another event—the Dinshawai incident—which was to prove the most controversial occurrence of these years. In June, 1906, a contingent of the British army was marching through Lower Egypt to Alexandria. While the army was bivouacked near Tanta, British soldiers went off to shoot pigeons near the village of Dinshawai. This form of sport, popular among the British in Egypt, was deeply resented by the Egyptian *fellahin* who regarded pigeons as their own domesticated animals. The soldiers were under the impression that the village *umdah* had been notified of their intention to shoot in the area and had passed this information along to the villagers. Actually, although the permission of the *umdah* had been obtained, he had failed to notify the Dinshawai villagers. Shortly after the soldiers began their shooting, an altercation ensued with the villagers, in the midst of which one soldier's gun went off accidentally (so he claimed), wounding a peasant woman. The *fellahin* then turned on the soldiers, beating them with sticks after the soldiers had allowed themselves to be disarmed. One of the soldiers who managed to break away ran for help. Overcome by heat and the effects of a head wound, he collapsed before reaching his destination and died.

When news of the incident reached Cromer, he reacted in strong and aggressive fashion. Although he still did not know the details of the quarrel, nor whether the villagers had known of the soldiers' intention to shoot in this area, he invoked a special military tribunal to try the case. This tribunal had been established in 1895 to try serious assaults against the army of occupation because

of the increasing number of offenses against the British
army and because Egyptian courts had proved unsatisfactory for handling these cases. It was composed of
the Minister of Justice, the British judicial adviser, the
British vice-president of the Egyptian Court of Appeal,
a British representative of the army of occupation, and
an Egyptian judge in the Egyptian Court of First Instance. Thus the special court was composed of British
military and judicial authorities and Egyptian officials
who held their position at the behest of the British. Its
composition, obviously, was not such as to create confidence in its fairness. It was not bound by the rules and
regulations of the Egyptian courts and could mete out
any punishment it chose.[36] The tribunal had met only
once previously, in 1897, when it exiled a group of Egyptians found guilty of assaulting members of the British
army of occupation.[37]

The court met late in June, 1906. Fifty-two men from
the village of Dinshawai were put on trial; thirty-one
were found not guilty and were released. The remainder
were found to have shared varying degrees of responsibility for the incident. The court supposedly found
premeditation in the actions of the *fellahin* and, therefore, dealt harshly with the offenders. The sentences, as
Edward Grey later remarked, were "severe, startlingly
so."[38] Four "ringleaders" were condemned to death by
hanging; two were condemned to penal servitude for
life; one, to 15 years; six, to seven years; three, to one
year and 50 lashes; and five, to 50 lashes. The execution of the sentences was even more brutal, for the hang-

[36] Cromer's reasons for creating the new tribunal are given in
Cromer to Kimberley, No. 233, February 17, 1895, PRO, FO
633/6, Cromer Papers.

[37] Cromer to Salisbury, No. 56, September 24, 1897, PRO, FO
407/144.

[38] Lord Grey of Fallodon, *Twenty-five Years* (New York, 1925),
I, 132.

ings and floggings were carried out just outside of Din-shawai, in front of the women and children, two men being flogged while the body of an executed man still remained hanging from the scaffold.[39]

The execution of the sentences sent a shudder through the educated Egyptian populace. Qasim Amin, a warm supporter of the occupation until this point, remarked: "Everyone I met had a broken heart and a lump in his throat. There was nervousness in every gesture—in their hand and their voices. Sadness was on every face, but it was a peculiar sort of sadness. It was confused, distracted and visibly subdued by superior force. . . . The spirits of the hanged men seemed to hover over every place in the city."[40] Others, like Ahmad Lutfi and Ahmad Amin, were stunned by the way in which the British had dealt with the villagers, especially since the British had not previously used such arbitrary techniques to maintain their position.[41] European public opinion was also aroused by the event. An article by Mustafa Kamil in *Le Figaro* carried news of the incident to the French public.[42] In England the left almost unanimously condemned the action of the tribunal. Bernard Shaw, in his play, *John Bull's Other Island*, unleashed a vitriolic attack against Cromer and the other British officials in Egypt. The leftist attacks against British policy in Egypt were followed by the formation of an Egyptian Committee in Parliament to keep a closer watch on Egyptian affairs. The Egyptian Committee was headed by men who had traditionally been critical of British rule

[39] File 23357, PRO, FO 371/67 contains some of the correspondence between the Foreign Office and Egypt and the speech of Edward Grey in the House of Commons.

[40] Quoted in J. M. Ahmed, *Intellectual Origins of Egyptian Nationalism*, p. 63.

[41] Ahmad Amin, *Hayati* [My Life] (Cairo, 1959), p. 83.

[42] The article is included in Adam, *Angleterre en Égypte*, pp. 151-59.

in Egypt. Although Grey defended the policy of the British and contended that severe action was warranted in the light of the growing Muslim fanaticism in Egypt, his defense was only lukewarm. The private correspondence of Liberal-imperialists like Grey reveals that they, too, were extremely embarrassed by the harshness of the British policy.

Cromer, in his Annual Report for 1907, attempted to defend the British actions in Egypt. He contended that Egypt was passing through a transitional phase. The old methods of keeping order had been replaced by the new, modern, legal system. But the Egyptian population had not yet adapted to this system, with the result that crime was on the increase. There could be no question, Cromer argued, of returning to the traditional way of maintaining order, but while Egypt was still accustoming itself to the new methods "punishment, more especially in exceptional cases, should be prompt and severe."[43] During 1906 the country had been aroused by Pan-Islamic sentiments, and there had been a consequent rise in crime throughout the countryside. The Dinshawai trial, Cromer said, was designed to deal with crime in an exemplary and peremptory fashion, thereby making it unnecessary to face similar incidents in the future.

To be sure, crime was on the increase in this period. But it scarcely could be argued that a special tribunal designed to hear only cases involving the army of occupation had been invoked for the purpose of dealing with the general problem of crime. If the British had contemplated such action, they had sufficient power to make changes in the Egyptian codes so that serious crime could be handled in a more peremptory fashion. Indeed, just two years before the Dinshawai incident, the Brit-

[43] Memorandum by Cromer, No. 15, 1906, *IICSP*, Egypt No. 3 (1906), Vol. cxxxvii, cd. 3086.

ish had reformed Egyptian courts by creating assize courts in the provinces. Their hope was that these courts would lower the crime rate; in 1906 they were still awaiting results.

In reality, the Dinshawai trial made clear that the British were not attempting to deal with crime in general, but with opposition to British rule. The tribunal viewed the incident as a premeditated assault against members of the British army of occupation, and as part of the growing discontent and violence against the occupation. The severe punishments were meant to show the Egyptian people that the British could enforce a strong policy. The trial must be seen as a reassertion of strength on the part of the British community in Egypt, which felt itself threatened by a hostile Egyptian populace and misunderstood at home. In addition to showing the Egyptian populace that its attacks on the occupation would be met by superior force, the trial was also designed to commit the British government at home, by a *fait accompli,* to a stronger policy than it seemed willing to support. Had the actual facts of the case warranted severe steps, such steps might have been justified. Colonial powers have often had to treat clear assaults against their authority by means of exemplary punishments. But the offense must be clear if the lesson is to have its desired effect, and even clearer if the severe policy is to be supported at home. The facts of the case did not, however, justify such a harsh policy. The justification that the trial was directed against nationalism and opposition to British rule had a drawback, though: the connection of the action of the villagers with nationalist discontent and antagonism to the British was not established. Although the court supposedly found premeditation, the evidence does not bear out this conclusion. The villagers were not informed of the soldiers' intention to shoot. They were provoked into resistance by the fact that the soldiers were hunting pigeons which the villagers regarded as private property, and finally by the wounding of one of their women. Hysteria, fear, and a feeling of lack of support seem to have dominated the thinking of the British officials in 1906. Even before Cromer had obtained sufficient information to warrant the invoking of a general tribunal, he had done so. Moreover, the severe sentences pronounced by the tribunal and carried out in such brutal manner did not produce the desired object lesson for the Egyptian populace. The sentences were so out of proportion to the crime that they only sent a feeling of revulsion through the people. Far from committing the British government to a stronger policy, the Dinshawai trial created more doubts about the British policy in Egypt, both in Parliament and in the Foreign Office. The chasm between the British in Egypt and the British community at home was widened further.

It is uncertain who was responsible for fixing the penalties of the Dinshawai offenders. It is difficult to believe that Cromer did not confer with the tribunal before it met and make his wishes known, since there were few official acts that he did not determine. In the previous trial involving the special military tribunal he had discussed penalties with the court and had determined on exile to the Sudan. Yet the evidence seems to indicate that neither he nor his subordinates interfered with the operation of the tribunal, once convoked. Indeed, Cromer was on the high seas, returning to England for his summer vacation when the penalties were assessed and carried out. He was, therefore, not consulted at this stage. In his first meeting with Grey, after his arrival in England, Grey stated that "he [Cromer] realized to the full the bad effect on public opinion; he said that if he had had any notion that such things might happen, he would never have left Egypt before the trial was over."[44] The evi-

[44] Grey of Fallodon, *Twenty-five Years*, I, 134.

dence, which is quite scanty, does seem to indicate that the punishments were determined by the special tribunal on its own accord. The court, undoubtedly, was influenced by the hysteria of the period and also by Cromer's desire to deal more severely with the occupation's critics.

*

Mustafa Kamil regarded the Dinshawai incident as one of the most decisive moments in the nationalist movement.[45] It is not surprising, therefore, that in the following year Egypt's first political parties were founded. The first one to be founded, the *Ummah* party, was composed of some of the wealthy, landed magnates in Egypt. Its general program was moderate. It was not in favor of raising the question of British evacuation; rather it wanted to work in cooperation with the British in liberalizing the administration and granting Egypt a greater amount of self-government. Its leaders had reason to believe that the party would receive encouragement from the British. Its very existence, as a moderate nationalist group, indicated the drift in Egyptian politics, for the party represented certain less extreme nationalist intellectuals and many wealthy landlords. The latter had traditionally worked with the British without espousing nationalist slogans. They were undoubtedly driven into this position by the popularity of nationalism. The party's newspaper, *al-Jaridah*, was edited by Ahmad Lutfi. While the *Ummah* party did not have a large following throughout the country, it was strongly represented in the Egyptian Legislative council and General Assembly, where high property qualifications prevailed.

The National party of Mustafa Kamil, and the Constitutional Reform party of Ali Yusuf were founded shortly

[45] An article in *al-Liwa*, April 12, 1907, excerpted in Abd al-Rahman al-Rafii, *Mustafa Kamil*, p. 237.

after the *Ummah*. The National party favored the
establishment of a responsible executive who would receive advice, not orders, from British advisers. The party
also supported improvements in education, replacement
of foreign officials with Egyptians, and a reform of the
capitulations. Its appeal continued to be strong among
student and professional classes; although it was poorly
represented in Egypt's legislative bodies, it was undeniably the largest and most influential organizer of public opinion. Ali Yusuf's Constitutional Reform party,
was, on the other hand, the court party, representing
the interests of Abbas, although its formal political program was similar to that of the National party.[46]

The foundation of political parties was proof that the
nationalist movement had reached a new level of articulation and organization. Nationalism had spread out from
small coteries meeting in secret societies, to formally
organized political structures making their appeal to increasingly larger audiences. Its leaders were in the process
of becoming proficient in the techniques of propaganda,
persuasion, and appeal. The nationalist elite group in this
period were specialists in symbols, that is, in defining
and propagandizing concepts.[47] Their skills were oratory,
journalism, and scholarship relating to the nation-state;
their activities were increasingly devoted to establishing
nationalism as the overriding ideology of their society—
as the intellectual and emotional value system that
would give sufficient unity to society to resist its rulers.

Yet the continued weakness of the movement was to
be seen, not only in its internal divisions, but in the
techniques for attaining its goals. The most vigorous

[46] These parties are discussed in some detail in "Political Parties
in Egypt," August 10, 1911, JJ 13, Vol. xxxvi, Kitchener Papers,
PRO 30/57.

[47] See some of the comments by Lasswell, Lerner, and Rothwell,
The Comparative Study of Elites (Stanford, 1952).

group, the National party, still looked to Europe for assistance, still placed a greater emphasis on propaganda and persuasion than on direct action. It hoped to organize a larger following in Egypt in order to make its claims seem more creditable to the European public and politicians. Spurred on in this line by the increased sympathy of the left wing in England and the founding of the Egyptian Committee in Parliament, the National party elected to issue English and French editions of its nationalist newspaper. The propagandistic emphasis was necessitated by the fact that the nationalist parties were too small and weakly organized to offer any other form of opposition to the occupation. None, as yet, had resorted to the practicing of violent, or non-violent, resistance to British rule, although the National party was gradually attaining this degree of organizational and emotional intensity.

*

In 1901 Cromer was 60 years old, but he was still anxious to remain in Egypt as long as health permitted. His health began to deteriorate rapidly, however, and he found himself out of sympathy with the policies of the Foreign Office. The events of 1906 brought him under increasing pressure to alter his policies. He did, in fact, make some changes toward liberalizing the administration, the most important being the appointment of Sad Zaghlul as Minister of Education. Zaghlul, a friend of Muhammad Abduh, was sympathetic to the aims of the *Ummah* party at this time. He was on good terms with the traditional ruling classes in Egypt, having married the daughter of the Prime Minister, Mustafa Fahmi. But he was known to be critical of some of Cromer's policies, yet willing to work with the British if some of these policies were liberalized. The appointment of Sad Zaghlul was the first attempt to win the favor of moderate nationalism, by making important concessions such as the appointment of a popular Egyptian figure to the Ministry. In his dispatches of 1907 Cromer also showed an awareness that the occupation had not done all that it could to promote talented Egyptians to top administrative positions or to give instruction in Arabic in the government schools, whenever possible.[48] Nevertheless, Cromer had no desire to implement any of this. Continual attacks from the nationalists in Egypt and the left-wing critics at home upset him. And he was convinced that Grey did not approve of his policies and was not prepared to support him fully. Consequently, he submitted his resignation in 1907 and was relieved of his post that year. Sir Eldon Gorst was chosen as his successor.

Cromer left Egypt under a barrage of criticism. The nationalists were quite elated over his resignation, and their parting remarks were only slightly tempered by their recognition of Cromer's great administrative skills and his personal integrity. *Al-Ahram*, an Egyptian opposition newspaper, wrote:

> If we regard Lord Cromer in the administration of our finances as a daring and courageous builder, we regard him in the administration of our government as a violent destroyer or a tyrant. He destroyed the Egyptian Sudan and built an English Sudan. He destroyed the Egyptian ministry and built an English advisory body. He pulled down the foundations of Abadin [center of the Egyptian government] in order to build Qasr al Dubarah [the British embassy] and he effaced the *Caisse de la Dette* in order to establish on its foundations the native bank.[49]

[48] Cromer to Grey, March 7, 1907, Cromer Papers, PRO, FO 633/13.
[49] Article of April 12, 1907, quoted in Ibrahim Abduh, *Jaridah al-Ahram* [*al-Ahram*] (Cairo, 1951), p. 269.

His critics in England were no kinder. The leadership of the Liberal party had decided to honor Cromer's services to the Empire by giving him a parliamentary grant of £50,000. The resulting parliamentary debate proved to be a full-scale debate on Cromer's policies, with his supporters thrown on the defensive by his critics.[50] Yet there can be no question of his great organizing skills, his leadership abilities, and his financial acumen. Without his indefatigible energies the early years of the occupation might well have ended in disaster for the British.

[50] See *Parliamentary Debates*, Fourth Series, 1907, CLXXIX, cols. 858-886.

CHAPTER IX

GORST AND KITCHENER:
NEW POLICIES

LORD CROMER's hand-picked successor, Sir Eldon Gorst, was quite a different person from his predecessor. Short, unprepossessing, and defensive, he was driven by boundless ambitions to achieve fame and prestige. Shortly after his graduation from Oxford and a short stint working with his father, one of the organizers of the Fourth party in the 1880's, Gorst went out to Egypt and joined Cromer's diplomatic staff. On Cromer's advice he entered the Egyptian government service and eventually became the financial adviser. He was later transferred to the Foreign Office as an Undersecretary of State, where, as the specialist on Egyptian affairs, he helped negotiate the Anglo-French Accord of 1904. Where Cromer, aggressive, domineering, abrupt, knew his own mind and had confidence in his abilities; Gorst's leadership talents were more forced: he was unsure of himself and uneasy in the face of criticism. When confronted with a variety of conflicting opinions on policy, his general tendency was to compromise these views. Gorst did have a knowledge of Arabic, though, and regarded himself as better informed about the feelings in Egypt than Cromer had been.

The failure of the Dinshawai trial and the outbursts of nationalist sentiments in 1906 had convinced the Foreign Office that a more liberal policy was needed in Egypt. In his last Annual Report (1907), Cromer had indicated the major lines of such a program. Gorst undertook this task with a vengeance. Whether the policies he carried out were his own or forced upon him by the Foreign Office is a much-debated, but irrelevant ques-

[*291*]

tion. He was, in fact, responsible for a more complete liberalization of the regime than British officials in Egypt had anticipated. His unpublished autobiographical notes give a good indication of his state of mind when he accepted the position of Consul-General. Gorst wrote:

> While outwardly proclaiming that Lord Cromer's policy was unchanged, [I decided] to apply the precepts laid down in his annual reports rather than to follow the actual practice of recent years—in a word to carry into execution the many excellent practical and statesmanlike maxims which abound in Lord Cromer's writings, but which had remained in the state of "pious opinions." . . . [I wanted] to render our rule more sympathetic to the Egyptians in general and to the *Muhammedans in particular* by restoring good feeling between the Anglo-Egyptian officials and the natives of the country and preventing the British element riding roughshod over the Egyptians by putting a check on the annual British invasion of new recruits, by giving greater encouragement to the Egyptian official class, and last, but not least, by giving a more national character to the educational system.[1]

Almost immediately after Gorst's arrival in Egypt he called together approximately 200 leading British officials in order to prepare them for the change in policy. Gorst told them, in essence, that the British should keep more to the forefront their avowed intention of preparing Egypt for its eventual independence. This policy would mean opening up more administrative positions to qualified Egyptians and sharing the formation of general policy with them.[2]

No doubt the new liberal policy in Egypt was designed to attain many of the goals of Cromer's autocracy. Coer-

[1] Gorst Papers, Autobiographical Notes, II.
[2] Manuscript of speech, November 2, 1907, Gorst Papers.

cion having failed to still nationalist agitation, the British now turned to a program of conciliation. It is clear that with the growing tension of European diplomacy the British were not prepared to relinquish control over an important base on the route to India and the Far East. At the same time, since they were involved in the armaments race in Europe, they did not want to have to divert attention, men, and money to their outlying possessions.

Gorst's policy must also be seen as an attempt to maintain the ideological and moral justifications of British imperialism in the face of mounting criticism. One of the concepts which gave imperialism its emotional fervor both at home and in colonial territories was the Victorian notion of carrying enlightenment to colonized peoples. This sentiment was consistently stated by Cromer in his official publications where the burden of his argument was that the British were governing Egypt in the interests of the Egyptians. The moral and ideological strength of this appeal contributed immensely to the type of personnel attracted into the colonial service and to Parliamentary support for imperialism. It was also an effective device for securing support among segments of the governed populace. The disturbances in Egypt in 1906 and the severe policies carried out by the British called into question the beneficial nature of British imperialism. Around 1900 there were repeated attacks upon British imperialism in general by leftist elements in England, particularly as a consequence of the Boer War. A great deal of this discontent was focused on Egypt with its growing nationalist agitation. Cromer's argument that nationalism was the work of a small group of discontented individuals and that the mass of the population remained attached to the occupation, appeared specious even to the Foreign Office. It was hoped, therefore, that Gorst would be able to conciliate the discontents and silence opposition to British rule. The pro-imperialist elements in England realized that if the Empire had to be maintained by force it would, to a certain extent, lose its ideological and moral appeal and receive less support among the English people.

Gorst's policy was based on quite different assumptions from Cromer's. He held that the nationalist movement had substance, that it had legitimate grievances, and that it could not be suppressed as Cromer had hoped. Instead, he intended to make some concessions to the more pressing grievances, such as the demands for self-government and the opening of administrative positions to the Egyptians. He also wanted to associate moderate nationalists with the occupation, while at the same time not hesitating to treat the extremists with severity.

Gorst, however, encountered formidable difficulties in implementing his new policy. A basic problem revolved around the hostility of his own British officials to the policy. These men, trained under Cromer and imbued with his political philosophy, felt no sympathy for the new liberal attitudes. Although Gorst slowly removed some of his bitterest critics, including Boyle, the Procurer-General, and the advisers to the Ministries of the Interior and Finance, and substituted men more amenable to his own ideals, he was unable to build up a staff of men loyal to his views, as Cromer had done. Many British officials felt their own positions jeopardized by the new policy of introducing Egyptians into top administrative positions. They also feared, largely because of their prejudices, that the Egyptians would not be able to run the complex machinery of government which had been built up over the years.

The first step in liberalizing the British administration was that of extending the powers of the provincial councils, a measure taken in response to Egyptian demands for increased powers of self-government. The Egyptians had demanded an increase in the powers of the central representative bodies, but the British were not willing to move that quickly. The provincial councils, which the British had reorganized in 1883 and theoretically endowed with a certain amount of power over the local needs of the country, had, in reality, exercised virtually no power. The British now undertook to define and to implement the councils' powers and to create local interest in them. The franchise was not altered, thus ensuring that the councils were still controlled by the wealthy magnates, but the size of the council was enlarged and its powers were increased. The councils were given a more definite control over local administration, the most important changes being in education. They were also given the power to increase the land tax by as much as 5 percent and to apply the money to projects approved by the Ministry of the Interior. In operation, wherever the surtax was collected, almost all of the revenue was used for the purpose of education. The provincial councils were also given greater control over the *kuttab* (village school) and primary education; eventually the government turned all the government primary and *kuttab* schools over to the provincial councils.[3]

The reform of the provincial councils did not silence the demands for endowing Egypt's central representative institutions with greater powers. The major nationalist groups continued to call for a constitution and for the creation of institutions with legislative rather than advisory powers. The provincial councils did not, therefore, become a focus of interest for the government activities of the populace, as the British had hoped. They carried out their increased responsibilities with efficiency,

[3] Gorst, Annual Report for 1909, *HCSP*, Egypt No. 1 (1910), Vol. cxii, cd. 5121.

although the exclusive interest in educational reform did not satisfy the British.

One of Gorst's pressing concerns was to define the relationship of the occupation to the nationalist movement. Here, Gorst reversed the policy established by Cromer, who had attempted to secure a working alliance with the moderate nationalists, or the *Ummah* party. Gorst broke this alliance and undertook to cultivate the friendship of Khedive Abbas II. Gorst had always maintained a good relationship with Abbas when he was in Egypt before his appointment as Consul-General. During the crises of 1893 and 1894 and afterwards, he had felt that Abbas's opposition to British rule could be explained by Cromer's intransigent attitude toward him. One of the major efforts of Gorst's policy in Egypt was to re-establish a rapport between the Khedive and himself. In this effort he was entirely successful. Even though Abbas had worked with the nationalists just prior to Cromer's resignation, Gorst was easily able to win him away from them. Through regular consultations with Abbas, and by treating the Khedive with more dignity than Cromer had accorded to him, Gorst was able to obtain the support of Abbas for British policies.[4] This transformation in the attitude of the Khedive may seem quite surprising on the surface, but actually it had a simple explanation. The nationalist movement, with its demands for constitutional government, constituted as great a threat to the position of Abbas and his family as it did to the British. The Khedive realized that if radicals like Mustafa Kamil triumphed or even if the moderate nationalists had their way, the royal prerogative would be severely limited. Abbas was continually caught in the nationalists-British crossfire, and was attracted to that side which seemed to press him less.

---

[4] Gorst Papers, Autobiographical Notes, II.

On the other hand, it is somewhat difficult to understand why Gorst placed so much stock in obtaining the friendship of the Khedive, a policy that was to cost Gorst and the British support among the moderate nationalists. Cromer had attempted to curry the favor of the moderates toward the end of his administration and had been fairly successful. The appointment of Sad Zaghlul, a friend of the *Ummah* party, was a step in this direction. The pro-British attitude of the *Ummah* party and its organ, *al-Jaridah,* was a clear indication of its willingness to work with the British. The Khedive, however, had had no sympathy for the group of men who were to form the *Ummah* party. One of the sources of his hostility was his antagonism toward Muhammad Abduh, the spiritual predecessor of the *Ummah* and one of the individuals who had been most opposed to the Khedive's corrupt activities in al-Azhar and in the Ministry of Waqfs. The Khedive, therefore, had resented the appointment of Zaghlul as Minister of Education in 1906 since he was known to have been a close friend of Muhammad Abduh. The promising relationship between the British and the moderate nationalists was injured, then, when Gorst made such a strong effort to cultivate the Khedive. At a time when the political base was still restricted, antagonisms between small groups were determinants in the political sphere. In its relations with the British, the *Ummah* party turned from cooperation to opposition. The party resented the fact that it was not closely consulted by the British and that its members were not given positions of power in the government. The newspaper of the *Ummah,* *al-Jaridah,* referring caustically to the policy of Gorst, as one of *wifaq* (accommodation) with the Khedive, became one of the most outspoken opponents of British rule.[5] During this period, its vehement attacks were

[5] See some of the articles by Ahmad Lutfi, the editor of *al-Jaridah,* in his work, *Safahat Matwiyah* [Forgotten Pages], pp. 25-39.

scarcely distinguishable from that of the extreme nationalists. Gorst's actions may, in fact, be understandable in the light of Cromer's opinion that the nationalist movement derived its strength from Abbas. Perhaps Gorst was working on this hypothesis and, recalling his previous friendship with the Khedive, believed he could squelch the nationalist agitation by winning the Khedive to his side.

In 1908 under increasing pressure from the nationalists and from Gorst, the government of Mustafa Fahmi resigned. Gorst, determined that the succeeding ministry would be composed of men of talent and not of puppet ministers, made almost a complete sweep of the ministry. The new ministry was headed by Butrus Ghali whom Gorst had been hesitant to name Prime Minister because he was a Coptic Christian. He was persuaded to do so by the Khedive. Sad Zaghlul, as Minister of Education, was the only person who continued to hold the same position he had held in the previous cabinet. Ismail Sirry, as Minister of Public Works, was the first fully qualified Egyptian to hold this position, and Muhammad Said, Minister of the Interior, was a moderate nationalist. This ministry, in contrast to previous ministries drawn from the old landed ruling class, had four men who held law degrees and one with an engineering diploma. Thus, it represented the new professional classes more fully than had previous cabinets.[6] On the whole, the new ministry was hailed by the nationalist groups.

These, then, were the liberal policies of the government. On a restricted scale, they had sought to endow local governing bodies with increased powers, to open more administrative positions to qualified Egyptians, and to establish a more representative ministry. Nevertheless, these liberal policies were accompanied by two of the most coercive acts yet introduced into Egypt: the press

[6] Gorst, Annual Report for 1908, HCSP, Egypt No. 1 (1909), Vol. cv, cd. 4580.

law and the criminals deportation act. The Egyptian legal codes had on their books a press law dating from 1881, which gave the government the power to grant licenses to newspapers before they could be published and also to warn, suspend, and suppress papers in the interests of public security. Cromer had never invoked the press law, although toward the end of his administration he had given the matter serious consideration. Cromer had allowed this relative freedom, in spite of criticism from his British colleagues, because he believed in the freedom of the press, at least as a symbol of British liberalism in the Empire. Cromer also realized the difficulties that would arise in applying such a law, since foreign newspapers would claim exemption from the law on the basis of the capitulations. The most vitriolic nationalist papers, although Egyptian-owned, could have easily come under the capitulations by creating dummy foreign owners.

Again, Gorst decided to reverse a policy of Cromer's: in 1909 he re-established the press law of 1881,[7] with the goal of bringing the nationalist press under control and curtailing the publication of articles inciting the population against the British. But there was difficulty in administering this law. Though Gorst attempted to apply the law to foreign papers on a few occasions, they remained exempt, claiming the immunity of the capitulations.[8] The Egyptian-owned papers found innumerable ways of dodging the full force of the law. As Cromer had feared earlier, they could claim immunity from the law by associating some kind of foreign interest with their papers. They were also able to circumvent the law by issuing the suppressed or suspended paper under a new name. The government forced the suppression of

[7] Gorst to Grey, No. 11, February 11, 1909, PRO 371/660, file 6829.

[8] Bertie to Grey, No. 416, October 20, 1909, PRO 371/660, file 6829, No. 38816.

al-Liwa, for instance, but its editors issued the same paper under a new name; when the government also suspended this paper, the editors issued their paper under still another name.[9] The press law, in short, did not enable the British to establish controls over the press or to restrict the intensity of the attacks on the occupation. Indeed, the press law itself seemed to have created just one more grievance for the nationalists to attack and exploit.

The British also felt dissatisfaction with the existing legal system and the growing crime rate in Egypt. They attempted to solve aspects of this problem by the criminals deportation act of 1909, which gave the government the power to place under police surveillance, without a regular court trial, known criminals not convicted in the regular courts. Especially troublesome brigands could be exiled to a labor colony in the Sahara. The reason for the law was the knowledge that many of the crimes of violence in the countryside were caused by men, singly or in bands, who terrorized villages to such an extent that no one would testify against them. The law called for the creation of committees composed of *umdah*s and notables who were to visit each village in the country and draw up lists of persons considered a danger to public security. In the first year of operation 12,000 names were compiled, but of this rather immense figure only 281 were sentenced. In succeeding years the number of convictions remained approximately the same.[10] The decline in the crime rate reported in 1909 and 1910 proved to be only a temporary phenomenon, and crime continued to increase. The law created another issue of opposition against the British. Upon replacing Gorst, Kitchener terminated the operation of both coercive measures.

[9] Abd al-Rahman al-Rafii, *Muhammad Farid*, p. 156.
[10] Gorst, Annual Report for 1909, *HCSP*, Egypt No. 1 (1910), Vol. cxii, cd. 5121.

Although Gorst's programs were designed to take the teeth out of the nationalist movement, nationalist feeling continued to grow during this period. Mustafa Kamil's considerable talents were devoted to spreading the newly emerging nationalist concepts among the Western-educated classes. In the later stages of nationalist activity prior to World War I the movement tended to focus on organizing and marshalling its followers, increasing its following among the nonprofessional classes, and establishing techniques of resistance to British rule. Though all of these tendencies were to be seen in the period just prior to the war, they did not culminate in active, organized resistance to British rule until the Egyptian riots and demontrations of 1919.

Mustafa Kamil died in 1908, shortly after Cromer's departure from Egypt. His funeral, which was attended almost *en masse* by the student population of Cairo, proved to be a remarkable demonstration of nationalist feeling. Leadership of the extreme nationalist group passed to Mustafa Kamil's hand-picked successor, Muhammad Farid. Although it was generally conceded that Farid was not the dynamic leader that Mustafa Kamil had been, he does seem to have initiated some significant developments within the movement. Under his leadership the National party was given a more formal organization. The party, *al-Hizb al-Watani*, founded in 1907, was now endowed with a formal executive body and with a congress that met approximately once a year, usually in Geneva or Brussels, to debate the events of the year and to define the general policy of the party.[11] Muhammad Farid also attempted to strengthen the relationship between Egyptian nationalism and the leftist elements in Europe, particularly the British left, which was extremely critical of the British occupation of Egypt. Mustafa Kamil,

[11] Abd al-Rahman al-Rafii, *Muhammad Farid*, p. 85.

it may be remembered, was willing to work with both the right and the left so long as their adherents were opposed to British rule. Farid, however, saw the illusory quality of Mustafa Kamil's alliance with the right and therefore concentrated his attention on the left. Egyptian nationalist delegates attended the various socialist congresses in Europe just prior to World War I. Although they may not have felt sympathetic toward the radical social and economic programs espoused by the socialists, they were in complete accord with the socialists' general condemnation of European imperialism. More important, Muhammad Farid and other extremist nationalists made efforts to associate left-wing English politicians with their own nationalist congresses held in Europe. Men like Keir Hardie attended the congresses in 1908, 1909, and 1910 and indicated their support for nationalist goals. Thus, Farid was far more successful in establishing an intellectual bridgehead with the European left than Mustafa Kamil had been.[12]

The extreme-nationalist movement secured its most vocal support in the government schools. Nationalist clubs were organized in all the higher schools and in the secondary schools; in addition, there was a general student nationalist association for all Egyptian students, tied in with the National party. The students were just beginning to realize their powers to disrupt the tranquility of the occupation, particularly by means of a strike or a boycott against the schools. Such a technique was used by the students of the Law School in 1906, protesting against British efforts to curtail the political activities of the students, and again in 1908, in protest over the resignation of the French director of the Law School. In both cases the strikes were only partially successful, but they clearly demonstrated the organized support for the

[12] *Ibid.*, p. 280.

nationalist movement to be found in the Law School. The efforts of the British to check political activities in the schools, by increasing the restrictions on the students, had no apparent effect on the growth of the movement.

Under Mustafa Kamil nationalism had confined its appeal to the urban classes, and the nationalist program had mirrored the interests of this class. But as new social groups with a certain amount of articulation and organization began to emerge, the nationalists made an effort to penetrate and dominate these groups. The most important of these groups was the industrial working class, still a relatively small class in Egypt, for industrialization had not been carried far during the occupation. The modern industrial force, as distinct from the traditional, still inefficiently organized artisan class, was centered in food and textile-processing industries and in communications. Most of the labor force was located in Cairo and Alexandria, with smaller pockets to be found in the larger delta cities, such as Damanhur and Mansurah. The first labor organizations were brought to Egypt by skilled and semi-skilled European workmen who had migrated to Egypt during the period of economic growth in the 1890's. The local, Egyptian unions that soon arose were imitative of European unions, but were organized partly in reaction to the discriminatory policies of the European unions against the Egyptian working force. The European unions were utilized, among other things, to secure and maintain differential treatment between European and Egyptian workmen. The first strike in Egypt occurred in 1899, in the tobacco workers union, and minor strikes that included Egyptian workmen took place in the tramway unions during the 1910's.[13]

[13] There is unfortunately little written on this subject for this period. Some information can be obtained in al-Rafii's life of Muhammad Farid. The only analysis by a Western scholar is Walter Laqueur, *Communism and Nationalism in the Middle East* (New York, 1956), p. 35.

[*303*]

Muhammad Farid was one of the guiding forces in carrying the nationalist movement to the urban proletariat. His speeches, unlike those of Mustafa Kamil, repeatedly called attention to the inferior working conditions, low pay, and depressed living standard of the Egyptian industrial worker. He contrasted the levels of pay of the European and Egyptian worker. The National party encouraged the workers to emulate their European counterparts, by organizing themselves and employing collective bargaining and the strike to win their goals. It was, of course, Muhammad Farid's hope that a well-organized, activist labor force, with the capacity to threaten the economic machinery of the country, would constitute a potent force in the nationalist movement. The National party began to infiltrate labor organizations around 1908-1909, organizing unions dominated by the nationalist leadership. The leader was Umar Lutfi, who organized the first nationalist dominated workers union in 1909 and then established additional unions in 1910 and 1911, located not only in Cairo and Alexandria but also in outlying urban centers.[14]

Economic and administrative growth during the occupation had also brought differentiation in the rural economy and a higher degree of organization to the rural proletariat. This group, now primarily wage earners for the large Egyptian and foreign landowners, began to display a rudimentary sense of group identity. It was the most uninformed segment of the population, the most tradition-minded element in society, but the National party took on the task of energizing this potential source of strength. Here, again, the leading figure was Umar Lutfi, who, after studying the cooperative movement in Italy, attempted to organize agricultural cooperatives in Egypt.[15] For the time being, though, the rural proletariat

[14] Abd al-Rahman al-Rafii, *Muhammad Farid*, p. 91.
[15] *Ibid.*, p. 296.

remained an unimportant factor in the political reckon-
ings of the occupation.

National party overtures to the urban and rural proletariat must be regarded as the first step in the emergence
of a mass, nationalist movement. Prior to this time, the
various groupings had represented special interests:
the *Ummah* representing the landed classes; the Constitutional Reform party, the Khedive; and the National
party under Mustafa Kamil, the aspirations of Egypt's professional classes. Originally, they were pressure groups,
rather than political parties. The *Ummah* and the Constitutional Reform party remained political pressure groups,
while the National party broadened its base. The change
in the National party occurred because its leadership
was more dynamic and progressive, less attached to the
traditional values of Egyptian society, thus placing the
party in a better position to appeal to other potentially
radical elements in Egypt. Natural, divisive tendencies
among the groups that supported the National party
were overcome by their common opposition to the
British, and their desire for economic and political independence. Nevertheless, the alliances within the National
party remained expediential, and could be broken should
the circumstances be altered, as they were after World
War I. At this juncture, the professional classes, repudiating some of their ties with radical, urban and peasant
forces, reached an accommodation with the wealthy
landed classes.

In an effort to broaden the base of the nationalist movement, some of the most extreme groups in the National
party attempted to strengthen ties with traditional-Is-
lamic leaders. These tendencies were not completely acceptable to the more moderate, Western-trained elements in the National party. The pro-Muslim orientation,
on the fringe of the nationalist movement, was especially
strong among activist, extremist, secret societies and

clubs. The Mutual Brotherhood Society, of which the assassin of Prime Minister Butrus Ghali was a member, was typical of this part of the nationalist movement. One of the goals of the Mutual Brotherhood was to place this organization in contact with Sufi *shaykhs* and other Muslim leaders, and to utilize these influential persons to marshal the population in favor of nationalist goals.[16]

An extremist leader of the National party, Abd al-Aziz Shawish, was one of the main proponents of using Islamic sentiments in his nationalist appeals. Abd al-Aziz Shawish, whose checkered background included training at al-Azhar, then a period of activity at Oxford, as *shaykh* for the Arabic language training program, was one of the editors of the nationalist papers, *al-Liwa* and *al-Alam*. His articles were the most consistently pro-Muslim and anti-Coptic published in the nationalist press. It was said of him that he wanted to rid the National party of its Christian elements and make it a pure-Islamic, Egyptian-nationalist organization. For a brief period Shawish published a periodical, *al-Hidaya*, "with the object of noticing and replying to all controversial religious statements made by Christian missionaries in this country."[17] No doubt extremist leaders like Shawish and those connected with the Mutual Brotherhood, in addition to being devout Muslims, saw the possibility of using the traditional ideological value system of the Egyptian people to increase the following of the nationalist movement. The Muslim tendencies within the nationalist movement, with its appeal to Islam and extremist anti-foreign attitude, appeared again after World War I, in the form of the Muslim Brotherhood, and became one of the most potent forces in the internal life of Egypt.

[16] Memorandum on the murder of Butrus Ghali, file 5946, No. 12737, PRO, FO 371/890.

[17] Gorst to Grey, No. 57, May 6, 1910, PRO, FO 371/892, file 17061.

[*306*]

The nationalists had not yet openly advocated the use of violence, but its possibilities were more generally discussed in this period. The moderate nationalists were still basically in favor of tactics of propaganda and persuasion, although they were impressed with the various techniques of non-violent resistance practiced by nationalist and other opposition groups outside Egypt. The extremist groups, on the other hand, were moving closer to the idea of using violence as a technique of opposition against the occupation. The Mutual Brotherhood, for instance, a small group of extreme nationalist students only partially integrated with the National party, had discussed the efficacy of using force, but had decided that the nationalist movement was not yet strong enough for such methods. Other secret, revolutionary groups arose in the years just before World War I, some of which also discussed, mostly in an academic fashion, the use of violence against the occupation.[18] Since these groups did not constitute the majority feeling of the nationalist leadership, force was not employed in an organized fashion. Nevertheless, individual acts of violence did occur, beginning with the assassination of Butrus Ghali in 1910, and the plot to assassinate Kitchener and others in 1912.

*

Although predominantly a Muslim country, Egypt has contained a substantial and influential Coptic minority community. The two religious groups had lived side by side with varying degrees of success in the past. The breakdown of the traditional relationships between the Copts and the Muslims, the result of modernization and the growth of the nationalist movement, produced tensions between them, which culminated in open discord during the latter part of the British occupation.

[18] Gorst to Grey, No. 76, June 4, 1910, PRO, FO 371/890, file 5946.

The Coptic community numbered about 700,000 before World War I. Although Coptic settlements were to be found throughout Egypt, the largest percentage lived in Upper Egypt. In districts around Asyut, Copts constituted over 20 percent of the population. Traditionally, they had been treated as had other minority groups in the Ottoman Empire. They had been permitted to adhere to their religion and to organize their own community distinct from the dominant Muslim community. In return, they did not threaten the existence of the state and paid an extra tax, which fell on all non-Muslim religious groups. Additionally, because of their clerical skills, the Copts had a virtual monopoly over the clerical positions in the Egyptian government.

The modernization of Egypt undermined the traditional positions of the Copts. The differentiation and specialization of economic and political institutions called for a wider variety of skills from personnel than had been necessary previously. Recruitment into these institutions gradually was made on the basis of skill and achievement. The Copts' privileged position as government clerks was thereby threatened. The Muslim community retained its dominant position in many political and economic institutions. The British, who the Copts had hoped would favor them at the expense of the Muslims, did not break this trend. The most responsible administrative positions, the offices of *mudir* and *mamur*, were reserved for Muslims on the grounds that only a Muslim could deal with the day-to-day problems of a predominantly Muslim populace. The educational institutions were to an even greater extent dominated by Muslim values. Traditionally, the Coptic and Muslim communities had maintained their separate educational establishments. But the modernization of the educational system had brought about the creation of Westernized, government schools. Although open to Copts and Muslims alike, the government schools provided religious instruction for only the Muslim students. The government-regulated *kuttabs*, also open to Copts and Muslims, still emphasized an Islamic curriculum through the extensive use of the Quran. The government maintained several Coptic village schools, but in the eyes of the Copts these were quite inadequate to meet their needs.

The forward-looking, secular-minded element in the Coptic community did not regret that the Copts had lost their privileges as a community. They did regret the fact that the modernization of Egypt had not been carried far enough to allow all positions to be filled on the basis of merit rather than religion. They also criticized the government for its conservative, pro-Muslim posture in the realm of education. These men, perhaps best represented by Salamah Musa, were attracted to the nationalist cause, with its promise of national rather than religious loyalty as the basis of society; but here, too, they were anxious about Islamic overtones in the nationalist movement.[19] The traditionalist-minded in the Coptic community, on the other hand, wished to preserve the old arrangements between the Copts and the Muslims. They therefore favored allotting a certain percentage of positions in the government to the Copts, a percentage of funds for Coptic education and a percentage of Coptic delegates in the various local and national representative bodies. They feared the nationalist movement, not merely because of its Muslim overtones, but for its secularist tendencies. Like the traditionalist Muslims, they viewed modernization as a threat to the existence of their religion.[20]

It was the nationalist movement, however, that

[19] See Salamah Musa, *Tarbiyah* [The Education of Salamah Musa], *passim*.

[20] Kyriakos Mikhail, *Copts and Moslems under British Control* (London, 1911), *passim*.

brought Coptic grievances to a head. The nationalist parties were predominantly Muslim; during the Gorst administration extremist elements in the National party had couched many of their propaganda appeals in the language of Islam. Christians, including Copts, were attacked as the enemy of the Egyptian Muslim. Moreover, the Muslim community seemed to have utilized many of the additional powers that Gorst gave to the provincial councils, especially in the realm of education, to enhance their own power at the expense of the Copts. The schools opened by the provincial councils under the new provisions, provided religious instruction for the Muslim student, but not the Copt.

The Copt-Muslim discord manifested itself most forcibly in an acrimonious press campaign. The leading newspapers were *al-Watan* for the Copts and the nationalist newspapers, *al-Alam* and *al-Liwa,* which were dominated at the time by Abd al-Aziz Shawish. In an article in *al-Liwa* the following appeared:

> The Copts should be kicked to death. They still have faces and bodies similar to those of demons and monkeys, which is proof that they hide poisonous spirits within their evil soul. The fact that they exist in the world confirms Darwin's theory that human beings are generated from monkeys: You sons of adulterous women, have you become so foolhardy that you should start and abuse the Muslim faith. The curse of Allah on you! . . . You tails of camels, with your monkey faces! You bones of bodies! You poor dreaming fools! You sons of mean rogues! Is it with such acts that people should win renown?[21]

The Coptic newspapers, in counterattack, were hardly more complimentary to the Muslims.

[21] Translated in the *Egyptian Gazette* and found in Douglas Sladen, *Egypt and the English* (London, 1908), pp. xxi and xxii.

Anti-Muslim feeling reached its height when a Coptic congress was called at Asyut in 1910-1911, shortly after the assassination of the Coptic Prime Minister, Butrus Ghali. The congress laid the grievances of the Copts before the occupation. Most of the complaints centered on the discriminatory treatment against the Coptic community in educational institutions and in the allocation of government positions. The congress recommended that the Copts be treated as minority groups were treated in certain European states: by apportioning a certain amount of government revenue for their needs and by giving them a certain number of representatives in the government. While the British recognized the validity of some of the grievances and attempted to put the educational institutions on a basis of equality by providing religious instruction for the Copts, they opposed the idea of treating the Copts as a privileged minority.[22] During this period it was quite common to charge the Gorst administration with having fomented discontent between the Coptic and Muslim communities for the purpose of strengthening the British position. There seems to be no basis for this charge whatsoever. The movement of discontent arose from certain obvious grievances suffered by the Copts; some of these stemmed from British policies, but they were not part of a general policy to set the Copts against the Muslims. The British worked throughout these years to eradicate these difficulties and to bring the Muslims and the Copts back into harmony. It is clear that the British did not want Egypt to be divided along religious lines. The discord dissipated when Kitchener, as Consul-General, in 1911 re-introduced more restrictive measures against the nationalists. Once again, the British became the common enemy, and the differences between the Copts and Muslims were relegated to a secondary position.

[22] Mikhail, *Copts and Moslems*, p. 20ff.

The growing tension in Egypt resulting from nationalist agitation and Copt-Muslim animosity, culminated in
1910. In the early part of the year a young nationalist
fanatic, Wardani, a member of the extremist Mutual
Brotherhood, which had discussed the idea of employing
violence against the occupation, shot and killed Butrus
Ghali, the Coptic Prime Minister. The assassination seems
to have been the work of a small coterie of nationalists
and was largely unrelated to the fact that Butrus Ghali
was a Copt. Although Butrus Ghali's administrative
abilities were widely recognized, he was regarded by nationalists as one of the puppets of the British regime. He
had, in fact, signed the resented Anglo-Egyptian accord for the Sudan in 1899, had been one of the members
of the Dinshawai tribunal, and was Prime Minister when
the press law and the criminals deportation act came into
being.

The second event of the year was the Egyptian General Assembly's unanimous condemnation of an agreement to extend the Suez Canal Concession for 40 years.
When the original Concession was signed in 1854, one
of the stipulations of the accord between the Suez Canal
Company and the Egyptian government was that the
Concession would expire 99 years after the opening
of the canal, and the canal would then be returned to
the Egyptian government. Since the canal had been
opened in 1869, the Concession was to run until 1968. In
the period 1900 to 1914 the Egyptian government found
itself under immense financial pressures, especially because of its growing financial commitments in the Sudan.
Failing to heed the example and advice of Cromer, Gorst
decided to attempt to obtain additional sources of revenue by extending the Concession of the Suez Canal
Company to 2008, in return for a percentage of the returns from the canal tolls to go to the Egyptian govern-

ment. Cromer had considered the possibility of negotiating such an accord with the Canal Company, but had decided against it, since he was well aware of the unpopularity of the Canal Company in Egypt. He realized that, to many Egyptian nationalists, the Canal Company was the symbol of rapacious, exploitative, European imperialism, and that the Egyptian people resented the fact that the canal was run by a foreign company and did not benefit Egypt. Gorst, however, seemed unmindful of these attitudes. He was, therefore, taken completely by surprise at the intensity of opposition to the agreement when the news of it leaked out. Under increasing pressure from the nationalist press to consider Egyptian opinion in this matter, Gorst agreed to submit the accord to the Egyptian General Assembly. The vote of the General Assembly was unanimously against the project, and Gorst was left with no alternative but to drop the idea.[23]

The nationalistic outbursts of 1910 brought the experiment in liberalizing the Egyptian administration to an end. Gorst was bitterly disillusioned. He was convinced that the nationalist agitation made good government impossible. Edward Grey, at the Foreign Office, felt that the British had gone as far as they could in endowing Egypt with responsible and representative institutions. Gorst's popularity in England, especially among the conservatives, was in marked decline. It was probable that he would have been replaced as Consul-General in the near future. But already in 1911 he was ill; he died the next summer, at the age of forty-one. Gorst's replacement, Lord Kitchener, well-known for his autocratic tendencies, gave an indication that Egyptian nationalism would no longer be appeased.

[23] See Gorst's Autobiographical Notes, ii, in the Gorst Papers for a discussion of this incident.

Gorst's administration must be considered a failure. It was only a brief interlude between the more restrictive administrations of Cromer and Kitchener. No doubt, part of the failure could be attributed to Gorst and his policies. In the first place, he failed to win the confidence of the British officials in Egypt who were responsible for implementing these policies. His efforts to liberalize the administration were inadequate to the extremist nationalists who wanted an increase in the powers of the Legislative Council and General Assembly and were not satisfied with the extension of the authority of the provincial councils. Moreover, what the British administration seemed to offer with one hand, it retracted with the other. The press law and criminals deportation act were probably the harshest measures yet introduced by the British administrators. The most serious error in judgment was that of alienating the moderate nationalists —the members of the *Ummah* party—by working so closely with the Khedive. The *Ummah*, while representative of only a small segment of the population, could at least have used its power in the press and in the legislative organs of the government in favor of the British. Instead, these papers were consistently turned against the British and proved embarrassing to Gorst, as the Suez Canal Company Concession debate showed. It seems clear, however, that no firm alliance could have been established with the National party; nothing short of a promise of evacuation would have conciliated its leading figures.

✿

Kitchener's appointment as Consul-General ushered in a period of more repressive measures against the nationalist movement. Following his early successes in Egypt and the Sudan, Kitchener had served in South Africa and India. An ambitious man like his predecessor,

Gorst, he had set his eye on the Consul-Generalship of Egypt. His appointment was cheered in England by pro-imperialist groups, including Cromer, all of whom were anxious to see the nationalist movement dealt with in a firmer fashion; it was also favored by pro-British elements among the Egyptian populace, who felt that the British had betrayed them when Gorst succeeded Cromer and attempted to make concessions to the nationalists.

Edward Grey's general instructions to Kitchener at the time of his appointment were that he should direct the energies of Egypt into more constructive work and away from nationalist agitation.[24] In his dealings with the nationalist movement, Kitchener revived the policy of Lord Cromer. He dealt with Abbas and the extremist harshly, while making concessions to the moderate nationalists of the *Ummah* party. The leaders of the National party— Muhammad Farid Abd al-Aziz Shawish, and others— were either imprisoned in Egypt or exiled. Many exiles took refuge in Constantinople, which became one of the centers of the nationalist movement. Khedive Abbas was shorn of some of his powers. The Ministry of Waqfs, which Abbas had controlled and utilized to his own ends, was brought under the control of a responsible minister over whom the British exercised some control. Governmental decorations and rewards were also partially taken out of the hands of the Khedive. These curtailments of Khedivial authority were accepted only by threatening Abbas with deposition, a step Kitchener seemed eager to take but was restrained from executing by the Foreign Office.[25] At the same time, Kitchener attempted to repair the damaged relations with the *Ummah* party. In this connection, the Consul-General amalgamated the two advisory bodies of the Egyptian govern-

[24] Magnus, *Kitchener*, p. 259.
[25] Memorandum of Lord Kitchener, July 1913, Grey Papers, General, Vol. IX.

ment, the Legislative Council and the General Assembly, into one body, called the Legislative Assembly. This new body, which had the same advisory powers as its predecessors, was elected on a basis of high property qualifications. Because of these requirements, it was dominated by the large landowners, mostly members of the *Ummah* party. The 2,000 registered electors returned 49 landowners, out of a total of 61 elected members, and when the new chamber met in 1913 the *Ummah* party held a majority.[26] The extreme nationalists were barely represented, since their members often did not qualify under the high property requirements or were not supported by an electorate dominated by wealthy landlords.

Kitchener's repressive policy, while not destroying the nationalist movement, did at least suppress its more overt aspects. With many of the leaders of the National party in exile and with the *Ummah* party enjoying the backing of the British, the extremist nationalists had to concentrate their energies outside the country, with Paris and Constantinople the centers of activity. The annual nationalist congresses, held in various European capitals, were the high points of the nationalist movement for the year. The Coptic-Muslim discontent, which had marred the last years of Gorst's administration, began to decline as nationalist feelings were once again brought under control. Many silent supporters of the British occupation, who had misgivings about their loyalty to the British during the Gorst administration, re-established their ties. No doubt, given enough time, there would have been open nationalist agitation in Egypt against the Kitchener administration, but for the three years of his rule the political situation in Egypt was largely untroubled. Except for sporadic outburst of violence on the part of the radical fringe of the nationalist movement the

[26] J. M. Ahmed, *The Intellectual Origins of Egyptian Nationalism*, p. 76.

Egyptian scene was once again quiet; there were no disturbances similar to those of 1906 and those that continually plagued the Gorst administrators.[27]

The second emphasis of Kitchener's program was the execution of public-works projects. He used reform projects to win support for the regime, and to divert attention from possible sources of discontent. It seems clear that, under the Kitchener administration, efforts to quiet political discontent by means of reforms aimed at securing the well-being of the population, were made more self-consciously than had been the case under Cromer. Kitchener himself took a great interest and delight in the public works, especially in the fields of agriculture and hydraulics. He supervised grandiose drainage schemes for Lower Egypt, regarding himself as a competent, amateur irrigation engineer. Kitchener was also intensely interested in improving the conditions of the *fellahin,* particularly depressed because of unfavorable economic circumstances during the Gorst administration. His five *feddans* law, and governmental distribution of land to the *fellahin* were attempts, though not very successful, to tackle some of the problems confronting the *fellahin.*[28]

Public health had long been a neglected area of British rule and reform. Except for the extensive activities in sanitation carried out in the wealthier, urban residential areas, little had been done to improve the health standard of the population. The Kitchener administration, along with its other tasks, tackled this problem. Here also, the first efforts were made to carry reform to the less privileged segments of the population, both in cities and

[27] There was an assassination plot on Kitchener, Abbas, and a leading minister in 1912. The plan was thwarted; and the evidence uncovered at the time indicated that only a small group of nationalist agitators were involved. Cheetham to Grey, No. 27, July 22, 1912, FO 407/76.

[28] See pp. 239-40.

rural areas. Urban sanitation projects, such as water filtration, sewerage, and street paving and cleaning, were introduced into some of the poorer quarters in all the major cities. Although rural health remained at an appallingly low level, the government did undertake for the first time to deal with bilharzia, hookworm, and ophthalmic infections, by means of travelling tent hospitals.

CHAPTER X

ADMINISTRATIVE CHANGE:
EDUCATION AND
PUBLIC HEALTH

THERE WERE other areas in which significant administrative reforms were carried out. In particular, important developments took place in the educational system and in the field of public health. The reforming activity was closely tied to the overarching aims of British policy in Egypt. It was only after financial solvency had been attained and money had been allotted for hydraulics and agriculture that funds were set aside for these two programs. Consequently, the important activity in these two areas was confined to the latter years of the occupation, to the last few years of Cromer's administration and to the Gorst and Kitchener periods. But, it is also quite clear that these two fields did not have a high priority even in these years and that the British had considerably less impact on Egyptian education and public health than they did on hydraulics and agriculture.

EDUCATION

The reforms carried out in Egypt throughout the nineteenth century had placed a strong emphasis on education. The introduction of a Westernized educational system had been regarded by the Egyptians as the fundamental method for transforming Egypt and adapting its institutions to the West. The British were subject to additional compelling reasons for stressing educational reform, since they had to prepare Egypt for the time when it would be capable of running its own affairs. Because of their Indian experiences, however, the British were cautious in sponsoring Western education for the Egyptian populace. Cromer and other British officials believed that the introduction of elaborate, literary Western-type education, as in India, would result in the creation of a Westernized political elite, a leadership for nationalist agitation that would be critical of British rule. In a despondent mood Cromer wrote to one of his colleagues that "whatever we do, education must produce its natural results, and one of these natural results, both in India and Egypt, will be the wish to get rid of the foreigner."[1] Cromer wanted to avoid such a situation in Egypt and hoped to do so by controlling and limiting the type of education given to the Egyptian population. Westernized schools were to concentrate on producing civil servants for the bureaucracy in addition to the necessary professional men—lawyers, engineers, and doctors. At the same time, efforts were to be made to give the population education in basic subjects such as arithmetic, reading, and writing, to be taught in the language of the country. It was hoped that this slight exposure would insulate the masses from the nationalist, should such a group arise.

Before the nineteenth century Egyptian education was dominated by religion.[2] Young people were educated at home by private tutors, in *kuttabs,* or in *madrasahs,* or schools in the larger cities. The instruction, provided by a person learned in religious subjects, concentrated on reading, writing, and simple arithmetic, with the Quran used as the source or guide book, for the reading and writing exercises. A great emphasis was placed on rote learning. The Quran itself was at the heart of the school curriculum, for memorization of the Quran was regarded

[1] Cromer to Gorst, March 12, 1908, The Cromer Papers, PRO, FO 633/14.
[2] See James Heyworth-Dunne, *An Introduction to the History of Education in Modern Egypt,* p. 184.

as the highest scholastic attainment. Higher education was given at al-Azhar, in Cairo, a religious institution founded during the Fatimid period. The goal was the assimilation of knowledge revealed in the first glorious centuries of Islam; those seeking knowledge were to learn and understand the laws set down in this period. At the center of al-Azhar's curriculum was dogmatic theology, language, and jurisprudence. Other subjects were regarded as subsidiary, useful only as they provided students with the tools for studying higher subjects or with corroborating evidence of the truth of the Islamic religious tenets. In this category were mathematics, astronomy, and physics. The French savants of Napoleon's expedition observed that scientific studies had virtually disappeared from al-Azhar. Neither astronomy nor mathematics were taught with precision.[3]

The new, Western-type schools were first created by Muhammad Ali. Though designed basically to train personnel for his military designs, they also included a number of important nonmilitary institutions, like the School of Medicine and the School of Translation. During the last years of Ismail's reign a considerable expansion of the education system at all levels was succeeded by a substantial reduction in the educational establishment, as a result of financial pressures. Many of the higher schools were consolidated—some even suppressed entirely—while enrollment figures in the primary and secondary schools dropped. Dufferin estimated that in the period 1873 to 1880 the number of pupils in the six most important government schools diminished by nine percent.[4]

When the British assumed control of Egypt they in-

[3] Material on al-Azhar may be found in Bayard Dodge, *al-Azhar; A Millennium of Muslim Learning* (Washington, D.C., 1961), pp. 129-37.

[4] Dufferin to Granville, No. 153, March 7, 1883, Granville Papers, PRO 30/29/296.

herited Egypt's dual educational system. Reductions in education budgets continued apace in the first decade of the occupation, as the British were under the same financial pressures as Ismail. The London Conference of 1885 suggested that the budget of the Department of Public Instruction be fixed at £E70,000; the budget did not vary much from that figure in this early period.[5] There was also further consolidation and abolishing of the higher schools, so that by 1892 the only ones left were the training schools for teachers, the military, and the police; and the Schools of Law, Medicine, and Engineering. At the lower levels the enrollments of the primary and secondary government schools were further reduced. The religious-educational establishment, ranging from the village *kuttabs* to al-Azhar, remained virtually independent of British influence.

In his Annual Report for 1902, Cromer laid down the major points of his educational program for Egypt.[6] The first point was to provide elementary education in the vernacular, to as many people as possible, by means of the *kuttabs*. The second point was to improve the Westernized, government school system to ensure "an efficient civil service." The third point called for restricting the enrollment of the government schools to those who could be absorbed by the economy and the administration. Fourth, Cromer wanted to emphasize technical education so that those who had talents, but did not qualify for the primary and secondary schools, could learn a useful trade. All of these had the overall purpose of securing a smooth-running administrative system, a group of Egyptian technicians for subordinate positions, and a modicum of education for the general population.

[5] Lord Cromer, Annual Report for 1903, *HCSP*, Egypt No. 1 (1904), Vol. cxi, cd. 1951.

[6] Lord Cromer, Annual Report for 1902, *HCSP*, Egypt No. 1 (1903), Vol. lxxxvii, cd. 1529.

It was hoped that all this could be done without running the risk of creating a class of dissatisfied intellectuals.

The primary and secondary schools, the core of Egypt's educational system, were rightly regarded by Egyptians as the stepping-stone to the civil service. Thus, there were always far more applicants than available positions. In one of the technical schools, for instance, a survey made in 1900 showed that of 792 graduates since 1889, all but 177 had elected to work for the state.[7] Cromer tied the educational system even more closely to the government bureaucracy by dividing the bureaucracy into two levels and requiring the possession of a primary or a secondary certificate for administrative positions. Between 1887 and 1892 a system of examinations was devised and certificates for primary and secondary levels were granted only to candidates who passed the examinations. Success in the examinations became the *sine qua non* for government employment.[8] The examinations were extremely difficult, and usually less than 50 percent of the candidates passed. Although candidates from private schools and private tutoring were eligible to take these exams, the government-school candidates had more success in passing them.[9]

The primary and secondary schools gave basic instruction in languages (Arabic, English, and French), geography, mathematics, and the elementary sciences. Most of the curriculum was devoted to languages, the indispensable tool of the Egyptian administrator. The number of students in the primary schools rose from 5,761 in 1890 to 8,644 in 1910; those in the secondary schools increased from 734 to 2,197 over the same twenty year

[7] Lord Cromer, Annual Report for 1900, *HCSP*, Egypt No. 1 (1901), Vol. xci, cd. 441.

[8] Lord Cromer, Annual Report for 1892, *HCSP*, Egypt No. 3 (1893), Vol. cxi, c. 6957.

[9] Eldon Gorst, Annual Report for 1909, *HCSP*, Egypt No. 1 (1910), Vol. cxii, cd. 5121.

period.[10] This, of course, was quite a small percentage of the youth of school age. Not surprisingly, the literacy rate was not high, for according to the census of 1897 only 11 percent of the males above the age of seven could read and write, and three-tenths of a percent of the females.[11]

Under Muhammad Ali and Ismail, the government had borne tuition charges for the government schools. Cromer reversed this policy. Egyptian families were now expected to pay their children's tuition. Whereas, in 1881, 70 percent of the students had received some form of financial assistance from the government—tuition, clothes, books—in 1892, 73 percent of the students paid all of their expenses.[12] A fundamental reason for this change of policy was the financial pressures on the government, and a concomitant desire to pare the budget to the minimum. Cromer used tuition receipts to support other, less popular branches of the education system: village schools, technical and teacher training colleges. But there were other reasons, as well. Cromer used tuition requirements to limit enrollment to a number that the government could absorb into the administration. In 1901, for instance, when it was brought to Cromer's attention that there were large numbers of graduates of the primary school who did not go on to the secondary schools and whom the government could employ only with difficulty, Cromer attempted to rectify the situation by raising tuition charges in the primary schools and by placing maximum limits on government salaries for those who held only a primary certificate.[13]

[10] Eldon Gorst, Annual Report for 1910, HCSP, Egypt No. 1 (1911), Vol. cIII, cd. 5633.

[11] Cromer to Grey, No. 29006, August 27, 1906, PRO, FO 371/67.

[12] Lord Cromer, Annual Report for 1892, HCSP, Egypt No. 3 (1893), Vol. cxI, c. 6957.

[13] Lord Cromer, Annual Report for 1901, HCSP, Egypt No. 1 (1902), Vol. cxxx, cd. 1012.

Another reason for the British decision to make Egyptians pay for their education in the government schools was the personal philosophy of men like Cromer that education was not the proper domain of the government. While willing to underwrite mass and technical education with government funds, Cromer felt that the upper classes should be made to pay for their own education. The British Consul-General believed that the intellectual life of the country was a private, or non-governmental, sphere, and that the only way the Egyptians would come to value education was by paying for it themselves. This attitude stemmed from Cromer's *laissez-faire*, liberal upbringing, his feeling that individualism was the cornerstone of society and that dependence on the government, especially among the ruling classes, was a sign of moral and intellectual decay. Such a policy, however, had the effect of allowing the wealthy classes to monopolize the schools and the top government positions. Only a small percentage of the country's needy students were granted financial assistance. No doubt, both the British and Egyptian ruling classes had a common interest in severely limiting the access to the educational establishment.

Language instruction was a particularly sensitive issue for the British. Under Ismail, although the schools had classes in English and French, most of the subjects had been taught in Arabic. French was the more popular foreign language, as the higher schools frequently employed French as a language of instruction if Arabic was not deemed suitable. The British were naturally inclined to foster the study of English, and were pressured by interested parties in England to do so. As English became the dominant foreign language of the bureaucracy, educated Egyptians were increasingly interested in having their sons learn English in the government schools.[14] As a result, there was an increase in the number of students who elected to take English rather than French in the primary and secondary schools. Arabic also began to give way to English in both the secondary and primary schools.[15]

The British were not reluctant to relegate Arabic to a secondary position, as many of the British officials regarded Arabic with ill-concealed contempt. According to one outside observer, the English adviser at the Department of Public Instruction was reported to have said that he would not have any Englishman under him who came to Egypt knowing a word of Arabic. "It only gave them romantic ideas about the natives, and they would waste their time explaining what they taught to the natives in Arabic instead of making them learn English."[16] Neither was Arabic considered a language of science; it was felt to be imprecise and lacking in the necessary vocabulary. If Western science was to be taken up, it should be done in European languages, the British argued. An increasing number of non-linguistic courses were offered in either English or French, rather than Arabic. The culmination of this program to establish English as the first language in the government schools occurred about 1900, when a large number of courses in the primary schools were given in English; in the secondary schools all subjects except Arabic and some mathematics were either in English or French.[17]

For students in the government schools, Arabic had become secondary. Examinations for the primary and secondary certificates were given in the languages in which the subject had been taught, thus compounding the burden on Egyptians.

[14] Cromer, *Ancient and Modern Imperialism*, p. 103.
[15] Cromer to Fremantle, December 17, 1896, Cromer Papers, PRO, FO 633/8.
[16] Blunt, *My Diaries*, ɪɪ, 39.
[17] Shafiq, *Mudhakkirati* [Memoirs], Vol. ɪɪ, Part ɪ, 88.

The nationalists, gaining strength at the turn of the century, launched a vigorous attack against the British for attempting to destroy Arabic as the language of the educated classes. Special criticism was directed against the British for putting English on a par with Arabic in the primary schools, in the teaching of elementary subject material. The nationalists had considerable success in their attacks, for they were taken up by sympathizers in the English Parliament. As part of an effort to conciliate nationalist feeling Cromer and his successors set out to reverse the British stance on the use of English. Arabic instruction was gradually reintroduced into the curriculum of primary and secondary schools. In the primary schools all courses were taught in Arabic. An increasing number of subjects in the secondary schools were taught in Arabic, as trained Egyptian teachers became available. The secondary certificate examinations could now be taken in Arabic or a foreign language.[18] Nevertheless, these curriculum changes did not go nearly as far as the nationalist critics desired. The latter still felt that the curriculum was too Western-oriented; they called for "a more comprehensive study of Mahommedan history, as well as Egyptian general history."[19]

A substantial number of the teachers in government primary and secondary schools were Englishmen, many of them serving only an apprentice period in the Department of Public Instruction prior to moving on to more responsible positions in other departments. Such a system did not, of course, develop esprit de corps or a commitment to the immediate task.[20] At the same time, there were permanent, English members of the Depart-

[18] Gorst to Grey, No. 17626, May 18, 1907, file 6662, PRO, FO 371/247.

[19] Lord Cromer, Annual Report for 1906, *HCSP*, Egypt No. 3 (1907), Vol. c, cd. 3451.

[20] See above, pp. 186-87.

ment. They were drawn from the lower strata of English society, poorly paid compared with their English colleagues in other departments, and were regarded condescendingly by the rest of the English community.[21] Some gave vent to their resentment by spurning their Egyptian colleagues and students; social discrimination was considerable. It was unusual for English teachers to entertain Egyptians in their homes; rather, it was far more common for the English instructor to spend his working hours at the school, then, if he happened to be a member of upper English society, to retreat for the afternoon and evening to the English Sporting or Turf club. The English teacher's attitude toward his Egyptian students was one of contempt and ill will. One Egyptian remarked in his memoirs that students in his class did not know the name of their teacher, nor he their names.[22] English teachers, like their Egyptian colleagues, often resorted to corporal punishments to discipline their students. The teacher who mixed with his Egyptian colleagues and had an open, sensitive, and sympathetic attitude toward his students was the clear exception.

The one English official whose personality pervaded the Department of Public Instruction was Douglas Dunlop. A Scotsman who went to Egypt as a missionary, he had caught Cromer's eye and was persuaded to join the Department. Dunlop rose under Cromer's guidance, eventually became the English adviser to the Department. He was rigorous, unbending, inflexible, a stickler for rules and contemptuous of the Egyptians. He attempted to enforce complete conformity throughout the government's educational system, even from his English staff. The staff was made aware of Department regulations by drawing the material for the mandatory Ara-

[21] Bowman, *Middle East Window*, p. 39.
[22] Salamah Musa, *Tarbiyah* [The Education of Salamah Musa], p. 31.

bic examination from the Department's book of rules and regulations. Dunlop's commitment to the rules produced a stultifying rigidity in the curriculum and teaching methods of the schools. As one British official remarked, the schools were "governed by a code of regulations, followed a syllabus, and a time-table which day to day and even hour to hour, was similar in every town from Port Said to Aswan."[23] Dunlop came under heavy attack from nationalist critics, but remained in control of education until after the First World War.

Egyptian teachers were hardly better than their English colleagues. Small pay and little prestige made it difficult to attract well-qualified men. Teachers of Arabic and Islamic subjects were drawn from a teachers training college, *Dar al-Ulum*, established under Ismail. It was composed mainly of Azhari students, to whom it attempted to give a more substantial secular training than al-Azhar. Those who taught subjects in English and French were educated at separate training colleges, schools (and their profession) so unattractive that the government had to finance student training there. Even so, the supply of graduates from these schools was severely restricted, and the majority of primary and secondary school teachers were not graduates.[24]

In 1898, the British drew on their Indian experience again, to set up a program for bringing the hitherto autonomous village *kuttabs* under government regulation.[25] The *kuttabs* were to receive government grants-in-aid for permitting government inspection, and for providing some instruction in reading, writing, and arithmetic in

[23] Bowman, *Middle East Window*, p. 66.

[24] Lord Cromer, Annual Report for 1892, *HCSP*, Egypt No. 3 (1893), Vol. cxi, c. 6957.

[25] Ismail had also attempted to bring the *kuttabs* under the control and inspection of the central government. For this program see Heyworth-Dunne, *A History of Education in Modern Egypt*.

Arabic, under government control. Such steps were in line with Cromer's policy of providing elementary education for the mass of the population. Mass education in Egypt, according to Cromer, was to consist of "the three R's in the vernacular language, nothing more."[26]

Kuttab children were taught by religious *shaykhs*, whose training varied greatly. Many were educated in al-Azhar, but their primary qualification was that they could read the Quran and recite it from memory. That the *shaykhs* had no real understanding of what they read or recited was probably only recognized by the few who went beyond the *kuttab* level in their education. The schoolhouse itself was poorly maintained, unkempt, and a breeding place for disease.[27] One of the major goals of British supervision was to ensure minimum standards of cleanliness. The number of schools under government regulation rose from 301 with 7,536 students to 4,432 with 156,542 students between 1898 and 1906.[28] The government attempted to give substance to its program by opening two schools, for training both men and women *kuttab* teachers. Nevertheless, the program had only a limited effectiveness. Only a small fraction of the total number of *kuttabs* in the country was drawn into the system of grants-in-aid. Although required inspections were designed to enforce standards of health and effective teaching in essential subjects, little could be done without well-trained teachers, and the number of *kuttab* teachers turned out by the government training schools was quite limited.

Three higher schools remained after the suppression

[26] Cromer to A. G. Fremantle, December 17, 1896, Cromer Papers, PRO, FO 633/8.

[27] There are several descriptions of the village *kuttab* system. Perhaps the most illuminating and entertaining is Taha Husayn, *al-Ayyam* [An Egyptian Childhood] (Cairo, 1945).

[28] Lord Cromer, Annual Report for 1906, *HCSP*, Egypt No. 1 (1907), Vol. c, cd. 3394.

and consolidation of schools in the last year of Ismail's reign and the first years of the occupation: the Law School, the School of Medicine, and the Engineering School. Possessors of the secondary certificate or its foreign equivalent were eligible for admission to these schools. None of these schools had any difficulty filling their available openings, as there was a great demand among the well-to-do, educated classes for positions. The most popular was the Law School since its graduates could aspire to fairly high-paying administrative and judicial positions, or become private attorneys. The School of Medicine followed in popularity. Private medical practice was not yet highly developed in Egypt, outside of Cairo and Alexandria, but the government sanitary service paid reasonable salaries which could be supplemented by private medical practice. The School of Engineering was the least attractive since the Public Works Department paid only small salaries and reserved most of the higher administrative and technical positions for British officials.

The School of Medicine, founded under Muhammad Ali, was a thoroughly Egyptian-Arabic institution when the British occupied Egypt.[29] Most of the teachers were Egyptians, trained mainly in Europe; lectures and books were in Arabic. The British did not interfere immediately in the activities of the School, which continued to function much as it had under the headship of Issa Hamdy during the reign of Ismail. According to an Egyptian historian, its instruction was of a high caliber, for it graduated 1,541 in the period 1883 to 1893, and continued to send students abroad to study medicine. The British, however, were not impressed with these statistics, and held a much lower opinion of the School.

[29] There is a general history of the school in Naguib Mahfouz, *The History of Medical Education in Egypt* (Cairo, 1935).

According to a report published in the *British Medical Journal* in 1885, the school had no physiological, pathological, or anatomical collection. Students learned by rote, and those who went to Europe for a medical education arrived in "an almost elementary stage of ignorance."[30] The British felt that the use of Arabic at the School was a great handicap, because it cut Egyptian doctors and medical researchers off from the most recent medical findings in Europe. This position was corroborated by the observations of a noted doctor, Rudolph Virchow, who visited Egypt in the 1880's. Although generally impressed with the School of Medicine, he had reservations about the use of Arabic as a medium of instruction: "The whole of the literature of civilized nations is closed to them. They know nothing of the satisfaction to be derived from the incessant conflicts in the arena of our sciences by all those who take part in them. The final results become known to them only at a late period in a most summary form. I have known many and can speak highly of their amiability, but have found not one who could be counted on to contribute in a useful manner to the program of the science and art of medicine."[31]

Whatever the opinion about the quality of instruction at the Medical School in this period, there is complete agreement among all observers that it was torn by severe, internal frictions in the next decade (1890-1899), as the British increased their influence. Egyptians resisted British interference, no group more vehemently than the students, whose opposition the British rather disdainfully regarded as a kind of "Muslim fanaticism." English influence was first felt when a small coterie of English medical experts were appointed to handle some of the School's clinical work. British control was gradually extended, until in 1897 E. Cooper Perry, from Guy's

[30] *British Medical Journal*, 1885, I, 812.
[31] Quoted in Milner, *England in Egypt*, p. 37.

Hospital in London, was sent out as a special agent to make recommendations for the complete reorganization of the School. As a result of his suggestions the course of study was reduced from six to four years, instruction was given in English, and a teaching staff of Englishmen was brought to Egypt.[32] The caliber of instruction improved; in 1902 the English Council of Royal Surgeons agreed to send an observer to the final examinations of the Egyptian Medical School so graduates of the school could qualify for graduate work at the Royal Surgeons College in England.[33] The great weakness of the School was the limited number of students admitted each year (see table). In 1911, for instance, the School of Pharmacy, attached to the Medical School, did not graduate a single student, while the Medical School graduated only six. The needs of the country in these areas were, of course, immense, for Egypt had a dangerously low ratio of doctors and pharmacists to the total population, even in the wealthier cities of Cairo and Alexandria. The restricted supply of graduates from the Medical School created a situation where foreign-trained doctors dominated the practice of medicine in Egypt. Because it was relatively easy to obtain a license to practice medicine, many opportunists were attracted to Egypt; unfortunately, these foreign-trained personnel frequently had failed to qualify to practice in Europe or other Near-Eastern countries.[34]

Egypt's most prestigious institution, the School of Law, attracted the most talented and most ambitious graduates of the secondary schools. Throughout the first decade of the British occupation, it was dominated by French influence; instruction was given in French, many

[32] E. Cooper Perry, *Report on the Medical School and Hospital* (Cairo, 1902).

[33] Cromer to Lansdowne, No. 1, January 2, 1903, PRO, FO 78/5301.

[34] Mahfouz, *The History of Medical Education in Egypt*, p. 55.

Egyptian Medical Students[35]

	Passed secondary exam	Entered Medical School	Left at parent's request	Dismissed	Died	To Europe	Still in School	Received Diploma
1902	131	28	1	2		1		24
1903	125	36	3	4		2		27
1904	136	24	2		1		2	18
1905	177	36		7	1	1	4	22
1906	366	53	6	1		1	14	28
1907	220	37	4	2	1	4	13	66
1908	228	50	2		2	1	34	
1909	329	50	1			1	47	
1910	396	50		1		2	46	
1911	445	50			1			

[35] Egypt, Department of Public Health, *Annual Report*, 1911, p. 25.

of the teachers were French, and Egyptian law was patterned after the *Code Napoléon*. With the increase of instruction in English in the primary and secondary schools, the Law School came under pressure to create an English section. Much to the chagrin of the French in Egypt, this was done in 1899. The English section grew rapidly and soon outstripped the French section. By 1906 there were more students in the English section than in the French, and the English section had a much faster rate of growth.[36]

There was a definite bitterness between the French and English staffs. The English felt that their counterparts in the French section were instilling in their students radical political ideas and a hatred of the English; the French viewed the British as attempting to undermine French influence in the School and throughout the country. Actually, both sides of the debate were justified: the School of Law was a center of revolutionary, nationalist discontent, its graduates being leaders of the nationalist movement, and the French staff was less cautious than the British in the ideas their students were exposed to. The British, in their turn, attempted to restrict French influence and to bring the School under English control. The resulting tensions culminated in the resignation of the French director of the School, Lambert, in 1907, and the appointment of an English successor. Lambert had protested against British interference in the activities of the School, and in the French section in particular. His charges, which were carried not only in the Egyptian press, but also in the leading French newspapers, were that the British adviser to the Department of Public Instruction, Dunlop, had attempted to make difficulties

[36] Gorst, Annual Report for 1907, *HCSP*, Egypt No. 1 (1908), Vol. cxxv, cd. 3966.

for the French teachers and had encouraged the students to go into the English rather than the French section.[37]

The basic reason for English interference in the Law School was that they wanted to control a School that was fast becoming a training ground for nationalist leaders. At the same time, the need for the English section was incontestable, with English supplanting French as the first language of instruction in the primary and secondary schools.

About 1900, when additional funds were available for the expansion of educational facilities in Egypt, Cromer argued that the money should be spent on mass elementary education in the vernacular, and on technical education. In accordance with his plans, the regulated *kuttab* system was extended and a number of new technical schools, workshops, and agricultural centers were created. Cromer's policies, however, set off a great controversy among the Egyptians. An important and influential group supported the British policies, the most representative being the editors of the Arabic newspaper, *al-Muqattam*, a staunch defender of most British policies. At the same time, critics of British rule levelled a vehement attack against the program: the most pressing need of the country was not the extension of mass education or technical schools, but the creation of an Egyptian university; Egypt lacked a major school where talented Egyptians could acquire a liberal, Western education at the highest level; and the higher schools concentrated on turning out efficient, but unimaginative technicians (rather than truly educated men) who could be utilized by the administrative apparatus of the country. One of the leading figures of the time, Muhammad Abduh, wrote:

[37] Bertie to Grey, No. 352, July 12, 1907, file 23418, PRO, FO 371/249.

The only schools which represent higher education in Egypt are the Schools of Law and Medicine and the Polytechnic. Of all the other sciences of which human knowledge is composed the Egyptian may sometimes obtain a superficial notion at the preparatory schools, but it is almost impossible for him to study them thoroughly, and often he is compelled to ignore them. . . . The result is that we possess judges and lawyers, physicians and engineers more or less capable of exercising their professions; but amongst the educated classes one looks in vain for the investigator, the thinker, the philosopher, the scholar, the man in fact of open mind, fine spirit, generous sentiments, whose whole life is found devoted to the ideal.[38]

Such men as this felt that underlying the British interest in mass education was a desire to prevent the educated classes from acquiring a deep exposure to Western education and culture.

Although a small segment of the British community favored the creation of an Egyptian university, British officials, on the whole, reacted negatively from the outset. The entire British colonial experience dictated such a position, for Cromer and his lieutenants most immediately feared that a university would be just another forum for nationalist sentiments, and a threat to British rule. They were also convinced that the full-scale introduction of Western institutions should come only in the latter stages of British rule, believing as they did that Egypt was not yet prepared for a university and that money could be expended more profitably on raising the educational levels of the masses.[39] Debate raged back and forth, but eventually the British were forced to give

[38] De Guerville, *The New Egypt*, p. 160.
[39] Information on this subject is to be found in August 1907, file 28843, PRO, FO 371/249, especially the letter from Judge Marshall to Gorst, August 18, 1907.

[337]

ground to conciliate nationalist opinion. Although the university was not to be sponsored by the government, the British did permit leading Egyptian figures to collect money for its founding. In 1908 the university was opened but on an extremely small scale. It offered fewer than ten courses and had a small, transient student body. While the government eventually allotted a small annual subsidy to it, the university remained on a limited and unimpressive scale for some time. The founders had envisioned the school as an institution of higher learning, oriented to Egypt's problems while providing well-rounded Western, yet general, education. They did, in fact, bring in talented European orientalists to teach courses in Arabic literature and Arab philosophy but the budget was so restricted that the school was not able to make any real mark on Egyptian education until after World War I.[40]

Under Muhammad Ali and Ismail, Egypt had sent numerous educational missions to Europe to provide talented students with training in European universities. Burdened with considerable financial problems in the 1880's, the British reduced this program and decided to send an educational mission to England as well as France. As more money became available, there was a gradual resumption of missions. In a representative period, 1907 to 1910, of the 59 students sent abroad at government expense the majority were studying mathematics and science. Another group prepared for teaching by taking education courses. Some took medicine; others, special branches of science.[41]

Yet there seems no question that even in educational missions the emphasis was still heavily on Westernized,

[40] Gorst, Annual Report for 1909, *HCSP*, Egypt No. 1 (1910), Vol. cxii, cd. 5121.

[41] Gorst, Annual Report for 1910, *HCSP*, Egypt No. 1 (1911), Vol. ciii, cd. 5633.

literary training, and the percentage of students working in the humanities was quite high. A scholar has attempted to collate these statistics and has suggested that more than two-thirds of the students studying abroad at government expense were studying humanities.[42]

Although the number of students sent by the government to study in Europe was restricted, the upper classes in Egypt maintained their traditional close connections with European education. It was common for wealthy families to send their sons to study in France or England when they failed to gain admittance to one of Egypt's higher schools. Since requirements for practicing law, medicine, or other specialties were not strict in Egypt, the person who did not qualify for Egyptian higher schools could study in Europe and return to practice in Egypt without great difficulty.

There were a number of European-run schools in Egypt, catering to both European and Egyptian students. Many of their graduates went on to Europe to complete their education. Students of these schools were permitted to take the primary and secondary certificate examinations, and to apply to the higher Egyptian schools if they passed them. A certain percentage of the students transferred to the government school system. A much larger percentage did not and continued in the private school system until graduation from secondary school. The French even had their own private Law School in Egypt, whose graduates were eligible to practice law there if they met the other Egyptian requirements.

The largest, private foreign school systems in Egypt were those of French and American missionaries. On the whole, these two groups ran highly competent, educational establishments and were able to place their

[42] Desmond Stewart, *Young Egypt* (London, 1958), p. 104.

graduates in good positions. Other schools varied in quality. Since there were few regulations governing licenses to run private schools, the caliber of education was not uniform. In general, private schools were not run as well as the government schools. They tended to be unkempt, to have a poorer staff, and to prepare their students less effectively for the decisive certificate examinations. The private schools did far less in the way of teaching students in the language of the country or in gearing education to the needs of the country. With some notable exceptions the private schools were mostly replicas of the schools at home. This situation was understandable, since the majority of students in the nonmissionary foreign schools were foreigners themselves. Among the Egyptian communities the Copts were the most vigorous in promoting private education for their own children. Traditionally the clerks in the Egyptian administration, they had attempted to maintain their positions in Egyptian society by means of an extensive educational program. The results were clear, for the Copts generally educated a larger percentage of their young people and were strongly represented in the government schools.[43] The Muslims lagged behind, but even they were caught up in the fervor for educational progress and opened a number of private schools. Under the guidance of Islamic reformers like Muhammad Abduh, a Muslim Benevolence Society was created, allotting a large part of its funds for educational reform.[44]

In spite of its defects, private education was an extremely important feature of general, Egyptian education. The private schools taught more students than the

[43] Lord Cromer, Annual Report for 1899, *HCSP*, Egypt No. 1 (1900), Vol. cv, cd. 95. While the Copts constituted only 6 per cent of the total population, they had 17 per cent of the students in the government schools.

[44] Uthman Amin, *Raid al-Fikr* [A Pioneer of Thought] (Cairo, 1955), p. 240.

government schools, especially more female students.[45] The major weakness of these schools was the same as that of the government schools: their concern for preparing Egyptian students for government certificate examinations as a preliminary step to entrance into the Egyptian civil service and their emphasis on linguistic training.

Western education for Egyptian women had its beginnings before the occupation, but for a long time it was confined to the royal household on a private tutor basis. Then, under Khedive Ismail, several European-operated schools were established for girls.[46] Women's education gained momentum and began to receive support from the upper classes. Its most ardent champion, Qasim Amin, published two books on the subject, both of which evoked strong responses. According to one Egyptian observer of the period uppermost in the minds of young, educated Egyptians were the nationalist movement and the women's rights movement initiated by Qasim Amin.[47] Cromer also remarked on "the change which has come over Egyptian public opinion during the last few years in the matter of female education."[48]

The efforts to expand women's education were part of a more general program for the emancipation and liberation of women. The women's rights movement was essentially stimulated by the Western educated. Although a few women participated in it, the majority were men from the urban areas. Most had travelled in Europe and had been struck by the influence of Western

[45] J. M. Ahmed, *Intellectual Origins of Egyptian Nationalism* (New York, 1960), p. 30.

[46] Yaooub Artin, *L'Instruction Publique en Égypte* (Paris, 1890), p. 156.

[47] Salamah Musa, *Tarbiyah* [The Education of Salamah Musa], p. 43.

[48] Lord Cromer, Annual Report for 1900, *HCSP*, Egypt No. 1 (1001), Vol. XCI, cd. 441.

women in society. Qasim Amin, as spokesman of the movement, favored restricting the use of the veil, giving women more educational opportunities, and generally raising their status *vis-à-vis* men. Proponents of women's rights argued that one of the causes of decay in the Islamic world was the regressive influence women had on their husbands and particularly on their children.

The movement had begun to make its influence felt by the turn of the century. Although the veil was still in wide use in the cities, women began to assume a larger role in Egypt's social life. They attended the opera in Cairo and sat behind gauze screens of the boxes so that they could not be observed by the men.[49] They were slowly drawn into the nationalist movement and participated in the 1919 riots. This movement of women's emancipation, it must be remembered, was essentially confined to the urban professional class.

The British attitude toward women's education was an ambiguous one. They felt sympathy for the ideals of women's emancipation; Cromer, for instance, believed that the inferior status of women in the Islamic world was one of the chief reasons for the backwardness of the East.[50] Under the British there was a slight extension of primary education for women and an accompanying expansion of a college for women primary school teachers. A few women from England came to Egypt to teach in the primary schools for girls. Cromer also set in motion a program to train women teachers for the *kuttabs* for girls.[51] But at the same time, the British were reluctant to interfere in a sensitive area of Egypt's religious and social life. In girls' schools, British officials actually enforced many of the traditional, rigid standards so as not to

[49] Ronald Storrs, *Orientations* (New York, 1937), p. 27.
[50] Cromer, *Modern Egypt*, II, 135.
[51] These efforts are described in the Lord Cromer Annual Report for 1900, *HCSP*, Egypt No. 1 (1901), Vol. XCI, cd. 441.

offend Egyptians. One English principal in Cairo ordered the girls in his elementary schools to wear veils when they reached the age of 12.[52] The British generally failed to respond to the demands for the extension of women's education as effectively as they might have. In the first years of the occupation they provided education for girls in primary schools at government expense, but as interest increased, they demanded that families pay the tuition charges. Female graduates of the primary schools had rather limited opportunities for furthering their education; they were eligible only for the School of Midwifery and the teacher-training school for primary teachers. Egyptians in general tended to look down on midwives and women teachers, so these schools usually did not attract girls from upper-class families. There were no government secondary schools for women in this period. Women could study at this level with private tutors or in private schools; yet from 1907 to 1929 only a few women took the secondary certificate examination and none passed it.[53]

Government progress in coeducation pales in comparison with Egypt's private schools. As late as 1914, government schools had only 786 women students, while the most energetic of the private schools—the American Mission Schools—had 5,517 female students in 1912.[54] Private schools were the greatest benefactors of women in Egypt; even after World War I they educated far more girls than did the government schools.

Throughout the nineteenth century, al-Azhar had a curious relation to the modernization of education in Egypt. As a staunch defender of traditional values, it was extremely slow to rise to the needs of the country and to

[52] Salamah Musa, *Tarbiyah* [The Education of Salamah Musa], p. 21.
[53] *Ibid.*, p. 42.
[54] Clayton S. Cooper, *The Women of Egypt* (London, 1910), p. 356.

the new knowledge being imported from the West. Muhammad Ali, Ismail, and after them, the British, did not modernize al-Azhar, but rather constructed a separate, secular, government educational establishment. Yet, since al-Azhar had been the center of education in the past, the government could not completely ignore it. Muhammad Ali utilized its graduates as teachers, translators, and even as students in some of his higher schools, at the outset of his educational reform. Ismail did the same when he created the *Dar al-Ulum* for training secondary school teachers for Arabic and Islamic subjects; *Dar al-Ulum* students were recruited from al-Azhar.[55] During the occupation, the School for Egyptian *Qadis* (Islamic judges) was established, and drew its personnel, both students and teachers, from al-Azhar. Although these schools were government-controlled, they remained attached to al-Azhar.

Al-Azhar remained relatively resistant to reform, and little was done before the British occupation. There had been rumblings of discontent during Ismail's reign, when Jamal al-Din al-Afghani and other forward-looking thinkers were associated with the school. The reforms enacted during the British occupation drew their inspiration from Muhammad Abduh, who himself had been a disgruntled student at al-Azhar when Jamal al-Din was there. In keeping with his own efforts to revitalize Islam and to accommodate its tenets and institutions to the modern world, Abduh turned his attention to al-Azhar. With the support of other liberals in al-Azhar, and that of the young Khedive, Abbas, a committee was created to supervise activities of al-Azhar and to propose changes in the school. Abduh was the dominating force on the committee until he ran into opposition from conservative elements and lost the patronage of the Khedive. His op-

[55] Heyworth-Dunne, *A History of Education in Modern Egypt*, *passim*.

ponents eventually drove him to resign, and his reform program was brought to a close, short of fulfillment. While he was in a position of power, however, he revised the curriculum, adding instruction in modern fields like Islamic history and government, put an emphasis on teaching from original sources rather than from commentaries on them, and fixed more rigidly the length of study at al-Azhar. Muhammad Abduh also attempted to improve the morale and physical conditions of the school. Gas lighting and filtered water were introduced. A hospital was established close to al-Azhar and a resident doctor was available at the school. Teachers' salaries were increased; the food and clothing of the student was improved.[56]

The British, holding to their general policy of not tampering with the religious life of the country, were reluctant to interfere with the operations of al-Azhar. Cromer observed the reforming activity of Muhammad Abduh with considerable satisfaction and used his indirect influence in favor of Abduh's program. Egyptians, even reformist-minded men like Muhammad Abduh, on the other hand, suspected the British of wishing to dominate and use al-Azhar and other Islamic institutions for their own ends.[57] These men hesitated to accept Cromer's proffered assistance, though many of them were quite willing to cooperate with the British outside the religious sphere. Their attitude, and that of the British, therefore, had the effect of insulating the religious institutions of Egypt from a great many outside influences.

In spite of the conservatism of al-Azhar (probably the most resistant to change of the traditional Egyptian institutions), its list of students who contributed to Egyp-

[56] Al-Muqtataf, 1905, xxx, 738ff., 918ff.
[57] Rashid Rida, Tarikh al-Ustadh al-Imam al-Shaykh Muhammad Abduh, I, 495.

tian modernization was most impressive: Muhammad Abduh, Sad Zaghlul, Taha Husayn, Ali Yusuf, and Ahmad Amin. In most cases they had been critical of their experiences at al-Azhar and regarded the approaches and teaching techniques of the institution as backward and uninspiring. Yet al-Azhar was never completely cut off from the modern even while training its students in the traditional. A limited number of students were influenced by these modernist currents within Islam, and attempted themselves to adapt Islam to the modern world. Because of this exposure to both the traditional and the modern these men were, in many respects, better equipped to lead the process of change in Egypt.

❋

Egyptians displayed an increasing interest in Westernized education throughout the occupation. Unlike the reign of Muhammad Ali, when people feared the government schools as institutions for taking their sons away from families and eventually enrolling them in the army, there was a great demand for education during the occupation. This demand could scarcely be met by the government schools, all of which were forced to turn away a large number of qualified students. In spite of the keen interest displayed by Egyptians, education remained one of the most underprivileged branches of the administration. In a report published in 1903, Lord Cromer gave the figures on government expenditures in Egypt from 1882 to 1902. The amount of money spent on education came to less than one percent of all Egyptian state expenditures. The budget rose from 1900 to 1914, but between 1907 and 1912, while steadily increasing, it never exceeded 3.4 percent of the total national budget. Moreover, this figure included fees paid by the families as tuition for their sons and daughters, a sum constituting one-third to one-half of the budget.[58] The number of persons affected by the state-administered schools was, therefore, quite restricted.

From his Indian experience Cromer felt that Indian education was too literary, not practical enough, and not fashioned to meet the needs of a backward, agricultural country. In Egypt he attempted to provide a more general, practical instruction through the creation of technical schools and regulated *kuttabs*. But the Westernized, government schools had the same literary bias as the Indian schools. Their devotion to producing government bureaucrats made it necessary to weight the curriculum with language courses. The study of language placed a premium on learning by rote, with the result that government schools had the same exaggerated emphasis on memory work as traditional Egyptian education; nor was the instruction geared to the needs of a backward, agricultural country. Primary and secondary schools had virtually no courses useful to a young man who wanted to return to his village. On the contrary, the schools which were located in the larger cities, were modelled after private, European schools, and devoted a large part of their curriculum to language, history, mathematics, and elementary sciences. The higher schools did, of course, give practical, science instruction, but it was given in English or French, with little thought to the peculiar needs of Egypt. None of them offered a vigorous, research program; they had to make do with applying the findings of European researchers to Egyptian conditions as best they could. There was a School of Agriculture, but it was a woeful institution; it attracted only a handful of students, most of whom were not native-born Egyptians and whose tuition had to be borne by the state.

The quality of education given in the government

[58] Bowman, *Middle East Window*, p. 49.

schools was relatively high in comparison with other schools in the Middle East. The caliber of instruction improved as one progressed to the higher levels. On the primary level there were a number of inadequately trained teachers, but in the higher schools, like the Medical and Law Schools, the teachers had impressive qualifications. Most of the teachers in the Medical School were Englishmen, trained in English universities. The examinations given at the end of the primary and secondary school years were rigorous and held the students up to high standards. Linguistic instruction, which was the core of the educational system, was effectively handled by employing Europeans to give instruction in their own languages.

Because of his Indian experience, Cromer had attempted to avoid the creation of a class of discontented intellectuals, an intelligentsia cut off from the rest of the population by education, regarding themselves as the natural leaders of society. His policies, however, had the effect of doing precisely what he wanted to avoid. By restricting enrollment and charging tuition, he made education the special privilege of a small, well-to-do class. Graduates of the secondary and higher schools, in particular the Law School, came to constitute Egypt's intelligentsia. Special status was accorded graduates of these schools. Their names were recorded faithfully in the Egyptian press and they came to regard themselves, much as the Indian intelligentsia had, as the elite of Egyptian society. And again, there was the rub: many, dissatisfied with the limited opportunities available to them after graduation, became outstanding critics of British rule.

PUBLIC HEALTH

Public health was one of the last areas to be affected by the modernizing tendencies at work in the occupation—for a variety of reasons. The goals of the British in Egypt were securing the material prosperity and economic development of the country, goals most easily achieved by means of agricultural and hydraulic modernizing. There were also the difficulties inherent in carrying out sanitation reforms. Egypt was a country wracked by poverty and disease. Eradication would require vast expenditures of money. Sanitation improvement also required an advanced level of governmental control over the habits and practices of the people, something hardly attainable in a country like Egypt. For elimination of disease implied basic alterations in numerous beliefs and practices, many of which had been established for centuries.

Although Egypt's modernizing rulers—Muhammad Ali and Ismail—had attempted to sponsor health reform, the country was still backward in matters of sanitation at the time of the British occupation. Indeed, in 1883, Egypt experienced one of its most frightful epidemics of cholera. Spreading from the delta throughout Egypt, the disease was estimated to have killed more than 100,000 people.[59]

The cholera epidemic of 1883 revealed the state of Egypt's unpreparedness in sanitation and public health. Except for the wealthy residential areas of Cairo and Alexandria, Egypt's major cities were hotbeds of infections. The streets were unpaved; drinking water was unfiltered, and there were no sewerage systems. Rural sanitation did not exist, and water-borne diseases like cholera spread rapidly whenever they got into the countryside. Egypt's irrigation and drainage canals, which were utilized for all purposes, including bathing, drinking, washing clothes, and relieving oneself, once infected with cholera or any other water-borne disease, carried the infection over the entire country.

[59] Colvin, *The Making of Modern Egypt*, p. 40.

The latter half of the nineteenth century was one of the extraordinary eras in the advancement of medicine in Europe. It was during this period that the microbes which caused many of the deadliest diseases were isolated. Immunizations against these dread diseases were developed. This knowledge was of immediate use in Egypt, which had repeatedly been ravaged by epidemics, the two most virulent being cholera and the bubonic plague. Beginning in the 1890's, when money was finally appropriated for public health purposes, an effort was made to secure the country against the outbreak and spread of these two destructive diseases.

Cholera and plague were not endemic in Egypt; usually they were imported from the East, most often from India, where both diseases were endemic. With a more accurate knowledge of how these diseases were spread Egyptian health authorities were better equipped to make sure that the country was not infected from the outside. Quarantining requirements which had existed throughout the nineteenth century, were modified in light of the new medical knowledge. Of special importance were the restrictions placed on Egyptian pilgrims to holy places in the Arabian peninsula who often transported infectious disease back to Egypt. In spite of severe opposition from the more traditional-minded segment of the populace, the British enforced rigid quarantining against the pilgrims. In years when the Arabian peninsula was known to be infected with cholera or plague, they restricted the number of individuals who made the pilgrimage. Techniques for stamping out infectious diseases once they had appeared in Egypt, were also developed. These focused on ensuring that infected villages and quarters of cities were adequately isolated from the rest of the population and that the canals remained free from infection.[60]

[60] Egypt, Department of Public Health, *Annual Report* for 1913, p. 15.

Cholera epidemics broke out in 1895-1896 and in 1902; the plague in 1899. Both were handled by means of the new techniques with more success than had been so in the past. The cholera epidemics of 1896 and 1902 both cost considerably less money to eradicate than had been the case in the past. Although the plague was never entirely eradicated prior to the outbreak of the war, it never reached epidemic proportions because of the careful attention of the Department of Public Health. Neither disease was to ravage Egypt again as it had in the past.[61]

The control of these infectious diseases gave clear proof of an increase in the government's power over the daily life of the people. Yet many of the measures taken by the government clashed with the traditional practices and routines of the populace and were often strongly resisted. The isolation of an infected village, disinfection practices, restrictions on places where drinking water could be drawn, autopsies, and immediate burials of the dead all constituted challenges to significant traditions and routines of peasant life. The peasantry bitterly resented restrictions on their traditional burial practices. The *fellahin* were inclined to regard disease as an integral part of life and to accept it fatalistically. So resentful were they of governmental interference with their traditional routines that they attempted to conceal the outbreak of any disease from the government health inspectors. This practice, of course, only had the effect of giving the disease a longer period of time to spread before detection, and immeasurably increased the difficulties of stamping it out. In the 1890's, part of the student body at al-Azhar resisted government efforts to quarantine some of its members infected by cholera; they were not brought under control until the police had shot

[61] Egypt, Sanitary Department, *Report on the Epidemic of Cholera in Egypt, 1897* and Egypt, Department of Public Health, *Plague in Egypt, 1899-1922.*

and killed two of the students.[62] The control of infectious diseases thus presents an example of the problems encountered in attempting to introduce Western scientific techniques where they clashed with the customary practices of the population.

In dealing with cholera and plague the government achieved a relative success by refusing to allow the recalcitrance of the population to stand in the way of its programs of keeping out these diseases and eradicating them once any part of the country had been attacked. Such was not the situation, however, with less severe infectious diseases—malaria, smallpox, eye diseases, and measles—which did not often reach epidemic proportions. Here the Public Health Department was virtually powerless to alter the unsanitary and unhygienic practices of the *fellahin*. Except among the wealthier classes, the population either allowed disease to run its course or sought the advice of barbers and other amateur practitioners. Measles was one of the deadliest diseases among children, either by itself or because it made the individual more vulnerable to other diseases. Parents avoided the assistance of competent doctors even when such assistance was available. The incidence of smallpox had been reduced somewhat through the program of training barbers in the technique of giving vaccinations, but only a minority of the population was vaccinated, and there was considerable question about the competence of the barber in giving vaccinations.[63]

The impetus for public health reform originated from a variety of sources. As in so many other areas, the British in Egypt agitated for these reforms. In particular, the public health officials who came in response to Egypt's medical needs during the cholera epidemic of 1883 maintained a steady pressure on Cromer and other high Brit-

[62] *Al-Muqtataf*, 1896, xx, 558.
[63] Egypt, Department of Public Health, *Annual Reports*.

ish officials for public health improvement. They were supported by interested professional groups in England, whose opinions were voiced in England's leading medical journals, *Lancet* and the *British Medical Journal*. The ruling groups in Egypt, along with the hierarchy of British officials, supported reforms in the field of sanitation without question where it could be shown that such would contribute to the economic development and prosperity of the country. It was because of this support that one of the first major sanitation reforms, designed to protect the country against the outbreak and spread of cholera and plague, came into being. Epidemics of these diseases brought Egyptian economic life to a virtual standstill. Probably the most active groups in agitating for sanitation reform were the wealthy Egyptian and European urban dwellers, who were responsible for a great deal of the urban, public health improvement effected during the occupation.

Urban health services were in their infancy when the British occupied Egypt in 1882. In this respect, both Muhammad Ali and Ismail had made efforts to modernize the expanding cities of Alexandria and Cairo. Under Ismail, particularly, there had been a concerted program to beautify the city of Cairo, in imitation of Haussmann's efforts in Paris. It was during this period that new, paved boulevards were constructed. Contracts were let both in Cairo and in Alexandria for supplying potable water and for gas lighting of streets in some of the wealthy, residential areas. The foreign community, which took a lively interest in the development of Alexandria, organized a municipal council to collect taxes and use the revenue for urban improvement programs.[64] But cities other than Cairo and Alexandria had almost no urban health programs. Paved streets had not come to the rest of Egypt. No sanitary systems of water supply or

[64] Marcel Clerget, *Le Caire* (Cairo, 1934), *passim.*

sewage disposal existed—except in the wealthier areas of Cairo and Alexandria.

There was a remarkable growth in the services to urban areas in the nineteenth century. Increasing pressure for sanitation reform was felt in all growing urban centers. A large number of municipal governments, with the power to tax their citizens and apply revenue to urban development programs, resulted. By 1914, 11 cities had modern systems of filtered water, distributed for the most part by private water companies to the wealthier residents.[65] Underground sewerage systems existed in Cairo, Alexandria, and Port Said, while some form of garbage disposal, usually by carts, was employed in most other large cities. Paved roads had arrived in most of the larger urban centers. Perhaps the most impressive example of urban development was that of Port Said. From a tiny work-center established on the Mediterranean at the outlet of the newly constructed Suez Canal, it grew to a city of 70,000 by 1914. Its urban development benefitted from financial and technical assistance provided by the Suez Canal Company. A modern, filtered-water system was installed in 1905; an underground-pipe sewerage system connected to private homes came before World War I. Paved streets, anti-malaria work, a regular health officer, and a municipal government all came into existence prior to the War. Infant mortality was also lower, largely because of public health reforms.[66]

But urban reform was tragically uneven. The wealthy benefitted; the poorer residents were hardly touched. Filtered water could not be supplied to the homes of the poor because of their dilapidated state; although filtered drinking water taps were installed at various places, they

[65] Égypte, Ministère du Finance, *Annuaire Statistique*, 1914, p. 62.

[66] Egypt, Department of Public Health, *Annual Report of the Office of Health at Port Said*, 1915-1916, p. 1.

were not as widely used as had been hoped. Sewage disposal was undertaken at the most rudimentary level, while there were few paved streets in these areas. Mortality rates were extremely high. In Cairo, for instance, mortality rates for the better residential areas were, in places, twice as low as those in the poor quarters.[67] This situation was allowed to exist without remedy for a long time, although just prior to the War, nationalist critics did call attention to it and compelled the government to introduce reforms.

Sanitation reform in rural Egypt was another area of public health almost completely neglected during the occupation. Egypt's villages were not provided with filtered water or with a sewerage system. Except for the barbers and the various inspectors of the Department of Public Health, the villages were without medical practitioners. Drinking water was drawn from the irrigation canals, which were used for many other purposes, including urination and the washing of clothes. The most widespread diseases in rural areas were bilharzia and hookworm, both worm diseases that infect the intestines and weaken the carrier. The bilharzia worm, the more widespread and dangerous, has a complex life cycle. The worm attacks the blood of the host spreading by human refuse in water. The eggs of the bilharzia worm are passed by human subjects and hatch into larvae which penetrate into and develop in water snails. Later, a second type of larvae hatch from the snail and enter human beings through the skin. This disease is widely distributed among many agricultural peoples because of their habit of depositing excrement and urine in canals or on canal banks. Because it is transmitted through water it is particularly difficult to control in heavily irrigated coun-

[67] Egypt, Department of Public Health, *Annual Report for 1913*, p. 52.

tries.[68] The introduction and spread of perennial irrigation raised the incidence of bilharzia in Egypt because canals carried water and the bilharzia snails throughout the year. In fact, studies made in Upper Egypt, where perennial irrigation was being introduced after World War I, showed that there were considerably more bilharzia worms in the perennially irrigated canals than there had been when basin irrigation was used. According to investigations carried out just before the War, and corroborated since, 70 to 80 percent of the Egyptian population was chronically infected by this disease.[69]

The first efforts to deal with rural health problems were made around 1900. Since such a large percentage of the population suffered from some form of eye disorder, travelling tent hospitals with trained ophthalmologists were sent out. The teams of medical practitioners assigned to these tent hospitals were equipped to diagnose and treat eye disorders, and to perform much-needed operations. This experiment in rural health proved so popular that tent hospitals were created at an increasing rate prior to the War.[70] Indeed, the whole program was so successful that the Department of Public Health decided to use the same general organization to deal with the equally important problems of bilharzia and hookworm; tent hospitals were created. The great defect in this program was that reinfection of the patient treated at the hospital was quite common. The *fellahin,* once discharged, would almost certainly be reinfected as soon as they returned to their villages. It was not until after the War that a program was launched to disinfect

[68] E. B. Worthington, *Middle East Science* (London, 1946), p. 150.

[69] Egypt, Department of Public Health, *Reports and Notes of the Public Health Laboratories, Ancylostomiasis and Bilharziasis in Egypt,* No. 6, p. 3.

[70] Egypt, Department of Public Health, *Annual Report of the Ophthalmic Section,* 1913, p. 5.

the canals. So, although the bilharzia and hookworm tent hospitals were as popular as the ophthalmic, it is to be doubted that their effect was commensurate with the goals of the program; without a program for the prevention of disease the hospitals could only provide temporary cures.

Aside from these rather rudimentary efforts to tackle some of the worst problems besetting the rural population, and aside from the work done by the sanitary barbers and other provincial officials of the Department of Public Health, rural public health standards in Egypt were barely altered during the occupation. The traditional practice of consulting unauthorized barbers for medical advice was maintained. The villagers remained fearful of government interference and attempted to conceal the outbreak of disease from the health authorities. Unsanitary habits continued to exist and villagers in general were not aware of the dangers of unsafe drinking water.

CHAPTER XI

BRITISH ADMINISTRATION
AND OTHER AGENTS
OF MODERNIZATION

OTHER IMPORTANT agents of change in Egypt besides that of the British administration were the private commercial and financial groups and the missionaries.[1] In some quite significant respects these groups changed Egyptian society more dramatically than did the administration, especially since the latter was committed to securing the tranquility of the people and was concerned with maintaining stability. The intrinsic importance of these groups, notwithstanding, it is beyond the scope of this study to examine them in detail. All that can be done in a history of the British administration *qua* administration is to indicate in general terms the nature of these groups and then to analyze their relationship with the British administrators.

At the outset, one point must be stressed: the role of the government in all spheres of Egyptian life—economic, political, and social—was immense. Prior, and during, the occupation the government was the major instrument for social change and economic development. The government dominated the hydraulic work for irrigation. Its influence over agriculture was great. It was a major force in sanitation and although there were numerous, private educational institutions, government schools were the pace-setters in most areas of education, giving access to the government bureaucracy and emulated by the private schools. It was within this framework of strong

[1] The missionaries will not be discussed in this chapter. Some mention has been made of them in the preceding chapter, in connection with the discussion of education.

governmental activity and control that the private groups operated. Their relationship to the government was then therefore a matter of great concern to all parties.

The British occupied an Egypt in a state of financial disintegration and virtual governmental bankruptcy. Private economic groups since Ismail's reign had played a major part in the economic development of the country,[2] but in the early years of administrative reorganization there was a quite natural diminution of the amount of new capital invested in Egypt. The British occupation was expected to be temporary and financiers were not anxious to invest in an area where the risks ran so high.[3] For the most part, then, during the first decade of British rule, the private economic groups were also involved in attempting to retrench and to protect their original investments. A vast amount of money had been invested in the Egyptian public debt. The Corporation of Foreign Bondholders represented the interests of European investors in government loans. During the first decade of British rule they struggled with the British administration to secure a realignment of Egyptian finances favorable to their own interests. As has been mentioned, the bondholders were often in conflict with the British administration over the appropriation of funds for the payment of this debt. Compromises were made on both sides as the debt was gradually consolidated and the interest rate reduced. On the whole, it can be said that the interests of the bondholders were certainly safeguarded by the relatively conservative financial changes engineered by Cromer during this period.

The next decade—1892-1902—saw a slow upswing of

[2] See above, pp. 40-41.

[3] There was a net increase of capital from abroad in the period 1883 to 1892 of only £E109,000. A. E. Crouchley, *The Investment of Foreign Capital in Egyptian Companies and Public Debt* (Cairo, 1936), p. 149.

European investment in Egypt. Because the Egyptian government was not permitted to borrow more than £E1 million without the consent of the Ottomans, the money was invested privately. A statistical table of paid-up capital and debentures of companies operating in Egypt, exclusive of the Suez Canal Company, indicates that the total capital rose from approximately £E6,500,-000 in 1883 to only £E7,300,000 in 1892. It almost quadrupled—to £E26,200,000—in the next decade.[4] But the major growth of private investing was to occur between 1902 and 1914. The reconquest of the Sudan, the construction of the Aswan Dam, and the signing of the Anglo-French Accord regarding Egypt opened vast opportunities to the European investor. Egyptian finances by this time were on solid foundations. Moreover, the continuation of British rule in Egypt seemed certain for many years to come. With new land coming under cultivation and the great possibilities for agricultural development in the Sudan, foreign investors came to regard Egypt as an area where high returns could be realized. Between 1900 and 1907, 160 new, joint stock companies were formed, representing £E43,335,000 authorized capital. By 1914 the total paid-up capital of joint stock companies operating in Egypt was £E100,152,000 (excluding the Suez Canal Company). The dividends of 1906, one of the peak years for these companies, represented an average rate of 9½ percent on the paid-up capital, and no less than 12 companies paid over 12 percent.[5]

One of the most striking facts about the investment in Egypt was that it was almost completely of foreign origin, whether the joint stock companies were incorporated in Egypt or abroad. Of the slightly more than £E100 million of paid-up capital in joint stock companies operating in Egypt in 1914, 92 million was controlled by foreign

[4] *Ibid.*, p. 147.
[5] *Ibid.*, p. 63 and p. 156.

interests, approximately 92 percent again excluding the Suez Canal Company.[6] Additionally, foreign interests held almost the entire public debt. Nor does this calculation take into account branches of European concerns or businesses other than joint stock companies, European-owned land, private loans, and investments by private insurance companies. The estimate of a scholar who made detailed studies of this problem is that considerably more than £E200 million was invested from the outside in Egypt. Of course, it must be assumed that a large part of this money was not new capital coming from Europe but rather the profits from enterprises already in Egypt. The annual payments to be made abroad on these various forms of investment amounted to nearly £E9 million.[7] The unreliability of these statistics cannot be too strongly emphasized, but they do constitute a picture of an economy dominated by foreign capital.

European capital tended to be consolidated in relatively large-scale economic enterprises. The average size of locally formed companies in 1900 was small, so that 33 locally subscribed companies represented paid-up capital and debentures of £E2,058,682, or an average of £E62,384. Companies formed on foreign capital were almost always big units. Three of them had a paid-up capital of over a million pounds, while the total paid-up capital and debentures of 45 foreign companies operating in 1900 amounted to £E19,108,893, an average of £E424,642. If the Suez Canal Company is taken into account, this average is raised to £E842,512.[8] The breakdown of these statistics according to country also presents great problems, but the general picture seems clear.

[6] Égypte, Ministère des Finances, Département de la Statistique Générale, *Annuaire Statistique de l'Égypte*, 1915, p. 362 and Crouchley, *The Investment of Foreign Capital*, p. 73.

[7] Crouchley, *The Investment of Foreign Capital*, p. 181.

[8] *Ibid.*, p. 43.

Surprisingly, the French were the heaviest investors, with a total capital of £E46,267,000 in 1914, followed by the British at £E30,250,000 and the Belgians, £E14,297,000. French capital tended to be concentrated in very large units; in 1902 six companies in which French capital had a controlling interest totalled £E11,548,000, while British capital, totalling £E9,977,000 was dispersed in 27 companies. Most of the French enterprises went back to the days before the occupation; the big firms were the *Crédit Foncier* and the Egyptian Sugar Company (see table below). Belgian capital was invested in land, transport, and industry. It provided a system of trams in Cairo and Alexandria, a light railway in the delta, two breweries, a cement company, and a cigarette company.

Companies containing Capital from Abroad,
grouped according to the controlling element in each case,
paid-up capital, 1914[9]*
(IN THOUSANDS OF EGYPTIAN POUNDS)

	England	France	Belgium	Others	Total
Mortgage cos.	13,493	39,102	1,974		54,569
Banks and Financial cos.	3,788	1,485	386	341	6,000
Agr. and Urban Land cos.	2,765	1,237	8,330		12,332
Transportation and Canal	2,724		2,495	514	5,744
Manufacturing, commerce and mining	7,480	4,443	1,109	373	13,405
Total	30,250	46,267	14,294	1,228	92,039

* excludes Suez Canal Company

The further breakdown of these statistics is also revealing of the areas into which this investment was attracted. It has been estimated that nearly three-fourths of this

[9] *Ibid.*, p. 72.

loan capital was in mortgage or land companies and that the mortgage debts in Egypt amounted to over £E60 million in 1914. There was also a large number of trading banks, mostly branches or subsidiaries of foreign banks. Their business was practically confined to the financing of external trade. Considerably less capital, but still important amounts, was attracted into the transportation system of Egypt and was related to the movement of the Egyptian export crops.

It is quite clear from this picture that the foreign financial community was a large and financially powerful group, that its money was attracted into the more modernized sectors of the economy, and was closely tied to Egypt's export crop, either directly or indirectly, when not invested for purely speculative purposes. One scholar, after studying the monetary system of Egypt, was led to conclude that the banking and joint stock company structure of Egypt was not well adapted to the needs of the country. The supply of money depended upon conditions frequently beyond Egypt's control. Only small amounts of capital were available for the small peasant landholders. Capital mainly served the foreign communities. There was an over-specialization of existing banks, an absence of credit facilities for local economic development, with the result that industrial development was hurt. This scholar adds:

> From the start, foreign banks have hardly adapted themselves to the real needs of the country. This they could not do, even if they tried. The forces at work were all making for disintegration. The regime of capitulations and its corollaries, the irresponsibility of foreign institutions, the separation, socially, politically, and economically, of the leading trading communities from the main body of the Egyptian society, the sharp division among these communities themselves, and

last, but not least, the lack of Egyptian enterprise—all these forces worked for segregation.[10]

In spite of the vast amounts of capital attracted to Egypt, little was allocated for industrial development. European financiers did not want to develop Egypt as a competitor with Europe in manufactured products. Rather, they wanted to extract the raw materials from Egypt, making it a consumer of European finished products. The few efforts to promote industrialization, usually the work of interlopers in the European financial community, were generally unsuccessful. In the 1890's, for example, a group of enterprising Englishmen tried to establish local textile factories in Egypt. These, of course, would have competed with the Lancashire factories aimed at the Egyptian consumer market. The British administrators in Egypt, realizing full well that they would be under attack from this powerful English lobby, impeded the venture, although Cromer was not able to prevent the establishment of the cotton mills. In fact, Cromer was aware of a similar controversy in India which had led to very strong attacks against the British administration by the Lancashire industrialists for allowing local textile factories to be established. To forestall this kind of criticism Cromer had an excise of 8 percent levied on locally manufactured goods, the tax being equivalent to the tariff on imported goods. Cromer's official reason for this excise was that he was opposed in theory to the practice of supporting industry behind protective tariff barriers. There is no reason to discount this reasoning, for Cromer was a dedicated apostle of free trade. But there can be no question that he also felt the pressure from the cotton manufacturing community in England, even before it had appeared.[11] In like fashion, excise

[10] M. A. Rifaat, *The Monetary System of Egypt* (London, 1935), p. 101.

[11] Findlay to Lansdowne, No. 53 A, PRO, FO 78/5233. The

taxes roughly equivalent to the tariffs on imported products were placed on other locally manufactured goods.[12]

There was, of course, a certain amount of industrial development accompanying the general economic activity of Egypt. Most of these changes occurred in the fields of food and raw material processing, and in transportation. Almost the entire industrial plant of Egypt before World War I was foreign owned. The most important industries were associated with the export of cotton, for there were relatively large British-owned plants for the ginning and packing of cotton for export. The cigarette and tobacco industries were quite large; Egypt even exported some of its finished products.[13] Public utilities industries—water, gas, electricity—existed in all the major cities. In addition, small, traditional, handicraft industries continued to function although they felt severely the competition from the new, modernized, foreign and Egyptian industrial enterprises. Egypt was almost completely dependent on Europe for its heavy industry. Its large machinery—locomotives, electrical equipment, water filtration systems, and so forth—were imported from Europe, the United States, and Japan. Moreover, Egypt was not self-sufficient in its power output, compelling it to import coal. The power of the Nile to produce elec-

---

marginal comment at the Foreign Office reads as follows: "The cotton mills case in which the commercial department was interested . . . is a long story, but the pith of it is that in order to avoid trouble which arose between Manchester manufacturers and the government of India owing to the alleged protectionist tendencies of the Indian cotton duties, and also in the interests of free trade, Lord Cromer obtained the imposition of the excise duty on cotton made in Egypt equivalent to the import duty on such goods manufactured abroad."

[12] The excises on Egyptian refined sugar and salt are described in Cheetham to Grey, No. 21570, No. 33, May 27, 1911, file 17894, PRO, FO 368/526.

[13] Georges LeCarpentier, *L'Égypte Moderne* (Paris, 1925), p. 91.

tricity had not yet been harnessed. In all, it was estimated that 366,000 people were engaged in industrial enterprises in 1917; that is, approximately 3 percent of the population.[14] Only a minority of these individuals worked in the modernized industries. A large segment of the labor force in the new industries, moreover, was composed of women and children, since Egypt had only rudimentary labor laws.

✻

An extremely difficult problem to resolve is the relationship between the administration and these private economic groups. The documentation clearly shows that there were numerous disputes between them, for, in many instances, they had conflicting interests. To provide any general estimate of the relative strength or preponderance of one or the other is to risk over-simplification. It would certainly be incorrect to assume either that the state was the handmaid of private economic groups or the reverse. Rather, the balance lies somewhere in the middle. Compromises were constantly being effected between the sometimes conflicting goals of these two major forces in Egypt; their relative strengths varied from one period to another.

The British administrators, of course, had no doctrinaire ideas about excluding foreign investment from Egypt. Quite the contrary, within certain limits, they welcomed foreign investment. These men had been raised in the Victorian *laissez-faire* climate and believed in the superiority of private initiative over government responsibility. Furthermore, as representatives of the British government, they were inclined to encourage the foreign investor to direct his capital to Egypt, and, of course, the British investor. Because of Egypt's peculiar international

[14] Alfred Bonne, *State and Economics in the Middle East* (London, 1955), p. 293.

obligations, however, the British administrators were usually precluded from favoring their own countrymen at the expense of others. The administration could not use tariffs (but could use excises) to favor British investors, since they were fixed by an international convention and could not be changed without complex negotiations. Moreover, the administration had developed the custom of awarding governmental contracts through open competition by bids. Although British officials were often under a great deal of pressure from the British community to use their influence for British capital, on the whole it is safe to say that very little discrimination and favoritism was practiced in Egypt.[15]

Since the Egyptian government was precluded from borrowing more than £E1 million without the consent of the Ottoman Empire, the government was under considerable pressure to invite private capital to Egypt for economic development programs. For this purpose, Cromer and his successors tried to attract European capital to Egypt by giving quite favorable concessions and privileges. In this way they were using the same kind of concessionary policies that had been employed by Ismail to divert capital to Egypt. Under Ismail concessions were granted to Europeans for a great variety of programs, such as street lighting and facilities for drinking water. This concession policy was held in abeyance to a great extent from 1875 to 1892, while Egypt was involved in a program of financial reconstruction.[16] But Cromer re-embarked upon it in a vigorous fashion during the last decade of his career in Egypt. Under the British there were concessions of immense amounts of land to European companies. The Behera Land Company obtained very large land concessions when its hydraulic

[15] See, for example, Cromer to Salisbury, No. 35, November 27, 1896, PRO, FO 78/4766.
[16] Crouchley, *The Investment of Foreign Capital*, p. 135.

rights were cancelled by the government. Privileged concessions were also made for tramway companies, water and electric companies, sugar factories, banks, and light railways. The privileged company was usually given monopoly rights, such as the right to sell land or to run the tramway system, in return for performing certain administrative and economic responsibilities.[17] This kind of arrangement clearly enabled the government to develop key aspects of the economy without itself being burdened with heavy expenditures. On the other hand, some of the concessions were made simply because of the financial pressures on the government. For example, a considerable amount of land was turned over to Ernest Cassel's land company because Cassel had provided a loan to the Egyptian government during the reconquest of the Sudan.[18]

In general, Cromer was able to exercise considerable control over the foreign financial community, though at the outset of his career, he had his difficulties with foreign bondholders. Many of his proposed reforms would have alienated this group, but with the more cautious guidance of the British Foreign Secretary, the British administration in Egypt was able to stand well with the bondholders on most occasions. As the years passed, and in the face of all the problems besetting the foreign community, Cromer became a symbol of responsible and stable government. The financial community was inclined, then, to trust his judgment and not make trouble. Indeed, in 1897 Cromer helped form the British Chamber of Commerce in Alexandria and constantly worked in close alliance with it. The other foreign communities, and especially the French, were more recalcitrant, but

[17] The tramway concession is described in Gorst to Grey, No. 24102, No. 70, July 4, 1908, file 22713, PRO, FO 371/451. There is also a long discussion of these concession companies in *al-Muqtataf*, 1900, xxiv, 124-25.

[18] See above, p. 245.

they preferred Cromer and his administration to the nationalists and to the threat of political and economic instability.

Of considerable significance in the lack of overt tension between the foreign financial community and Cromer was Cromer's close relationship with Ernest Cassel. Cassel was one of the great international financiers of the late nineteenth century. Born in Cologne, he had risen rapidly in the Anglo-Egyptian Bank at Paris and then with Bischoffsheim and Goldschmidt in London. He made a fortune with these firms and then set up independently in 1884. His overseas interests included Swedish and American railways, but probably the area in which he exercised the greatest economic influence was Egypt. He was one of the prime movers in the foundation of the National Bank of Egypt, the Agricultural Bank, the *Daira Sania* Company, the *Daira Sania* Sugar Corporation, and various land companies.[19] He and Cromer were able to work very closely together on Egyptian matters. Cassel provided funds for the reconquest of the Sudan and the creation of the National Bank, and at times when money was desperately required

Thus, it seems fair to say that in the decade and a half before Cromer's retirement there was a marked forging of interests between the administration and the financial community. The growing prosperity of the country undoubtedly sealed this alliance and generally precluded any strong divergences of interests. In the last few years of Cromer's administration, however, there was an increase of tension between the administration and the financial community. The conflicts came to a head afterward, when Gorst was Consul-General. The basic source of the conflict stemmed from a financial crisis covering roughly the years 1907 to 1910 and the divergent reac-

[19] See the biographical sketch of Cassel in the *Dictionary of National Biography.*

tions to the financial crisis by the Gorst administration and the foreign financial community. The relations between these two groups were exacerbated, however, by Egyptian nationalism and by the criticisms of Gorst's conciliatory policies by major segments of the financial community.

Inflation and speculation on Egyptian stocks and land had been rife since 1900. Cromer had warned that the current speculative policies of the financial groups were dangerous and that a great deal of Egypt's prosperity was constructed on false foundations.[20] In 1907, Cromer's last year in Egypt, the recession came. It was brought on by a recession in Europe and a diminution of the total amount of European capital available to Egypt. The Egyptian economy was so closely tied to that of Europe that any slackening of European investment had wide ramifications. Furthermore, speculation had driven Egyptian prices to a peak in the early part of the year. A loss of confidence ensued. The economic setback was heralded when in 1907 one of Egypt's foreign banks, Sconto e di Rispormio was forced to close its doors.[21] A number of other companies followed it into liquidation.

Although the crisis had begun in 1907, its resolution fell to Gorst, who in the process of doing so, aroused the hostility of the financial community. In the first place, the Gorst administration, although under heavy pressure from leading financiers in Egypt, refused to appropriate government funds to reconstitute some of the defaulting companies.[22] Also, the British administration was taking steps to restrict the freedom of the foreign community

[20] Cromer, Annual Report for 1904, *HCSP*, Egypt No. 1 (1905), Vol. ciii, cd. 2409.
[21] Gorst, Annual Report for 1907, *HCSP*, Egypt No. 1 (1908), Vol. cxxv, cd. 3966.
[22] Gorst refused to advance £E2 million to the *Crédit Foncier* in 1908. *Le Bourse Égyptienne*, May 6, 1908, as found in the Gorst Papers, Cuttings from Newspapers, iii.

and to curtail financial speculation, then so rife in Egypt. In 1906 companies incorporated in Egypt were required to utilize founders' shares only when these shares constituted the remuneration for the contribution of a patent or a government concession. Until this regulation it had been customary for certain unprincipled speculators to make immense profits simply by selling worthless founders' shares in non-existent companies to a gullible public.[23] Further steps were taken to regulate the Egyptian companies. The Egyptian stock market was regularized somewhat during the Gorst administration. The government prohibited the opening of any exchange without government sanction.[24] Earlier the government had ruled that no application for incorporation would be considered unless the articles of association were in conformity with certain provisions laid down by the government. No united company was to have fewer than seven members. All capital was to be subscribed and every shareholder was to have paid a minimum 25 percent of the nominal value of the shares for which he had subscribed.[25]

These steps were mere palliatives, however, since it was still possible for joint stock companies to be incorporated in foreign countries and then operate in Egypt free from the Egyptian regulations. English laws of incorporation were notably lax, and speculators interested in quick profits in Egypt, for example, were able to sell their founders' shares in Egypt freely if the companies were incorporated in England. In 1908 the Mixed Tribunals rendered a most significant decision in these matters. It ruled that companies formed solely with the object

[23] Gorst, Annual Report for 1910, HCSP, Egypt No. 1 (1911), Vol. ciii, cd. 5633.
[24] Cheetham to Mallet, September 24, 1910, file 35788, PRO, FO 371/894.
[25] Lord Cromer, Annual Report for 1899, HCSP, Egypt No. 1 (1900), Vol. cv, cd. 95.

of exploiting an enterprise in Egypt, which had their seat of affairs and their meetings of shareholders in Egypt, even if they were incorporated in foreign countries, must be treated as Egyptian companies and would have to meet the more rigid Egyptian laws of incorporation.[26] Although there were many companies not affected by this ruling, it greatly increased the control of the administration over the operations of the foreign financial community.

These were but the first measures to make business organizations more responsive to the needs of Egypt by bringing them under governmental regulations. They pale in comparison with the latter measures in the next century. In particular, in the 1920's, regulations were passed to increase the personnel of Egyptians in all companies registered in Egypt and to compel these companies to employ a certain number of Egyptians. (The more recent nationalizations of the Nasser government have brought the economy firmly under the control of the state.) One of the major reasons for the independent position of these companies during British rule was the existence of the Mixed Tribunals. Staffed in the majority by European judges, they tended to protect foreign interests. They were a large obstacle to be overcome in the elaboration of economic laws which could bring the foreign financial groups more firmly under government controls.

Gorst's difficulties with the foreign business community were greatly intensified by his more liberal policy toward Egyptian nationalism. Large and influential segments of this community were bitterly opposed to these policies. They disliked the growing political instability of Egypt, the attacks on the British administration, and the indirect attacks on the foreign business interests operating in Egypt, and generally favored a more severe and re-

[26] Gorst to Grey, No. 36, May 22, 1908, PRO, FO 368/181.

[372]

pressive policy toward the nationalists. One man in particular, Ernest Cassel, a powerful figure in these financial
groups, was quite active in his criticisms of the Gorst
administration. He was exceedingly well-connected in
English society, for he had the ear of King Edward and
many leading English politicians. The various press organs of the financial community—in Egypt the *Egyptian
Gazette* and in England the different financial periodicals
—consistently subjected Gorst's policies to a scathing
criticism. There can be no question that this influential
opinion played a major role in terminating the conciliatory policies toward Egyptian nationalism and securing
the appointment of Kitchener as successor to Gorst.[27]

*

Throughout the British occupation of Egypt there
were obvious differences of goals between the financial
community and the British administration. The administration regarded Egypt as valuable because of its
strategic location. Their overarching goal was to secure
the stability and tranquility of the country. For this
reason they were inclined to be cautious in the development program they sponsored for the country, attempting
at all times to mitigate the effects of social change. The
financial community, on the other hand, favored a more
rapid development of the country: to be sure, there were
limits to the kinds of change they supported. Most did not
want Egypt to be turned into a competitor for European-
manufactured goods so they were not eager to support
the industrialization of the country. Many were also opposed to the growth of nationalism and any changes
which might stimulate these forces. What they wanted
to do was to develop the agriculture of Egypt--its cotton
crop—and make it a profitable area for foreign invest-

[27] The newspaper cuttings in the Gorst Papers, Vol. III, give a
good picture of these press attacks.

ment. Under Cromer these tensions were suppressed. Except for some difficulties with the foreign bondholders and with a group of industrialists who wanted to construct cotton mills in the country, this period was marked by a convergence of interests. Cromer created maximum conditions of political security and encouraged Europeans to invest in the agricultural sphere of the economy. Paradoxically, as Britain's hold on Egypt became more secure, the relationship between the financial community and the British administration became more precarious. The community was growing in size; more capital and companies were being attracted to Egypt. It was becoming more diversified in its interests. Conflicts were bound to arise among important segments of this community, as the dispute over textile manufacturing in Egypt indicated. Under Gorst and, to a lesser extent Kitchener, the administration was less successful in channelling the energies of these groups. The administration felt the need at this time to regulate the foreign financial community in the interests of economic and political stability. In the past the British administrators had been more interested in attempting to create favorable conditions to attract these investors. Thus, conditions favoring open conflict were created, and the last decade of British rule before the War was marked by bitter, though generally concealed, disputes between these two powerful interests.

CHAPTER XII

EGYPT IN 1914

Two BASIC generalizations should be made about Egypt in 1914 before examining it in greater detail. The first is that the impact of the British administration on Egypt tended to strengthen existing trends and patterns of development. It is interesting how little the British fundamentally altered the path in which Egypt had been transforming itself earlier in the century. The emphasis on change continued in hydraulics, in the exporting of a cash crop, and in the rationalization of the bureaucracy. But the influence of the British upon Egypt should not be discounted. Egypt had reached a crisis condition in the 1870's, on the verge not only of financial bankruptcy but administrative disintegration as well. There is no saying how the Egyptians would have weathered this storm themselves. They might have responded magnificently to the crisis and continued the transformation of the country, although this is unlikely. Egypt would certainly have been hard pressed for capital and skilled personnel and would not have been in a strong position to attract either from abroad. Although the British occupation should be seen, not as a radical transformation and modernization of Egypt, but as a consolidation and continuation of established trends, this view should in no way minimize its importance in shaping the development of modern Egypt.

A second fundamental generalization should be made in evaluating British rule in Egypt and the state of Egypt in 1914. As this chapter will attempt to show, Egyptian institutions were developing at different rates of growth. Certain of them, to use the terminology of modernization already employed, were characterized increasingly by their specialization, their functional specificity, their interdependence with other institutions, and their recruitment of personnel on the basis of merit. Other institutions remained relatively non-modernized, or, as the case may be, less modernized, characterized to some degree by their functional diffuseness, self-sufficiency, and recruitment of personnel on the basis of ascriptive rights. It is clear that the British administration, while not entirely responsible for these different rates of growth, did influence institutional development. The requirement and goals of the British, as an imperial power in Egypt, necessitated a severe limitation of the development of Egyptian institutions in certain areas while stimulating their growth in others.

*

One of the most impressive developments in Egypt was the growth of the population. The statistics compiled by the Egyptian government must be used with great care, and though they cannot be relied upon in detail, they can give a general picture. During the French invasion of Egypt French scholars estimated the population of the country at approximately 2,500,000. The first real governmental census taken in Egypt in 1882 showed that this population had grown to 6,900,000. It is generally conceded now that the latter figure was an undercount, a result of the troubled conditions in Egypt in 1882. Subsequent censuses, however, clearly indicated a rapidly growing population. The census for 1917 showed the population to have reached 12,750,000.

The figures from these census reports do suggest that while both rural and urban areas were growing, the urban areas were growing slightly faster. According to the census of 1917 Cairo, Alexandria, Port Said, Damanhur, Tanta, Mansura, and Asyut all had populations of over 50,000. Damietta, Suez, Zagazig, Chibin al-Kom, Beni Suef, Fayum, Minya, Sohag, and Kena had populations of 20,000 to 50,000. Moreover, the figures showed that in the various provinces of Egypt the highest rates of increase were to be found in these cities, rather than in the rural areas. The major cities—Cairo, Alexandria, and the canal cities—had a rate of increase well over 20 percent between 1907 and 1917, while the rest of the country had a growth rate slightly under 20 percent during this same ten-year period. Whereas close to 33 percent of the male population in the major cities was literate, in the rural areas and smaller cities the percentage was considerably less.[1]

The growth of Cairo and Alexandria was quite remarkable. In 1800 the French had estimated the population of Cairo at 260,000. By 1917 it was reported to have a population of 790,000. The population of Alexandria had grown to 445,000 in 1917. When the French first saw these cities they were unsanitary, divided into quarters with gates separating one quarter from another, without filtered water supplies, with the most rudimentary system for the removal of refuse, and without adequate roads. By 1917 both were much more like integrated cities than clusters of separate quarters. The various areas of the cities were connected by new, modern, paved boulevards, by electric railroads, and by tramways. They both had companies for filtered water and gas lighting of the streets. Sewer piping had also been installed. To be sure, these benefits were enjoyed primarily by the wealthier classes, living in the modernized sections, but the contrast with the Cairo and Alexandria of 1800 is still quite astonishing.[2]

The urban environment was the real crucible of social change in Egypt. It was here that the Egyptians were given the most complete exposure to the West, that they obtained their Westernized education, that they sought

[1] The figures in this chapter are compiled from the various *Annuairs Statistiques* of the Egyptian government, issued from 1909.
[2] Marcel Clerget, *Le Caire, passim.*

their new forms of employment as professional men or as a new urban proletariat. As others studying the development of African societies in the modern era have pointed out, it was within the urban environment that the individual was often at odds with his traditional bases of loyalty, such as family and religion. He sought to establish new sources of loyalty, new bases of integration. Educated Egyptians in the urban areas, particularly, created their own new associations to give themselves a new sense of identity and integration. Student and alumni associations flourished. Professional organizations were created. Muslim clubs, with a new attitude toward modernity, were also springing up. The urban proletariat were gradually being organized into trade unions. All these groups were attracted to nationalism, although their understanding and definition of nationalism varied a great deal. The urban areas then spread their influence and their ideas slowly out into the rural areas.

It has been customary to attribute the rapid growth of the population in non-Western areas in the nineteenth and twentieth centuries to the introduction of advanced, Western medical techniques, with their effect on mortality rates. To a limited extent this was true of Egypt during the occupation. Once again, the statistics fail to provide firm conclusions, but there does seem to be reasonable evidence that in certain wealthier urban areas, in cities like Port Said, Cairo, Alexandria, and others, there was a decline in both adult and infant mortality rates without a decline in the birth rates. The reductions in mortality were definitely tied to the improved standards of urban health in these areas. Even more decisive were the efforts to safeguard Egypt from the outbreak of epidemic disease. It is difficult to calculate the effect of greater control over cholera and plague on population growth, but it probably was considerable, because

Egypt had been periodically ravaged by these diseases throughout the nineteenth century, up to the occupation. Public health reform, therefore, did have the effect of stabilizing the mortality rates against sharp increases produced by epidemic diseases.

Public health reform, however, was by no means the decisive factor in the growth of the Egyptian population in this period. Of greater importance were the hydraulic and agricultural reforms which increased the economic potential of the country. The substitution of perennial irrigation for the basin system enabled the land to support a greater population density and reduced the incidence of famine among the population. The development of the communications and transportation systems in Egypt, as was the case in India, allowed for the better distribution of food supplies throughout the country. The tragic situation in which surpluses were produced in one section of the country while another section suffered severely from food shortages was brought to an end. Egypt had been beset with famines in the eighteenth and, on occasions, the nineteenth century, the last one before the occupation occurring in the last years of Ismail's reign. Although a large part of the population suffered from malnutrition and undoubtedly many died from a lack of food, particularly among infants, there were no widespread famines during the occupation. Statistics indicate that increases in the amount of soil available for cultivation did not keep pace with the growth of the population. But the rise in yields, the substitution of cash crops (cotton) for grains, the development of rudimentary forms of industry compensated for slower growth in the amount of arable land available. It seems clear that the general technological developments, especially in agriculture and hydraulics, were more responsible for the growth of the population than the introduction of new medical techniques.

One of the curious features of the British occupation was the fact that the British tended to regard the growing population as a healthy sign for Egypt. In his annual reports, Cromer cited the increase in population as an indication of the general prosperity of Egypt and the effectiveness of British rule. There was no awareness that a growing population might in fact constitute one of Egypt's greatest difficulties. The first informed statement of warning was not made until 1917 when, in a scholarly publication, one of the British demographic and statistical experts pointed to some of the dangerous trends in Egyptian population growth.[3] Up to this time, of course, the British had made no efforts by means of propaganda and education to restrict the growth of the population.

The different impacts of British rule and Western influence can be seen quite clearly in the economic sphere. One of the most important developments was the growth of business firms, mostly controlled by Europeans. These were mainly large-scale economic organizations, but they dealt with only a small portion of the economic activity of Egypt. As indicated, they were generally involved in the sale of land, the providing of capital to the modernized sectors of the economy and to the large landholders, the modernized transportation and communications systems, and the movement of Egypt's export crop. Nevertheless, much of the country's economic activity was carried on as in the past—on the basis of subsistence farming, organized around the village community. Moreover, there were few modernized and specialized organizations in the industrial sphere. Egypt either imported its industrial products from Europe or manufactured them locally by means of the artisan and handicraft system.

Clearly, one of the major developments of the late nine-

[3] S. Craig, "The Census of Egypt," *L'Égypte Contemporaine,* 1917, pp. 209-34.

teenth century was the growth of Egypt's transportation
system. Rail transportation played a primary role. The
first railroad was not constructed in Egypt until the
1850's, but by the First World War Egypt had 2,614
kilometers of state-controlled railroad. These rails connected Cairo with the principal cities of Lower Egypt, including the canal cities—Alexandria, Damanhur, Mahalla,
Benha, Zagazig, Mansura, Tanta, and Rosetta. It also
connected Cairo with Upper Egypt, the line running
along the Nile into the Sudan. Shorter railroads joined
Cairo and Alexandria with their suburbs. In Middle
Egypt, Fayum was linked with Cairo. During the British
occupation the administration gave concessions to several
private companies to develop light railways linking smaller agricultural centers in Lower and Middle Egypt with
the major railroad lines. There was also a considerable
development of the postal system, of telegraph and tele-
phone lines, and road and river transportation. By 1914,
for example, almost 2,000 post offices and stations existed
in Egypt, and rural postal service had begun.

The importance of this impressive extension of the
transportation system throughout Egypt should not be
underestimated. The primary aim, it seems clear, was
to enable Egypt to move goods easily within the country
and ultimately to export some of the products overseas.
The railroads allowed for an increase in economic specialization, particularly in the rural sphere, and, thus, tended
to break down the traditional agricultural self-sufficiency.
The transportation network linked certain segments of
the Egyptian economy to the world economy. It also
allowed for the movement of populations on a vaster
scale than had existed previously. The smaller, light railways in Lower and Middle Egypt were important, for
they connected previously isolated areas to the modernized sectors of the economy and provided a stimulant for
the development of agricultural specialization in these

areas. Moreover, the transportation system had wider implications. It linked the peasant more closely to his district capital. In particular, he had easier access to the new modernizing administrative system being established in these areas, its health services and especially its judicial organization. It seems reasonable to assume, though, that a certain percentage of the peasant population did not take advantage of the administrative, health, and judicial organizations, once access to them had become easier.

The major alterations within the Egyptian economy occurred, of course, in the agricultural sphere. The agricultural specialization of the nineteenth century is truly remarkable, for Egypt, starting almost from scratch, became one of the world's leading exporters of cotton. This agricultural specialization necessitated more rational farming practices, research work adapted to the needs of Egypt, the creation of agricultural societies, the publication of farm journals, and the introduction of new technology. All of these developments were taking place under the British and were actively supported by them. Moreover, through the hydraulic reforms carried out by the British, the amount of arable land was increased from 5 million *feddans* in 1896 to 5,490,000 in 1914. The total cultivated area—including land cultivated more than once a year under perennial irrigation—rose from 6,350,000 *feddans* in 1893 to 7,620,000 in 1914. The increase of cotton exports accompanied these changes in land under cultivation.

Even within this sphere of intensive change, differing impacts must be emphasized. The benefactors of these developments were the large landholders who cultivated an estimated two-thirds or more of the cotton crop. The smaller landholders existed as before on subsistence farming, often supplementing income by working on the larger farms. An important corollary of agricultural specialization was the introduction of the market exchange system into rural areas. Here, the smaller peasantry were involved. The government created its own markets, not only for the collection of taxes as before, but also for small loans to peasants, the sale of cotton seeds, and the purchase of the cotton crop. These government-controlled markets were a significant force in breaking down peasant agricultural self-sufficiency and linking the village to the central economic system.

The configuration of varying rates of growth can be observed within the political sphere. The varying rates of differentiation and specialization of these institutions were crucially influenced by the British administration.

The Egyptian governmental bureaucracy was probably the most highly developed political institution within Egypt. It had grown not only in the personnel employed, but, much more significantly, in the specialized tasks that it undertook. Specialized departments, such as public health, agriculture, and so forth, required skilled personnel, at least to staff the higher ranks of the bureaucracy. Accordingly, recruitment into these branches emphasized technical qualifications and the capacity to discharge tasks requiring specialized knowledge. To be sure, the bureaucracy still had a large redundancy of employees possessing no special skills; they staffed the minor posts and were probably not removed because the British feared the discontent that might result. But the significant point is that the upper ranks of the bureaucracy were being staffed by professionally trained men, that specialized knowledge was called for, and that there was a resultant corps of experts in Egypt. Additionally, the bureaucracy was performing considerably more tasks than it had traditionally. It was exercising more control over the domestic life of the country, even rural Egypt; in this connection rural officials, through regulation from the central government and through special training, were gradually becoming more the agents of the central government than an extension of the village community and kinship system.

The British administration, however, placed limits on the autonomy of the bureaucracy; virtually all positions of power within the various ministries were reserved for British officials. While emphasizing merit and technical qualifications in the recruitment of personnel, the British also attempted to ensure obedience to their system of alien rule. The most ambitious Egyptians, no matter what their talents, found it difficult to advance. Many of them renounced careers in the government for just such reasons and became nationalist leaders in opposition to British rule.

The military was far more under the control of the British and its development much more carefully regulated. The military school in Egypt had less professional status than Egypt's other educational institutions. The top positions within the army were held by the British, and every effort was made to ferret out discontent and deal with it firmly. The military crisis of 1894 only intensified these tendencies within the British administration. Egyptian officers could hardly expect promotions unless they had demonstrated loyalty to British rule. The military, then, did not develop in as autonomous a fashion as the bureaucracy.

Legislative bodies and political parties ranked lower on the scale of developed political institutions in the Egypt of 1914. Here, it is clear that opposition by the British administration delayed the emergence of these political structures. The British permitted the creation of a Legislative Council, a General Assembly, and provincial councils. But they limited them primarily to an advisory capacity. When demands were made to increase the powers of these bodies and endow them with real legislative authority, the British were willing to make only rather minor adjustments and then only in the powers of the provincial councils. Additionally, the administration set property qualifications for membership so high that only the landed element of the society were represented—a group essentially conservative and disinclined to remake these institutions into instruments of public welfare and public interests. By 1914 embryonic political parties had begun to emerge, much to the displeasure of the administration. And they were still far from being mass political organs. Their organization was rudimentary and they were dominated by a few popular leaders; therefore, their continued existence as political parties was still problematic.

*

The extensive economic changes taking place in Egypt between 1880 and 1914 were producing alterations in the class structure of the country. Many of the changes that did occur were already clearly established before the British occupation and were given a greater impetus by British policies. The agricultural and administrative reforms sponsored by the British tended to increase the economic power of the large, landholding classes, groups in a strong position to add to their already extensive holdings because of the sale of lands by competitive auctioning. Furthermore, the continued extension of private landholding rights and the rationalization of the judiciary enabled the big landholders to aggrandize their holdings at the expense of the smaller peasantry. Segments of the peasantry were gradually being turned into a rural proletariat. The emergence of both urban and rural proletariats in Egypt indicated the fragmentation of communal and kinship Egypt into distinct social and economic classes. These groups no longer stood in a corporate relationship with the other elements of the society.

By the same token, the spread of Western education

[385]

throughout Egypt was creating a new group of leaders with new knowledge, able to perform tasks not well developed in Egypt before 1800: this was the dynamic element in Egypt. They had the most radical political and economic goals and high aspirations for themselves as a group. Many of these aspirations could be realized only in a society modernizing as Egypt was. Men could aspire to professions accorded new status and prestige. They could move into upper ranks of the bureaucracy, where their specialized knowledge was so essential. But they also felt the resistance of the alliance of British administration and landholding classes excluding them from the exercise of political power and the implementation of economic programs which would have favored their interests. The new Western-educated class was, then, to varying degrees, antagonistic to the administration and interested in promoting changes in the allocation of political power and economic resources. The most vocal elements were those who constituted the nationalist movement.

The continued elaboration of educational institutions taking place under the British administration accelerated the division of Egyptian society into definite groups according to educational attainments. There were those who acquired Westernized educations and therefore had access to the better positions within the bureaucracy. There were those educated in the Muslim schools, still very much centered around al-Azhar. In the reign of Muhammad Ali the government had used personnel from the religious schools in the Westernized, education system. But by 1914 the gap between the two school systems was quite distinct. Nowhere did one system lead into the other. The Westernized schools trained young men in Western knowledge and prepared them for service in the modernizing administration. The Islamic schools, although they were influenced by modernity, trained

young men basically in religious subjects and prepared
them for the traditional semi-religious and religious roles
of *shaykh, imam, mufti,* and school teacher. Only a few
men had the ability, energy, vision, or opportunity, to
move from one system to the other, since regular channels
of access did not exist.

It is difficult to determine the relationships between
these two elites—the traditional and the modern. Their
members were clearly trained to do different tasks.
It could be anticipated that there would be conflict between them, especially as the status and prestige attached to mastering modern knowledge increased at the
expense of the traditional. These tensions were to culminate in the founding of the Muslim Brotherhood in the
1920's, a movement largely representing the interests of
the more traditionally educated, and aimed at a restoration of the group's status and power. In large part, the
modern and the traditional did not cooperate, but existed
separately in their own spheres. Within the nationalist
movement, however, there was often a coalition, for the
groups were able to cooperate in their opposition to
British rule. The National party contained within its own
ranks members of both elites, often at odds with each
other on methods of opposition and goals but capable of
setting aside these differences for the common goal of a
rather vague Egyptian nationalism. In all of the periods
of intense nationalist activity before the War—1882, 1893-
1894, and 1906-1914—certain members of the two elites
were able to act very much in unison.

Below these two, educated elites was the great mass
of the population, which had no education at all or only
the rudimentary education provided in the village
kuttabs. The educational system tended to re-enforce the
existing class structure, for when tuitional charges were
introduced in the Westernized schools, only the wealthy
could afford them. To be sure, the *kuttabs* did provide

access to the higher Islamic schools and to al-Azhar, but there was no access from there to the Westernized schools. Also, unless a family had some wealth or was motivated by great ambition for its sons, it was unusual for the family to send its sons on to the advanced Muslim schools. Most of the *fellahin* felt that they could not spare their children from work in the fields. Thus, education, far from stimulating mobility, tended to freeze the existing class structure. The major shifts in class alignment were occurring exclusively among the wealthier classes, and were related to access to the Westernized schools.

❊

One of the most significant changes taking place throughout the nineteenth century pertained to the roles and functions of the kinship system. The various central institutions were assuming greater controls over functions previously discharged largely through the kinship system. In the political sphere the village officers—the *umdah,* the *ghaffir,* the *shaykh*—were now more closely regulated by the officers of the central government. Even remote villages were drawn into the central economic system, exchanging their products in local markets and engaging in trade outside the confines of the village. The gradual penetration of judicial institutions into the villages was breaking the family hold on the resolution of village disputes. The new, Westernized schools tended to take the task of imparting knowledge away from the family and the village elders, thereby further lessening the control that the village and kinship systems had over an individual's life.

As has been observed in so many transitional societies undergoing these kinds of changes, there was a decline in the system of social control and a rise in the amount of deviant behavior. The results can be seen most visibly in the problems encountered by the new judicial system and the increase of crime in Egypt. Many of the crimes occurring in rural Egypt reflected the erosion of the traditional system of social controls. The inability of the new judicial and administrative apparatus to cope with this mounting crime rate further indicated that the institutions of the central government were not as capable of securing the same level of social controls as the old system.

CHAPTER XIII

SOME CONCLUSIONS ON
BRITISH RULE IN EGYPT

As ROBINSON AND GALLAGHER have pointed out in their important work, *Africa and the Victorians*, British Victorian statesmen preferred informal empire to direct political controls. They favored a system of treaties, informal persuasion, and the *threat* of force to safeguard their essential economic and political interests, over a system of direct administration of colonial territories. Robinson and Gallagher argue that the occupation of Egypt was a decisive event in the breakdown of the old order of informal empire. The strategic importance of Egypt to the British was so great that the British could not permit Egypt the luxury of a proto-nationalist movement in the form of the Arabi revolt. The occupation ensued. The French were alienated because of their rival interests in Egypt, and the forces of national imperialism were let loose on the African continent. The British were forced to expand up the Nile valley to protect their control over Egypt, and, to divert foreign attention from Egypt, were compelled to allow other powers to grab territory in Africa.

The analysis of the British administration in this book largely corroborates and extends the findings of Robinson and Gallagher for Egypt. The strategic importance of Egypt informed the administrative programs of the British while in Egypt. Of paramount importance was the maintenance of conditions of tranquility and stability, so that external powers could not meddle in Egyptian affairs and the country would not be torn by a repetition of the Arabi revolt. For these reasons, the British administration pursued essentially conservative political

and social policies. While developing the agricultural resources of the country to attain at a minimum financial
solvency, at best economic prosperity, the administration
was disinclined to sponsor any radical alterations in the
political and economic powers enjoyed by the privileged
classes in Egypt. The upper, landholding elite remained
the benefactors of the agricultural development and the
wielders of political power not assumed by the British.

In the analysis presented here the occupation in 1882
does not appear to have been so decisive a change for
the relationship of Egypt and Great Britain as might
appear on the surface. To be sure, the dual control was
brought to an end. The British now monopolized the
powers that had been wielded by both the British and
French before 1882. But they did not at first greatly extend these powers. The British preference for informal
empire was quite clear in the early years of the occupation. The British administrators wished to create in Egypt
conditions which would enable them to withdraw without jeopardizing their strategic interests. Thus, they concentrated their attention on the Ministries of Finance and
Public Works, allowing other Egyptian branches of the
government to go largely unregulated. This emphasis
was, in fact, the same that had existed under the dual
control system, when British and French officials were appointed to supervise the activities of the two ministries.
That this policy of withdrawal was incapable of realization is probably true. It seems clear that the British
would never have been satisfied that conditions were
such as to permit them to withdraw in safety. The only
formula that might have worked was that put forward
in Drummond Wolff's negotiations with the Ottoman
Empire: an arrangement that would have given the English the right of re-entry if conditions became disturbed
in Egypt. The French, however, were unwilling to allow
the British such a great privilege and persuaded the

Turks not to ratify the convention. Other events, such as the Mahdist revolt in the Sudan, reduced even more drastically the likelihood of British withdrawal.

Gradually the Foreign Office, especially under the leadership of Salisbury, came to a more positive evaluation of the strategic importance of Egypt to Great Britain. The British became less inclined to countenance evacuation. The Foreign Office became disillusioned with the strength of the Ottoman Empire and felt it necessary to hold Egypt in the event of a dissolution of Ottoman control, with resulting European scramble for power. At the same time, the British administration in Egypt was beginning to extend its control into other important branches of the Egyptian government. Beginning in 1892, the British took steps to establish dominant influence over the Ministries of Justice and the Interior. The 1894 crisis, which involved the Egyptian army, also resulted in tighter controls over the Ministry of War. The primary impetus for the extension of British influence seems to have come from British officials themselves, although it is clear that overseas financial groups were again taking an interest in Egypt and were in favor of these programs. British officials felt that their programs of reform were being jeopardized by inefficient operation of the Ministries of the Interior and Justice. In particular, the rising crime rate in the country concerned them, and they believed that a reorganization of these ministries would result in a solution to this vexing problem.

Between 1892 and 1914 there was a steady growth of British influence over the Egyptian administrative system. Inspectors and sub-inspectors were appointed in virtually all branches of the government, as they had been earlier in the Ministry of Public Works. These British officials, although technically the subordinates of the Egyptian officials, became the real executive power in the country. No Egyptian official could afford to disregard the advice they proffered. By the time of Kitchener's administration (1911-1914), the British had even gone so far as to regulate the Ministry of Waqfs, previously untouched because it related to the religious life of the country.

During this period there was a growth of other forces outside the administration, forcing decisive changes in the administrative programs of the British. The two most important were Egyptian nationalism and European finance in Egypt. They both came to a head during the Gorst administration (1907 to 1911). After Gorst's brief efforts at liberalizing the administration, to appease the nationalist movement the British returned to a more severe policy under Kitchener. Equally important for the modernization of Egypt was the growth of European financial interests in Egypt. Whereas, in the first decade of British rule in Egypt, the administrative reforms carried out were in accord with the interests and goals of the administrators themselves, in the latter years of the occupation these programs also had to be tailored to the interests of these financial groups. The interests of these two groups often diverged. The strength of the financial community can be clearly seen in the tensions that developed between it and the Gorst administration over financial policies during the recession of 1907-1910, and over Gorst's liberal policies toward the nationalists.

*

The techniques of rule employed by the British also varied from one period to another. In the first decade severe limitations in men and money were placed upon the British. It was during this period that Cromer boasted of the achievements that were obtained with only a handful of British advisers. The British administration rested upon a few key personnel whose influence was maximized by giving them control over the most important branches of the administration. As the years passed and as the occupation became more permanent, the size of the British staff grew almost out of control. Although the administration still ruled—theoretically—in an advisory capacity, the advisers increasingly became the executive apparatus of the country. Egyptian authority was bypassed, even at the local levels. The lower Egyptian officials, the *umdahs, ghaffirs,* and barbers, felt the influence of British officialdom. As the Milner Commission discovered at the conclusion of the First World War, the large British staff in Egypt was one of the most deeply felt grievances in Egypt.

It must be remembered that Egypt was never, before the First World War, a colony of the British Empire. Legally, the British could not govern this territory as they would have governed a regular imperial possession. The British personnel in Egypt were under the direction of the Foreign Office, not the Colonial Office. They were forced to leave intact the Egyptian administrative apparatus, always controlling it indirectly in their role as advisers and inspectors. But, of course, with the growth of the British staff and the presence of a British army in Egypt, the British found it easier to dominate Egyptian officials. It was the presence of a foreign community and foreign interests, rather than the anomalous relationship of the British to the Egyptian administration, that limited the authority of the British. The foreigners enjoyed extra-territorial rights of long standing. Taxes had to be specially negotiated before they could be applied to the foreigners. The same was true of administrative decrees and legislation. The foreign powers did not give up these rights at the time of the British occupation because of the promised British evacuation of Egypt. Since the foreign community in Egypt was large and extremely important in all segments of the modernized part of the economy, significant changes in the administration required the consent of the foreign powers.

Recent analyses of the British occupation, drawing their evidence largely from Cromer's publications, have stressed the popularity of the British administration of Egypt before the First World War. Repeating the arguments of Cromer, these writers have stated that the peasantry were more contented than they had ever been in the nineteenth century. To be sure, there was an impressive economic growth during these years. Whether the peasantry were more contented or less so, seems impossible to prove, however. British sources argue one way, Egyptian sources another; and the peasantry are completely silent. It does seem clear, however, that the British employed coercion to supplement whatever consent they received in ruling Egypt. This element of coercion has not been adequately pointed out. The British treated any threat to their rule with severity. Although the British army was small, it was the primary source of their power in Egypt. During periods of greatest strain between Egypt and Great Britain, the British were not slow to increase its size. The Egyptian army was also an instrument of coercion. It was staffed by British officers in the higher ranks, and Egyptian officers were watched very carefully. Studied isolation and aloofness was a conscious technique of the British administrators. That Cromer was accessible to the most insignificant peasant, as some writers have claimed, appears largely to have been a myth, at least in the latter years of Cromer's rule in Egypt. The British used their isolation and their separation from the Egyptian population to enhance their image of moral and physical superiority over the Egyptians.

*

The British administration of Egypt was undeniably an agency of social change in Egypt. But this remark does not imply that the British administrators were committed to the complete transformation and modernization of Egypt. As the analysis presented here has indicated, the British tended to draw limits beyond which they did not favor programs of social change. Consequently, the transformation of Egypt was marked by different rates of change. Indeed, in many crucial areas, such as the reallocation of political power in accordance with changing social and economic conditions, the British tended to obstruct the forces and pressures for change. Of special significance in an analysis of the modernizing impact of the British administration on Egypt is the way in which the administrators perceived their own role in Egypt. Did they see themselves as transformers and modernizers of Egypt? How did they foresee the future of Egypt? Would Egyptian society be transformed along the lines of the West or remain very much as it had before?

The British administrators centainly did see themselves as transformers of traditional Egyptian society. They realized that the impact of the West, under a system of colonial rule, would decisively alter that society's basic institutions and values. Egyptian society could never be the same after this crucial exposure. Since, by and large, British officials were not sympathetic to many aspects of traditional Egyptian society, they took pride in their role as transforming agents. They were hopeful of destroying the despotism and tyranny of Egyptian political institutions; they favored, intellectually at least, if not in actual practice, the movement for women's emancipation. They were certainly unfavorably disposed to Islam. Consequently, they welcomed the modernizing changes within it, although once again at a distance. The British were especially aware that the economic changes introduced by them would have far-reaching

[*396*]

effects, not simply on the standards of life but on the value system of the population.

These men, however, generally did not believe in the universality of Western ideals and institutions. Unlike earlier generations of colonial reformers, such as the Benthamites in India, they did not believe that they could make Egyptian society over in the image of England. Indeed, they felt that basic changes in values and mentality would have to spring from the Egyptian peoples themselves and that the most that colonial rulers could do was to prepare the material and economic conditions for such changes. Many were exceedingly more pessimistic about the modernizing capacities within Egyptian society. They were impressed with the strength of the traditional society, its resistance to change, and its ability to absorb and transform the modernizing influences, within the framework of the old. On many occasions British officials stated that they felt Egypt could obtain economic prosperity, but that the old political and religious institutions would probably persist. The impact of the West, they believed, would basically be confined to elevated standards of living and a greater measure of political stability. But the political institutions of the West and its values of individualism and self-reliance would not thrive once British influence had been withdrawn.

Nearly all British officials felt that Britain's dominant position in Egypt would be sustained for generations, if not for centuries. They believed that they would have a lengthy period of time in which to effect their changes. Indeed, questions about Egypt's future as an autonomous state were always dealt with in a vague and abstract way, for the British officials did not see this problem as a pressing matter. They were not prepared intellectually in this generation or in later generations for the rapid growth and strength of Egyptian nationalism. In these early years they tended to regard Egyptian nationalism as the work of a few, discontented demagogues, not representative of the will of the people. For these reasons they did not prepare Egypt as thoroughly for its independence as they would have if their perceptions of the future of Egypt had been clearer.

SELECTED BIBLIOGRAPHY

THIS is not an exhaustive bibliography, but rather an annotated bibliography of the most significant materials used for this study. There are good bibliographies for Egypt, especially René Maunier, *Bibliographie Economique, Juridique, et Sociale de l'Égypte Moderne, 1798-1916* (Cairo, 1918) and the New York Public Library, *Modern Egypt, A List of References to Materials in the New York Public Library*, compiled by Ida Pratt (New York, 1929), and the student interested in pursuing any subject further should consult these works first.

Manuscripts

The most important single source for the study of British rule in Egypt is the Foreign Office archives of the British government, located at the Public Record Office in London. These archives contain the dispatches between England and Egypt from the Foreign Office to the Consul-Generals and other officials in Egypt and are to be found mainly under classifications FO 78 and 371.

The Egyptian archives are considerably more difficult to use, as they have not been so well catalogued as the British documents. I was permitted to see technical documents on my visit to Egypt in 1960, and these, along with other materials from this period, are located at the Citadel, Dar al-Mahfuzat, in Cairo. Archival materials for earlier periods in the nineteenth century are to be found at Abdin Palace in Cairo. I was also able to look at departmental archives located at the various ministries and found the departmental orders of the Department of Public Health to be quite helpful.

The private papers of British officials, in Egypt and at the Foreign Office, were another valuable source of information. Of great interest are the papers of the three Consul-Generals, Lord Cromer, Eldon Gorst, and Lord

Kitchener. Cromer's papers are the fullest; Kitchener's the least interesting for Egypt; and Gorst's not so full, but useful if only for the diary. The private papers of the Foreign Secretaries help to supplement the records of the Consul-Generals. These papers include the private correspondence as distinct from the official correspondence of the Foreign Secretaries and the Consuls, and therefore, often provide more revealing information about Egypt. Those records consulted were: Lord Granville, Lord Salisbury, Lord Lansdowne, and Edward Grey.

While the above private and official collections undoubtedly provide the fullest picture of British activities in Egypt, they do not always give the best idea of the way in which the theoretical programs were actually administered in Egypt and what kinds of responses they evoked in the populace. This kind of information I have attempted to obtain from a variety of sources, one of the most valuable of which has been the private papers of British officials in Egypt who occupied lower ranks in the administrative hierarchy. Of great interest here are the papers of Alfred, Lord Milner, who served in Egypt from 1889 to 1892 and kept his contacts with Egypt over a long period of time; Harry Boyle, Cromer's Oriental Secretary; Reginald Wingate, the Commanding-General of the Egyptian army and Governor-General of the Sudan; Edgar Vincent, later Baron d'Abernon, financial adviser in Egypt in the 1880's; and Thomas Russell, an inspector of the Ministry of the Interior and later Commandant of the Cairo police force.

Published Primary Sources

Government Papers

There is a vast body of material dealing with Egypt in published government documents. The Annual Report of the British Consul-General in Egypt, published in the

House of Commons Sessional Papers, is a primary source. This report grew with each passing year to over a hundred pages and gives a great deal of statistical information about the administration of Egypt. Economic reports from the various consuls located at Cairo, Alexandria, Port Said, and Suez can also be found in the *Sessional Papers*.

Nearly all of the existing Egyptian government ministries and departments issued a wealth of information about their work, from which the Consul-General's Annual Report was compiled. Although the statistics to be found in these reports must be used with great caution, they are an extremely detailed and useful body of documents for studying Egyptian administration under the British. A good list of these can be found in Winifred Gregory, ed., *List of the Serial Publications of Foreign Governments, 1815-1931* (New York, 1932).

Memoirs

The memoirs of Englishmen, mostly officials serving in Egypt, give considerable information on British rule and also British attitudes toward governing Egypt:

Blunt, Wilfrid Scawen. *My Diaries*, 2 vols. (New York, 1921).

————. *Secret History of the English Occupation of Egypt* (New York, 1922).

Bowman, Humphrey. *Middle East Window* (London, 1942).

Boyle, Clara. *A Servant of the Empire: A Memoir of Harry Boyle* (London, 1938).

Broadley, Alexander M. *How We Defended Arabi and his Friends* (London, 1884).

Chamberlain, Joseph. *A Political Memoir, 1880-92*, ed. C. H. D. Howard (London, 1953).

Coles Pasha, C. E. *Recollections and Reflections* (London, 1918).

[*401*]

Colvin, Auckland. *The Making of Modern Egypt* (New York, 1906).

Cromer, *Abbas II* (London, 1915).

———. *Ancient and Modern Imperialism* (New York, 1910).

———. *Modern Egypt*, 2 vols. (London, 1908).

———. *Political and Literary Essays*, 3 vols. (London, 1908-1916).

Dicey, Edward. *England and Egypt* (London, 1881).

Marshall, J. E. *The Egyptian Enigma, 1890-1928* (London, 1928).

Milner, Alfred. *England in Egypt* (London, 1892).

Ramm, Agatha, ed., *The Political Correspondence of Mr. Gladstone and Lord Granville, 1876-1886*, 2 vols. (Oxford, 1962).

Rodd, Rennell. *Social and Diplomatic Memories, 1884-1893* (London, 1922).

Russell, Thomas. *Egyptian Service, 1902-1946* (London, 1949).

Storrs, Ronald. *Orientations* (New York, 1937).

Willcocks, William. *Sixty Years in the East* (London, 1935).

These works must be supplemented by works written by Egyptians, or in some cases, by non-English sympathizers with the Egyptian nationalists:

Abbas, "Mudhakkirat al-Khidiwi Abbas" [Memoirs of Khedive Abbas] *al-Misr*, May 1951.

Adam, Juliette. *Angleterre en Égypte* (Paris, 1922).

Amin, Ahmad. *Hayati* [My Life] (Cairo, 1959).

Lutfi, Ahmad. "Mudhakkirat" [Memoirs] *al-Musawwar*, September 1 to December 1, 1950.

———. *Safahat Matwiyah min Tarikh al-Harakat al-Istiqlaliyah fi Misr* [Forgotten Pages from the History of the Movement for Egyptian Independence] (Cairo, 1946).

Musa, Salamah. *Tarbiyah Salamah Musa* [The Education of Salamah Musa] (Cairo, 1948).

Shafiq, Ahmad. *Mudhakkirati fi Nisf Qarn* [My Memoirs over a half Century], 2 vols. (Cairo, 1936).

Al-Subki, Muhammad Fakhr al-Din. *Mudhakkirat Tabib fi al-Aryaf* [Memoirs of a Rural Doctor] (Cairo, 1946).

Periodicals

A great deal of information was garnered from newspaper and periodical sources, much of it of a technical nature, related to the administrative and scientific programs of the British in Egypt. It would be tedious to list all of the articles utilized. Reference to the most important may be found in the footnotes. The periodicals found most helpful were:

Jaridah al-Ahram (Cairo, 1951). This is a collection of some of the most important articles published in this newspaper, ed. by Ibrahim Abduh.

The Agricultural Journal of Egypt
British Medical Journal
Bulletin de l'Institut d'Égypte
Cairo Scientific Journal
L'Égypte Contemporaine
Al-Muqtataf
The Nineteenth Century
The London Times

Secondary Sources

In most cases, biographies have been used because of extensive quotations from private papers found in them:

Amin, Uthman. *Muhammad Abduh* (Washington, 1953).
———. *Raid al-Fikr* [A Pioneer of Thought] (Cairo, 1955).

Al-Aqqad, Abbas Mahmud. *Sad Zaghlul* (Cairo, 1936).

Cecil, Gwendolyn. *Life of Robert, Marquis of Salisbury,* 4 vols. (London, 1921-32).

Crewe, *Lord Rosebery* (New York, 1931).

Gardiner, A. G. *The Life of Sir William Harcourt* (London, 1923).

Garvin, James L. *Life of Joseph Chamberlain,* 3 vols. (London, 1932-1951).

Gwynn, Stephen and Tuckwell, Gertrude M. *The Life of Sir Charles Dilke,* 2 vols. (New York, 1917).

Hamzah, Abd al-Latif. *Adab al-Maqalah al-Sahafiyah fi Misr* [Journalistic Articles in Egypt], 5 vols. (Cairo, 1951).

Hollings, Mary A. *The Life of Sir Colin C. Scott-Moncrieff* (London, 1917).

Lyall, Alfred. *The Life of the Marquis of Dufferin,* 2 vols. (London, 1905).

Magnus, Philip. *Gladstone, A Biography* (London, 1954).

———. *Kitchener, Portrait of an Imperialist* (New York, 1959).

Makhluf, Najib. *Nubar Pasha* (Cairo, 1899).

Morley, John. *Life of William Ewart Gladstone* (London, 1903).

Al-Rafii, Abd al-Rahman. *Muhammad Farid* (Cairo, 1948).

———. *Mustafa Kamil* (Cairo, 1950).

Thorold, Algar. *The Life of Henry Labouchere* (London, 1913).

Wolf, Lucian. *The Life of the First Marquess of Ripon,* 2 vols. (London, 1921).

Zaydan, Jurji. *Tarajim Mashahir al-Sharq* [Biographies of the Great Men of the East], 2 vols. (Cairo, 1922).

Zetland, *Lord Cromer* (London, 1932).

Others

Addison, Herbert. *Sun and Shadow at Aswan* (London, 1959).

Ahmed, J. M. *The Intellectual Origins of Egyptian Nationalism* (New York, 1960).

Ammar, Hamed. *Growing up in an Egyptian Village* (London, 1954).

Baer, Gabriel. *A History of Landownership in Modern Egypt, 1800-1950* (New York, 1962).

Balls, Lawrence. *The Cotton Plant in Egypt* (London, 1912).

Barois, Julien. *Irrigation in Egypt*, tr. from the French by A. M. Miller (Washington, 1889).

Berger, Morroe. *Bureaucracy and Society in Modern Egypt* (Princeton, 1957).

Cleland, Wendell. *The Population Problem in Egypt* (Lancaster, Pennsylvania, 1936).

Crouchley, A. E. *The Economic Development of Modern Egypt* (New York, 1938).

————. *The Investment of Foreign Capital in Egyptian Companies and Public Debt* (Cairo, 1936).

Dhuhni, Salah al-Din. *Misr Bain al-Ihtilal wa-l-Thawrah* [Egypt between Occupation and Revolution] (Cairo, 1939).

Haim, Sylvia G. *Arab Nationalism* (Berkeley, 1962).

Hamza, Abdel Maksud. *The Public Debt of Egypt, 1854-1867* (Cairo, 1944).

Heyworth-Dunne, James. *An Introduction to the History of Education in Modern Egypt* (London, 1938).

Hourani, Albert. *Arabic Thought in the Liberal Age, 1798-1939* (London, 1962).

Hurst, Harold. *The Nile* (London, 1952).

Issawi, Charles. *Egypt at Mid-Century* (London, 1954).

Landau, Jacob. *Parliaments and Parties* (Tel Aviv, 1953).

Landes, David. *Bankers and Pashas, International Finance and Economic Imperialism in Egypt* (Cambridge, Massachusetts, 1958).

Lozach, Jean and Hug, G. *L'Habitat Rural en Égypte* (Cairo, 1930).

Abu-Lughod, Ibrahim. *Arab Rediscovery of Europe* (Princeton, 1963).

Mahfouz, Naguib. *The History of Medical Education in Egypt* (Cairo, 1935).

National Bank of Egypt, *The National Bank of Egypt, 1898-1948* (Cairo, 1949).

Al-Rafii, Abd al-Rahman. *Asr Ismail* [The Reign of Ismail], 2 vols. (Cairo, 1948).

——. *Misr wa-l-Sudan* [Egypt and the Sudan] (Cairo, 1948).

——. *Al-Thawrah al-Arabiyah* [The Arabi Revolt] (Cairo, 1949).

Rifaat, M. A. *The Monetary System of Egypt* (London, 1935).

Robinson, Ronald and Gallagher, John. *Africa and the Victorians* (New York, 1961).

Sandes, Edward W. C. *The Royal Engineers in Egypt and the Sudan* (Chatham, England, 1937).

Wallace, Donald MacKenzie. *Egypt and the Egyptian Question* (London, 1883).

Willcocks, William. *Egyptian Irrigation* (London, 1889).

INDEX

Abbas II, Khedive of Egypt (1892-1914), 35, 38, 146, 147, 179n47; succeeds Tawfiq, 154; dispute with Cromer, 154-79; loss of influence, 179; and nationalism, 263, 269; and Mustafa Kamil, 269; and Gorst, 296-98; and Kitchener, 315; and Muhammad Abduh, 344-45

Abduh, Muhammad, 39, 129, 151n4, 151, 152, 153, 154, 158, 176, 179n47, 183, 249, 252, 257, 258, 336, 340, 346; and Abbas II, 297, 344-45; and reform of al-Azhar, 344-45

Adam, Juliette, 267

al-Afghani, Jamal al-Din, 15, 17, 39, 152, 344

agriculture, 42-43, 80; premodern, 28; modernization under Muhammad Ali, 35-37; modernization under Ismail, 38-39; modernization of, 219-48, 381-82; mechanization of, 234; under Kitchener, 317; and population growth, 379. See also cotton, irrigation

Agricultural Bank, 237-40, 369

Agricultural Society, 230

al-Ahram, 40, 249, 270, 289

Aird and Company, 222

Akaba crisis, 278-79

al-Alam, 306, 310

Alexandria, 349, 378, 381; municipal government, 70; public health reform, 353-55; population growth, 376-77; modernization of, 377

Ali, Muhammad (ruler of Egypt, 1805-1848), 25; modernizes Egypt, 31-38; develops Egyptian bureaucracy,

202; and reform of education, 321; and al-Azhar, 344

Amin, Ahmad, 282, 346

Amin, Qasim, 254, 257, 258, 266, 282, 341, 342

Anglo-Egyptian Bank, 369

Anglo-French Accord of 1904, 268

Arabi, Ahmad, 15-16, 18, 148, 149, trial of, 67-68

Arabi revolt, 11-24, 40, 43, 54, 84, 127, 148, 176, 390; and Egyptian bureaucracy, 203

Arendt, Hannah, 196

army of occupation (British), 81, 104, 194, 280, 394, 395

army (Egyptian), 43, 52, 64, 104, 395; in Arabi revolt, 16-24; reform of under Muhammad Ali, 32-33; nationalist agitation in, 168; under British rule, 384. See also Ministry of War

Aswan Dam, 216, 220-24. See also William Willcocks

Asyut, 376

Awdah al-Ruh, 251

Balls, Lawrence, 228

banks, 362, 363-64

barbers, 29, 394; changing role of, 210-12

Baring Brothers, 57-58

Baring, Evelyn. See Lord Cromer

barley, 230

beans, 230

Behera Land Company, 245, 367

Belgium: investment in Egypt, 362

Benha, 381

Beni Suef, 376

bersim, 231